Turning Points in Historiography

Rochester Studies in Historiography

ISSN 1533-7014
Senior Editor: Georg G. Iggers
Professor Emeritus of History
State University of New York at Buffalo

Turning Points in Historiography:
A Cross-Cultural Perspective

Edited by

Q. Edward Wang
Georg G. Iggers

THE UNIVERSITY OF ROCHESTER PRESS

First published 2002
Soft cover edition published 2006

University of Rochester Press
668 Mt. Hope Avenue, Rochester, NY 14620, USA
www.urpress.com
and Boydell & Brewer Limited
PO Box 9, Woodbridge, Suffolk IP12 3DF, UK
www.boydellandbrewer.com

Cloth ISBN-13: 978–1–58046–097–2
Cloth ISBN-10: 1–58046–097–6
Paperback ISBN-13: 978–1–58046–269–3
Paperback ISBN-10: 1–58046–269–3

ISSN: 1533–7014

Library of Congress Cataloging-in-Publication Data

Turning points in historiography: a cross-cultural perspective / edited by
    Q. Edward Wang and Georg G. Iggers
        p. cm. — (Rochester studies in historiography, ISSN 1533–7014; v. 1)
    Includes bibliographical references and index.
    ISBN 1–58046–097–6 (alk. paper)
        1. Historiography—History. 2. History—Philosophy. 3. Historiography—
Europe—History. 4. Historiography—Asia—History. 5. History—
Methodology. I. Wang, Q. Edward, 1958-. II. Iggers, Georg G. III. Series.

    D13 .T87 2001
    907'.1—dc21   2001035597

A catalogue record for this title is available from the British Library.

Designed and typeset by Christine Menendez.
This publication is printed on acid-free paper.
Printed in the United States of America.

Contents

Preface

This volume discusses and analyzes innovative changes in historical thinking and historical writings in world cultures. Our intent with this book is to expand the horizon of our study of historiography, an academic field that was carved out more or less by modern Western scholars, and take into account the contributions of other cultures to our knowledge of the changes in the world over the past few millennia. As a project, it originated from a small conference held in West Point, New York, in 1995, organized by Professor Thomas H.C. Lee of the City University of New York and sponsored by the Chiang Ch'ing-kuo Foundation. It was part of a larger project called "Chinese and Comparative Historiography," which Thomas Lee initiated and led from that time onward. Some of the contributors to this volume have participated in the project, along with many others from Asia, Europe, and North America. It was at Williams College, one of the subsequent meetings Thomas Lee organized in 1998, that the proposal for organizing an international conference on "Turning Points in Historical Thinking: A Comparative Perspective," was finalized. We appreciate the suggestions and comments made toward the proposal by the participants at the meeting, including Peter Bol, James Hargett, Thomas Lee, Conrad Schirokauer, and Richard Vann. We are also grateful to the Chiang Ch'ing-kuo Foundation for funding the proposal, which provided the essential resources for organizing the conference at the State University of New York at Buffalo, in August 1999.

Dr. Thomas Burkman, director of the Asian Studies Program at SUNY Buffalo, played a key role in organizing the conference. Assisted by his office staff, especially Patricia Kratz, Dr. Burkman not only took care of all the logistics that ensured its success, but also contributed his ideas to the design of its program. We also would like to thank SUNY Buffalo and its Asian Studies Program for providing additional financial assistance for the conference. The conference also benefited from the participation and/or comments of Peter Bol (Harvard), Chou Liang-kai (Chung-hsing University, Taiwan), Roger Des Forges (Buffalo), Carol Gluck (Columbia), Hsu Cho-yun (Pittsburgh), Thomas Keirstead (Buffalo), Achim Mittag (Bielefeld, Germany), Carlos Antonio Rojas (Mexico), Jörn Rüsen (Essen, Germany), Stefan Tanaka (University of California at San Diego), Yü Ying-shih viii

(Princeton), and Zhang Zhilian (Peking University). To Professor Hsu Cho-yun, we owe our thanks for his support of the project on Chinese and Comparative Historiography in general and of the conference in particular. Professor Yü Ying-shih gave a thoughtful speech at the closing ceremony, which led to much discussion and enthusiasm among the participants. We hope the volume presented here reflects adequately the comments and concerns all the participants made and raised at the conference with regard to our comparative study of historical cultures.

We are thankful to the contributors to this volume for their promptness in revising their papers and to Professor Toyin Falola of the University of Texas at Austin for suggestions on publication. Our appreciation also goes to Mr. Timothy Madigan, editorial director of the University of Rochester Press, for showing a strong interest in this volume. In preparing this volume for publication, we are indebted to the editorial board of the series for suggestions and to Wilma Iggers and Linda Pirolli for proofreading some of the chapters. We also would like to thank Louise Goldberg, copyeditor at the University of Rochester Press, and Molly Cort for their proficiency and care in ensuring the quality of this book. The interest shown on their part in this book is indeed a great encouragement and assurance for our ongoing project on comparative historiography.

Q. Edward Wang and Georg G. Iggers
January 28, 2001

1. Introduction

Q. Edward Wang and Georg G. Iggers

"Turning point" as a metaphor has a broad appeal to people interested in change. It has hitherto been used by psychologists, sociologists, educators, philosophers, and most of all, historians, to identify a major event, or a series of events, in the history of a life, a discipline, an institution, a society, or civilization.[1] Such an event is seen in retrospect to have influenced the future course of development of the society being scrutinized. In his lecture series on the rise of Europe delivered in Japan, Geoffrey Barraclough, an eminent English historian, offered an example of how to identify turning points in history. He argued that the major turnings points at which Europe distinguished itself from the rest of the world and eventually gained prominence and dominance, occurred first in the period between 1076 and 1122, and secondly during the Scientific Revolution of the seventeenth century. Why these two periods, rather than the more commonly known events such as the Renaissance and the Reformation, or the French Revolution? Because, Barraclough explained, those conventional "turning points" had only regional impacts, whereas the church-state conflict of the eleventh and twelfth centuries and the Scientific Revolution of the seventeenth caused more significant changes in European history and helped Europe exert a greater impact on the course of world history.[2]

Barraclough's observation may still be debatable among European historians. But his interest in identifying turning points in history from a world perspective was shared by A. L. Macfie, who authored *The End of the Ottoman Empire, 1908–1923* in Longman's new Turning Points series. To Macfie, although in the Near and Middle East there had not been many historical turning points, "few, if any, can compare in the range and profundity of its consequence with the collapse of the Ottoman Empire." The magnitude of the collapse was unprecedented in Macfie's opinion, because Macfie, like Barraclough, viewed its impact from a global perspective. The empire's fall constituted the ultimate cause for the outbreak of World War I.[3]

Although historians seem fond of identifying turning points in history, they have not done so for the development of their own discipline. Since the nineteenth century, when the history of history emerged to become an important field in the study of history itself, we have seen a number of scholars produce valuable works that offered useful and insightful surveys for the history of historiography, including the delineation of important phases in its development. But few of them have done it from a global perspective, as recommended by Barraclough. In his own work on the global trends of historical writings, *Main Trends in History*, Barraclough also made observations based largely on the works of Western historians, referring especially to the modern development in historiography in the nineteenth century, which he regarded as unique to the Europeans and a model for non-Western historians.[4] Barraclough, of course, has not been alone. In the study of historiography, which has so far attracted mostly Western scholars, what has been commonly done in the past few decades was that most scholars, limited by their history knowledge and language proficiency, simply substituted a Europe-centered approach for a global approach. The triplet designations ancient, medieval, and modern, first invented by the humanists in Renaissance Italy to assert the importance of their own accomplishment and later adopted by historians to periodize both European and world history, also constituted the basic framework for the development in historical writing.[5] As stated above, Barraclough opposed such tripartite historical periodization for failing to consider the global nexus of European history, though it seems that he too was unable to eschew completely Eurocentric views in the history of history.

Although a true world perspective is hard to attain, many have appreciated and supported the effort. In 1979, the same year Barraclough's *Main Trends in History* appeared, Georg Iggers and Harold Parker co-edited *The International Handbook of Historical Studies*, which included chapters on China, Japan, and Africa, similar to those Barraclough constructed in his book; the latter covered new developments in historiography outside the European continent, while paying a particular attention to Soviet Russia.[6] Although the proportion of non-Western historiography in both volumes remained smaller than its Western counterpart, these two anthologies pioneered the study of comparative historiography in the English-speaking world. While demonstrating an increasing interest in the subject, the publication of these works also suggests that if one wished to discuss issues in historiography from a worldwide and cross-cultural perspective, much remained still to be done.

In the last twenty years from 1979 to the present, we have seen more attempts to broaden the scope of historiography. For example, D. R. Woolf edited an impressive two-volume *Global Encyclopedia of Historical Writing*, in which the number of entries on Africa, Asia, and Latin America rivals that on Western historiography and has reached a remarkable proportion. This resulted from a conscientious effort pursued by the editor as well as the editorial board, although the board was comprised entirely of historians in the West. In his introduction, Woolf explains the coverage of the encyclopedia. "The inclusion of little-known Chinese historians," he writes, "at the expense of greater space that might have been allotted to Livy, Matthew Paris, or Carl Becker is intended to correct a Western bias in most comparable textbooks and dictionaries on historical writing without ignoring the usual case of characters found in such works, from Thucydides to Toynbee." At the same time, the encyclopedia also noted the contributions made by female historians through the ages.[7]

Woolf's desire to expand the horizon of historiographical study is well appreciated by more and more historians in today's world. At the most recent convention of the International Congress of Historical Science, held in Oslo in August 2000, we found that many panel organizers intended a global and comparative presentation. For example, Rolf Torstendahl, a Swedish historian, organized a panel discussion on assessing the historical writings in the twentieth century. In his pursuit of this ambitious project, Torstendahl assembled an international team of historians and produced a book that covers almost all the continents, including Australia, whose historiographical enterprise was often either overlooked by or lumped together with the Western world in previous works. Although the organization of Torstendahl's book still reminds us of the Hegelian outlook of world history, beginning in the Far East with Japan and China and moving westward to Europe and America, it nevertheless presents a valiant attempt at breaking down the Western domination in historiography, expanding the cause pioneered by earlier works.[8]

Not only has this interest in comparative historiography led to the inclusion of non-Western historical writings, it has also resulted in a global perspective on the study of the Western historiographical tradition. *Westliches Geschichtsdenken, Eine interkulturelle Debatte* (Western historical thinking: An intercultural debate), edited by Jörn Rüsen, is a good example. Although the title suggests that it is a book on Western historical thinking, it presents its theme from a cross-cultural perspective. The organization of the book revolves around a paper given by Peter Burke, an English cultural and intellectual historian, on ten most important characteristics of Western historical thinking, at an international conference organized by Jörn Rüsen at the University of Bielefeld in 1995. In presenting his thesis, Burke adopted a comparative perspective. "Unlike some earlier historians, Hans Baron for example," he states, "I shall not be referring to the 'awaking' of historical thought at a particular moment (in his case, the early Renaissance), nor will I be assuming or arguing, like Hegel, that historical thought is a monopoly of the West. On the contrary, interest in the past appears to have existed everywhere and in all periods."[9] Provided such an intention, Burke offered his insights on the characteristics of Western historical thinking by comparing and contrasting them, whenever and wherever he could in a cursory manner, with those of non-Western regions. His observation aroused interest, as the book shows, not only from historians in the West but also from the experts on non-Western historical writings, such as Chinese, Indian, Japanese, Islamic, and African. While not all the contributors to the volume agreed with Burke in regard to his observations of both Western and non-Western historiography, they all seemed appreciative of his effort. This appreciation derived largely from the fact that although Burke explained the distinctiveness of Western historical thinking, he had no intention to suggest "that the Western style of historical writing is superior in everyway to the alternatives."[10]

Well-intended goals notwithstanding, both Burke and Rüsen recognized the difficulty in pursuing historiography from a cross-cultural perspective. For Burke, "it is obviously foolhardy for a single individual to offer conclusions on this huge subject [characteristics of Western historical thinking]."[11] For Rüsen, the challenge is not only directed to one's academic preparation, but also to his/her cultural prejudice. Such prejudice is inherent in one's cultural identity. "The identity-building difference between self and other is working in each memory, and any effort to remember in itself an asymmetrical normative relation. Ethnocentrism (in all its different forms) is quasi-naturally inherent in human identity." In forming one's identity, Rüsen argues, historical consciousness (*Geschichtsbewußtsein*), or a sense of one's own past, played an indispensable role. In order to reach a new understanding of one's relations with others in this globalizing world, or to redraw the self/other distinction interculturally, we need to reconfigure historical consciousness through cross-cultural communication. But, Rüsen laments, "historical thinking is not well prepared to solve the questions objectively rising from the context of international and intra-national constellations."[12]

Perhaps for these reasons, comparative historiography faces many challenges and remains a fledgling field in the historical profession.[13] Rüsen is certainly right when he said that the key to the problem is to reconfigure our historical consciousness. Before comparative historiography is possible there has to be a reorientation in the ways in which historians approach historical study. History became a professional discipline in the West during the nineteenth century. This professionalization both enriched and impoverished historical studies. The gain for history was a greater methodological awareness, a more critical approach to the sources, and at least a professed desire to reconstruct the past as objectively as possible. But the very formation of history as a discipline also involved a narrowing of scope. The eighteenth century witnessed serious attempts at writing a universal, transcultural history. The most massive of these attempts was the English *Universal History* launched in 1736, which in over thirty volumes attempted to tell the history of all the peoples of the world—Europeans, Asians, native and European Americans, and Africans north and south of the Sahara. But it was in no sense a comparative history. It was criticized for being in fact not a history of mankind, but rather a collection of particular histories each largely independent of the other.

The theory of history that underlay historical research, sometimes labeled historicism, drew a sharp distinction between history (which in its narrative form was concerned with recapturing unique aspects of the past, as they were revealed in the archives) and the social sciences (which proceeded analytically on the basis of empirical data to formulate generalizations). The emergence of history as a discipline went hand in hand with the rise of nationalism. On the one hand professionalization was to guarantee the objectivity of historical studies; on the other hand it consciously assisted in constructing national identities. Thus while giving lip service to the objectivity, impartiality, and honesty of the historian, it in fact too often utilized scholarship to legitimize nationalistic aspirations. Comparative history was left to writers outside the profession who constructed great systems, such as Hegel, Comte, Marx, and later Max Weber, and who, while they transcended national boundaries, operated from a conception of world history which assumed the cultural superiority of the Western world and viewed the non-Western world from the perspective of this Western superiority.

Although modern historiography has its inherent problems in pursuing a cross-cultural presentation, it nonetheless provides us with a useful basis for our project. The rise of scientific history was once regarded as the mark for historical professionalization. The pre-eminence of scientific history coincided with the writing of national histories in most parts of the world. This phenomenon allows us to take two different approaches to our identification of turning points in historical cultures, hence the division in our book. The pursuit of scientific history, given its emphasis on source criticism, resulted in a narrowing of the scope of historical study, as we mentioned above. Yet due to its association with the undertaking of national history, it gained popularity across many nations. This worldwide popularity of national history, at least from the late nineteenth century onward, was of course an outcome of many factors, of which Western expansion through military conquest and economic coercion into other continents was certainly most notable. But it helps to divide the study of historiography into two periods: one when the contact of historians from among many regions appeared minimal to non-existent, and the other, when such contact, through the spread of nationalism, imperialism, positivism, Marxism, modernism, and most recently, postmodernism and postcolonialism, became frequent and regular. In other words, though we agree that a turning point in history should have a worldwide impact, we must also note that the world itself has never been so large and global as we have seen since the last century. In different historical periods, in fact, the world appeared very differently to many of its inhabitants.

What we consider as a turning point in historiography refers to a fundamental change in the perception of the past in a certain culture that occurs in a historical time, and has a far-reaching influence in the later period. This change often leads to the rise of new schools in historical writing and new ideas of history, which constitute a form of historical thinking that shapes or reshapes one's vision of the past, the present, and the future. The impact of these turning points varies greatly from one historical period to another. But if we take a long-term perspective, almost all of them had a cross-cultural influence on historiography, even before the world was globalized as a result of the expansion of capitalism. The invention of narrative history by Greek historians, demonstrated in the work of Herodotus (ca. 484–424 B.C.), so elegantly analyzed here by François Hartog, constituted a form of historical writing not only for many ancient historians in classical Greece and Rome, but also later for modern European historians. Moreover, it provided the basic form of national history for non-Western historians throughout the twentieth century. However, the form itself, Hartog reveals in his research, was a cultural mixture even in its own time. The "pre-history" of Greek historiography suggested that there were multiple reasons for the Greeks to adopt this particular form; it not only reflected the cultural influences from Egypt and Mesopotamia, but also perpetuated a relationship among history, divination, and epics.

If Greek historiography provided Western historians a basic form of historical writing that later exerted a cross-cultural influence, in the East, Chinese historiography was also regarded as a model practiced by many Asian historians, especially in Japan, Korea, and Vietnam before the nineteenth century. During the Ch'in-Han period (221 B.C.–220 A.D.), which was marked by the rise and fall of two great Chinese dynasties, the canonization of Confucianism as a political ideology also came to shape the form of historical thinking and turned it into an orthodoxy in Chinese historiography. It was characterized by one's effort to understand the movement of history from the perspective of person-cosmos correlation. Influenced by the humanist emphasis of the Confucian teaching, historians also placed individuals at the center of history, which led to the adoption of the "annals-biographic" form in dynastic historical writing, the mainstay of traditional Chinese historiography. The correlative idea suggested that the ultimate goal of historical writing was to present and preserve Tao, or the perfect correspondence between nature and people. By contrast, the use of the annals-biographic form indicated that such action, or the proper execution of the mandate of Heaven, was always a human one, involving both the rulers and the ruled, for the will of Heaven was reflected in the behavior of the people.

In his essay on the unification of the Ch'in Dynasty in 221 B.C., Chünchieh Huang offers us a comprehensive yet succinct analysis on the implication of the Ch'in unification. The unification was traditionally considered a turning point in Chinese history since it was thought by Chinese historians to have laid the foundation for later empires. He shows that the concern for reaching an ideal person-cosmos correspondence prompted historians to debate upon the significance of the event, namely the question whether Emperor Shih-huang (259–210 B.C.), the dynasty founder, actually carried out the mandate of Heaven in his action. If he did, then why did the dynasty only last some thirty years? If not, then how could he even accomplish his task? The debate, which lasted over two millennia in imperial China according to Huang, showed that once the correlative idea entered the domain of history, it could be translated into a moral issue: whether or not Tao was present in a certain period of history was to be reflected in the moral behavior of the ruler (his relation with his people), which, in turn, also determined the fate (rise or fall) of the dynasty. In the case of the Ch'in Dynasty, while historians generally appreciated the unification, they also assailed Ch'in-shih-huang's brutal policy toward his subjects, especially the intellectuals, which, the historians believed, led to the quick downfall of the dynasty and its loss of the mandate of Heaven. This morality-bound historiography, or the so-called "praise-and-blame historiography" (p'ao-pien shih-hsüeh), was prevalent in imperial China as well as in most of East Asia.[14]

The rise and fall of a dynasty, or an empire, was important not only to Chinese historians, but also to European historians in both ancient and medieval times. In his thoughtful discussion on the transformation of European historiography in the fourth and fifth centuries, Ernst Breisach shows us that one of the key issues was how historians and Christian fathers accounted for the role of pagan empires in the linear progress of human history. In other words, what challenged Christian historians was how to find an "accommodation model," to borrow Breisach's term, that could not only relieve the tension between the world of the sacred and the world of the mundane, but also blend them into one. Their success in doing so, needless to say, would constitute a major turning point in Western historical thinking. But at the time, namely between 313 and 420, according to Breisach, this task seemed increasingly difficult to accomplish. For a long time, three "accommodation models" vied for prominence, offered respectively by Eusebius (ca. 260–340), Orosius (ca. 380–420), and St. Augustine (354–430). Each had its attractions and, at the same time, deficiencies. For whether or not one theory could gain popularity was not decided by its own persuasiveness; it rather depended on the unfolding of history because "human experience and theoretical endeavors," Breisach reminds us, "are . . . inextricably intertwined." As the success of the Germanic invasion brought down the unity of the Roman Empire, gone with it was the idea of universality of the world, which undermined significantly Orosius's effort at merging sacred and pagan histories into one. By contrast, St. Augustine's theory was a beneficiary of the fall of the Roman Empire because it favored the separation of the City of God from the mundane world. But throughout the medieval period, Breisach argues, the idea of universality was never completely forsaken. That was why Eusebius's model prevailed at last, for it pointed to a potential unity in the future while recognizing the difficulties and agonies in the present.

Indeed, although it is difficult to identify a critical moment for the transition from classical period to the medieval period in European historical culture, many agree that the fall of the Roman Empire and the rise of Christianity brought dramatic new changes to the Western tradition of historical writing during the fourth and fifth centuries. Back to the East in China, the fall of the Han Dynasty in the third century, which resulted in the decline of classical Confucian culture, suggested that a similar cultural transformation was also occurring during the third and fifth centuries. For as the influence of Confucianism in Chinese society waned, it created an opportunity for the intrusion of foreign culture. Buddhism, which had made its presence known in China as early as the first century, gained a remarkable headway during this period, spreading not only from the north to the south in China but also to Korea and Japan. In the late sixth century, the rise of the Sui and ensuing T'ang Dynasties ended China's political division, but it did not bring back the dominance of Confucianism as we had seen in the Han. Rather, Chinese culture in the T'ang times was characterized by its eclecticism. As a result, when Chu Hsi (1130–1200) and his friends in the Northern Sung Dynasty of the tenth century attempted to revive Confucianism, they were no longer able to cleanse the Buddhist influence. In fact, Chu Hsi's new interpretation of Confucian classics, known as Neo-

Confucianism in English, was known for its metaphysical and ontological consideration of the morality issue raised by classical Confucianism. This consideration clearly bore the imprint of Buddhism.

Witnessing the ebb and flow of Chinese culture and the rise and fall of political powers during the third and tenth centuries not only urged Neo-Confucians to search for a new cultural order but also prompted historians to look for a new historical interpretation. In his well-researched essay, Thomas Lee argues that in the course of Chinese historiography a new direction was taken from the tenth century onward, and that this new direction influenced both the idea and style of historical writing. The former was marked, thanks to Neo-Confucianism, by a renewed emphasis on moral teaching in history and a political concern for the legitimacy (*cheng-t'ung*) question in historical interpretation. The latter was shown in many new historiographical changes at the time, including the experiment with a new genre in historical narrative, an improvement in historical commentaries, and an increased sensitivity in exercising historical criticism. The Neo-Confucian interest in moral teaching in history was a reflection of a political concern shared by many intellectuals at the time; due to the dramatic political changes associated with the fall of the Han, historians began to develop a sense of "anachronism," or an awareness of a cultural breakdown, which required them to consider, on moral ground, the legitimacy question in their studies of the histories of those post-Han dynasties. For Sung historians, especially Ou-yang Hsiu (1007–1072), as Lee analyzes for us, the desire for finding a moral meaning in historical writing amounted to a search for historical truth because the highest moral accorded with Tao, the ultimate truth in human history. Acting on the belief that Tao will reveal itself in the process of history, Sung historians paid high attention to historical criticism in order to ensure that in their historical narratives, there would be the least amount of factual mistakes and that Tao would make its full revelation. Finally, as the form of narrative gained currency in the historical practice of the Sung, historians also attempted to address the question of historical causality, or in Lee's term, the "inter-connectedness" of historical events. This interest in historical causality resulted in the writing of many general histories, among them Ssu-ma Kuang's (1010–1086) famous *Tzu-chih t'ung-chien* (A comprehensive mirror of aid for government), as well as commentaries on existing historical texts, such as Liu Chih-chi's (661–721) *Shih-t'ung* (Perspectives on historiography).

The Chinese concern for the revelation of Tao, or the perfect Heaven-person correlation, in history, therefore, accounted mainly for the changes in Sung historical writing. In the West, this concern was shown in the relationship between the sacred world and the mundane world, as analyzed by Breisach in his essay. In the Middle East, it took yet another form in historical practice, which appeared a bit more complex. Stephen Humphreys shows us in his essay that the Muslims' relation with their God followed the Covenant-Betrayal-Redemption paradigm, which provided the master narrative for all the historical accounts of early Islamic culture. The paradigm was so widely received in Muslim society that when the so-called Abbasid

Revolution took place in the mid-eighth century, historians were forced to come up with answers for the question of whether the Revolution redeemed the caliphate from Muslims' past sins, or betrayed the Muslim covenant with God. But no matter how historians thought of the Abbasid Revolution, it ushered in a new phase of Islamic history concurrent with a newly founded empire, which in turn shifted the focus of history from religion to politics. The rise of political history, or dynastic histories focusing on court life, characterized the Islamic experience in historiography in the ninth century. Considering its content and interest, it bore some superficial resemblance to the Chinese experience in dynastic historiography. But the emergence of Islamic historical writing, in Persian, in the late tenth century, which represented another historiographical shift in Islam, according to Humphreys, indicated that there were more differences than similarities. Persian-language historiography was not merely an account of history in another language, it also provided a new narrative style that had been absent in dynastic histories. If the turning points in Islamic historiography in the ninth and tenth centuries were associated with the revolutionary events going on in the Middle East at that time, the trend intensified in the subsequent centuries. In the fourteenth century, for example, the great work of Ibn Khaldun (1332–1406), probably the greatest history ever written by an Arab historian prior to the modern times, showed a direct concern not only for the political turmoil in his world but also the aftermath of the Black Death. Although it was a reflection upon his own time, Ibn Khaldun's work was so comprehensive and profound that it has amazed readers ever since its appearance.

If the above shifts and turns prove that "Islamic historiographic traditions were hardly stagnant" prior to the nineteenth century (Humphreys), the same can also be said about the Chinese tradition. In his extensive essay on historical culture in late imperial China, especially the Ch'ing Dynasty (1644–1911), Benjamin Elman offers us an excellent example for the changes in traditional historiography. From the Han Dynasty (206 B.C.–220 A.D.) onward when Confucianism gained and maintained, for most of the time, its prominence in Chinese culture, the relationship between classical study and historical study became a perennial concern for the Chinese literati. The former, needless to say, referred to the study of Confucian Classics and their commentaries, and the latter to history texts, especially the dynastic histories that had been produced over the centuries since Ssu-ma Ch'ien (ca. 145–87 B.C.). Viewed in a different perspective, such a relationship reflected a perception, held by both the rulers and the literati at a certain time, of the role of history in Chinese politics. Through his painstaking study of how the knowledge of history was scrutinized in civil service examination, Elman has enabled us to look into the historical thinking of the Chinese people in the late imperial period and compare it with that in the previous period. From the Ch'in-Han period onward, history as a subject of knowledge witnessed a continuous growth. It became an important category in the official division of knowledge during the middle imperial period. While its interest in moral didacticism remained unchanged through the centuries, it did take different forms of expression, especially in the way in which history was incorporated into the civil service examination. As shown in Thomas Lee's essay but also discussed here by Elman, the rise of Neo-Confucianism led to a new interest in seeking a unity between the Classics and history, namely to expound moral principles in the Classics through the help of accurate history examples. Such attempt affected the role the knowledge of history played in the civil service examination. Elman shows that in the later imperial period, a new turning point, or historicization, of classic learning, seemed to have taken place, evidenced not only by the effort made by historians to redefine the nature of the Classics as history, but also by the amplification of the use of history in the civil service examination. More important, Elman argues, this historicization in Ch'ing China bore similarity to the approach of German historicism and paved the way for modern Chinese historians to further desacralize the Classics in the twentieth century.

Although the change of historical culture in late imperial China, as Elman argued elsewhere,[15] had something to do with the contact between the Chinese literati and the Jesuits in the sixteenth and seventeenth centuries, this type of exchange did not compare, either in scale or frequency, with the communication between the West and non-West from the nineteenth century onward. In the history arena, this kind of cultural exchange was initiated, as we briefly discussed earlier, by the project on writing scientific history for modern nation-states. The attempt was first made by nineteenth century European historians and was later emulated and extended by historians of other regions in the world. Taking a comparative approach, Eckhardt Fuchs presents us a careful analysis of the emergence of scientific history in modern Europe. Although he has confined his study largely to nations in Western Europe and North America, he has convincingly demonstrated that the undertaking of scientific history, at its early formation, had acquired an international dimension. This internationalization of scientific history did not mean that historians of all nations shared the same idea about its goal, practice, and method, nor did it mean that there was no resistance to its spread. Rather, Fuchs contends, even within the Western nations, there were various models of "scientific history"; the German model exemplified by Rankean historiography, in spite of its wide influence, was only one of them.

As Fuchs offers a critical view of the practice of scientific history, Christopher Hill extends the criticism into the writing of national history. Taking a similar "international" approach, Hill discusses the worldwide influence of national history as a genre of historiography, using France, Japan, and the United States as examples. Although the writing of national history was naturally associated with and in service for the nation-building project, he argues, it was never pursued within the scope, or territory, of a single nation. Instead, the aim of national history was to create a space in which historians could imagine the past not only of the focal country but also with its counterparts in the world. In other words, while the nation-building project was for strengthening the nation, this strengthening was for the purpose of constructing a relationship between the focal nation and others in the world, especially at a time when capitalism was making impressive headway. In early twentieth-century Japan, for example, Fukuzawa Yukichi's

(1835–1901) advocacy of "history of civilization" (*bunmeishi*) was aimed directly at finding a path for his country to join other "civilized" nations in the world. Like Fuchs's, therefore, Hill's comparative approach has enabled him to note an often-ignored aspect of the subject: the international connection in national historiography. However, he has made it clear, this international connection has little to do with the promotion of transnational historiography proposed recently by some historians. Rather, it is a useful mirror for showing the latter's potential problems.

Hill's finding is consonant with the Chinese experience. In the early twentieth century, when Japanese, American, and European historians were plowing the field of national history, Chinese historians, too, embarked on the project. And their attempt was inspired by their foreign counterparts, especially those in Japan, where the first group of Chinese national historians, or the National Essence (*kuo-tsui* or *kokusui* in Japanese) scholars, received part of their education. What prompted these historians, as Q. Edward Wang shows us in his essay, to search for a history of the Chinese nation was a series of defeats the country had suffered since the mid nineteenth century in confronting other nations. The national history project, therefore, was designed to make changes to the humiliating relationship between China and the outside world in order to earn respect, if not the honor and glory China used to enjoy among other nations. To accomplish such a task required, of course, some imagining, in which these historians conjured up an ideal past in a remote time and identified it as the basis of the National Essence. But they also had to deal with the less ideal yet more accessible past, namely the Confucian-centered Chinese cultural tradition over the past two millennia. The reconstruction of China's national past, therefore, turned out to be much more than the job of imagining; it involved a good deal of effort at negotiating between the ideal and the substantial, the native and the foreign, the past and the present. Such negotiations often caused agonies on the part of the historians, for no matter how lofty and compelling their goal seemed, they could not reach it through self-denial. Nonetheless, viewed from the perspective of historiography, the Chinese experiment with national history was a sharp departure from their age-old tradition in writing and recording history.

The cultural agonies experienced by Chinese historians in the early twentieth century were repeated in the African experience in the mid twentieth century, when Africans began to establish the history discipline of their own. On the one hand, as Toyin Falola describes for us, there was a clear goal: to refute the claims made by European colonialists on racial inferiority and emphasize not only the continent's glorious past but also its ability to build modern nations. On the other hand, however, Falola contends, there was a serious problem embedded in this kind of nationalist historiography, for while it intended to correct the distortion of Africa in the colonial presentation, it also pursued an avowed goal of making history available to the making of African nations. Moreover, nationalist historiography seemed to have followed the same way of thinking as that of the European colonists, only conversely. In contrast to the colonial claim that Europe was a model for Africa, for example, African nationalist historians argued that Africa was the model for Europe, either in a remote past or in a foreseeable future. In the areas of historiography, nationalist historians also followed the elitist and conservative approach to the past and the empirical emphasis on source criticism that thwarted, to a new generation of historians, the potentials for future change.

The above four essays help reveal the fact that national history based on scientific rigor constituted a major turning point in historiography in the world. These essays have also revealed its inherent problems. Since the 1970s, while the writing of national history has retained much of its attraction to many historians in the world, it has no longer been a dominant trend in historiography. The major challenge to national historians, especially those in the non-Western regions as shown in Wang's and Falola's essays, has been addressing the conflict between "imitation" and "identity," as observed by Partha Chatterjee.[16] As an international trend in historical writing, national history, while supplying basis for national identity, extended its influence across national borders and hence had a paradoxical impact on its practice, especially among non-Western historians. Moreover, in the non-Western regions, while the paradox was easily detected in nationalist historiography, it was so pervasive and persistent that that also affected the work of its critics.

In his penetrating analysis of the Subaltern School in modern Indian historiography, to which Chatterjee belonged, Vinay Lal discusses this paradox in great detail. On the one hand, Lal writes, the Subaltern School, formed in the 1980s by a group of India-born, Western-educated scholars in both India and abroad, constituted a high point in modern Indian historiography. It received international attention and praise for its success, not only in shifting the interest of the historian from above to below, but also in experimenting with new approaches to historical study. On the other hand, he finds, despite the novelty claim by the school and its challenge to the colonial "Cambridge School" and the nationalist school that preceded it, it was not immune to the influence of its opponents. For example, the Subaltern interpretation of the British colonization of India resonated with the claims of the colonialists; they blamed the failure of the Indian bourgeoisie to launch a successful revolution and establish a sustainable democracy. Even the adoption of the term "subaltern," a word rarely used in modern English, let alone by non-English speaking peoples, indicated that although their cause claimed autonomous status for a colonized people, it was very much Western-bound in both theoretical inspiration and methodological experimentation. Indeed, the Subaltern scholars studied and mastered Western theories, ranging from Marxism and structuralism to post-structuralism and postmodernism. This suggests that the School's success, or "ascendancy" in Lal's words, lay not so much in its expression of a subaltern voice in India (the School recently has developed more interest in the middle class) as in its ability to negotiate and navigate between new Western theories and Indian or Third World historical experiences. Although it offered a powerful critique of colonial and nationalist historiography, it ultimately failed to rid itself of the elitism that had plagued its opponents. The same can also be said, as argued by Arif Dirlik and others,[17] about the crusade of postcolonial criticism in general.

Although the Subaltern School may not deserve worldwide acclaim as a viable alternative to national and scientific history—the latter pretty much drew the parameters of modern historiography—it has no doubt called attention to the ongoing challenge to the study of history as an academic discipline. That challenge is postmodernism. Drawing on the traditional affinity between history and literature seen in many cultures, postmodernists shed considerable doubt on the central position of rationality in historical interpretation and the emphasis on source criticism in historical methodology. Needless to say, these two constituted the cornerstones of modern historiography and were built on the ideas and notions advanced by the *philosophes* during the Enlightenment. For a long while, historians chose to ignore postmodern critique. Hayden White's *Metahistory*, published in 1973, has since been regarded as a classic of the genre and has received more attention from the literary circle than from the historians.[18] Beginning in the 1990s, however, it seems that it was no longer possible to ignore postmodernism for "[it] is a movement that turns the writing of history into a blind alley and leads up to a dead end." Convinced by such a belief, Keith Windschuttle published an influential book, *The Killing of History*, and launched a serious counterattack.[19] In his essay written for this volume, Windschuttle reiterates his position and offers a review of current literature on postmodernism and history. It is clear to him that while more and more titles have been published on the subject, introducing postmodern theories and critiques to historical study, there also seems to be a valiant and effective defense shored up by seasoned historians in the profession. By contrast, as Windschuttle notes, despite the increased attention of historians to postmodern theory, there have not been many attempts at postmodernist historiography.

Nevertheless, given the magnitude of the postmodern challenge to the history profession, it may well become a foundation for a major change, or a new turning point, in historiography. Chinese historians, to some extent, are drawn to postmodernism. Using the Chinese interest as an example, Arif Dirlik offers an analytical discussion of the postmodern influence on the study of history in general, and of Chinese history in particular. Compared with Windschuttle's unremitting criticism of it, Dirlik sees some of its benefit: the postmodern critique "has legitimized ways of thinking about the past that may rescue history from the teleologies of modernity, and enrich our understanding of the past, and its relationship to the present." The key issue here, he believes, is not whether historians should accept or reject postmodernism, but how to historicize it in order to reach a fair understanding and assessment of its content and influence. In so doing, one has to consider both modernism and postmodernism and their ambiguous connection. The experience of modernism, Dirlik argues, was not the same for European nations and the nations outside Europe. It did not for example lead to the assertion of tradition in non-Western regions as in Western Europe. It is postmodernism that seems to have offered non-Western historians a chance to reclaim some of their tradition in a positive light. Insofar as historical thinking is concerned, the ideas of plurality and temporality espoused by postmodernists have enabled scholars to overcome the China-West, or East-West, dichotomy that was prevalent for quite some time among historians in both China and the West. To a great extent, such dichotomous thinking also existed in many other regions in the world.

Dirlik, of course, is not entirely taken by postmodernism; his essay critically examines the emergence of postmodernism both as an intellectual concept and an historical phenomenon. But he does open a new door to our understanding and evaluation of the influences of modernism and postmodernism in the world. It is clear that if we broaden our horizon and take a cross-cultural approach, we will see things differently and understand them in a different way. This does not mean that we should negate some of the contributions some cultures made in the past, including scientific reasoning and rational thinking, just as we should not slight other accomplishments of other cultures in other periods of time. If historiography is a memory of humankind, this memory ought to be a collective one, contributed by all the peoples in the world. It is to this end that we present this small volume, along with regrettable omissions and unintended mistakes, only hoping to do it better next time.

References

1. A quick search of the Yale University Library resulted in a finding that there have been over one hundred books bearing the title "turning points" across many disciplines, from literature, psychology, and economics to history, art, and education. But it was historians who first adopted the term in the late nineteenth century and have used it most frequently.

2. Geoffrey Barraclough, *Turning Points in World History* (London: Thames and Hudson, 1977), especially chapter 1.

3. A. L. Macfie, *The End of the Ottoman Empire, 1908–1923* (London: Longman, 1998). The quote is on page 1. The other titles published in the Turning Points series so far are Robert Tombs's *Paris Commune, 1871* and Beatrice Heuser's *Bomb: Nuclear Weapons in Their Historical, Strategic and Ethical Context*.

. 4. Barraclough believed that modern European historiography was benefited by two schools, that of Ranke and that of Marx, which helped cause a great change that "had no parallel elsewhere." *Main Trends in History* (New York: Holmes and Meier Publishers, 1979), p. 96.

5. See, for example, Ernst Breisach's *Historiography: Ancient, Medieval, and Modern* (Chicago: University of Chicago Press, 1983).

6. Its subtitle is *Contemporary Research and Theory* (Westport, CT: Greenwood Press, 1979).

7. D. R. Woolf, "Introduction and Editorial Conventions," *A Global Encyclopedia of Historical Writing*, 2 vols. (New York: Garland Publishing, 1998), 1: xiv.

8. Rolf Torstendahl, ed. *An Assessment of Twentieth-Century Historiography: Professionalism, Methodologies, Writings* (Stockholm: The Royal Academy of Letters History and Antiquities, 2000).

9. Peter Burke, "Westliches historisches Denken in globaler Perspektive—10 Thesen," *Westliches Geschichtsdenken, Eine interkulturelle Debatte,* ed. Jörn Rüsen (Göttingen: Vandenhoeck & Ruprecht, 1999), p. 31.

10. Ibid., p. 32.

11. Ibid.

12. Jörn Rüsen, "Einleitung: Geschichtsdenken im interkulturellen Diskurs," in ibid., p. 14 and p. 21. Also, see his "Some Theoretical Approaches to Intercultural Comparative Historiography," *History and Theory* 35 (1996): 5–22.

13. There has been some work done by German scholars, such as *Geschichte und Vergleich: Ansätze und Ergebnisse international vergleichender Geschichtsschreibung*, ed. Heinz-Gerhard Haupt and Jürgen Kocka (Frankfurt: Campus Verlag, 1996). But it remains within the scope of Western historiography.

14. Cf. Masayuki Sato, "Historiographical Encounters: The Chinese and Western Traditions in Turn-of-the-Century Japan," *Storia della Storiografia,* 19 (1992): 38–43; and his "Kognitive Geschichtsschreibung—Normative Geschichtsschreibung," in *Westliches Geschichtsdenken,* ed. Jörn Rüsen, pp. 204–22.

15. See Benjamin Elman, *From Philosophy to Philology: Intellectual and Social Aspects of Change in Late Imperial China* (Cambridge, MA: Harvard University Press, 1984).

16. Cf. Partha Chatterjee, *Nationalist Thought and the Colonial World: A Derivative Discourse* (London: Zed Books Ltd., 1986), pp. 1–35.

17. See Arif Dirlik, *The Postcolonial Aura: Third World Criticism in the Age of Global Capitalism* (Boulder, CO: Westview Press, 1997) and Aijaz Ahmad, "The Politics of Literary Postcoloniality," *Race and Class*, 36:3 (1995):1–20.

18. See Richard T. Vann, "The Reception of Hayden White," *History and Theory* 37 (1998): 143–61.

19. Its subtitle is *How a Discipline Is Being Murdered by Literary Critics and Social Theories* (Sydney: Macleay Press, 1994; New York: Free Press, 1997). Windschuttle is of course not alone. In the 1990s, we have seen quite a few texts that have dealt with the postmodern challenge to historiography, such as Joyce Appleby, Lynn Hunt, and Margaret Jacob, *Telling the Truth about History* (New York: W. W. Norton, 1994); Georg Iggers, *Historiography in the Twentieth Century: From Scientific Objectivity to the Postmodern Challenge* (Hanover, NH: Wesleyan University Press, 1997); and Richard Evans, *In Defense of History* (New York: W. W. Norton, 1999).

PART I

2. The Invention of History: From Homer to Herodotus

François Hartog[1]

The Greeks are considered to be the first inventors of history, and Greece is seen as the place from which everything began. Isn't Herodotus thought to be the "father of history," at least since Cicero (although Cicero quickly added, "even if [with him] there are innumerable fables.")? Father, surely, but for whom and meaning what? For the ancients? Or for us, the moderns, inheritors of a historical culture fashioned by and through the Western tradition?

Two approaches offer themselves, as a starting point, for answering these questions: decentering and historicization. To decenter and historicize Greek experience would be to confront it with other cultures and show how it constituted itself through a series of choices.

To move in this direction, consider four other ancient traditions concerned with the past. It is well known that history and its writing did not begin in Greece; rather it began further to the east and earlier. In Egypt, where continuity was so crucial, the royal lists go back to the end of the fourth millennium B.C.E. The Egyptians started by inscribing pictograms on wooden and ivory tablets; then, later, their compilations on papyrus were at the origins of the first annals. The annals kept the records of the prominent deeds of the kings (or at least of what was viewed as important to record at that time). But perhaps the most striking feature of Egyptian civilization is its autochthony (to use a Greek notion). As far as they looked into the past, the Egyptians didn't see anybody but themselves and the gods. And, as is well known, their monuments have something unique: instead of expressing an interest in the past, they exhibit a desire for eternity, but a material one or a petrified one, which contrasts sharply with the Greek epic and its celebration of an "immortal glory" (*kleos aphthiton*).[1]

In Mesopotamia, at the end of the third millennium B.C.E., the monarchy of Akkade was the first to unite the country under its authority and to enlist scribes to write its history, thereby legitimating its power in the pres-

---

1. Copyright © 2000 Wesleyan University. Reprinted with permission from *History and Theory* 39 (2000): 384–95.

ent. This historiography was a royal history (only kings made history), a monumental one (making itself visible especially through enormous inscriptions), and an exclusive one (held in the hands of a caste of intellectuals, masters of writing).[2]

To the East also, the sacred books of the ancient Hebrews were always fundamentally considered as history. However, although the Bible is inhabited throughout by the demands of remembrance, it never displays any curiosity for the past as such. The principal danger was to forget the ancestors' experiences and no longer believe in their truth. To quote Y. H. Yerushalmi: Israel "receives the order to become a dynasty of priests and a holy nation: nowhere is it suggested that it would become a nation of historians."[3]

A last meaningful example, coming from the Far East, is Vedic India, because there too revelation and the emphasis placed on memory is enormous. But the context, the logic, and the aims are deeply different from those found in Greece. The texts grouped under the name Veda are holy books that only address the sacred. Veda or "knowledge" is "revelation" or more literally "hearing" (audition). Extraordinary characters, "prophets" (the translation is only an approximation), at once human and more than gods, "during the originary times, have in effect had visions, of this or that portion of that knowledge, and have transmitted it to humanity."[4] They have "seen" that knowledge, then have given it, in the form of a text, to be heard, that is to say to be learned and repeated by future Brahmans: to be memorized. Here, memory plays a far greater part than the writing. My only point is that such revelation turns its back on history. The whole process of memorization (long, codified, and demanding) turns away from any historicization of the tradition.[5]

What place can we then assign the Greeks, these people who have never been visited by revelation and who did not know the imperatives or duty of remembrance? Housed in their narrow settlements on the border of the Orient, are they not actually "late-comers" who managed to pass themselves off as "first comers"? (They themselves never claimed to be first in historiography, and Herodotus never proclaimed himself the first inventor of history.)

They were indeed late-comers. They only discovered or rediscovered writing relatively recently (during the eighth century B.C.E.) by adopting the Syro-Phoenician alphabet, and it took them another three centuries or so before they would begin to write their first histories. But the Greek world knew neither the text as revelation nor writing as a preserve for a caste of specialists (as was still the case in the Mycenian kingdoms).

Epistemologically, the Greeks always privileged seeing (over hearing) as the mode of knowledge. To see, to see by oneself, and to know, were one and the same thing. Ontologically, their presence in the world made no question for them: it was self-evident. To be present, to be there, to see, and to know all go together for the Greeks.[6]

Earlier I promised to decenter and to historicize the Greek experience. To historicize would mean to follow or, better yet, to retrace the path from the Greeks to us: the long arch of Western historiography from the Founding

Fathers. I cannot make such a trip here, but I will raise a general question. On what types of continuity does it repose? How does one distinguish between founding, recuperated, or reactivated texts that shape this history? For instance, how and why did Thucydides become, mostly in the nineteenth century, the father of "scientific" history, or to phrase it in David Hume's words, why is "the first page of Thucydides the beginning of real history"?

I. Divination and History

If I were to sketch out an archeology of "historical thinking" in the West, I would first begin by "measuring the possibilities that were excluded as we became Western." If this formulation comes from the philosopher Maurice Merleau-Ponty, who was dealing with the arts of India and China, it seems to me possible to make use of it to reflect on the beginnings of historiography.[7]

Here I will limit myself to a few remarks on the "pre-history" of historical thinking. It is not out of a preference for origins, but because we can set up an experimental situation. We can grasp the configurations (intellectual, political, and so on) from which choices and bifurcations were made that did not have to be, or that could have been otherwise (and later, to be forgotten or to become so self-evident that no one any longer dreamed of questioning them). We can also measure the distance between "an interest in the past" (which exists everywhere under various forms collective and personal) and the emergence of "historical thought," which is, I think, above all concerned with the present.

Let us go back, for a moment, to Mesopotamia at the end of the second millennium. Without pausing over the first model of monumental and royal historiography, whose methods are as incontestable as they are simple, I would like to focus briefly on an exchange which seems to have linked divination and history. In ancient Mesopotamia, as we know, divination played an important role in decision making. How did the soothsayers work? They accumulated and classified oracles, made lists, compiled cases, and created real libraries.[8] The soothsayer was guided by an ideal of exhaustivity (to collect all the examples), and was always looking for precedents. The way a soothsayer works is comparable to the way a judge works. In other words, divination, before being a science of the future, is first of all a science of the past.

A series of oracles were found at Mari (a great palace in Syria) dating from the beginning of the second millennium that modern researchers dubbed "historical oracles." Why historical? Instead of employing the canonical modality—"If the liver of the animal (sacrificed, a sheep) is thus, it is a sign that the king *will take* (in the future) the town in such a way"—the oracle says "If the liver of the animal is thus, it is a sign that the king *has taken* (already) the town in such a way (a very precise one)." This passage from the future to the perfect tense is truly surprising, even more so since the events to which they refer are thought (by the moderns) to have actually taken place. That is why some assyriologists have wanted to see in such oracles the very beginnings of Mesopotamian historiography: first divination, then history (if you leave out the first half of the oracle dealing with the liver).[9] Some sinologists held the same view in regard to Chinese historiography (from divination to historiography).[10]

My lack of competence keeps me from taking sides, but the point that interests me here is that the *two disciplines*, divination and historiography, seem to have shared or inhabited (peacefully enough) the same intellectual space. Surely, they could be and were practiced by the same intellectuals. The Mesopotamian king came in search of assistance and the oracle helped him make a decision. For the specialist consulted, the scribe, to take note of a "historical" oracle, to transcribe it and to study it, meant to add a new oracular configuration to his lists and thereby to increase his stock of precedents. We might also imagine the process reversed. The seer might start from the *event* (the news of the taking of the town by the king) in order to decipher (that is, to verify by doing a sacrifice on the spot) the signs inscribed on the liver. Another possibility might be that the scribes would recopy the historical record, relating this or that act by the king—some part of a royal inscription, for example—and then, using their lists of oracles as databases, they could confront the event and the state of the liver that would normally correspond to such an event. They reconstitute it or invent it and, by doing so, they accumulate new knowledge and increase their capacity for finding new oracles. Of course, even if I don't really know how they worked, it appears, once again, that divination and historiography could work hand in hand.

We could extend this investigation to ancient Rome through an examination of the famous *Annales maximi*, which are all the more famous for having disappeared. Each year the *pontifex maximus* was supposed to write a "chronicle" (*tabula*) that he hung on the front of his house. Cicero interprets this transcription as the very beginning, albeit clumsy and unrefined, of Roman historiography. In a recent re-examination of this vexed question, my colleague John Scheid suggests that this document, delivered at the end of each year, must have functioned as a kind of report on the state of the relations between the city and its gods.[11] It was left to the *pontifex maximus* to compile it in his capacity to "retain on his *tabula* the memory of events." He played the role of a master of time. What *events*? What is an *event*? Victories, defeats, calamities, omens: they were collected and registered, not for themselves, but as signs that allowed for the keeping of records of piety. Particularly important in this regard were the omens: first, one has to decide whether something (strange, extraordinary) is or is not an omen, and if the answer is yes, then what will be the appropriate answer (how to "expiate" it). To do the job, the *pontifex* too needs archives and has to look for precedent.

This compilation could rightly be called an "official" history or a "religious" history of Rome. But it is worth noticing that the temporality at work here is a civic or political one. The report has to be written every year for the new consuls, addressing the following questions: Where do we stand with the gods? Have we done what was necessary? What should we do? The *pontifex* is, as I said, a man of the archives guided by research into precedent (most particularly concerning omens) but his main concern is with the present. Each year he furnishes the new consuls with a report on the City's religious situation.

The choices of the Greek city were different. Divination was certainly present and collections of oracles did exist. But, what was historiography for the Greeks, and later would become for the moderns in the West "history," took a different path. This historiography presupposed the epic. Herodotus wished to rival Homer; what he became, ultimately, was Herodotus.

II. The Epic As Generative Matrix

In Greece all begins with the epic. With it, through it, the Trojan War, which for ten years pitted the Acheans against the Trojans, became the "axial" event situated at the edge of history. At first it was only a Greek event, then a Roman one, and finally a Western one. Today, the Trojan war is disputed and even denied, but it was for centuries a shared point of reference.[12] Thucydides saw it as the first enterprise of any scope undertaken "together" by the Greeks. In fact, it is what constituted them as "Greeks." Retrospectively, the Persian Wars (fifth century B.C.E.) transformed the Trojans into Barbarians (a denomination unknown to Homer) and the Achean expedition into the first and decisive victory over Asia. Five centuries later, Virgil will rediscover for the Romans the very beginning of their history in the ashes of Troy and in the exile of Aeneas. And, nineteen centuries later, Hegel will still celebrate the Trojan War as the victory of Europe over what he called "the asiatic principle."

But the Homeric epic is in no way history, even if the first history—that of Herodotus—makes use of it and of the original pact of the epic, but for its own ends in a completely different world.

III. The Discovery of Historicity

Odysseus's journey is now nearly finished. His companions are dead, he is treated as a guest of honor at the court of the Phaeacians. During the feast given by their king, Odysseus asks the bard Demodocus to sing the famous episode of the wooden horse. In this scene in which the hero is placed in front of the bard who sings of his own adventure, Hannah Arendt saw the beginning, poetically speaking at least, of the category of history. "What had been sheer occurrences now became *history*," she wrote.[13] Indeed, we witness the first telling of the event (which constitutes it as such): the first making of history. With this peculiarity: the very presence of Odysseus proves that "it" really took place. This is an unprecedented configuration, or even an anomaly, since in the epic the truth of the bard's words depended completely and only on the authority of the Muse—both inspiration and guarantor. Going even further, Hannah Arendt saw this scene as paradigmatic for history and poetry because "the reconciliation with reality, *catharsis* (purification), which according to Aristotle was the essence of tragedy, and, according to Hegel, was the ultimate purpose of history, came about through the tears of remembrance."[14]

Could we follow Hannah Arendt in this short-cut that leads us from Homer to Hegel via the Aristotelian *catharsis*? Are we witness to the "first" Greek historical narrative? And for whom? For us, perhaps, but only as a kind of primal scene. For Demodocus, assuredly not. He is the bard as usual. Nor is it such for the Phaeacians. They listen to their bard as usual. Their world situated on the border puts them already in the position of those "people of the future" evoked by Alcinoos: the gods, he says, "have spun out doom for men so that there may be song for those to come," in which they would take pleasure.[15] For Homer's audience (whatever the meaning of such an expression)? How did they perceive that "anomaly"? Did they perceive it at all, and if so, how did they make sense of it?

But the person for whom this question is first posed is Odysseus, because he is the only person who knows, from experience, that what has been sung by Demodocus is at once *his own* story and history. So, how does he react? He cries. Are they "tears of remembrance"? But he also makes a certain number of gestures and utters certain words. To Demodocus, who has already sung twice, he has a messenger bring a choice piece of meat—an obvious way of honoring him—and through this act he celebrates the role of the bard. The *Odyssey*, unlike the *Iliad*, takes pleasure in putting the character of the bard and his performance of the epic on stage.

Then, Odysseus continues: "Demodocus, I consider you outstanding among all men; indeed either The Muse, child of Zeus, instructed you, or Apollo." With this invocation of the close tie that binds the poet to the Muse (or Apollo), we recognize a form of conventional and expected praise: the bard is a visionary. But what comes next is more surprising: "For all in due order (*liên kata kosmon*) you sing the fate of the Greeks / all what they did and endured and suffered, / as if (*hôs*) you yourself were present, or heard it from another (*akousas*)."[16] The register changes here. The visionary became one who saw for himself, or more exactly his description fits so well, is so perfect, or even too (*liên*) perfect, that Odysseus is tempted to believe that Demodocus actually saw what he sings, but all the while knowing that this is absolutely impossible. Demodocus, bard and blind, is in no manner a witness. Odysseus is *the* witness.

Certainly, all listeners of the epic, and Odysseus first among them, are well aware of the omniscience and omnivision of the Muse that depends on her presence, on her being there. "Tell me now, Muses," asks the poet, "who have your homes on Olympus / for you are goddesses, are present, and know all things; we hear only rumor (*kleos*), nor have sure knowledge of anything."[17] The Muses know everything because they are always there. And the bards, under the influence of inspiration, see *like* the Muse, as if they themselves were present. So, why this detour, by Odysseus himself, through human vision, this valorization, historical *avant la lettre*, of the autopsy and this distinction between the eye and the ear, which will become later the main methodological point of Greek historiography?

Demodocus's account is too adequate, perfect (*lién kata kosmon*) not to be the result of actual vision, Odysseus seems to say. For him, actor and witness, this ability to say all, exactly as it happened, is the sure marker of the truth of the song. In effect, to see, to know, and to say are all of a piece. For the Muse, the famous nineteenth-century Rankean motto—to say *wie es eigentlich gewesen ist* (how it actually was)—was never a problem for her! The epic pact thus presupposes this convergence. But, for Odysseus, by a curious and striking reversal, it is human vision that he promotes (at least for these three verses) as the scale by which to measure the correctness of divine vision. A Demodocus as "bard" is juxtaposed, if I may say so, to a Demodocus as "historian," even if the latter only appears here to "authenticate" the other, the bard. Of course, the Muse has the last word. But the shift of register, even so brief, or the quasi doubling of Demodocus as "bard" and as "historian," is nevertheless, poetically speaking (in the sense of a poetics of knowledge), important. What counts is the very fact that Odysseus was able to utter such a proposition. This change of register appears as a flash of light illuminating another possible configuration of knowledge, as the designation of a place that does not yet have a name. It does not make it necessary or even probable but merely possible; indeed, only a few centuries later would Herodotus fill the place and name it: *historia*.

Demodocus obviously does not answer Odysseus's false questions and no one expects him to answer them. He is the bard playing his role. His song enchants the Phaeacians. But Odysseus himself cries. Why? Are these, to quote Arendt once again, "the tears of remembrance"? When the misfortunes of the Greeks are evoked, is he like Penelope or Menelaus, a victim of *pothos* (mourning)? Is the work of mourning not yet complete? This is in fact the sense of Alcinoos' question when, noticing his tears, he asks Odysseus if he lost a family member or someone close to him at Troy. Odysseus does not respond.

But well before Alcinoos' question about the reason for his tears, a surprising simile, a clear marker of the poet's intervention, had already underlined their strangeness and importance. "And just as a woman laments falling about her dear husband who falls before his city and his people as he wards off from city and children the pitiless day, and she seeing him dying and gasping pours herself around him and shrieks shrilly, but the soldiers behind her strike her back and shoulders with their spears and lead her off as a slave to have toil and woe, and her cheeks wither in grief most pitiable: so pitiful a tear did Odysseus let drip beneath his brows."[18]

That Odysseus cries we might understand, but why like a wife? For whom are these tears of pity shed? The woman who is devastated by mourning, who cries for her absent husband, is Penelope. The woman who saw her husband die in front of his city and his people, before being harnessed like a slave, is Andromaque. Through its evocative power, this simile sums up and universalizes Odysseus' suffering which becomes the suffering of all victims of war and is another manifestation of that "art of allusion," so characteristic of how the *Odyssey* functions.[19] At the same time, this simile contributes depth to the text and as such would temper Eric Auerbach's stylistic notations in his great book *Mimesis* where he confronts the Homeric epic with Biblical narrative.[20] The epic style is "externalized, in a perpetual foreground." However, here we discover background.

Odysseus cries? It seems to me that the weeping Odysseus is in mourning for himself: his tears are shed for himself. From the beginning of his wanderings in the non-human world entered into from Cape Malea, he is a missing person: neither dead nor alive, he has lost everything, even his name. He is *like* a wife who, from the day of her husband's death, has nothing more, is nothing. The heroic, "masculine" part of him, that part of him to which his glory is attached, was left, so to speak, on the shores of Troy. Now, landed on the shores of the Phaeacians, these mediators who are about to bring him back home to the real world, he hears himself celebrated by the songs of Demodocus under his glorious name. The "husband" rejoins the "wife." Very soon he will be able to say again: "I am Odysseus, son of Laertes, who for all wiles am famous among men, and my fame reaches heaven."[21]

But for that, or before that, there is a price to pay. Odysseus finds himself in the terrible position of having to listen to the story of his adventures, told in the third person, as if he were absent, as if he were dead. He discovers himself occupying the place of the dead. At the very moment when Odysseus hopes finally to be reunited with his past glory, in the midst of the Phaeacians and through the very words of Demodocus, he experiences a kind of death. Is he dead, is he alive? He hears what a living man normally would never hear. In a sense, this last experience is even more radical than his descent down into Hades because in Hades, though he may have traveled to the outer limits that separate the living from the dead, he remained without ambiguity on the shores of the living. But now he experiences what it means to be beyond that limit. This part of the scene too is emblematic.

I suggest that this brief moment when he is *no longer* Odysseus and *not yet* Odysseus is a poetic translation of a painful discovery of the non-coincidence of oneself with oneself (or self with self?). This is a discovery that does not yet have words to name it, but that Homer makes visible through tears. Is it not actually the experience of time itself that resides in the gap between otherness and identity? I am not referring here to the experience of finitude or historicality, but rather the shock of the temporal difference that separates oneself from oneself: not yet and no longer, the first encounter with "historicity."

The epic separates past and present through simple juxtaposition. As soon as the bard, any bard, begins to sing, the caesura divides: the *klea andrôn*, the great deeds of heroes, are transformed into acts performed by men of yore and the dead become men of the past. The *Odyssey* would also like to be able to *juxtapose* but, having chosen to sing of the return, finds it impossible to do so. As with Odysseus, the poem also experiences time and discovers historicity. Or, to put it differently, the *Odyssey* is perhaps caught between two regimes of narrative: the epic one in which it would like to believe, and another one, dimly present for the moment, but which seeks to take account of time itself. To be overly schematic: the poem can no longer simply "juxtapose" and it does not yet know how to "chronologize." Does the fascination of the *Odyssey* not stem also from its evocation of the epic as nostalgia? Is it not itself a desired and impossible return to the epic—the *Iliad*?

Such were what I called the choices of the epic.

IV. Historein/Sêmainein

"Tell me, O Muse, of the man of many devices . . ." was the inaugural pact of the epic. The Muse, daughter of memory and source of inspiration, was the guarantor of the poet's song. With the first history, the realm of the spoken world is over. Prose replaces verse; writing dominates; the Muse disappears. In its place a new word and a new narrative economy emerge: "What Herodotus the Halicarnassian has learned by inquiry is set forth (the exposition of his *historiê*. . . ." In the service of no particular power, with his very first words he begins to define and claim the narrative form which begins with the use of his own name. He is the author of his account (*logos*) and it is this account that establishes his authority. The paradox lies in the fact that, at the same time, this newly claimed authority has yet to be fully constructed. Such a narrative strategy, characteristic of this moment in Greek intellectual history, marks a break with the eastern historiographers. If the Greeks were inventors of anything, they invented the historian rather than the history. (Such a mode of self-affirmation and writing was far from a purely historiographical phenomenon. To the contrary, it is a marker or even the signature of this period of intellectual history [sixth–fifth century B.C.E.] which witnessed the rise of "egotism" among artists, philosophers, doctors.[22])

The life of Herodotus unfolded between two major conflicts: the Persian wars (which he had not known firsthand but which he chose to relate), a period of threats to, and consolidation of, the polis; and the Peloponnesian war, inextricably linked to Thucydides' account, also a perilous time of profound questioning. The period Herodotus describes in his work (550–480 B.C.E., with several additional flashbacks) saw important changes. To the east, the Persian empire arose and prospered; in Greece, first Sparta and then Athens came to prominence. Politically, the ancient ideal of "eunomy" was replaced by that of "isonomy" (equality of political rights for all citizens), and finally by an entirely new notion, that of democracy.

When the *Histories* opens, the Barbarians were already situated geographically, forming with the Greeks a pair of opposites. To Herodotus, the division between them is obvious: there is no need to explain or justify it, although it was absent from Homer's poems. The distinction had appeared between the sixth and fifth centuries, starting with the Persian Wars, which territorialized the Barbarians geographically and gave them a face: that of the Persians. In the *Histories*, Herodotus bore witness to this phenomenon and actively contributed to it. He went even further, however, in constructing a political rationale for distinguishing between Greeks and Barbarians, which also offered a political perspective on the Greek past. As a result, the word

"Barbarian" came to signify not primarily, or necessarily, barbarism (cruelty, excess, laxity), but political difference; it separated those who chose to live in city-states from those who never managed to get along without kings. The Greek is "political," in other words free, while the Barbarian is "royal" meaning submissive to a master (*despotês*).[23]

This new form of discourse and this singular figure did not emerge from a vacuum. Herodotus undertook for the Persian Wars what Homer had done for the Trojan War. To write history means to begin with a conflict and tell the story of a great war on both sides and by fixing the "origins" (*aitia*, truest cause). In contrast to the Bible which tells a continuous story from the beginning of time, the first Greek historians fixed a point of departure and limited themselves to recounting a specific sets of events.[24]

Like the bard, the historian deals with memory, oblivion, and death. The bard of old was a master of glory (*kleos*), a dispenser of immortal encomia to the heroes who died gloriously in war. Herodotus sought only to ensure that the traces of the markings of men, the monuments that they produced, would not disappear (like the colors of a painting that fade with time), would not cease to be recounted and celebrated (he used, characteristically, the term *aklea*, stripped of glory). The shift from *kleos* to *aklea* indicates that the historian refers continually to the epic, but also makes more modest claims than the bard.[25] It is as if he knew that the ancient promise of immortality could never again be uttered except as a negative: as a promise to delay oblivion. Similarly, where the bard's area of expertise covered "the deeds of heroes and gods," the historian limits himself to the "deeds of man," in a time which is itself defined as "the time of man." He adds one principle of selection: to choose that which is great and elicits astonishment. Thus he gives himself a means of measuring difference in events and of ordering multiplicity in the world.

The emblematic word, *historiê* (the Ionic form of *historia*) little by little took hold (although Thucydides, for his part, took pains never to use it). It is an abstract word, formed from the verb *historein*, to inquire. To inquire, in all the meaning of the word, means to go and see for oneself. It expresses more a state of mind and an approach than a specific field. *Historia* is derived from *histôr*, which is related to *idein*, to see, and *oida*, I know. Thus the *histôr* is present in the epic where he appears several times, but not as an eyewitness, only as an arbiter, or better yet a guarantor in a context of *neikos* (quarrel): he has never seen for himself what is at stake.

Herodotus is neither bard nor even *histôr*: he *historei* (investigates). He does not possess the natural authority of the *histôr*, nor does he benefit from the divine vision of the bard. He has only *historiê*, a certain form of inquiry which is the first step in his historiographical practice. Produced as a substitute, *historiê* operates in a way analogous to the omniscient vision of the Muse, who knows because her divine nature allowed her to be present everywhere. The historian, acting on no authority but his own, intends from now on to "go forward with his account, and speak of small and great cities alike. For many states that were once great have now become small."[26]

If the inquiry (thus defined) both evokes the wisdom of the bard and breaks with it, Herodotus also appeals to a second register of knowledge (that we have already met), the divinatory one. Herodotus *historei* but he also *sêmainei*. He investigates and he shows, reveals, signifies. *Sêmainein* is used for someone who sees what others do not or could not see, and makes his report. The verb specifically designates oracular knowledge.[27] Since the epic, the seer, who knows the present, future, and also the past, is portrayed as a man of knowledge. Epimenides of Crete, a famous soothsayer, was reputed to have applied his divination skills not to what ought to be, but to what, having already happened, still remained obscure. Here too divination is a science of the past. We are also reminded of Heraclitus' formula, according to which the oracle neither speaks nor hides, but "means" (*sêmainei*).[28]

In the Prologue, precisely at the moment when Herodotus speaks for the first time saying "I," he "signifies" (*sêmainei*). Drawing on his own personal knowledge, he reveals, designates who first took offensive action against the Greeks, Croesus, the king of Lydia. The first to subjugate the Greeks, Croesus is designated as "responsible," or "guilty" (*aitios*). Through this investigation and designation, Herodotus is certainly not a seer, but he arrogates to himself a type of oracular authority. So, even if it is in a very different way from what we saw before in Mesopotamia, divination and history with Herodotus have still something in common.

The two verbs *historein* and *sêmainein* are crossroads verbs where ancient and contemporary knowledge come together and intertwine, as attested in a unique way by the work of Herodotus himself. They are two intellectual tools by which to "see clearly" further, beyond the visible, in space or time; they characterize and shape the intellectual style of the first historian. He is neither bard nor soothsayer but between the two; he is Herodotus.

References

1. J. Assmann, *Das Kulturelle Gedächtnis: Schrift, Erinnerung und politische Identität in frühen Hochkulturen* (Munich, 1997), 169–74.

2. J. J. Glassner, *Chroniques mésopotamiennes* (Paris, 1993).

3. Y. H. Yerushalmi, *Zakhor: Jewish History and Jewish Memory* (Seattle, 1982).

4. C. Malamoud, "Inde védique," in *Dictionnaire des mythologies*, ed. Y. Bonnefoy (Paris, 1981), 541.

5. C. Malamoud, *Cuire le monde: Rite et pensée dans l'Inde ancienne* (Paris, 1989), 305.

6. R. Brague, *Aristote et la question du monde* (Paris, 1988), 28; J. Strauss Clay, *The Wrath of Athena: Gods and Men in the Odyssey* (Princeton, 1983), 12, 13.

7. See *Westliches Geschichtsdenken: Eine interkulturelle Debate*, ed. Jörn Rüsen (Göttingen, 1999).

8. J. Bottero, "Symptômes, signes, écriture," in *Divination et Rationalité*, ed. J. P. Vernant (Paris, 1974), 70–86.

9. Glassner, *Chroniques mésopotamiennes*, 26–28.

10. L. Vandermeersch, "L'imaginaire divinatoire dans l'histoire en Chine," in *Transcrire les mythologies*, ed. M. Detienne (Paris, 1994), 103–13.

11. John Scheid, "Le temps de la cité et l'histoire des prêtres," in *Transcrire les mythologies*, 149–158.

12. See, for example, M. I. Finley, "Lost: The Trojan War," in *Aspects of Antiquity: Discoveries and Controversies* (New York, 1972), 31–42.

13. H. Arendt, *Between Past and Future* (New York, 1954), 45.

14. Ibid., 45.

15. Homer, *Odyssey*, 8, 580.

16. Homer, *Odyssey*, 8, 487–91.

17. Homer, *Iliad*, 2, 484–86; Clay, *The Wrath of Athena*, 19.

18. Homer, *Odyssey*, 8, 521–31.

19. P. Pucci, *Ulysses Polutropos: Intertextual Readings in the* Odyssey *and* Iliad (Ithaca, N.Y., 1987).

20. E. Auerbach, *Mimesis: The Representation of Reality in Western Literature* (Princeton, 1953).

21. Homer, *Odyssey*, 9, 19–20.

22. G.E.R. Lloyd, *The Revolution of Wisdom* (Berkeley, 1987).

23. F. Hartog, *Mémoire d'Ulysse: Récits sur la frontière en Grèce ancienne* (Paris, 1996), 87–95.

24. A. Momigliano, *The Classical Foundations of Modern Historiography* (Berkeley, 1990), 18ff.

25. Herodotus, I, 1.

26. Herodotus, I, 5.

27. M. Detienne, *Apollon le couteau à la main* (Paris, 1998), 138ff.; F. Hartog, "Myth into *Logos*: The Case of Croesus or the Historian at Work," in *From Myth to Reason?*, ed. R. Buxton (Oxford, 1999), 183–95.

28. Heraclitus, fr. 93.

3. The Ch'in Unification (221 B.C.) in Chinese Historiography

Chun-chieh Huang

I. Introduction

"Six warring states seized to complete the unification of great lands and far seas; great forests on Mt. Shu balded only to erect A-fang Palace," bemoaned the T'ang Dynasty (618–907) poet Tu Mu (803–852). The Ch'in state, located in the wild west of China proper, with its *"Sturm und Drang"* militant power, conquered disparate kingdoms and unified the land in 221 B.C. However, this very first Chinese Dynasty prospered only fifteen years before it melted into thin air. Nonetheless, the quick rise and decline of the Ch'in Dynasty (221–206 B.C.) constituted a major turning point in Chinese history, marking its transformation from classical China to imperial China both in historical reality and in the Chinese mind. The Chinese have since then often returned to the experience of the unification and downfall of the Ch'in Dynasty as a source of guidance and inspiration. It seems as if the impressive rise and quick collapse of the Ch'in Dynasty became an immanent mirror, in which the Chinese could constantly reflect their own pains and gains. The question is: What exactly did the Ch'in experience offer to the Chinese? To answer this question, namely how and why the Chinese dwelled on the Ch'in experience, we need to consider certain characteristics of Chinese historical thinking.

But first, let us take a look at how Chinese historians approached the importance of the Ch'in unification in Chinese history. In general, Chinese historians believe that the unification of the Ch'in Dynasty made a major contribution to the development of Chinese culture. And this belief has been shared by historians in both imperial and modern China. In 1924, for example, Lü Ssu-mien (Ch'eng-chih, 1884–1959), an acclaimed historian known for his Classical learning, observed that "China before the Three Dynasties was a feudalistic world, and China after the Ch'in and Han Dynasties became an imperial one, which was essentially different. It was because the Ch'in Dynasty unified China."[1] In 1939, Ch'ien Mu (Pin-ssu, 1895–1990), a famous Confucian scholar and historian, expressed a similar viewpoint. Ch'ien summarized the historical significance of the Ch'in's unification as follows: a) mapping out the imperial realm of China; b) unifying the Chinese people; c) laying the foundation for the Chinese political system; and d) establishing a basis for the future development of Chinese scholarship.[2]

Lü and Ch'ien's observation of the position of the Ch'in Dynasty in history went unchallenged among many Chinese scholars throughout the twentieth century. For instance, more recently Cho-yün Hsü, an American-trained social historian of ancient China, offered his view of the role of the Ch'in Dynasty in developing Chinese culture. According to him, in the long evolution of Chinese culture, there have been only two periods, demarcated by the Ch'in. The time from the ancient period to the Ch'in and Han Dynasties was the first period, which was characterized by the emergence of the first "universal order." From that time onward to the present day was the second period. The first universal order, established in the Ch'in-Han period, collapsed during the period of disunion (220–589), which consequently led to the establishment of the second universal order in the Sui (581–618) and Tang (618–907) Dynasties. The second universal order was modified through the Sung (960–1279) and Ming (1368–1644) times. However, it collapsed during the Ch'ing (1644–1911) Dynasty. From that time onward, or in the second period, Chinese culture was darkened by thick clouds.

The universal order in the Ch'in and Han Dynasties included political, economic, social, and cultural dimensions. Politically, this universal order was founded on an imperial and bureaucratic system. Economically, there was a national market network operating together with small-scale agricultural systems. Culturally, there was a prevalent form of Chinese thought that blended elements of Confucianism, Taoism, Legalism, and Yin-yang thought. It was soon to be developed into a philosophical system that could be applied throughout the world. Hsü also notes that at a social level, there was a group of intellectuals who endeavored to preserve and promote Chinese culture.[3]

Historians in imperial China, though believing that the unification of the Ch'in Dynasty marked a crucial turning point in Chinese history, assessed the significance of the event mainly from a moral perspective. As the rise of the Ch'in Dynasty marked the beginning of autocratic rule in China, its decline was regarded as an unavoidable outcome of moral corruption at the imperial court. To some, the historical experience of the Ch'in Dynasty even suggested a degradation of moral principle (*tao*).

This essay attempts to scrutinize the peculiarities of Chinese historical thinking via a study of the Chinese reflection on the Ch'in experience. We will review the opinions of Chinese intellectuals and historians about the Ch'in empire, especially their moral perspective. We argue that Chinese historical thinking is essentially moral thought; traditional Chinese historical scholarship is a study of ethics. To better analyze the ethical concerns in Chinese historical thinking, we will discuss some general characteristics of Chinese thinking in the second section. In the third section we will review both the negative and positive moral judgments that Chinese intellectuals passed on to the Ch'in experience. The fourth section will inquire into the twofold-ness of the notion of *tao* in Chinese historical thinking. In the last section we will conclude the essay with some reflections on the characteristics of Chinese historical thinking.

II. Chinese Historical Thinking as Moral Thinking

Before considering the Ch'in experience, I have to clarify what I meant by the moral dimension of Chinese historical thinking in two respects. (2.1) It seems to me that the Chinese often establish moral imperatives through historical narrative and historical interpretation. Chinese historical narrative is more than "exemplary."[4] It goes beyond supplying solid examples for extracting moral lessons from the deeds of historical characters or historical events. The Chinese mode of thinking is also concrete; it seeks to contextualize itself in solid examples. (2:2) There was never a *l'histoire pour l'histoire* in the Chinese tradition; the Chinese wrote history of the "past" for the betterment of the "future." Chinese historians focused their historical narrative on the moment here and now, so that it could serve as guidance for the future. For this didactic purpose, they extracted universal moral ideals from concrete historical facts. The following paragraphs will explore these two aspects in further detail.

(2:1) As I have argued elsewhere,[5] the so-called "cognitive" activity in Chinese historical thinking actually moves back and forth in time, first going to the past for information, then coming back to the present with lessons to pattern our own actions by. Then it goes back once again to ascribe meaning and significance to the past, then it comes back with inspirations for living accordingly in the present moment. And this "back-and-forth" movement is itself self-consciously historical. Although this is not a full-fledged theory of history, it is undoubtedly a dynamic view of history particular to the Chinese people, which is also frequently exhibited and practiced in their day-to-day thinking and living.

Mencius (ca. 371–289 B.C.) was most explicit in stating and executing this back-and-forth movement in historical thinking. He noted that just as no artists or artisans could perform their tasks without squares, compasses, and pipes, no benevolent ruler could govern without historical precedents. The Way of the Former Kings and the sages were the compasses and squares for a benevolent government.[6] Mencius also used the historical examples of the famous figures—Shun, Fu Yüeh, Chiao Ke, Kuan Chung, Sun Shu-ao, and Po-li Hsi—to suggest that Heaven often tests one's fortitude through starvation, hardship, and frustration before placing on him a great task or responsibility. Hence he concluded a principle: men flourish in adversity and wither in comfort.[7] This example shows that Chinese thinkers not only extract moral principles from history, they also use historical examples to expound these principles, hence, the back-and-forth movement.

Mencious' use of history suggests that Chinese thinkers, as well as historians, follow a concrete mode of thinking, which refers to an approach that regards historical facts as the basis of abstract theories. Chang Hsüeh-ch'eng (Shih-chai, 1728–1801), a Ch'ing historian, once remarked, "Ancient sages never discuss principles without giving solid examples."[8] Chang's observation offers a good example for the concrete mode of thinking—it reasons with solid and specific examples rather than with metaphysical speculation. Of course, while based on specific examples, the principle it draws from also points to the "universal." However it is the "concrete universal."

(2:2) It is precisely because the Chinese tend to extract universal ethical principles from historical events, Chinese historical thinking is never very distant from the present, nor from the future. The grand historian Ssu-ma Ch'ien (145–86 B.C.) expressed this idea in an exemplary manner. In his magnum opus *Shih Chi* (or the *Grand Scribe's Records*), Ssu-ma Ch'ien comments on several "truly extraordinary men" and their writings of history:[9]

> All these men had a rankling in their hearts, for they were not able to accomplish what they wished. Therefore they wrote of past affairs in order to pass on their thoughts to future generations. . . . I have examined the deeds and events of the past and investigated the principles behind their success and failure, their rise and decay, in one hundred and thirty chapters. I wished to examine all that concerns heaven and man, to penetrate the changes of the past and present, completing all as the work of one family. But before I had finished my rough manuscripts, I met with this calamity. It is because I regretted that it had not been completed that I submitted to the extreme penalty without rancor. When I have truly completed this work, I shall deposit it in some safe place. If it may be handed down to men who will appreciate it and penetrate to the villages and great cities, then though I should suffer a thousand mutilations, what regret would I have?

As Ssu-ma Ch'ien said, Chinese historians record "past affairs" for the sake of "future generations." Historians seek to find the principles behind successes and failures in history, so that their historical records can serve as a guidance for the present and for the future.

III. The Ch'in Empire as a Negative and Positive Mirror

In this section, we will analyze the unification and downfall of the Ch'in empire as (3:1) a negative mirror that manifests the eternal principle in history—that any empire is doomed to decline if it fails to rule with humanity and righteousness; and (3:2) a positive mirror that reflects the principle that unification brings peace and prosperity to the people. These two points are further analyzed in the following passages.

(3:1) Why did the Ch'in Dynasty decline? This question, which readily arose from observing the Ch'in experience, has been central to Chinese historical thinking ever since the Han times. During the Tien-an Men Square Incident on April 5, 1978, for example, Peking citizens mourned the death of Chou En-lai and put up signs with slogans such as, "The Age of Emperor Ch'in Is Vanished," and "Folks Today Are No Longer Simple-Minded." It shows that the Ch'in experience remains a vivid memory for the modern-day Chinese. Over the past two millennia, indeed, the Chinese people by and large grunted and sweated under a weary life, due largely to the oppressors' wrongs and insolence and their monopoly of power. The Chinese who suffered under the slings and arrows of this monopoly politics often pointed to the Ch'in Dynasty and regarded it as the source of their suffering. In the meantime, they also longed about a new departure from the Ch'in experience. Thus viewed, the Ch'in Dynasty has never completely vanished from one's memory, nor have all the unpleasant experiences associated with it. History therefore becomes an endless cycle of memory and a continuous interaction between past and present. Despite the postmodernist challenge, I would still like to say that what history becomes today is actually formed and engendered by the past; what seems past is never passed by completely.[10]

The Ch'in as a negative mirror rendered tremendous historical lessons for the Chinese since the founding of the Former Han Dynasty (206 B.C.–8 A.D.). This was due to the fact that the Han emperors and ministers had to deal with the legitimacy question of their dynasty.[11] As the story goes, the founding Emperor Han Kao-tsu (r. 202–195 B.C.) considered his own empire as a "spear-won land," and once blustered at a Confucian scholar Lu Chia (216–176 B.C.): "I established my empire on horseback. Why should I study the *Book of Odes* and the *Book of History*?" However, after Han Kao-tsu had been on the throne for a short period, he quickly realized the importance of the legitimacy question. In fact, Han Kao-tsu later became almost fascinated with the "reasons why the Ch'in lost control of All Under Heaven."[12] It is because as the immediate successor to the Ch'in Dynasty, the Han rulers must develop a good explanation for the Ch'in's fall in order to prove that the establishment of the Han Dynasty was not only legitimate but also necessary. Lu Chia's *Hsin Yü* (New Discourse) was written exactly for that purpose. It explained the failure of the Ch'in and drew historical "lessons" from its experience. The most important "lesson" drawn from the Ch'in experience was the principle that any emperor has to rule his subjects with humanity and rationality, which was espoused most eloquently by Chia Yi (201–169 B.C.), another well-known Confucian in the Han period:

> Ch'in, beginning with an insignificant amount of territory, reached the power of a great state and for a hundred years made all the other great lords pay homage to it. Yet after it had become master of the whole empire and established itself within the fastness of the pass, a single commoner opposed it and its ancestral temples toppled, its ruler died by the hands of men, and it became the laughingstock of the world. Why? Because it failed to rule with humanity and righteousness and to realize that the power to attack and the power to retain what one has thereby won are not the same.[13]

Chia Yi's comments, to a large extent, suggested the attitude of Chinese intellectuals toward the Ch'in experience throughout the imperial period. What the Chinese intellectuals meant by "the Ch'in failed to rule with humanity and righteousness" is to be understood in the following contexts:

(3:1a) *Ch'in's application of strict laws and heavy punishment*: the most prevalent stereotype against the Ch'in empire lies in its rigid laws and inhuman punishment. Again, let us quote Chia Yi:

> The First Emperor of Ch'in, harboring an avaricious heart and following a self-assertive mind, not trusting his meritorious vassals or keeping close to intellectuals and commoners, abolished the kingly way of ruling, established his personal authority, banned writings and books, stiffened punitive laws, promoted craftness and power, neglected benevolence and righteousness, and made tyranny the first rule of the world.[14]

For Chinese historians, "rigid enforcement of harsh punishment" has become a collective memory about the Ch'in's Dynasty in Chinese history. In *Shih Chi*, Ssu-ma Ch'ien quoted the words of the Ch'in Shih-huang's contemporaries to describe the cruel punishment under the Ch'in:

> The way the First Emperor is, he has a disposition to be obstinant and self-willed. Arising from a feudal lord and having united the world, he attained all he intended and fulfilled all he desired. He thinks no one who ever lived is his match. He exclusively employs legal officials, and they are close to him and favored by him. The Erudites, although there are seventy of them, vainly fill their positions but are not used. The chancellors and other great vassals all receive assignments for tasks His Highness alone determines and rely on himself to accomplish things. His Highness enjoys establishing his prestige through punishment and killing. As the officials in the world are afraid of offending him and want to keep their salaries, none would venture not to devote their loyalty to him. Since His Highness has never been informed of his mistakes, he becomes more arrogant daily. And his subordinates either submit in awe of him or deceive him to win his acceptance.[15]

Pan Ku (Meng-chien, 32–92), author of *The History of Former Han*, also criticized Emperor Shih-huang for relying solely upon punishment in government.[16] His criticism was shared by official historians of later periods. In the section called "The Treatises on Punishments and Laws" of many dynastic histories, we find the same criticism of the "unrighteous" use of harsh punishment in the Ch'in Dynasty. However, what is interesting was that although historians regarded the Ch'in political experience as a negative mirror for later rulers, they were more or less impressed by Emperor Shih-huang's success in unifying China proper. After the unification, Emperor Shih-huang inscribed his travels and visitations throughout the land on the stones, in which he perceived himself as having "set up imperial etiquette and social graces,"[17] putting "social relationships in order and the society in peace,"[18] and making "politics and the bureaucratic system operate smoothly."[19] Nonetheless, it seems that historians could not excuse the emperor's cruel rule despite his military success. A grand canyon, therefore, lies between Emperor Shih-huang's self-image and later historians' perception of his deeds.

(3:1b) *Destroying the cultural heritage and abandoning traditional values*: the second "lesson" the Chinese learned from the experience of the rise and decline of the Ch'in empire was that the Ch'in fell because it neglected traditional values. Chia Yi described Emperor Shih-huang as a ruler who "discarded the ways of the former kings and burned the writings of the hundred schools in order to make the people ignorant."[20] From that time on, "burning the books and burying scholars" became the most memorable scandal associated with the reign of Emperor Shih-Huang and registered permanently in the minds of many Chinese, especially among historians. Ssu-ma Ch'ien, for instance, considered Emperor Shih-huang responsible for destroying time-honored ceremonies.[21] Pan Ku went even further. He suggested that Emperor Shih-huang's hostility toward the Confucianists was a major cause for the fall of the Ch'in Dynasty shortly after the emperor's death. The Confucianists were so alienated that when Ch'en She rebelled against the Ch'in, they offered their help to him.[22] Other dynastic histories echoed Ssu-ma and Pan's criticisms of the Ch'in Dynasty.

Again, what was generally agreed upon by Chinese historians contradicted to Emperor Shih-huang's self-perception of his position in history. Emperor Shih-huang thought that in unifying China, he also unified the thoughts and opinions of the Chinese people, upon which he could establish a "political and bureaucratic system." It would "operate smoothly and bring forth an economic boom." Moreover, this system was so perfect that "the great way of ruling manifests itself and never needs changing."[23] In other words, Emperor Shih-huang hoped that the thoughts he had unified would be passed on to later generations without alteration. What happened after his death showed that he was totally wrong.

(3:2) Although the Ch'in system did not become perpetual as Emperor Shih-huang had hoped, its impact proved to be far-reaching. In the Chinese tradition, there was another consideration of the Ch'in experience, which regarded it as a positive mirror. Chia Yi, the same Han scholar who vehemently criticized Emperor Shih-huang's hostility toward intellectuals, praised the emperor's contributions to unifying China at that time:

> After this the First Emperor arose to carry on the glorious achievements of six generations. Cracking his long whip, he drove the universe before him, swallowing up the eastern and western Chou and overthrowing the feudal lords. He ascended to the highest position and ruled the six directions, scourging the world with his rod, and his might shook the four seas. In the south he seized the land of Yueh and made of it the Cassia Forest and Elephant com-

manderies, and the hundred lords of Yueh bowed their heads, hung halters from their necks, and pleaded for their lives with the lowest officials of Ch'in. Then he caused Meng T'ien to build the Great Wall and defend the borders, driving back the Hsiung-nu over seven hundred li so that the barbarians no longer dared to come south to pasture their horses and their men dared not take up their bows to avenge their hatred.[24]

Indeed, it was because the Ch'in Empire unified China proper, it put an end to slings and arrows across five hundred years during the Spring and Autumn Period (722–464 B.C.) and the Warring States Period (463–222 B.C.). Butchery of common people was commonplace before the unification of Ch'in. "In wars to gain land, the dead fill the plains; in wars to gain cities, the dead fill the cities," described Mencius.[25] And the terrible warfare was often followed by years of great famine. Modern statistics tell us that if we count a large scale warfare, namely a war fought between two big states, as "1" and small scale warfare as "0.5," then 468.5 wars were fought during the 242 years of the Warring State Period.[26] What is more alarming was that the frequency of war and bloodshed increased as the years went on until the Ch'in put an end to it. Ssu-ma Ch'ien, another critic of the Ch'in, also recorded that the Ch'in unification resulted in a standardization of "the measurements of capacity, weight, and length." In the Ch'in Empire, "all carts had the same width between wheels, and all writings used the same characters."[27] All this helped bring peace and prosperity to the common people.

Following Chia Yi and Ssu-ma Ch'ien, more people in the later periods evaluated the Ch'in experience favorably. Pan Piao (3–30 A.D.), for example, who witnessed the chaos associated with the transition from the Former Han Dynasty (206 B.C.–23 A.D.) to the Later Han Dynasty (25–220 A.D.) in the first century, explained to his friend Kui Hsiao (?–33 A.D.) that according to his observation, the Han would last a long time. Pan's optimism was based on the fact that "the Han inherited new administrative divisions from the Ch'in Empire in which no feudal lords could be in power for hundreds of years."[28] In other words, Pan believed that the Ch'in unification had destroyed the feudal warlords, the potential challenger to a centralized empire, and had laid the foundation for a unified dynasty. In his recent study of Han intellectuals, Wang Chien-wen points out that in regard to the Ch'in experience, the attitude of the Han intellectuals was ambivalent. On the one hand, they loathed the dictatorial rule of Emperor Shih-huang and his successor. On the other hand, they credited the Ch'in for creating a bureaucratic and administrative system, the very first in Chinese history, that, after inheriting it with some modification, the Han rulers used to keep their Dynasty together for a long period of time.[29]

Thus viewed, the Ch'in Empire's unification did put an end to the bloody Warring States period of hundreds of years and pave the way for a stable life and economic revival. This fact, despite Ch'in's favoring of harsh punishment toward its subjects, strikes later historians as having a positive impact, especially when they consider other difficult times in Chinese history. For modern historians, the Ch'in experience often helps them to reflect critically their own war experience in the twentieth century.

IV. The Twofold-ness of Tao and Its Problems in Chinese Historical Thinking

The foregoing description of the Ch'in as both a negative and a positive mirror in Chinese historiography gives rise to a question: If the Ch'in did apply harsh laws and destroy traditional culture, how can the Ch'in unification have a positive impact on history? In order to answer this question, it seems that we must consider *tao*, the central concept in Chinese historical thinking. To many Chinese historians, (4:1) history is best taken as a concrete manifestation of abstract and transcendental *tao* in this mundane human world. (4:2) In the meantime, *tao* is both the *modus operandi* of the universe (the "to be") and the moral guiding norms of human affairs (the "ought to be"). (4:3) Given this emphasis on the "ought to be" in history, Chinese historical thinking becomes inadequate to offer a satisfactory explanation for the role the "evils" played in history. In the following, we will explain why this is so.

(4:1) First of all, let us see how the Ch'in experience was viewed from the perspective of *tao*. In the Han period, it was commonplace for people to attack the Ch'in for turning against *tao*, the general governing rule of the universe. This was often done to justify the Han replacement of the Ch'in. For instance, in a conversation among Li Yi-chi (?–177 B.C.) and Chang Liang (?–189 B.C.), two scholar-officials, and Liu Pang (r. 202–195 B.C.), the founding emperor of the Han Dynasty, the Ch'in was characterized by them as a regime "without *tao*" (*wu tao*).[30] This assessment by and large went unchallenged through the Han times; some even took it as a major reason for the quick downfall of the Ch'in.[31] In other words, *tao* was understood as transcendental and eternal "natural laws" that governed the movement of history. In this sense, history is nothing but the manifestations, in positive or negative manners, of *tao* in the human world. This *tao*-centered view of history could be found in Ssu-ma Ch'ien. Yet it was the Neo-Confucians from the Sung Dynasty onward who developed it into a full-fledged form.

Ssu-ma Ch'ien declared that his *Shih Chi* was written to carry on the noble cause of Confucius (551–479 B.C.). He quoted Tung Chung-shu (179–104 B.C.) in stating that Confucius' *Spring and Autumn Annual* "has commented on major events during the 242 years to offer a universal norm and guidance for moral actions; [it] has also criticized the Son of Heaven, the feudal lords, and the marquis, only to picture the kingly *tao* (or the Way)."[32] It is evident that Chinese historians, most notably Ssu-ma Ch'ien, wrote about the past with an eye on the future. *Tao* or the Way therefore became the yardstick Chinese historians employed to narrate and judge the past in order to help construct a better future.

However, it is not an easy task to combine factual judgment with value or moral judgment in historical narration. In his "biography of Po Yi and Shu Ch'i," Ssu-ma Ch'ien already encountered the difficulty in convincing people, including himself, that history is always governed by the righteous heavenly *tao*. He shared his doubts with readers by giving two famous examples:

> Some people say: "It is Heaven's way, without distinction of persons, to keep the good perpetually supplied." Can we say then that Po Yi and Shu Ch'i were good men or not? They clung to righteousness and were pure in their deeds, as we have seen, and yet they starved to death. Of his seventy disciples, Confucius singled out Yen Hui for praise because of his diligence in learning, yet Yen Hui was often in want, never getting his fill of even the poorest food, and in the end suffered an untimely death. Is this the way Heaven reward the good man?[33]

Indeed, if the heavenly *tao* (or the Way) really rewarded the good man on a fair basis, how could it be Emperor Shih-huang who accomplished the task of unifying China in 221 B.C., given his cruel character? More often than not, history did not move in accord with the righteous heavenly *tao*. As the twelfth-century Neo-Confucian philosopher Chu Hsi (Hui-an, 1130–1200) acutely observed, "the regulations of Ch'in are all affairs of honoring rulers and demeaning subjects, and so later generations could not change."[34] In Chu Hsi's view, all the emperors in Chinese history since Emperor Shih-huang of the Ch'in were motivated by "selfish desire" instead of the "Heavenly way."[35] The Ch'in experience demonstrated most powerfully the fundamental incongruity between the world of "to be" and the world of "ought to be."

(4:2) The passe-partout of this problem is the Chinese tradition of incorporating value judgment in historical narrative. To traditional Chinese thinkers, history was a manifestation of moral principles. What were considered heroes in history were those who supposedly understood *tao* in history and acted accordingly. Due to the influence of this kind of thinking, Chinese historiography also focused on the moral issue in history; namely the way in which the Chinese came to understand *tao* or Principle in different historical periods. From that perspective, we can see both the breakthrough and the limitation of Chinese historical thinking.

Let us take Chu Hsi as an example to see this affinity of morality and history. Chu Hsi provided a systematic explanation for the development of Chinese history. His explanation could be considered a "regressive view of history" and could be summarized as follows:

1. The development of Chinese history was divided into two major periods, with Ch'in's unification as the turning point.
2. The golden age of Chinese history occurred during the Three Dynasties (Hsia, Shang, and Chou Dynasties) before the Ch'in uni-

fication. After the Ch'in, ancient politics and culture were in a steady decline.

3. These two periods were differentiated by whether or not the rulers' abiding to the Way or Principle: the heavenly Way prevailed during the Three Dynasties, whereas after Ch'in and Han times only "human desires" took command.[36]

Hence, Chu Hsi denounced the Ch'in experience:

> The regulations of Ch'in's administration are all matters of venerating rulers and downgrading subordinates. That is why later generations did not wish to change them. Moreover, the Three Rulers titled themselves "Huang," the Five Rulers titled themselves "Ti," while the Ch'in ruler [went so far as to] title himself both "Huang [and] Ti." [In view of] this single event alone, how could later generations be willing to change?[37]

From Ssu-ma Ch'ien to Chu Hsi, Chinese historians agreed that the Ch'in empire ruled against *tao*, the Way or Principle.

What then is the "Principle" in Chinese historical thinking? As I have previously suggested,[38] *tao* or the "Principle" in history is the consistent One throughout the ages. This "One Principle" manifests itself in various ways throughout history and remains undisturbed by time and space. At the same time, this Principle depends on the sages' enlightened leadership to prosper and expand in this world. The Principle in history is the unity of both the cosmic principle of operation and the moral norms for human conduct.

The final characteristic of *tao* in history is of paramount importance. As Chu Hsi said, the Principle or the Way is the "natural course of the Heavenly principle" (*t'ien-li chih tzu-jan*). However, Chu Hsi also took the Way to be the "required norms of human world" (*jen-shih tang-jan chih li*).[39] In other words, *tao* was perceived of both as an objective, neutral, natural *principle*, and as subjective, moral *norms* in Chinese historical thinking. Moreover, many Chinese thinkers, such as Chu Hsi, asserted that *tao* "always exists independently of human expectations, imperishable throughout the ages. Not even thousands of years of human abuses can destroy it, nor can any so-called wise rulers help it prosper."[40]

Taking the Chinese interpretation of the Ch'in experience as an example, we find that *tao* serves the sole abstract yardstick for Chinese historians in interpreting historical changes. All the concrete historical facts only serve to illustrate, positively or negatively, the eternal essence of *tao*. Therefore, *tao* becomes an ideal transcending historical facts. It is a "spiritual leverage" for Chinese historians when interpreting or making judgments on history.

In this sense, traditional Chinese historical interpretations are, to a certain extent, characterized by an ahistorical or even anti-historical way of thinking. A supra-temporal moral stance is taken when interpreting temporal history. Chinese historians illustrate the only regulative and normative *tao* or the Way by offering explanations for the rise and decline of dynasties as well as for cultural changes in different times. Finding historical facts per se is never the only goal of Chinese historians in studying history. Rather, reading history is taken as a means to achieve their goal in manifesting and espousing *tao*. Historical knowledge provides service to moral judgment. In the intellectual pursuit for Chinese historians, historical studies were inevitably diminished to become a handmaiden of ethics and moral teaching.

V. Conclusion

The Ch'in as a turning point in Chinese history has left an imprint in the minds of the Chinese that is not easy to eradicate. Since the Han, Chinese historians and thinkers kept drawing moral lessons from the Ch'in experience. In this sense, the Ch'in unification and downfall is not a dead mummy in the museum but an accessible library from which one can enjoy reading and extrapolating "lessons."

Our study of the Chinese reflections upon the Ch'in experience also shows that *tao* in Chinese historical thinking is both moral principle and norm. This *tao* is eternal. Thus defined and viewed, how are we to interpret the cultural diminution and political abuse during certain historical periods? *Tao* does not always find its best representation in the human world, as seen in the Ch'in experience. And it is unfortunately often the case that evil gets its way. When that happened, the good was abused, politics was mistreated, and civilization was darkened. How are we going to offer a "reasonable" interpretation for these historical occurrences, particularly the rise and fall of the Ch'in? Chinese historians had their way; they looked up to certain heroes, such as the legendary sage-kings (King Yao, Shun, Yü, Duke Chou, and Confucius), to take the responsibility of reviving and persevering *tao*. Traditional Chinese historiography, therefore, became sheer biographies of a few "heroes" rather than the records of the people as a whole, as charged by modern historian Liang Ch'i-ch'ao (1873-1929).[41] However, such "history for the heroes" in traditional China is challenged by a problem: if the cultural well-informed sages or politically *tao*-aware rulers do not come to power in a timely fashion, how could history operate in order to correspond with *tao*?

To conclude, Chinese historical thinking as exhibited in the interpretations of the Ch'in Empire is a sort of ethical thinking. However, ethics in Chinese historical thinking is grounded in metaphysics, which is centered upon the notion of *tao* that comprises both principle and norm. This twofold-ness of metaphysics in Chinese historiography is, on the one hand, a very powerful leverage by which historians can judge any historical figures, but it is, on the other hand, a double-edged sword that cut short historians' explanatory power in accounting for the evils in history.

References

1. Lü Ssu-mien, *Pai-hau Pen-kuo-shih* (Vernacular history of the nation) (Taipei: Lan-t'ing Bookstore Photo-reproduction of 1924 edition, 1973), p. 201.

2. Ch'ien Mu, *Kuo-shih Ta-kang* (An outline of Chinese history) (Taipei: T'ai-wan Shang-wu Yin-shu-kuan, 1966), vol. I, pp. 116–20.

3. Hsü Cho-yun, *Chung-Kuo Wen-hua ti fa-chan Kuo-cheng* (The developmental process of Chinese culture) (Hong Kong: Chinese University of Hong Kong Press, 1992), preface, pp. 22, 47.

4. Jörn Rüsen, "Historical Narration: Foundation, Types, Reason," *History and Theory*, 26: 4 (1987): 87–97.

5. Chün-chieh Huang, "Historical Thinking in Classical Confucianism: Historical Argumentation from the Three Dynasties," in *Time and Space in Chinese Culture, ed.* Chün-chieh Huang and Erik Zürcher (Leiden: E. J. Brill, 1995).

6. D. C. Lau, tr., *Mencius* (Hong Kong: Chinese University of Hong Kong Press, 1979), 4:A:2, p. 137.

7. Lau, tr., *Mencius*, 4:B:15, pp. 261–63.

8. Chang Hsüeh-cheng, *Weng-shih Tung-i* (Comprehensive meaning of literature and history) (Taipei: Hua-shih Publishing Co., 1980), p. 1.

9. William Theodore de Bary et al., comp., *Sources of Chinese Tradition* (New York: Columbia University Press, 1960), p. 235.

10. Cf. Keith Jenkins, *On 'What is History?': Carr and Elton to Rorty and White* (London and New York: Routledge, 1995).

11. Cf. Wang Chien-wen, "Li-shih chieh-shih ti hsien-shih i-yi: yi Han-tai jen tui Ch'in cheng-ch'üan hsing-wang ti ch'üan-shih yü li-chieh wei li," (Historical explanation in the actual world: understanding the Ch'in Experience in Han China), *Hsin Shih-hsüeh* (New history), 5, no. 4 (Dec. 1994): 79–124.

12. Ssu-ma Chien, "Biographies of Li sheng and Lu Chia," in *Shi Chi* (Taipei: T'ai-shun Bookstore Photo-reproduction of new punctuated edition), chüan, p. 2699.

13. Chia Yi, "The Faults of Ch'in," in *Anthology of Chinese Literature: From Early Times to the Fourteenth Century,* comp. and ed. Cyril Birch (New York: Grove Press, Inc., 1965), p. 48.

14. Ssu-ma Ch'ien, *Shih Chi* (Taipei: T'ai-shun Bookstore Photo-reproduction of new punctuated edition), chüan 6, "Basic Annals of Emperor Shih-huang," p. 283. English translation adopted from William H. Nienhauser, Jr., ed., *The Grand Scribe's Records* (Bloomington: Indiana University Press, 1994), vol. 1, *The First Emperor of Ch'in, Basic Annals 6*, p. 168.

15. Ssu-ma Chien, *Shi Chi*, chüan 6, "Basic Annals of Emperor Shih-huang," William H. Nienhauser, Jr., ed., *The Grand Scribe's Records*, vol. 1, *The First Emperor of Ch'in, Basic Annals 6*, p. 149.

16. Pan Ku, *Han Shu*, chüan 23, "Treatise on Punishments and Laws," p. 11a.

17. Ssu-ma Chien, *Shih Chi*, chüan 6, "Basic Annals of Emperor Shih-huang," p. 249.

18. *Shih Chi*, chüan 6, p. 261.

19. *Shih Chi*, chüan 6, p. 262.

20. Chia Yi, "The Faults of Ch'in," in *Anthology of Chinese Literature*, comp. and ed. Cyril Birch, p. 47.

21. Pan Ku, *Han Shu*, chüan 88, "Biographies of Confucian Scholars," p. 16.

22. Ssu-ma Ch'ien, *Shih Chi*, chüan 6, "Basic Annals of Emperor Shih-huang," p. 16.

23. "Inscriptions on the Mt. T'ai" in *Shih Chi*, chüan 6, "Basic Annals of Emperor Shih-huang," p. 243.

24. Chia Yi, "The Faults of Ch'in," in *Anthology of Chinese Literature*, comp. and ed. Cyril Birch, p. 47.

25. Lau, tr., *Mencius* , 4:A:14, vol. I, p. 149.

26. Cho-yün Hsü, *Ancient China in Transition: An Analysis of Social Mobility, 722–222 B.C.* (Stanford, Calif.: Stanford University Press, 1965), pp.24–52.

27. Ssu-ma Ch'ien, in his *Shih Chi*, chüan 6, "Biography of Emperor Shih-huang," p. 239; Nienhauser, Jr. ed., *The Grand Scribe's Record*, 6, "The First Emperor of Ch'in," Basic Annals 6, p. 137.

28. Wang Hsien-ch'ien, *Hou Han-shu Chi-chieh* (Collected annotations of history of later Han) (Ch'ang-sha: Hsü-shou-t'ang, 1879; woodblock edition), chüan 30a, p. 16.

29. Wang Ch'ien-wen, *Fung-t'ien Ch'eng-yün: Ku-tai Chung-kuo ti Kuo-chia Kai-nien chi ch'i Cheng-tang-hsing Chi-ch'u* (Providence and fortune: Foundation for the legitimacy and conception of state in ancient China) (Taipei: Tung-Ta Publishing, Inc., 1995), pp. 271–76.

30. Ssu-ma Ch'ien, *Shih Chi*, chüan 8, "Biographies of Emperor Kao-tzu," p. 358.

31. Wang Hsien-ch'ien, *Han-shu Pu-chu* (Annotations of history of former Han) (Ch'ang-sha: Hsü-shou-t'ang, 1879; woodblock edition), chüan 45, pp. 1–20.

32. Ssu-ma Ch'ien, *Shih-Chi*, chüan 130, "The Grand Scribe's Preface," p. 3297.

33. Burton Watson. tr., "The Biography of Po Yi and Shu Ch'i," in *Anthology of Chinese Literature*, comp. and ed. Cyril Birch, p. 104.

34. Li Ching-te, ed., *Chu-tzu Yü-lei* (Peking: Chung-hua shu-chü, 1981), chüan 134, p. 3218. Hereafter cited as *Yü-lei*.

35. *Yü-Lei*, chüan 135, p. 3219.

36. Huang, Chün-chieh, "Chu Tzu Tui Chung-Kuo li-shih ti chieh-shih," in Chung Ts'ai-chun, ed., *Kuo-chi chu-tzu-hsüeh hui-i lun-wen-chi* (Taipei: Academia Sinica, 1993), pp. 1083–1114.

37. *Yü-lei*, chüan 134, p. 3218.

38. Chün-chieh Huang, "Imperial Rulership in Cultural History: Chu Hsi's Interpretation," in *Imperial Rulership and Cultural Change in Traditional China, ed.* Chün-chieh Huang et al. (Seattle: University of Washington Press, 1994), pp. 188–205.

39. Chu Hsi, "Meng Tzu chi-chu," in his *Ssu-shu chang-chu chi-chu* (Peking: Chung-hua shu-chü, 1982), chüan 3, p. 231.

40. Chu Hsi, *Hui-an hsien-sheng Chu Wen-kung wen-chi* (Collection of writings of Chu Hsi) (Taipei: Chung-wen ch'u-pan-she Photo-reproduction of the *kinsei kanseki sokan* edition), chüan 36, p. 2306.

41. See Liang Ch'i-ch'ao, "Hsin shih-hsueh," (New history) in *Liang Ch'i-ch'ao shih-hsueh lun-chu san-chung* (Liang Ch'i-ch'ao's three works in history) (Hong Kong: San-lien shu-tien, 1980), pp. 2–5.

4. From Ancient to Medieval Historical Thinking

Ernst Breisach

Few assertions of a turning point in history have been so firmly and success-fully asserted as the one concerning the change from the ancient to the medieval period in Europe. Its importance is proven by its incorporation into the basic periodization scheme of Western civilization: ancient, medieval, and modern.[1] The assertion of a change that involved all of life also implied a change in historical understanding. But there was no consensus on what took place, how and when. The use of the concept of a turning point invites us to ponder the question of how to explain a large-scale change occurring within a short time span in the long development of human history.

For scholars who believe that history was shaped by the actions of pow-erful individuals and events, it was not hard to locate the ancient-to-medieval turning point. Some of them simply identified the turning point with the deposition of the last Roman Emperor (of the West), Romulus Augustulus, by Odovacar in 476. For social historians, who have favored explanations in terms of social, economic, demographic, or other grand forces, changes often extended over long periods. Thus the turning point became a turning period. In postmodernist perspectives, the problem of the change of histor-ical periods has become a matter of linguistic constructs, far from the com-plexities of the actual past to which scholars presumably had no access at all.

The present inquiry recognizes the element of construction in the con-cept of a turning point but stipulates an ultimate referentiality. Human expe-rience and theoretical endeavors are treated as inextricably intertwined. The full historicity of human life necessitates the rejection of any reductionism—objective or linguistic. Human life must be seen as a web of phenomena with constantly shifting hierarchies.

The concept of a turning point from the ancient to the medieval period, particularly in reference to historical understanding, has one crucial implica-tion. In contrast to the word "break," the term "turning point" implies a con-tinuous development that is redirected and not simply interrupted. This def-inition accords well with the very mechanism that has so far governed the understanding of human historicity: the building of a nexus among the past,

the present, and the expectations for the future. Never permanently successful, each nexus nevertheless offers a temporary but necessary balance
between the two basic kinds of human experience: change and continuity. A
proper nexus can temporarily achieve that balance because in it each of the
time dimensions, far from being independent of the other, was part of a
dynamic whole. Much as in William James's concept of the "specious present," the brief present has a dynamic relationship of interdependence with
the other two dimensions of time.[2] Any new understanding of the present,
itself shaped by memories (the past) and the expectations for the future,
brings in its wake a new understanding of the past and altered expectations
for the future. Turning points refer to changes in the nexus—its accents, sub-
stances of interpretations, and rhetorical forms—that marked important
changes in historical understanding. Thus, the inquiry into the ancient-to-
medieval turning point in historical understanding will become a search for
a specific change in the perception of human historicity. And such a change
is best seen in the nexus built at the time.

   On this point, the initially noted certainty concerning the turning point
from the ancient to the medieval period has had its specific historiographical
counterpart in the certainty about the change from the cyclical to the linear
pattern of historical understanding. Both of these patterns represented a type
of nexus building. But is the equation of ancient with cyclical and medieval
with linear appropriate?

   The long-held view that the cyclical model was dominant in the ancient
period is, with some exceptions, correct. Cyclical, however, refers here not to
the full circle, as it had in Polybius's cycle of governments, but to the
inescapably recurrent pattern which states, empires, or cultures have been
subject to: origin, rise to power and prominence, flourishing, and decadence
and decay.[3] Historians have perceived a pattern that runs its course relentlessly—against the wishes of the members of a group who are usually mistaken about their expectations for the future. The cyclical model has certainly been favored by analysts who have studied Rome in its late period of
prominence. From Machiavelli to the American populists and to the "Fall of
Rome" literature since 1880, theories of decadence or decline have prevailed.
Yet was the cyclical interpretation of history truly the preferred mode of the
phase of Roman culture from Augustus to the fourth century? Although
Pompeius Trogus's cyclical view of history and some intimations of a cyclical historical pattern (Velleius Paterculus) were present at that time in Rome,
the answer must be a "no."[4] Contrary to the prevailing opinion, the typical
historical understanding in the Roman Empire was a linear one. The experience of nearly a millennium of Roman security and success in dominating
what is known as the ancient world made for a historical understanding
expressed in the idea of *Roma aeterna*. (See Virgil and Ammianus
Marcellinus).[5]

   With Roman linearity meeting Christian linearity, was there then no fundamental change in the pattern of how the nexus was built and hence no
ancient-to-medieval turning point? Such doubts can be dispelled by a closer look at the term linearity. In its formal sense, the term asserted only that

the development of history—whether understood segmentally or universal-ly—followed a straight line. In historical theory it stipulated the prevalence of continuity over any change that would disturb the linear pattern. Such might be the case with the writings of dynastic histories in both ancient China and Egypt. Chronology tied such histories together on the basis of a routine sequence of important aspects of human life. Continuity was expect-ed to be endless. Events that could have been turning points were defused as transition points within the set course of history.

The linearity of medieval historiography, however, would be of a kind that would be understood only if one abandoned the purely formal (geo-metrical) or morphological approach. The change from the linearity of *Roma aeterna* to that of *Christiana aeterna* concerned the substance, not the form of human development. Surprisingly, the best guidance for historians in their attempt to grasp what occurred in the ancient-to-medieval change has come from a look at the debate concerning the turning point from medieval to modern historical understanding. There the debate also centered on the change of one type of linearity to another. The difference between the two linearities was a substantial rather than a formal or morphological one and has been routinely referred to as secularization. It does not matter whether one agreed with those scholars who saw secularization as a radical break from the medieval world or with the moderate claimants who understood the transition as a transposing of medieval into modern concepts.[6] What mat-ters here is that at the core of the term secularization stood a basic change in the view of the world and of the human condition, which separated the mod-ern use of the term linear from the medieval. That change made it feasible to speak of a turning point despite two linear conceptions meeting at the medieval-to-modern juncture.

The crucial feature of medieval linearity is highlighted most effectively if one points to the decisive difference between the medieval and the modern understanding of the concept of an end stage in history. Both in the enlight-ened and in the medieval usage, the term linearity referred to a historical development toward a stage of human existence that would no longer exhib-it the characteristics of the historical age. For the Enlightenment thinkers, that age brought the final and full human emancipation by perfect rationali-ty, which was shown in the transition from the "empire of fate" to the "empire of virtue" in Condorcet.[7] In medieval historical thought, the end stage also was perfect albeit outside of human control and human history.

In the Middle Ages that post-historic stage was seen as being embedded in a conception of the cosmos with two ontic levels. The higher one was sta-ble, permanent, perfect, and the locus of God's Providence that directed his-tory. The lower level, with its temporary and imperfect phenomena, was, in its existence, direction of development, and ending, fully dependent on the higher one. Chronologically, the historical world was suspended between two states of perfection—with neither being under human control. This new view of the cosmos drew a sharp line of separation from the ancient mode of understanding. The latter, although acknowledging gods and the power of fate (Tyche), knew only a sporadically effective and hazily conceived second ontic level. There seemed to be an exception in the case of Platonic and neo-Platonic notions of essences and ideas, in which a higher ontic level was signified. Yet though they introduced anonymous qualities of permanence and hierarchy into the human condition and into historical understanding, these Platonic notions influenced history only in a general way through inspiring models of perfection, but not through a planning and governing God. A comparison of any typical work of ancient historiography with an equally typical medieval chronicle demonstrated convincingly that the change in cosmologies had profound repercussions in historical understanding.

The tentative conclusion seems justified here, that, in its widest sense, the effective acceptance of the new Christian view of the world and of the human condition also connoted the general turning point from the ancient to the medieval period. At this juncture the chronological location to which the term "effective" refers will be left open. Effective acceptance cannot mean, as in some older versions of intellectual history, the simple presence of a set of concepts and ideas, no matter how dominant they appeared at the time. These concepts and ideas need to be woven into the fullness of life—its habits, institutions, ideals, politics, and more. These realities, in turn, act as shaping forces. This interweaving makes it difficult to ascertain the "effective" moment of the turning point from the ancient to the medieval period of human life and its counterpart in historical understanding. Simultaneity cannot be simply assumed.

Theoretically speaking, the turning point toward the medieval historical understanding was reached when a new view of the world and the human condition found its lasting appropriate historical nexus. The story of historiography however showed scholars struggling to arrive at that new nexus. Between intent and realization lay the difficult task to bridge the gap between the ontologically different realms: the sacred and the mundane. In historiographical practice that meant to grapple with the task of constructing a historical nexus which needed to reflect a partially known providential design while being bound by the limits of human experience, logic, concepts, and language. The realm of absolute universality met the limits of temporal existence. Although authors of historical accounts had partial access to the higher ontic level through the Bible, historians found the task at incorporating the demands of that ontic level into their accounts in the midst of specific contexts extremely challenging. Therefore, instead of one definitive solution the inquirer finds three major ventures in attempting to "translate" sacred certainties into the dimensions of the mundane world fraught with contingencies. And the turning point in historiography would be determined by that "translation" which would be most effective for explaining the changes from late antiquity and to the early Middle Ages.

Despite their considerable differences, all three of the ventures strove to create either frameworks for historiography or actual historical accounts which told the human story in human terms but were in accord with the structures and forces of the higher ontic level. That meant to fulfill five major conditions:

1. Recognition of the absolute sovereignty of the sacred over the mundane,
2. Affirmation of the entrance of God, at one point, into history in human form,
3. Interpretation of human actions in terms of inescapable human sinfulness (with resultant human fallibility),
4. Acceptance of time as a created dimension limited to the historical period, and
5. Projection of the conversion of all people as preparation for the end of history.

These five conditions would supply the major guiding themes to the medieval understanding of history. A reasonable expectation for the present inquiry therefore would be to locate the first historical account, which not only accomplished the nexus among past, present, and expectations for the future in accord with the five principles, but also found a lasting acceptance. It would thereby signal the ancient-to-medieval turning point in historical understanding.

Of the five conditions, the first (with the fourth and fifth as its corollaries) was the origin of the basic need for the difficult translation process. It actually created the tension that pervaded all medieval historical endeavors. The third condition was easily satisfied, since the fallibility of human beings could be shown from the course of history; it was indeed maintained even by ancient historians. The second condition was most directly relevant to the turning point issue. And it also was the most difficult one to translate into terms of historiography. The affirmation of the Incarnation constituted a direct and visible intermingling of the two ontic levels. As an event in mundane space and time it represented a cosmic element that became an historical one. In the new view of the world and the human condition, it represented a demarcation point, separating the old from the new dispensation— a turning point in its own right. Its positioning in a new historical understanding presented a major problem and proceeded only gradually.[8] Much like the pertinent theological debate, the historical debate about the issue occurred in the late ancient period in the context of the formative epoch of the Christian tradition—in the ancient period usually referred to as the patristic one. Portending developments in historiography, the patristic theological debate showed that, despite the common reliance on the biblical text, the Christian view of the world and of the human condition could vary considerably within generally recognized parameters. In time, accents would shift even within the same interpretation, which boded ill for the expectation that one could locate easily the first and prototypical medieval work of history and, with it, a precise turning point. What actually happened justifies that cautionary note.

The formation process brought forth four seemingly appropriate models of historical understanding, which define the turning away from the ancient model. Yet the earliest of them left the strict separation of the sacred and mundane spheres intact and thus made no attempt at "translation." It flourished in the time of the persecutions and was fueled by the resultant antagonism toward the Roman Empire. The oppressed Christians derived hope from their chiliastic expectations of an imminent end of the world with the Parousia. The inherent dynamics in the Christian cosmological system produced here a view of human development virtually untranslatable into a historical form. In it, only the Incarnation represented a unique turning point in historical understanding. Compared with it, historical turning points of the kind figuring in the ancient-to-medieval turning point inquiry became insignificant. With the end of the world so close, mundane history lost all of its importance. Translation was restricted narrowly to the explanation of the persecutions in the divinely governed world. When done, it relied on the continuity with the past (the Old Testament) as allegorically established, in this case through linkage to the seven Egyptian plagues. The Old Testament deliverance of the oppressed yielded the hope of deliverance to those oppressed at the present.

While this model could not even accommodate the notion of an ancient-medieval turning point, it stimulated the computation of the world's expected duration by critics. In effect, it supplied to contemporary eschatologists and their critics alike a means of arbitration on the issue of the time span left before the expected end of history. Universal chronicles, such as the one of Sextus Julius Africanus (ca. 180–250), would compute the present age of the world and then figure out the years left to six thousand years—the expected duration of the world.[9] The most significant result for medieval historiography would not be the widely different calculations of the age of the world but the concept of a universal human development, divided into six world ages.[10] Up to the transition from the fourth to the fifth age various Old Testament figures served as period markers. The Incarnation, as the key turning point, divided the fifth from the sixth and last age. Thus, the most significant turning point in all of history fell into the reign of Augustus. But it did not divide the ancient from the medieval period but the old from the new dispensation. What historians would eventually see as the turning point between the ancient and medieval periods would be of a different order. In the end, the immediate rationale for the early chronicles proved of less importance than their demonstration that the new understanding of history would be one of universal scope.

In contrast, the three later models of historical understanding were ventures in the reconciliation of the two ontic levels, undertaken between 313 and 420 A. D. In modern terminology, these models would be identified as philosophies or theologies of history, metahistories, or (in postmodernist terminology) metanarratives. All of them strove to satisfy the five conditions for a proper "translation" and hence were candidates for providing the turning point in historical understanding. But they also responded clearly to the mandate of universal validity for the Christian view of the world and the human condition. It would matter very much that in satisfying that mandate, they found a congenial context in the still intact Roman world with its own claim to universality. At the least, the *Roma aeterna* view seemed to supply much strength to the new nexus with its affine expectations for the future.

Once more the contextual web of ideas and life's practices showed its influence. Far from being products of free linguistic play or poetic choices, the new models of historical understanding were creative efforts focused on the solution of specific problems under given conditions, with their opportunities and limits.

The three models of historical understanding, which followed that of a strict separation, differed from one another in how they intended to reconcile the tension between the two ontic levels in historical accounts. The first model strove for an accommodation between the two ontic levels, sometimes to the point of near fusion. The second conceded a degree of necessary cooperation between the two but insisted on the separateness and superiority of the sacred, which must be recognized as irreconcilable with the mundane world. The third relied on a syncretism that integrated the sacred into a world whose development combined the cyclical and linear orders.

1. The strict, even hostile separation of the ontic spheres became less and less tenable as the antagonism between the Christian community and the Roman state lessened. The preparation for the eventual turning point was made by Melito of Sardis in his argument that the Roman Empire—still the embodiment of *Roma aeterna*—was divinely willed to facilitate the spread of the faith.[11] The Roman concept of a linear history prepared the way for the Christian one, with the latter claiming a greater finality and universality. Melito's argument provided the basis for what would become the accommodation model in the venture to relieve the tension between the sacred and mundane levels of historical understanding.

Eusebius of Caesarea's works represented the best known and, in the end, most effective argument for the accommodation model. It was helpful when the thesis that the Roman empire was the auxiliary instrument of the *Christiana aeterna* became utterly persuasive after the Edict of Milan in 313. Eusebius created the foundations for a Christian understanding of history that corresponded to the new situation. His *Chronicon* and the connected Chronological Tables showed the predestined convergence of all known histories, as many life lines of ancient empires and states gradually flowed into only two: Roman history and the Jewish-Christian development. Eternal Rome and the eternal Christianity became one at the Incarnation, although the actual unity did not take place until the accommodation was accomplished in the years after 313.

The *Ecclesiastical History* did its part by extending the Jewish-Christian historical development, recorded in the Old and the New Testaments, from the end of the Book of Acts to the recognition of Christianity as the permitted and soon favored religion. But that history did not only extend the chronological chart, it also signaled the beginning of the weaving of Christianity into the practice of Roman life. Eusebius's *Ecclesiastical History* supported this process when it anchored the sacred in a mundane institution (the church) and gave it a history. As the church became eventually an all-pervasive feature of medieval society, its history would become the most significant part in medieval historiography. The universal chronicle, which Eusebius did not invent but pushed into prominence, stood as the potent symbol of the new unity between the sacred and the mundane in historical development. The chronicle supplied the nexus with both the past and the expectations for the future in conformity with the five conditions, but also with a present that in historical understanding and in the praxis of life favored the intermingling of the sacred and the mundane. Because of its conceptual and institutional impact, Eusebius's work can, at least tentatively, be considered a turning point from ancient to medieval historical understanding.

2. Nearly a century after 313, what had seemed to be the definitive turning point in historical understanding was put in question by a new overall context. In 410, the Visigoths had conquered the city of Rome. The sense of security fostered during eight centuries was shattered and so was the concept of eternal Rome. The Christian view of history in its accommodation version had lost much of its mundane supporting context. The visible signs of Rome's decline as a power even brought the return of decadence theories in which Christianity was portrayed as the corrosive force. The period of easy accommodations between Roman and Christian history had passed. At that point, Augustine, Bishop of Hippo, set out to create a new historical understanding that would satisfy the five conditions and would be universal without relying on affirmation from the perceived universality of the Roman Empire. His model would be one of separation that involved neither support by the affinity to the Roman sense of history nor expectations of an imminent end of the world.

Augustine used a moral argument for the separation of the history of Christianity from that of Rome. Far from being a benevolent state with an auxiliary function for Christianity, Rome was doomed from the beginning by Romulus's fratricide. And the Roman state did not fulfill the conditions that alone justified the existence of a state: proper worship and maintenance of justice. While he recognized the Roman Empire as the actual context of Christian life and actively cooperated with it, Augustine denied the pre-destined union that had been at the center of the accommodation view. The entirely different natures of the sacred and the mundane made any true and lasting union between them impossible. The two faced each other in a relationship of hierarchy and not of equality. Far from showing any development toward a union between the two ontic levels, which Augustine saw manifested as the *civitas Dei* (the community of God) and the *civitas mundi* (the Community of the world), history proved that the two were destined by their fundamentally different orders to remain separate and unequal.[12] Although state and Christianity could cooperate, due to the flawed human condition, the *civitas Dei*'s perfect order could never be realized on earth. Hence, the tension between the two realms would never lessen. History, far from demonstrating an existing or a future unity between the two, proved the impossibility of such a unity. The only exception to that was the Incarnation, which however was not intended to bring about the Kingdom of God on earth.

Mundane history was cast adrift. With the order of the *civitas Dei* not transferable to the *civitas mundi*, Augustine recited a number of organizing models for the latter (cyclical, ages of life, *vaticinium Eliae*, world ages) without endorsing any of them. His decision left historians with no proper guidance for dealing with the relationship between the sacred and mundane dimensions in their accounts. The void, however, was filled by the syncretistic model suggested in the work of the Iberian cleric, Orosius, who had joined Augustine with the intention to assist him in the designing of a response to the post-410 aftermath.

3. Orosius's *Historiae adversus paganos* seemed to lack originality, relating as it did a long series of calamities that had befallen Rome due to divine displeasure with a city and its empire that was founded on fratricide, injustice, and the worship of the wrong gods. Yet when Orosius reintroduced into historiography the cyclical model—although one with a linear component—he suggested a way of looking at history destined to be used in a number of medieval universal chronicles. In which sense, then, could it be seen as an important part of the issue of the turning point?

Orosius combined Christian linear thinking about history with the cyclical model of a special kind: the four empire theory. Gleaned from the Book of Daniel (2:31–45), that view of history knew a world history consisting of four successive empires, each of which experienced its cultural cycle. Orosius chose a version that identified the empires as Babylon, Macedonia, Carthage, and Rome. Of them, Babylon and Rome had the longest life spans.[13] The succession of empires introduced a clear and important linear component in which Christianity was seen as part of the last phase of the Roman cycle. Orosious, therefore, made it possible to see Christianity as the apex of history, but at the constant risk of submerging the claim to a unique Christian development and chronology. Both seemed tightly integrated into a mundane cultural cycle.

The most perplexing problem in the Orosian model was that the apocalypse coincided with the end of Rome. In terms of the nexus, the expectations for the future conflated the sacred and mundane end points. In order to avoid this conflation, a series of efforts was made to extend the deadline for the end of Rome. As far as the ancient-to-medieval turning point in historical understanding is concerned, the Orosian model, by its very logic, had no direct relevance. Nevertheless, quite a few medieval interpreters of history liked its fusion of the mundane and sacred histories, while disregarding its internal contradictions.

With Orosius the attempts at translating the Christian views of the cosmos and the human condition into a corresponding historical understanding shaped decisively by the context of the Roman Empire came to an end. Without this context, these models, while exerting to various degrees a shaping influence on medieval historiography, became chronologically puzzling. It became clear that the ancient-to-medieval turning point in historiography, that is the crucial part of the translation process toward medieval historiography, had come in an epoch usually considered to be late antiquity—well before the dates routinely suggested as those for the beginning of the Middle Ages. This incongruence in timing could be written off as essentially an issue of construction and remedied simply by redefining the beginning of the medieval period. But a better account for the incongruence would simply concede that the turning point in historiography was properly located some-where between 313 and 420, regardless of the current periodization for the beginning of the Middle Ages. The new models were able to satisfy the five conditions and the demand for universal validity in reference to and with support of the concept of universality espoused for the Roman Empire. For nearly a century, a fortuitous moment prevailed with a seemingly ideal coin-cidence of two universalities. The accommodationist and syncretistic models benefited from it. The separatist models, one eschatological and the other non-eschatological (Augustine), created in a time of doubts about Rome's benevolence supportiveness, could not take full advantage of it.

The century after 313 can best be seen as experiencing a turning process in which the ancient-to-medieval turning point in historical understanding took place. While its models did not shape medieval historiography in detail, they offered views of history on the basis of the five conditions that focused on their common and central theme of universality. With that, historiogra-phy contributed its part to giving the medieval world its sense of unity. With the demise of Roman power, the ensuing struggles to keep that universal sense effective in medieval historiography assumed a more than technical character. Universality was threatened by two contrary dynamic forces.

First, none of the models created did satisfy the quest for the ultimate "translation" of the sacred into the mundane. The quest for a perfect "trans-lation" went on in the form of modifying the models and, late in the Middle Ages, of the creation of a few new ones.

Second in sequence was the impact of a grand contextual change: the Roman Empire gave way gradually to the world of the Germanic migrations. Once that happened, historical understanding could no longer be shaped and reshaped with the help of the assumed and convenient correspondence between sacred and mundane universality. In the vastly different world of the Middle Ages proper, heterogeneity dominated most aspects of life (apart from the church and the world of learning). The universality basic to the three models would soon be under a creeping siege.

Since the five conditions and their universal validity were at the core of the medieval sense of history, the question of the turning point seems to come down to which model proved able to maintain that universality in his-toriography under conditions adverse to it.

Least affected, but also least consistently influential, was the model that was independent from mundane contexts because it mandated a strict sepa-ration of the sacred. Still, it was evoked in the Middle Ages intermittently as a source of hope in periods of extraordinary stress, such as when eschatolog-ical expectations rose at the turn of the year 1000 and in especially tense social, religious, and political conditions. But since the medieval period was characterized by a deliberate intermingling of the mundane and the sacred in all aspects of life, the eschatological and separatist approach remained most-ly ineffectual. The theological or cosmic nexus was the only appropriate one.

The Orosian model remained relatively popular as it could be updated by extending the end of the Roman cycle. Yet the extension of that cycle's duration had existential importance only in the case of the Holy Roman Empire of the German Nation. As the time went on, the repeated postponements of the end of Rome and history and the receding awe of the now past Roman Empire decreased the persuasiveness of the Orosian model. Its systemic problems proved grave: the close link to a fading and morally condemned empire as well as the impossibility of properly merging the ancient cyclical view, emphasizing the recurrence of the same, with the Christian linear one which claimed utter uniqueness.[14]   Orosian influences did shape medieval historiography but not decisively.

Writing well after Eusebius, Augustine had the opportunity to create a different turning point toward medieval history. While, a century earlier, the historical context had wrought the accommodation model, logic and the new context would lead Augustine to a new model of historical understanding on the basis of the separation of the two ontic realms. This time no expectation of an imminent Parousia figured in it, only a long difficult process of finding a modus vivendi between the City of God and the City of the World in a new context. But such a separation did not appeal to a period in which the church and the wider society would for many centuries try to exist intertwined. The medieval preference went to a nexus among past, present, and the expectations for the future that intertwined the sacred and the mundane. With Augustine rejecting such an intertwining, his influence on medieval historiography was sporadic. As for the inquiry into the ancient-to-medieval turning point, Augustine's work was effective theologically, but not historically.

Eusebius's work proved more successful in suggesting how to integrate the essential elements of the new Christian worldview into a historical nexus. The past retained its usefulness through a balance between rejections and acceptances. That made possible the maintenance of continuity between the past and expectations for the future (the Christian stipulation of universality in time).

Eusebius's *Chronicon*, *Chronological Canon*, and *Ecclesiastical History* favored the universal chronicle, which ideally expressed the medieval view of the cosmos and the human condition. In it the past and the present were firmly connected to the expectations for the future. The *Ecclesiastical History* supplied the actual connecting piece that facilitated the transition from the ancient to the new age. By lifting into dominance the ecclesiastical developments, this work fostered a historical understanding that supported the symbiosis of historical thought and medieval life, in which the institutional church remained central.

Eusebius's oeuvre, therefore, can be justifiably considered the sought-for turning point since it gave to medieval historiography the elements of a workable historical nexus. Taking effectiveness and endurance as criteria, centuries of development confirmed the judgment. It took nearly one thousand years to erode the medieval historical nexus. The gradual discovery of the global world deprived the medieval worldview of its claim to universal validity in spatial terms, and the emergence of the modern state would lessen the centrality of the institutional church.

References

1. In the 1690s Christopher Cellarius used the tripartite scheme of ancient, medieval, and modern in his *Universal History*. Renaissance humanists had already suggested a similar scheme: ancient time (peak in learning)—middle period (often referred to as declination)—and rebirth of learning. Only the twentieth-century maturation of the globalization process and the stipulation of a postmodernity have begun to weaken the traditional scheme.

2. William James, in his *Principles of Psychology* (New York, 1990), p. 606, defined the term: *The knowledge of some other part of the stream [of time], past and future, near or remote, is always mixed in with our knowledge of the present thing* (emphasis in the original). However, he gave credit for the phrase to E.R. Clay on p. 609.

3. For this rare, fully cyclical model see Polybius *The Histories*, trans. by Evelyn S. Shuckburgh (Bloomington, 1962), 6:6-9.

4. Velleius Paterculus, *Compendium of Roman History*, I:16–18, in *Sallust, Florus and Velleius Paterculus*, trans. by John Selby Watson (Washington, DC, 1964). His focus was on the rising and ebbing of cultural creativity.

5. Vergil(ius Maro, Publius), *The Aeneid*, trans. by Frank O. Copley with an introduction by Brooks Otis (Indianapolis, 1965). See Jupiter's declaration: For them [Romans] I set no bounds of place and time; rule without end I grant them. I:275. Also, Ammianus Marcellinus, *Res gestae*, trans. J. C. Rolfe (Cambridge, MA, 1956), 14.6.4. He views Rome's obvious crisis as merely "declining into old age . . . Rome has come to a quieter period of life."

6. For the best juxtaposition of these two views see Carl L. Becker *The Heavenly City of the Eighteenth Century Philosophers* (New Haven, 1932), and for a radical break Hans Blumenberg, *The Legitimacy of the Modern Age*, trans. Robert M. Wallace (Cambridge, MA, 1983).

7. For the release from the "empire of fate" see Condorcet, *Selected Writings,* ed. Keith Michael Baker (Indianapolis, 1976), p. 281.

8. The acceptance of a chronological scheme anchored in the Incarnation year, established by Dionysius Exiguus in the sixth century, occurred only slowly. The acceptance of the backward counting from the Incarnation year (suggested by Bede c. 700 and widely since the seventeenth century) proved to be even slower.

9. The figure of 6,000 was derived from the six days of Creation and the distinction between human and divine temporal concepts from Psalm 90:4 and 2 Peter 3:8.

10. The six ages of the world spanning the time from Creation to Last Judgment were patterned after the biblical story of Creation, with the seventh age, the world sabbath, constituting the end of historical time. Their authority was established by Augustine, Isidore of Seville, and Bede.

11. See Melito's petition to Emperor Marcus Aurelius in Eusebius, *Ecclesiastical History*, trans. and with commentary by Paul L. Maier, 4:26.

12. For Augustine's definition of the two communities see Augustine, *The City of God*, trans. by Marcus Dods, introduction by Thomas Merton (New York, 1950), pp. 336, 477. The perennial and universal confrontation gave the Augustianian view

independence from the contexts of time and space. But this, however, came at the price of the lost hope for a perfect state on earth as well as an irremediable distance from whole-hearted affirmation of any existing condition.

13. Paulus Orosius, *The Seven Books of History against the Pagans* (Historiae adversus paganos), trans. Roy J. Defarri (Washington, DC, 1964), 2:44. The middle two empires experienced quite a few variations by other proponents. The case of Rome was complicated since Orosius hesitated to ever state that figure since, with the end of Rome coinciding with the end of the world, he did not wish to appear presumptuous and read the mind of God.

14. The Orosian model enjoyed a greater popularity in the early Middle Ages than the Augustinian one. However, with the link to the Roman Empire losing its importance and the absence of the "end," that popularity faded, except for a residual one in the German area where, as late as the sixteenth century, *On the Four World Empires* by Johann Philip of Schleiden (Sleidanus) proved a great success.

5. New Directions in Northern Sung Historical Thinking (960-1126)

Thomas H. C. Lee

I. Introduction

Scholars generally agree that Chinese historical thinking reached a turning point and underwent significant changes in Sung China (960–1278). The changes included the Neo-Confucian interest in the moral purpose of historical studies,[1] a more practical approach to the idea of *cheng-t'ung* (legitimate political transmission),[2] a significant refinement in historical criticism and, last but not least, an increased sophistication in the writing historical commentaries (*shih-p'ing*).[3] There are also other features that were characteristically new, such as the broadened definition of source materials and the creation of new categories of historical writing, including notably the compilation of local gazetteers.[4]

Most of these changes were fundamental, and marked a significant shift in direction towards a more moralist understanding of the purpose and method of historical knowledge.

The points listed above do not, however, cover the complete spectrum and the immensely challenging breadth of the Sung achievement in historical writing. Rather, there was also a powerful trend during this transitional period to search for a rationalist unity between factual exactitude and moral purpose. Briefly speaking, the Sung thinkers held an exciting belief that moral and political lessons had to be grounded on correct knowledge of history, based on the complete, that is, perfect collection of precise records. Such a conviction led to massive and even dilettantish compilations of historical materials, more sophisticated theory and method for examining documents and historical records, and the creation of new types of historical writing.

In what follows I will try to place these changes in a modern perspective, to explain what new ways of understanding history in the Sung, especially during the first half of the dynasty (960–1126), really means for a modern student who wishes reliably to comprehend Sung sense of the past. I shall use the following four characteristics to summarize it: the first is the sense of "anachronism," that changes did actually happen in the past, and that history was not just merely repetitions of the past events. The second is the belief that literary style affects the way of presenting truth, that is, historical truth is made evident only with a reliable or truthful narrative. To put it more radically, only historical truth is to be displayed in the exact or perfect narrative. The third is the continuation and expansion of the idea of historical criticism that had risen since the ninth century, but was in the Sung starting to take a central stage in the theory and practice of historical studies. The final characteristic is an incipient awareness of "interconnectedness" of facts that helped to strengthen the ideal of broad learning and an encyclopedic approach to historical records.

II. Sense of Changes and Anachronism

Although the Chinese idea of the past was always informed by a keen awareness of constant changes, as suggested at least by the title of one of China's most ancient books, *The Book of Changes* (*I-ching*), it is questionable if historians always applied the principle of "changing circumstances" to comprehend history. Traditionally, "change" means changing composition of all the existing elements within a certain unit (block) of time.[5] This is to say that "ebb and grow" (*hsiao-chang*) of factors or elements in their perennial search for harmony or equilibrium were the norm;[6] "change" had to be understood as such a process. Simply put, this is a cyclical view of history; it precludes the idea of "invention." It also denies the possibility of the rise or appearance of "new elements." On the other hand, I do not think that the pattern of repetition was evident or definite in the conventional historical wisdom of traditional China.

The Sung perhaps was the first time in Chinese history that there had been a degree of awareness that "change" could be somewhat more than simply the changing configuration of the perennially existing elements within a system (time block). "Change" for the Sung people could mean irreplaceable or irreversible loss of certain things: although not necessarily linear, this new historical consciousness views history as a process of accumulated changes, and that the present is to be understood as a result of the immediate preceding past, but not as a stage of repetitive pattern. I shall use the interest in two new areas to demonstrate my point: one is the appreciation of the antiquity and collection of historical relics, and the other is the keen interest in the T'ang history, which the Sung considered more immediately relevant than the histories of the earlier dynasties for the understanding of their own. The intense interest in collecting historical relics, especially bronze wares, reflected a kind of awareness similar to the antiquarian interest in Europe during the "Age of Erudition."[7] Erudite collection of historical relics does not necessarily imply an awareness of "change," or in the words of Myron Gilmore: a "sense of anachronism,"[8] but such interests could certainly lead in that direction. Ou-yang Hsiu's (1007–72) antiquarian collection, compared with that of Chao Ming-ch'eng (1081–1129) and Li Ch'ing-chao (1084–1147), shows how within half a century, the idea of "change" had shifted from "ebb and grow" to "sense of anachronism." Ou-yang Hsiu writes in his Preface to the *Records of Antique Collection (Chi-ku lu)*[9]:

> People laugh at me, saying that it is naturally easy to collect things when there are plenty of them, that all collections will eventually disperse, and that I should therefore not pay attention to such objects [and much less to collect them]. I would answer: "this is nothing but a personal hobby. All that I do is not more than spending time to enjoy them. However precious the collections are, including ivory, rhinoceros horns, gold or jewels, none of them will not eventually disperse. But I will not exchange them for other things."

Ou-yang's interest had little to do with history, and he talked only about the "dispersal" (*san*), not "disappearance" or "loss" (*shih*[b]) of the objects. What was dispersed is not necessarily lost forever; similar (or even same) objects will return in a different time. He was clearly not concerned with the possible significance of these objects as historical evidence. His interest was characteristically antiquarian. From the traditional Chinese viewpoint, this was very much within the range of "ebb and flow" idea. The possibility for "loss" of these antique items did not seem to concern him at all, especially what this could mean to historical knowledge. Some fifty years later, when Chao Ming-ch'eng wrote the preface to *his Records of Bronzes and Stones (Chin-shih lu)*, we notice a change of thinking:

> After the publication of *Books of Poetry* and *History*, [people began to think that] the deeds of rulers and their subjects have been properly recorded. . . . However, the dates, places, offices, and genealogies [found in these books], when checked with records found in the bronze or stone inscriptions, are often found to contain errors. I have examined the similarities and differences [between inscriptions and written documents], and compared them with various other records. The result of all these works is *Records of Bronze and Stones*, in thirty chapters. . . .
>
> Alas, the remains of the sages and worthies since the Three Dynasties are often found in the bronze and stone monuments. Wind and rain, shepherd boys and woodcutters have destroyed most of them, whatever left are found in this small book. Bronze vessels and stone monuments can not preserve themselves . . . and will eventually disappear.[10]

For Chao Ming-ch'eng, the collection and study of remains from the past not only has its own intrinsic values, but has significance for historical criticism, too. A strong sense of the need to preserve them, in the face of their permanent loss, was Chao's purpose. To use antique for studying history was for Chao a purpose. Chao and his wife, Li Ch'ing-chao, were saying that collection of the antiques was important, because they could disappear forever if not properly collected and studied.

A comparison between Ou-yang's and Chao's prefaces shows that there was a distinct difference in the purpose between two major eleventh-century intellectuals in their attitudes towards the remains from the past. It is true that Ou-yang Hsiu also used inscriptions to critique written records, and his interests were not solely antiquarian, but he was not as clear about it as Chao was. In all, by the eleventh century, Chinese thinkers had advanced to a new stage and understood how historical relics could serve a greater purpose than hobby and connoisseurship.[11]

The awareness that historical events are unique and are meaningful only when they are presented in their original narrative form is another indication of the sense of anachronism. Chu Hsi's (1130–1200) criticism of Ssu-ma Kuang (1019–86) is a good example. Commenting on Ssu-ma Kuang's *Tzu-chih t'ung-chien (Comprehensive Mirror for Assistance in Government)*, Chu Hsi pointed out that terms that Ssu-ma used to describe Han history were improper because they were not Han terms.[12] For Chu, Ssu-ma was engaging in anachronistic use of terms. This criticism on Ssu-ma is reflective of the Sung awareness of anachronism.[13]

Sung thinkers were the first to say openly that the history of their preceding legitimate dynasty, that of the T'ang, was most relevant to the Sung in terms of supplying historical analogies. This explains the appearance of many histories of the T'ang. Shih Chieh (1005–45), Fan Tzu-yu (1041–98), and Sun Fu (998–1057) were the more notable authors.[14] Fan Tzu-yü clearly stated in his "Memorial to the Emperor on the Completion of the *T'ang Mirror (T'ang-chien)*":

> I am born in a time when Your Majesty has just taken on the great responsibility (ascended). I have noticed that Your Majesty, supremely intelligent and hard-working everyday, consulted senior and learned men. The result is the enlightening of the sagely scholarship. What we can now hope best to use as a mirror is appropriately the T'ang."[15]

This attitude was partly a result of the awareness among Sung scholars that there were many inaccuracies in historical texts. But more importantly, they must have felt that historical changes made it imperative that one look to the most immediate past as most closely relevant, because of the lack of accumulated changes. The passing of time leads to qualitative changes. The preliminary consciousness about possible qualitative change had made its debut in the ninth century, and is found suggestively in the writings of Tu Yu (735–812).[16] The idea of qualitative change, and perhaps even progress, had begun to appeal to some thinkers. It would be difficult to argue that Tu Yu and his followers had adopted the idea of linear progress,[17] but the idea that the distant past was different from the most recent past was becoming widely accepted. This suggests that history for them was a process of incremental changes, not repeating itself, and hence probably not even going through a predictable cycle.[18] In Ch'en Shun-yü's (?–1074) hilarious remark:

> There are those who say that the *tao* of the Three Kings (Dynasties) repeats itself like a cycle, and change is the cyclic repetition of differing distribution of loyalty (*chung*), substance (*chih*), and culture (*wen*). Anyone who makes such a statement is making a thief out of the *tao*. . . . The ancients say: "governing the state is like fine-tuning string musical instruments like the lute (*ch'in*) and zither (*se*). When the strings do not resonate, then one may wish to go to the extreme by putting on new ones. This is how you get the music right. When the state is in discord, then one must reform it."[19]

A similar argument for the need of change in social or even natural orders is also found in Su Hsün's many historical essays (*lun*). For Su (1009–66), history was full of changes, and although changes were natural, constant, and occurring according to some rules, there were also contingencies.[20] Su Hsün actually did not even talk about repetition and regularity within historical cycles; he refrained from promoting the cyclic view of history. Shorn of cyclical patterns, historical changes were interplay between general trends and human actions. Furthermore, Su Hsün argued that the classics could only be fully understood if one studied history.[21] Su Ch'e, (1039–1112) his son, continued the belief in the importance of historical knowledge. He further argued how powerful *shih*[a] (circumstances, historical forces) was in affecting the course of historical development. He argued, for example, that what was said about the antiquity might not be trustworthy: "We have doubts about what is said of the peace and chaos, prosperity and decline in ancient times."[22]

Their contemporary, Wang An-shih, (1021–86) held a similar attitude. Wang's criticism of historical knowledge is well known. But his anti-historical attitude is a result of his impatience with continuous piecemeal changes that occurred constantly in history. He was forever looking for bringing the final stage of history, the utopia universal, to realization. His attitude is thus a paradoxical affirmation that the very nature of history is change, not constancy: reform was needed and was justifiable because past history as such, in its nature of change, could not provide perennial guidance. In Peter Bol's interpretation, it is the "intentions" of the ancient sages that were constant, not institutions. Historical changes dictate that we have to act with prudence, that is, to weigh the circumstances. History does not readily provide with us any constant truth, and if universal constancy existed (Wang did not question this), it is to be sought beyond history.[23] Wang An-shih's interests in the *Rites of Chou* (*Chou-li*), a work of utopian apocrypha, is indicative of his absorption with the unchanging idealized world presumably existing in the antiquity. He had no patience with the fleeting reality of human affairs in time.

The willingness to surpass the historical reality in order to effect the change to achieve the utopian "end of history" is found in Wang's important compatriot, Tseng Kung. (1019–83) Tseng's argument that *fa* (best interpreted also as "institutions" here) changed in history is another example of the idea that institutional changes in history were plentiful and cannot be denied, and yet a qualitative reform in institutions was needed.[24]

Sung people's interest in the more recent historical period of the T'ang and even their own dynastic precedents is reflective of this awareness of persistent but incremental changes in historical process. Piecemeal changes occurred constantly; accumulated, they disrupted the equilibrium. To understand the present is therefore to understand the immediately preceding period; historical pattern, even if knowable, does not help very much. In this connection, it is understandable that the eighteenth-century historical commentator Chao I (1727–1814) would note that it was a Sung habit to cite almost exclusively Sung dynasty's own precedents in policy discussions in the Court.[25] To me, the awareness that history was constantly changing and did not follow any regular pattern definitely was in accord with the idea of "anachronism" as Chu Hsi had expressed.

Of the leading Northern Sung historical thinkers, Su Hsün was by far the most sophisticated. Most of his contemporaries accepted the view that historical truth was self-evident and could be found in the classics; they largely fell within the traditional Chinese mode of historical thinking. Still, Su and others also wrote about the gradual change in history, and that one could not detect any clear pattern in them. The emergence of the idea demonstrates that the sense of anachronism was making its debut in Sung times. It also demonstrated that they believed in changes as accumulative, and that "modern" history can better be used for guidance. The new ideas of change and sense of anachronism are significant. They certainly were new in China's tradition of historical thinking.[26]

Having said this, I must hasten to add that the sense of "anachronism" remained a stillborn in Sung historical thinking. Perhaps this is an idea that had chronically made its appearance in the long history of Chinese historical thinking before and after the Sung, without growing into an ideology with a defined contour. In any case, by the thirteenth century, this sense of anachronism was dealt a big blow by the powerful surge of moralist philosophy of history, in which the idea of universalism and supra-historical constancy of human order became dominant. The new direction stresses the traditional view that Chinese history after the Ch'in unification was a history of permanent decline and perpetual loss of equilibrium. They promoted the idea that there was nothing new or meaningful in the development or change that had occurred after the unification. For them, one studies the post-Ch'in history simply to affirm the evident fact that it was a history of deviation from the perfect norm that was the antiquity. The purpose of historical knowledge for them is to enable humankind to return to the perfect *san-tai* (Three Dynasties) world of antiquity.

Chu Hsi is a great champion of this kind of historical view:

> Things eventually degenerate. From Ch'in and Han on, the two
> *ch'i* and five agents naturally became rather turbid and lost their

clarity and purity in high antiquity. For example, from the time of Yao to the present, the central stars (*chung-hsing*) have already deviated by 50 degrees. From Ch'in and Han on, things have naturally degenerated. When [Han Emepror] Kuang-wu (r. 25–57) appeared, there was a slight correction, but afterwards it again became bad. Again, after [T'ang Emperor] T'ai-tsung (r. 627–649) appeared there was a slight correction, but afterwards it again became bad. In the end, it could not be as in antiquity."[27]

The new turn had its important merits, which I will examine later in the article. For now, it is useful to note that they had now relegated the idea that historical change per se is worth investigation to a secondary importance. For them, a better way of understanding the interaction between humans and changing historical circumstances is to recreate or restore the past than to understand the change as such. In short, the early flowering of a "sense of anachronism" had by now outlived its brief and temporary attraction. However, its appearance, especially in its stress of modern history and discussion on *shih*[a] (circumstances, historical forces) did become widely accepted, which later historians only were happy to use from time to time.[28]

III. The Idea of Narrative

The literary accomplishment of one of the most important Sung historians, Ou-yang Hsiu, directs us to the idea that history required a special kind of narrative. He was almost like saying that "wen" (writing) and "shih" (history) should be one. The idea of the unity between "wen" and "shih" was not new, but Ou-yang Hsiu and Tseng Kung, among the Northern Sung essayists, were the first to advance a theory for an authentic narrative for historical writing.[29]

Traditionally, a "narrative" was considered to be not more than an exposition that was in accord with the *tao* (the way) or, that, in the Western expression, could bear witness to it. Early Northern Sung literary theory was specifically concerned with how to combat the popular style of writing in flowery and extravagant verses, so that literary pieces could be an effective vessel for carrying the *tao*. By the time of Ou-yang Hsiu, the success of earlier critiques provided him with a foundation based on which he could articulate the new literary theory systematically. He pointed out: "People of the later ages are confused. They see that literary pieces get transmitted, and think that the authors learned only 'wen.' As a result, the more efforts they put into writing, the less they accomplish." As for the necessity of *wen* in historical writing, Ou-yang's position shows an appreciation that historical changes necessitated an effort to collect as much material as possible for evidence. "History" as such is more than the "standard history" could record, because the latter was primarily to serve as a carrier of a "view" (*ta-t'i*).[30] As such, it should be and only be the perfect literary embodiment of the *tao*.

Ou-yang Hsiu therefore distinguished *hsiao-shuo* (miscellaneous sayings, records, minor tales) from the *cheng-shih* (orthodox or standard history).[31]

All *hsiao-shuo* materials, if not edited into a cohesive whole, were not history, even though they are important for historical criticism.[32] Only a structured narrative in proper literary form could carry the "truth" which is readily found in the classics. A narrative was an integrated part of this search and a witness or even embodiment of truth.

Ou-yang Hsiu further acknowledged the difficulty in finding the truth that was *tao*. However, he believed that historical knowledge was a reliable way to achieve the discovery. The complicated experiences of human and social life made it especially important that historical knowledge be placed in correct and exact narratives. Once this is done, then we will find that historical truth is indeed exactly what are found in the classics, as this was the case in the antiquity as depicted by Confucius, especially in his *Spring and Autumn Annals*.[33] This is a normative view of history and quite optimistic indeed. But he was willing to go to the extreme to argue that historical records would not be worth keeping, should moral truth not be directing the course of human affairs.[34] His occasional desperation over the failure of the heavenly *tao* in manifesting itself in human affairs does not preclude him from privileging the records found in the Confucian classics over those of other historical writings.[35] He faulted Ssu-ma ch'ien precisely on this ground.[36] In this, Ou-yang may be said to be a-historical.[37]

However, Ou-yang held on to the belief that truth would certainly be found in historical development. He was absolutely serious about it. He trusted that historical records would witness the *tao* or the permanent moral order. Not swayed by the fact that history is full of contradictions and tragedies, he remained committed to such moral ideas as *cheng-t'ung* (legitimate succession of dynasties). This may sound paradoxical, because he was quite a realist when it came to this idea. But what he actually was defending was twofold: the idea of legitimate dynastic succession was so morally correct that it had to be also historically realistic. Moreover, the many interpretations of it advanced by generations of thinkers before him were in any case not in accord with the classics, which made no proclamation on it.[38]

Ou-yang Hsiu may therefore sound anti-historical. Nevertheless, he championed the importance of truthful narrative so that the course of changes in human affairs would eventually reflect the ultimate truth. Truth reveals itself in historical process. This is almost Hegelian: if we seem not to understand it, it is because the time has not come for the "actuality" (*Wirklichkeit*),[39] Ou-yang could have argued.

Tseng Kung, as a close compatriot of Ou-yang, was less sanguine about the belief that the ultimate truth (which had to be also moral) would indeed reveal itself in history. But he shared a similar belief about the importance of historical narratives or literary writings in general for understanding the changes in human experiences. Tseng Kung was above all a believer in the theory that writing as such participated in the reproductive process of *tao* in time, however contentious the different interpretations of it could be:

> "Since the institutions of the Three Dynasties fell, and humanity
> and benevolence of the ancient kings declined, scholars have been

advancing different ideas, and philosophers establishing their own contending schools of theories. . . . A gentleman living in such a [fragmented] world will find it exceedingly difficult to talk about (find) the true "principle" (*li*, truth). The various writings of different merits could indeed show us [the logic of] the rise and fall of good governments."[40]

His attempt to distinguish "memorial/commemorative writings" (inscriptions, *ming*) and true history (*shih*) similarly reflects the belief in the need for a truthful "narrative." This in itself is another indication that he, like Ou-yang, shared the view that there is such a thing as "ultimate history" or "standard history."

The stress on the need for a truthful narrative is reflective of the awareness that there are records that, in written form, were different from fictions. Fictional writings (if not yet novels) had become increasingly popular and numerous since the mid-T'ang, but they were traditionally categorized as "*hsiao-shuo*." While Ou-yang Hsiu was hammering home the need to relegate certain historical records to the category of "hsiao-shuo," Sung Ch'i (998–1061) was articulating a theory on it. Written often in a style that by the Sung times had become a literary genre and begun to be called "*pi-chi*" (miscellaneous notes), the *hsiao-shuo* writing had functions more than those of merely *belles lettres* and entertainment.[41] For him, while many *hsiao-shuo* works could not be properly considered as history in the traditional sense, they were so valuable that they should be carefully preserved, because they could help humankind better understand the past.[42] Sung Ch'i's theory was not lost to Ou-yang Hsiu, who, appointed to succeed Sung Ch'i in the compilation of the *New T'ang History*, also significantly incorporated *hsiao-shuo* materials into his *New T'ang History*.[43] It is true that Ou-yang's belief is that not all the historical materials (including secondary histories, that is, histories in the second sense) could or should be included in the official standard histories. However, precisely because of this, certain *hsiao-shuo* materials found in the "miscellaneous notes" could have significance as historical works or at least serve as sources.

Sung Ch'i, while concurring with Ou-yang's theory, felt that since so much information was to be found in the "miscellaneous notes," scholars should affirm the value of them at least as historical sources. Now that "miscellaneous notes" provided information of historical significance, they should not be grouped indiscriminately with the traditional *hsiao-shuo* works or especially fictions. The latter were increasing so rapidly that they were forming a major category of published works. A new sense of historical narrative emerged, and it caused the traditional concept of *hsiao-shuo* to change, and the criterion for "historicity" became sharpened in the process. It is a modern idea that all materials could serve the purpose of various kinds of historical research. We the moderns therefore could scarcely appreciate how important a breakthrough for the Sung people to realize, for the first time, that "miscellaneous notes" materials could also serve as historical sources. Moreover, to realize that "miscellaneous notes" or *hsiao-shuo* works may include information that could supplement the moral goal of historical knowledge is a significant change.

Most "miscellaneous notes" works had yet to exhibit any tendency in employing causal interpretation, but there was a visible qualitative uniformity in their contents: grouping together information of similar historical events or institutions for interpretative use. In other words, a "miscellaneous notes" piece typically seeks to present a "story." This is evident in the great works of Hung Mai's (1123–1202) four volumes of *sui-pi* (*Casual notes*), although there were important "miscellaneous notes" works before Hung, such as Sung Ch'i's own work. Su Shih (1036–1101) is also famous of his *chih-lin* (*Forest of Records*) which includes mainly fictional miscellany, but also his discussion on historical events. The tradition in recording fictional stories is continued in Hung Mai's *I-chien chih* (*Records by I-chien, the Listener*).

Each piece of Hung's "miscellaneous notes" is a complete story. Still, what J. B. Brumfit attributes to Voltaire of doing, Sung "miscellaneous notes" writers did not do, because they had not fully developed the notion of secondary or particularized causes.[44] What Hung Mai did was to entertain a rudimentary notion of an inner logic that gives cohesion to a story, however outlandish it might be. The rise of "miscellaneous notes" style of *hsiao-shuo* writing is the second part of a Northern Sung conception of "narrative."

The quest for a story eventually led to the rise of *chi-shih pen-mo* ("recording the root and branches of events") style of writing in history, and the writing of novel in literature. The *chi-shih pen-mo* style of writing is, as is well known, an attempt to make sense of chronological writings. Once annals developed to its height and most sophisticated, like the *Mirror*, their readers found it necessary to sort through the enormous pool of data to construct a "historical event." What Denys Hay had to say about medieval European annals is instructive here: "There thus came into being a great deal of chronological material, relatively exactly dated, which could be extended backwards or forwards by writers anxious to write more comprehensive or less rigidly annalistic history." From such writings, we see "continuous or connected exposition," that is, "narrative."[45] The purpose of Yuan Shu (1131–1205), who coined this term and compiled the first *chi-shih pen-mo* (1176), is precisely to construct a narrative that can show the logic of historical development. What he did was to rearrange the materials of Ssu-ma Kuang' annalist *Comprehensive Mirror to Assist in Government* (*T'ung-chien*) so that related facts were grouped together to present a narrative. The great *T'ung-chien* thus became a collection of 239 "topical histories," such as "The intrigues of the eunuchs in later Han," "The campaigns for the founding of the T'ang" or "The An Lu-shan Rebellion." The search for genuine and particularized causal relations was about there: the way Yuan collected the relevant facts under the heading of "An Lu-shan's Rebellion" (755) naturally suggested a certain set of causes. Yang Wan-li (1127–1206), commenting on the work, quite rightly touched on how causes were indeed multi-faceted, for he must have felt that certain facts that Yuan included in the topic should not have been selected, while other should.[46] Obviously, this prompted him to remark on the multiplicity of causes. One almost wants to say that Yang was a pre-modern post-modernist. Yuan's effort is in fundamental contradiction to the conventional but deep-rooted preoccupation with moral causality, shaped by both Confucian and Buddhist thinking. Because of the powerful influence of moral causality, one expects that the search for historical causation would remain a stillborn, as it turned out to be. However, it can not be denied that a new notion of narrative was on the horizon in twelfth-century China.

Accompanying the development of this type of narrative was the ability to compose novels of complicated anecdotes: this is evident in the evolution of the *Water Margin* (*Shui-hu*) cycle of stories. In a sense, the fictional elements aside, the early *Water Margin* cycles quite resemble John of Froissart's (1337–c. 1404) entertaining panoramic *Chronicle of England, France, Spain and the Adjoining Countries*, which is the example *par excellence* of how chronicles evolved out of the medieval annals.[47] Let me explain.

By the end of the Northern Sung, that is, in the early twelfth century, the technique of expanding historical facts into stories was already commonplace. A famous example is the half-historical and half-fictional *Ta-Sung hsuan-ho i-shih* (*Vignettes of the Hsuan-ho era [1119–25] of the Great Sung.*) It exhibited a chronicle-like resemblance. The author constantly entered facts not mentioned in their proper places (dates under which they should appear). He did so to provide a causal context for the central event with a purpose of providing a story line. The way to do so is to begin by saying, "earlier," and then introduce the "causes" that could explain why the event concerned should take place in a certain point of time.[48] Obviously this is a chronicle. It is true that some "facts" in the book are fictional, but most are based on reliable records. It is hard for a historian not to detect an affinity between Yuan Shu's search for a story and this kind of writing style that evolved into the famous sixteenth century novel, the *Water Margin*. The rise of many Chinese novels understandably reflected the experiment on narrative expansion of basically historical sources.

Historians disavowed the *chi-shih pen-mo* style of writing, judging it as not much more than a rearrangement of materials of the great *Mirror* without adding any new information. There were few followers of Yuan Shu.[49] But this does not obliterate the fact and indeed the irony that it was a product of the search for a coherent narrative. It was not until the late nineteenth century that the Chinese began successfully and confidently to write history in very much Yuan Shu's style, now, though, under Western influence.

The rise of new ideas on narrative is reflective of the massive new historical materials available to historians, partly as a consequence of the widespread use of printing technology. For a conventional moralist historian, a correct narrative is the key to truth as found in the Confucian classics. Other materials, useful as they were, did not need to be included in *the* historical narrative per se. The increase in information necessitated a narrative device to present stories, and this was realized in the increased use of "miscellaneous notes" for recording of "miscellaneous" facts and for historical criticism. It also resulted in the rise of *chi-shih pen-mo* style of writing, which was centered in a rudimentary causal narrative of a story cycle. No wonder literary scholars agree that novels rose in the Sung times.

IV. Historical Criticism

I remain a believer that Ssu-ma Kuang's greatest achievement in historiography was in textual criticism. Although Chinese historians, like historians in other societies, were committed to recording historical events factually, they never developed a theory of historical criticism, at least until the end of the eighth century when Liu Chih-chi wrote the first comprehensive treatise on historiography. For example, skepticism directed towards the records found in the venerated Confucian classics, such as the *Spring and Autumn Annals*, was found sporadically before him, but Liu Chih-chi went as far as to write lengthy essays questioning the validity of many of their records.[50]

A preliminary method for arriving at historical truth, combining the expurgation of supernatural forces for historical interpretation and the reliance on "common sense" approach to historical probability thus began to develop in the Northern Sung times.[51] Although Ssu-ma Kuang described his method as somewhat like "scissors and paste," his method at least is a secularized one, exorcising elements of dubious or mythical origins. For example, the *Mirror* does not mention that the ancient Ch'u patriot poet Ch'ü Yüan committed suicide, as most quasi-historical works would readily do. After all, Ch'ü Yüan's suicide was an indispensable part of a mythical story of patriotic martyrdom, but Ssu-ma had the prudence to question its authenticity.[52] Another example shows how common sense and a nascent concept of causal relations had prevailed in his historical criticism: Ssu-ma Ch'ien's biography on Su Ch'in (?–317 B.C.E.) says that "Su Ch'in succeeded in fashioning an alliance of the six states. [And as a result,] the Ch'in army did not dare to advance beyond Han-ku Pass for fifteen years."[111] The way Ssu-ma Ch'ien wrote this sentence suggests that he was assigning the "cause" of Ch'in's policy as a result of Su Ch'in's success in fashioning the alliance of Ch'in's enemies against Ch'in. And it is true that for fifteen years, Ch'in rulers did not move against the six states. However, whether this could be causally credited to Su Ch'in's strategy is open to question. Ssu-ma Kuang chose to strike out the second sentence and reproduce only the first sentence.[53] This reflects his judgment on the causal relations of the matter. An even more instructive example is found in his careful narration on the narrow escape by Chang shou-kuei, a rebel general of the T'ang, from the execution by An Lu-shan, (?–757) then still in T'ang emperor's service. One can see how common sense had to be employed for deciding on the cause why Emperor Hsuan-tsung (r. 712–755) exonerated An in this particular incident.[54] Thus, one could say that the idea that particularized causes had to be carefully assigned had emerged as an acceptable norm for at least some historians by the Northern Sung.[55] The process was to insist on using secularized common sense as a basis for historical criticism, and on precision, however preliminary, in the assignment of causal interpretations.[56]

Historical criticism as described above obviously had gone beyond simple comparison of texts and textual criticism, and had shown a kind of "higher criticism" that one sees in eighteenth-century Biblical studies. Of course, the latter was based on careful theoretical reflection on methodology, something the former did not have. Suffice it to say that secular rationalism made its first appearance in Northern Sung historical works. This use of secular rationalist approach to historical records or stories was to become well accepted by people like Chu Hsi, and especially Cheng Ch'iao (1104–62) during the Southern Sung (1127–1278). It is a very important development indeed.[57]

Critical scholarship often came hand in hand with skepticism. There was another source for a broadened critical attitude towards received wisdom. A reflection on the influences of Geographic Discovery on the rise of skeptical tradition in Western thought may help us understand some Sung skeptical tradition. The appearance of a wide range of information because of an expanded horizon of knowledge, a lot of which contradicting the accepted truth, forced people to become skeptical of Christian teaching, especially after the Geographic Discovery.[58]

Let me start with a little anecdote. It illustrates how the opening up of the South affected Sung people's horizon of knowledge. Wang An-shih wrote a poem cherishing the golden color of fallen petals of chrysanthemum in the autumn. Su Shih criticized the poem by saying that no flowers would last to the autumn. It is said that Wang An-shih was greatly irritated by Su's criticism, and machinated for him to get demoted to Huang-chou prefecture (modern Huang-kang of Hupeh). Once in Huang-chou, Su then realized that indeed chrysanthemum flowers lasted well into the fall, and that Wang An-shih was right in his cherishing their golden colors. Upon hearing this, Wang An-shih said: "did he not read the *Songs of the Ch'u* (*Ch'u-tz'u*): 'in the evening, I shall feed [my eyes] with the fallen petals of autumn chrysanthemum'?"[59] The little story is interesting because it tells us how broadened geographic experiences were affecting intellectual pursuits and literary imagination.

The geographic expansion into the south since the mid-T'ang, but especially during the Five Dynasties Period, is a well-known fact, although few scholars have related the phenomenon to the new erudite tradition. It is well known that the Geographic Discovery of the fifteenth and sixteenth centuries stimulated the rise of late Medieval travel literature and such historical writings as William Robertson's *History of America*. Similarly, it is only natural that Chinese scholars would also be curious about the new landscape and life in the South and looked at it with an awareness of difference.[60] The rise of local gazetteers was undoubtedly a result of the push to the South, but more importantly, the erudite tradition was also a part of this exciting process of discoveries. The several well-documented works during the Northern Sung on medical flora in particular, and on various plants in general, attested to the discoveries over the centuries of expansion and migration that now caught the attention of scholars.[61] Not only detailed studies of tea were published in the Sung, but other works, such as investigations on lychee or orange were also compiled at the same time.[62] Their publications were consequences of changed perceptions about geography and its role in human life and experience.[63] In short, the erudite character of Northern Sung scholarship was at least partly a result of the two centuries of intensive southward expansion and the mass emigration from the North.

Another force at work in making knowledge more readily available to a wider range of people was of course the use of printing technology. I shall not discuss this matter in any length, as this is a well-known story. Any student of Chinese history and culture will be instantly impressed by how much more information is available for studying the Sung than for the pre-Sung times.

Broad knowledge also characterized classical learning, and provided a foundation for more sophisticated critical scholarship. The erudite approach in classical learning was represented especially by Hu Yuan (993–1059) who laid the methodological foundation, although Sun Fu's (992–1057) creative and liberal interpretations were the real fountainhead of Sung understanding of the *Spring and Autumn Annals*.[64] Hu's contribution is in textual exactitude. It came from his early experiences in working with Hsing Ping (932–1010) who was involved in the massive collation work on the officially sanctioned classics in the early Sung. The history of Sung classical learning could thus be characterized as a tension between the stress on textual exactness and the emphasis on creative understanding of the canons.

However, the tradition of textual studies paradoxically reinforced the determination and confidence of those who sought to exercise liberal interpretation of the texts. The works of Chu Hsi and his disciples exemplified such a paradox. For them, classical learning was a process of amassing as much information as possible to assist critical understanding. The erudite tradition commented on by so many students of the Sung was actually founded on this methodological premise in classical learning. Its relationship with the Sung historiography is evident. Moreover, the idea of broad learning as such is a notable element of Sung historical thinking. To this I will present a more detailed discussion in the next section.

In short, the significant development in textual criticism in particular, and a more critical attitude towards classical learning and actually all kinds of knowledge in general, provided a defining characteristic of Northern Sung historiography. Not only did textual criticism progress to a new height, a skeptical attitude towards received wisdom made it possible to expurgate mythical elements in historical records. I have characterized this attitude as "commonsensical," as the Sung had yet to develop rationalism, but clearly, it was on the horizon.

V. Encyclopedic History and Interconnectedness of Events

Undoubtedly the main feature of Sung historical compilations was its massiveness. Ssu-ma Kuang's history, despite the author's effort to present only "historical" facts, run 294 chapters. Li T'ao's *Draft Continuation of the*

Mirrors was even more voluminous. Other works of historical interests, such as Yüeh Shih's *T'ai-p'ing huan-yu chi (Gazette or Monumenta of the Territories during the T'ai-p'ing Era)* or Wang Ch'in-jo's *Ts'e-fu yuan-kuei (Mansion of Documents [for Conducting] Major Divinations)*, were also massive, and these were only two of a whole series of comprehensive compendia of various subjects that were put together in the tenth and eleventh centuries. No other dynasty before the Sung ever launched on comparable compilation efforts.[65]

As is well known, bibliographic control and a classification scheme developed significantly in the Sung, in response to the mass appearance of published works. When scholars (and especially bibliographers) decided on how to classify facts in different categories, it became necessary to consider the relationship between facts, and to decide how and why they could be grouped under one heading.[66] This was particularly true in the prefatory note of *T'ai-p'ing kuang-chi (Extended Records of the T'ai-p'ing Era)* which is also a clear if preliminary statement on fictionality or historicity, as well as on categorization (classification) of knowledge. The nature of this work makes its classification as "lei-shu" (encyclopedias; lit. books with categories) very dubious, because a lot of records found in this work are fictional. However, it is Ou-yang Hsiu and Sung Ch'i, while compiling the *New T'ang History*, who invented this new genre of "lei-shu," so as to classify an entire assortment of publications.[67] The development of this new classifying unit provides a context for understanding the erudition tradition and the nature of works like the *Extended Records*. For the editors of this work, and for those who felt the need to create a new classifying scheme for *lei-shu* books, the decision on what kind of information could be included into an encyclopedic work had to be made because they were relevant to the understanding of the whole knowledge proper and that, more importantly, this body of knowledge reveals an internally connected unity. In the opinion of Vincent of Beauvais, reflecting on the purposes of medieval *speculum*, the compilers of such encyclopedias believed that a good summary as such of the knowledge of the universe would reflect the image of God.[68] This is to say that the correct collection and classification of all knowledge could lead to truth itself.

A related point is that with a need to sort through the enormously expanded collection of source materials (hence the need to distinguish what is and what is not *shih*, that is, written history, or standard history), there must have risen a feeling that facts were related to each other in more ways than existing *relevant* records suggested. There had to be more than one way to regroup facts surrounding a particular historical event, so as to offer new interpretations. The skeptical attitude towards the "received wisdom" was lurking behind this thought.

The development of the idea of a "story," as discussed above, is the first step towards understanding that pattern or unity existed in historical events. But such searches could easily lead to the desire to "reorganize" or "rearrange" source materials. This sequence deserves some discussion here. Some thinkers must have believed that the way to understand historical truth (in both moral and causal senses) is to gather all the right and relevant facts and to re-arrange them, if necessary, so that they could be in accord with or bear witness to both moral and causal truth. Here, a preliminary conscious-ness of the nearly tragic "historical inevitability" became possible, because of the strengthened consciousness of causation. In other words, the rising awareness of the existence of an inner logic in historical development only made humans more aware of the tragic nature of human hopelessness than before.

Su Hsün's famous essay, "Investigating Shih[a]" is a good example. It is perhaps the first systematic exposition on the idea of "causal fatalism."[69] Paradoxically, he argued that historical changes were such that moral gov-ernment could only succeed if the ruler understands the so-called shih[a] in its operation:

> "The shih[a] of the universe acts sometimes strongly and sometimes weakly. The sage examines the changes of shih[a] and responds to it with the idea of expediency (ch'üan). . . . This is why some rulers are not judged as illegitimate hegemons even though they practice despotic government, while others are not awarded the title of legitimate kings even though they practiced moral government."[70]

Here, shih[a] should still be translated into "circumstance," though many modern interpreters have interpreted it as "contingency." By "contingency," one may mistake Su as if he considered history as fundamentally incompre-hensible because of its contingent or accidental nature. Su actually meant by shih[a] the malicious or ephemeral nature of historical changes, but they were not entirely incomprehensible. The nature of change in history was for him only nearly incomprehensible, and especially incomprehensible morally. Rather, humans should accept that malice with a fatalist sense of tragedy. Because of the predictably malicious nature, historical circumstances are not completely incomprehensible or accidental (contingent). They are pre-dictably "inevitable."[71] In short, history is predictably full of undesirable and immoral elements.

If, for Su Hsün, contingencies were not totally unpredictable or incom-prehensible, then expediency was necessary and morally. He wrote many essays extolling the virtue of expediency, showing that he must have believed in the possibility to discover the inner working of shih[a], the contingency, in history.

Discussions on the idea of shih[a] appear in many Sung writings,[72] and it is Tseng Kung who echoed Su Hsün's point:

> The rise and fall of a dynasty depends on[, first of all,] whether it governs according to the great moral principle and great law. And then it depends on how it institutes its local administration: to set up a local government so that the Court could exercise easy con-trol, or to follow what the circumstances (shih[a]) dictate and insti-tute accordingly, both are fine. The worst thing is to seek to gov-ern directly too big a territory [without delegating the power], or that the circumstances (shih[a]) on the local level threaten the power of the court.[73]

What Tseng Kung was concerned with was the historical circumstances that determined the way local administration should be set up, and it was obviously his opinion that a ruler should not seek to intervene beyond what the circumstances allowed him. While conceding that the great moral principle and heavenly law ultimately determined historical changes, whether one could comprehend the circumstances also contributed to the results.[74]

This realistic attitude provided a foundation for people to seek what I referred to above as the "secondary causes," but more importantly, it led to the belief that comprehensiveness in knowledge of the relevant facts could serve as the basis for true understanding. In this way, erudition that characterized Sung thinkers and intellectual activities was linked to historiography.

The widespread use of the word *t'ung* (lit. to connect, to pass through, to penetrate, etc.) after Liu Chih-chi's *Shih-t'ung* (lit. comprehending history) demonstrates that the idea that events were related in more ways than their primary records superficially or ostensibly suggested. After Liu, *t'ung* appeared in important works by such as Tu Yu (*T'ung-tien*, Comprehensive institutions, ninth century), Chou Tun-i (*T'ung-shu*, Penetrating the *Book of Changes*, eleventh century) and above all, Ssu-ma Kuang's *Tzu-chih t'ung-chien* (also eleventh century). While the purposes of these books varied, there was one fundamental consensus in their belief that facts and ideas were "interconnected."[75] Clearly, the choice of *t'ung* is to demonstrate their conviction that proper learning via organizing and carefully examining all relevant facts, placing them in a comprehensive but comprehensible (classified) manner, will lead to truth, especially the historical truth.

To amass all relevant materials, to investigate or examine them in a critical (or even rational) manner, and to place them in a correct narrative, so as to determine their causal or moral relations—these were the way to truth. Historical truth, once established, will of course show that the moral force indeed was at work in time. I mentioned that Ou-yang Hsiu had hinted at how correct narrative was tentative to revealing the historical truth. Now, erudition was added to this methodological formulation.

Erudition without recognizing that knowledge had to have consistency and cohesiveness would be the last thing that Sung thinkers, especially those articulate on the purpose or method of historical writing, desired. This is at least evident in Ssu-ma Kuang, and was later expanded by Chu Hsi.

Ssu-ma Kuang's *Comprehensive Mirror* (*Tzu-chih t'ung-chien*) is the most famous work that used the word "t'ung"; it is therefore important to reflect on how Ssu-ma understood it. The readers need to be reminded of two things: first, Ssu-ma had in 1064 submitted to the Ying-tsung Emperor (r. 1063–67) a short work, entitled *T'ung-chih* (*Comprehensive Records*) which was an eight-chapter work covering the history of 403–220 B.C.E. The second is that when Emperor Shen-tsung formally commissioned him to compile a history of "Deeds of Rulers and Officials of the Dynasties" ("li-tai chün-ch'en shih-chi"), the name *Tzu-chih t'ung-chien* was already decided by the emperor himself. Shen-tsung's choice apparently came from Ssu-ma's *Comprehensive Records*, a name Cheng Ch'iao (1104–62) later used more famously for his own encyclopedia, also called *Comprehensive Records*. Ssu-ma

Kuang said nothing about how he understood *t'ung*.73 Rather, it was in commenting how one should learn that he referred to *t'ung*, citing Hsün-tzu's famous adage: "thinking hard and then one comprehends (*t'ung*)." Chu Hsi, concurring, told his disciples that *t'ung* meant (speaking undoubtedly for Ssu-ma): "It is only after one has repeatedly studied the book(s) that one is thoroughly versed in its content. Without repeatedly studying the book(s) to become thoroughly versed, then how can he think hard on it (them)?"[77]

The remark may sound simplistic, but it is actualized in Ssu-ma's methodological acumen: his purpose was to achieve a comprehensive platitude, without loosing sight of the inherent unity that could bear witness to the permanence of moral force at work in history.

T'ung thus meant erudition, but supplemented by a commitment for thorough understanding of the inner logic that was moral in nature. When all the relevant facts are put together, and carefully collated and criticized, put in a precise narrative, the truth will then reveal itself.

This conviction continued to inform many Southern Sung thinkers cum historians, climaxing in Cheng Ch'iao's famous *Comprehensive Records* (*T'ung-chih*, often translated as "Comprehensive Treatises"). For him, unity is behind all ideas, and all histories or events were connected.[78] Cheng Ch'iao paid less attention to narrative exactitude, but recent studies show that he did try to rewrite some narratives: not based on historical criticism, but to place the texts in a new narrative, so as to reveal the connection between events.[79]

The significance of erudition for historical criticism is enormous, and I am tempted to say that Cheng Ch'iao's work is like a distant echo of what the Benedictine Monks at St. Maur, among them the famous Jean Mabillon, and the Bollandists did for historical criticism and the analytical spirit of the Enlightenment.[80] What epigraphy and other activities of Sung erudites did for the eighteenth century Chinese philologists is undoubtedly comparable.[81]

I would like to offer one final comment, that is, the social and economic factors in historical interpretation. When one believes that events are "connected," then one will easily realize that causes can often be more complex and variegated than what contemporaries believe them to be. In his analysis of Edward Gibbon's *Decline and Fall of the Roman Empire*, Arnaldo Momigliano argued that Gibbon was able to use the Enlightenment analytical spirit to present an entirely new understanding of the enormous materials accumulated over the century before him, and that this constituted Gibbon's most important contribution.[82] Of course, Gibbon's most original contribution is in his chapters 15 and 16 when he analyzed the "causes" of the decline and fall of the Western Empire, much to the dismay of Christian demagogues. From the combination of broad learning and analytical spirit, modern historical scholarship began to rise, and the ideas of social and economic causes emerged as an indispensable part of historical interpretation of our days.

I admit that I have searched in vain for this analytical approach. The idea of causation, incipient as it was, did not continue to attract historical thinkers in imperial China; concern for supra-historical causes prevailed and overwhelmed the post-Sung thinkers. Still, if one performs a detailed analysis of works by Yuan Shu, examining the principle he employed to determine which facts were to be included in a certain event, then one may find that there existed a painstaking process in the seemingly simple intellectual exercise. The same must be true also for Cheng Ch'iao. Ultimately, Ma Tuan-lin's (1254–1325) work, in the tradition that began with Tu Yu, shows that he believed that there was a causal nexus behind the evolution of social and political institutions.[83] Perhaps Sung histroriography, or Cheng Ch'iao at least, is still awaiting a modern interpreter to do it full justice, like what Cornford did for Thuscydides in terms of the latter's notion of causation.[84]

Chinese ideas of causation are an important subject that few modern students of Chinese history have examined. Clearly, the idea of *shih*[a] and the writings suggestive of an awareness of secondary or particularized causes all indicate that many Sung historians were struggling with the validity of the comprehensive moralist causal interpretation. This is significant, because this was a time when the Buddhist conception of causation (*karma*) was being replaced by Neo-Confucian moral cum historical causality or judgment.[85] The frustration of many compilers of historical works in the Southern Sung, including such as Hu Hung (1106–62), Lo Pi (c. twelfth century) and Chin Lü-hsiang (1232–1303) was because they could not find within history itself adequate normative evidences to support the ideal of "history teaching by its own examples." It thus fell on the more realist Chu Hsi, in a genuine empathy of Ssu-ma Kuang's historical acumen, to continue to separate historical writing itself (text) and historian's own judgments.[86] Chu Hsi argued for a clear-cut division between the distressingly unpredictable and incomprehensible reality of history, and the tranquil, supra-historical world of moral truth.[87] Students of history must employ such a distinction to make sense of the historical forces and changes.[88] The famous *Kang-mu* (*Outlines and Details [of the Comprehensive Mirror]*) inspired by Chu Hsi, eventually proved to be stale history, providing an unique way of understanding history from a genuinely Chinese viewpoint.[89] The compromise, however subtly struck, effectively goaded Chinese historians away from systematic searches of secondary, social and economic, causes in histories. In the historical world of Chu Hsi, there is no place for the idea of a nexus of variegated, connected, though not unified, causes, much less Goethe's "tout comprendre; tout pardonner."

In all, a new *mentalité* was about to dawn in the eleventh and twelfth centuries. An incipient search for a more sophisticated system or hierarchy of causes, informed by the ideal of "interconnectedness" (*t'ung*), appeared in the writing of Chinese historians. There was at least the awareness that it was important to collect all the relevant materials for precise presentation. For many of them, a correct narrative will help humans to overcome the complex and confusing context that had prevented them from seeing the truth. Once that exact narrative is constructed, then the truth would avail itself to humankind. In short, when all the evidence is examined and properly arranged into a correct narrative, we shall see all the moral lessons operating flawlessly as they did in antiquity and as they were spelled out so clearly in the Confucian canons.

One may say that Sung historians and philosophers in the end failed in their experiments in erudition and in their search for "interconnectedness." However, they were the first in Chinese historians to practice systematic collection and criticism of sources. They also were the first to broaden the range of historical sources for evidence. These developments went hand in hand with a new thinking on what constituted an event. The series of development eventually contributed to the further sophistication that one finds in the eighteenth century philological and epigraphic studies.

All in all, one of the many exciting developments in Northern Sung historical thinking led to the discovery of the idea, if not practice, of "interconnectedness." Many people echoed such concern by naming their books as some kind of "*t'ung*." Such an idea would have helped to stimulate a more systematic search for particularized causes that are not usually detected by contemporary chroniclers. However, in the swift and powerful change in Sung thought effected by Neo-Confucian thinkers whose agenda was larger than historiography, a new and influential perspective of historical causation that was at once moral and supra-historical was created. Its influence and persuasiveness ultimately prevented the full development of the notion of "interconnectedness" in actual historical writing and interpretation. Nonetheless, the fact that many books were named "*t'ung*," and the compilation during and after the Northern Sung of encyclopedic works and histories indicate the widespread anticipation of that lofty, if premature, idea of "interconnectedness."

VI. Conclusion

The story of Northern Sung historical thinking, like that of the political debates at the time, is one of effervescence, full of exciting new possibilities. These included the development of anachronistic sense, the search for literary refinement and coherent narrative, an improved sophistication of textual and general historical criticism, a rudimentary awareness of interconnected relations of facts, which went hand in hand with a broadened definition of what constitutes a "fact" or historical source. Not all of them developed fully in the subsequent centuries. Textual criticism flowered again in the eighteenth century and prepared Chinese historiography for a transition into its modern phase. The search for a story helped the development of novels. As for the search for "causal relations," one could argue that the search for a "story" or a coherent narrative is a part of the enterprise, and in this sense, it saw an incipient beginning. But any systematic search for particularized causes, or indirect social, economic, geographic or political causes for interpreting historical changes, however, remained a stillborn. Such efforts were overshadowed by the Neo-Confucian drive to continue using supra-historical moral principles to pass on judgments on recorded historical facts. Yes, these records were now meticulously and methodically criticized, collated, and verified, so that history could indeed fulfill the role of "philosophy teaching by examples."

References

1. Conrad Schirokauer, "Chu Hsi's Sense of History," in Conrad Schirokauer and Robert Hymes, eds., *Ordering the World* (Berkeley: University of California Press, 1993), pp. 193–220.

2. Hok Lam Chan, *Legitimation in Imperial China: Discussions under the Jurchen-Chin Dynasty* (Seattle: Washington University Press, 1984).

3. Chin Yü-fu's *Chung-kuo shih-hsüeh-shih* (Shang-hai: Shang-wu, 1938, and expanded edition by Hong Kong: Wen-lo, no date) remains a widely used work. See also Yin Ta, *Chung-kuo shih-hsüeh fa-chan shih* (K'ai-feng: Chung-chou, 1985). See also W. G. Beasley and E. G. Pulleyblank, eds., *Historians of China and Japan* (Osford: Oxford University Press, 1961).

4. James Hargett, "Song Dynasty Local Gazetteers and Their Place in the History of *Difangzhi* Writing in China," *Harvard Journal of Asiatic Studies*, 56, 2 (1996): 405–42.

5. Joseph Needham, "Time and Knowledge in China and the West," in J. T. Fraser, ed., *The Voices of Time* (New York: George Braziller, 1966), pp. 92–135.

6. Thomas H. C. Lee: "Muß die Geschichte einem rationalen Deutungsmuster folgen? Eine kritische Anfrage aus chinesischer Perspektive," Jörn Rüsen, ed., *Westliches Geschichtsdenken: Eine interk-ulturelle Debatte* (Göttingen: Vandenhoeck & Ruprecht, 1999), pp. 269–75.

7. See works by Harry L. Barnes, Denys Hay, and Arnold Momigliano cited later in this article.

8. Myron Gilmore: "The Renaissance Conception of the Lessons of History," in his *Humanists and Jesuits: Six Studies in the Renaissance* (Cam bridge: Harvard University Press, 1963), pp. 1–37.

9. Ou-yang Hsiu, "*Chi-ku lu* mu-hsü," in Ssu-ch'üan ta-hsüeh ku-chi cheng-li yen-chiu so, ed. *Ch'üan*-Sung wen (Chengdu: Pa-shu shu-she, 1989-) (CSW hereafter), vol. 17, 716 (54): 419-20.

10. Chao Ming-ch'eng: "Chin-shih lu hsü," in his Chin-shih lu, collated and punctuated by Chin Wen-ming, entitled Chin-shih lu k'ao-cheng (Shanghai: Shanghai shu-hua she, 1985), pp. 1-2.

11. For Ou-yang Hsiu's historical criticism using historical remains, see Chao Lü-fu: "Ou-yang Hsiu shih-hsüeh ch'u-t'an," in Wu Tse, ed., *Chung-kuo shih-hsüeh shih lun-chi* (Shanghai: Jen-min, 1980), 2:201–25. Chao gives actual examples to demonstrate how Ou-yang used inscriptions from historical remains to collate written records.

12. Chu Hsi: *Hui-an chi*, ed., Wen-yüan ko Ssu-k'u ch'üan-shu (SKCS) (Taipei: Shang-wu, 1986), 44/4b–5a.

13. Chu Hsi made many comments on how commentary writers often distorted the original meaning of classical texts by ignoring the very mundane and folk style and ideas in the texts, and use embellished flowery style to comment on them. See the many comments in his *Chu-tzu yü-lei*, ed. Li Ching-te (Peking: Chung-hua, 1983), ch. 139, passim.

14. Both Fan and Shih published studies on T'ang history and both works were called *T'ang Mirror*. Sun Fu compiled a *Discussions and Judgments on T'ang History*

(*T'ang-shih lun-tuan*); see T'uo-t'uo, comp., *Sung-shih* (Peking: Chung-hua, 1977), 203: 5099. T'eng Tzu-ching's collection of T'ang edicts, perhaps modeled on Sung Min-ch'iu's *T'ang Ta-chao-ling chi,* might have not been published; see Fan Chung-yen, "Fen Wen-cheng kung chi," in Hsing-cheng yuan wen-hua chien-she wei-yuan hui, ed., *Fan Chung-yen yen-chiu tzu-liao hui-pien* (Taipei: the author, 1989), 3: 248–51.

15. Fan Tsu-yü, "Chin *T'ang-chien* piao," in Tseng Tsao-chuang and Liu Lin, eds., *Ch'uan Sung-wen* (*CSW* hereafter, Ch'eng-tu: Pa-shu, 1989–), vol. 48, 2128 (14): 390.

16. Li Chih-ch'in: "Tu Yu te li-shih chin-hua lun," in Wu Tse, ed., *Chung-kuo shih-hsüeh shih-lun,* pp. 170–91.

17. Machiavelli's famous chapter xxv of *Il Principe* is characteristic of this broad outline (river) of *foutuna* and man's *virtù* as dykes and barriers (banks) which do not change the course, but could make the river not "so wild and dangerous." Where *necessità* dictates the general course, human actions, adaptive to circumstances, may change half of the course. According to Felix Gilbert, it was Machiavelli's great friend, Guicciardini, who returned to the idea of *ricorsi.* Felix Gilbert, *Machiavelli and Guicciardini* (Princeton: Princeton University Press, 1965), pp. 192–96, 287–301.

18. Tseng Tsao-chuang and Liu Lin, eds.: *CSW,* vol. 36, 1540 (7):32.

19. George Hatch, "Su Hsün's Pragmatic Statecraft," in Hymes and Schirokauer, eds., *Ordering the World,* pp. 59–75. For more discussion on this matter, see later.

20. Su Hsün, "Shih-lun, shang," in *CSW,* vol. 22, 925(7):138: "The classics, with histories [to provide actual examples] to confirm its praise and blame; the histories without classics [to provide perennial rules] could not be used to judge between light and heavy (right and wrong)." The same opinion is repeated by his son Su Ch'e, see next note.

21. Su Ch'e, *Luan-ch'eng hou-chi,* 14, in Ch'en Hung-t'ien & Kao Hsiu-fang, eds., *Su Ch'e chi* (Peking: Chung-hua, 1990), p. 1046. See also his many comments on the complex relationship between *shih*[a] and the human virtue, on pp. 959, 956, ("The Han mandate was a result of circumstances, not human action.") 971, (The loss of the Han mandate was partly fate, partly human error.") 976, ("[Li] Ku's attempt to support a worthy ruler so as to maintain the Han mandate can not succeed because of circumstances. . . . He refused to budge to the enormous changes and adapt himself to change. This led to his execution. . . .") and passim. For Su Ch'e's writings on the importance of history, see "Luan-ch'eng ying-chao chi," in ibid., pp. 1346–47. For Su Ch'e's criticism on anachronistic behavior, see, for example, "Luan-ch'eng ying-chao chi," in ibid., pp.1268–69.

22. Peter Bol, *"This Culture of Ours"* (Stanford: Stanford University Press, 1992), pp. 216–18. See also the policy discussion question Wang composed: "The question: 'Hsia institutions are changed in the Shang times. Shang institutions are changed in the Chou times. These changes are necessitated by the times (circumstances) to meet the desire of the people. Are we not to say that the intentions remained the method in the succession?'" See Wang, *Lin-ch'uan hsien-sheng wen-chi* (Hong Kong: Chung-hua, 1971), 70: 748. Wang An-shih's historical thinking is best articulated in his many utterances advocating reforms: "Those who understand historical vicissitudes will naturally talk about how to reform (transform). They say: 'to return to primitive times (*t'ai-ku*) is foolish or devilish'" (Ibid., 69: 731); "If the *tao*

of all sages and worthies are the same, and do not change according to circumstances, then how could they be worth the names of sages and worthies!" (Ibid., 69: 730), and so on.

23. Tseng Kung, "*Tsan-kuo ts'e* mu-lu hsü," in *CSW*, vol. 29, 1252 (22): 336.

24. Chao I, *Nian-erh shih cha-chi* (Taipei: Shih-chieh, 1958), 26: 360–62. Chao I was discussing mainly poetic (rhapsodic) writings, but this was quite applicable to other writings.

25. The idea of progress, commonly considered to have been characteristic in the legalist sense of the past, and thought to have been resuscitated since Liu Chih-chi and especially Tu Yu of the ninth century, could be considered as part of this complex of ideas discussed here. Although following Donald Kelley, and later Denys Hay, one may wish to say that this is a kind of "historicism," or even just history as an independent knowledge, I prefer to think that this whole complex of ideas was only reflective of the times. They never grew into a tangible movement. I will therefore not use the labels of "progress" or "historicism" to characterize them. For Kelley, see *Foundations of Modern Historical Scholarship* (New York: Columbia University Press, 1970). For Denys Hay, see his *Annalists and Historians* (Cambridge: Cambridge University Press, 1977), pp. 91–92.

26. Chu Hsi, *Chu-tzu yü-lei*, 134: 3208–9. Translation is quoted from Conrad Schirokauer, "Chu Hsi's Sense of History," in Hymes and Schirokauer, *Ordering the World*, p. 214.

27. See later in this essay for more discussion on the idea of *shih*[a].

28. Ou-yang was primarily concerned with how best to construct literary pieces that could reflect the *tao*. See Steve van Zoeren, *Poetry and Personality: Reading, Exegesis, and Hermeneutics in Traditional China* (Stanford: Stanford University Press, 1991), pp. 178–81. In a similar vein, Ou-yang believed that historical writings were useful or meaningful only if they showed that the *tao* was at work. An extension of the idea is that only perfect narrative could reveal the *tao* in historical world. See also my *Education in Traditional China: A History* (Leiden, Netherlands: E. J. Brill, 2000), pp. 296–97 for a brief discussion of this matter and on modern Chinese studies of this matter.

29. "Grand structure" in Peter Bol's translation; see his *"This Culture of Ours,"* pp. 228, 241.

30. Ou-yang Hsiu, in *CSW*, vol. 17, 698 (36): 83. The discussions on the idea of "standard history" (*cheng-shih*) began with Liu Chih-chi (661–721), although the idea originated at least in the early T'ang times. See Liu's *Shih-t'ung*, annotated by P'u Ch'i-lung (*Shih-t'ung t'ung-lun*, Shang-hai: Ku-chi, 1978), 12: 329–78. For "minor tales," (*hsiao-shuo*), see a recent article by Laura Hua Wu, "From *Xiaoshuo* to Fiction: Hu Ying-lin's Genre Study of *Xiaoshuo*," *Harvard Journal of Asiatic Studies*, 56 (1996): 339–71. It is useful to note here that Wu's concern is more about *hsiao-shuo* (*xiaoshuo*) as a literary genre than its historiographic significance, but she agrees that there is a significant change in its definition in the Sung, and emphasizes the difference between a traditional Chinese *hsiao-shuo* and the modern fiction or novel. In this connection it is useful to note that Hung Mai (1123–1202), the noted compiler of "hsiao-shuo" in the Sung times consciously made a distinction between "minor tales" and "standard history" or even just "history."

31. Wang Ming-sheng, in his *Shih-ch'i shih shang-ch'ueh* (Peking: Chung-kuo, 1987), however, repeatedly pointed out that Ou-yang Hsiu used *hsiao-shuo* materials

while revising the *Old T'ang History* for his new compilation. See, for example, 69/2a–4a, 93/3b–5b. For another reference to Ou-yang's emphasis on a concise narrative, see *CSW*, vol. 17, 718 (56): 454. For a more complete discussion on the relationship between "minor tales" (*hsiao-shuo*) and *shih* (especially standard histories), and between "minor tales" and the "miscellaneous notes" that was championed by Sung Ch'i, see later. As a corollary of Ou-yang's distinction between minor tales and standard histories, let me cite an interesting comment by Chu Hsi: "Except for the materials that are chosen and written into Ssu-ma Kuang's *Comprehensive Mirror*, all the rest of the *Southern* and *Northern Histories* by Li Yen-shou are not more than an interesting collection of minor tales." See Chu , *Chu-tzu yu-lei*, cited from P'u Ch'i-lung, ed., *[Liu Chi-chih,] Shih-t'ung t'ung-shih*, 17:486.

32. In Ou-yang Hsiu's characterization, the *Spring and Autumn Annals* accomplished a perfect unity between exact narrative and truth and that the historical events were also major and important enough to warrant its classical status. What do not appear in the classics are facts that we no longer can fully "understand," that is, we can no longer derive moral lessons from these facts and they should not be subject-matter for attention. See his many utterances found in, *CSW*, vol. 17, 697 (35): 67, 698 (36): 75–76, 716 (54): 417–18, 718 (56): 454; vol. 18, 734 (72), 22–23, passim; his criticism of Ssu-ma Ch'ien's *Historical Records* is also based on this argument.

33. See his challenging "Pen-mo lun" (On roots and branches), in *CSW, vol. 8*: 734 (72), 16–18. What are found in the classics are root truth, and should be studied, as for historical records that are doubtful, these were for Ou-yang, "branches," and "to bracket them and leave them unknown" is acceptable.

34. See his "Ch'un-ch'iu lun" (On *Spring and Autumn Annals*) in ibid., vol. 17, 731 (69): 740–45. See also, for other examples, vol. 18, 733 (71): 3, 6.

35. See *ibid.*, vol. 17, 716 (54): 431–32.

36. Almost like Jean Mabillion, actually a great historian, who believed that certain things can in fact be established with moral certainty.

37. I take a slightly different reading of Ou-yang Hsiu's famous essays on the *cheng-t'ung*. For me, Ou-yang's "realist" position was in being courageous to question whether the ancient ideals could work. He attacked many theoretical assumptions (mainly based on the naturalist "Yin-Yang" and "Five Phases" ideas) as not trustworthy, because they were not based on Confucius' original teaching. His belief that history and truth could be one only if the classical teaching was followed became ever surer in another of his essays, often neglected, "Wei-Liang lun," in *CSW*, vol. 17, 730 (68): 731–32. His realism therefore is different from the kind of realism one sees in Su Hsün and Su Ch'e, discussed later. For an English work on *cheng-t'ung*, see Hok Lam Chan, *Legitimation in Imperial China: Discourses under the Jerchen-Chin Dynasty* (Seattle: University of Washington Press, 1984), pp. 38–39, passim. For a good collection of traditional Chinese essays on "cheng-t'ung," see Jao Tsung-i, *Chung-kuo shih-hsueh shang te cheng-t'ung lun* (Hong Kong: Lung-men, 1977). It is to be noted that as Ou-yang Hsiu grew old, his attitudes towards *cheng-t'ung* and the purpose of history as witnessing the truth of the classics became less flexible.

38. For discussion on "actuality," see the introduction in Hegel, *Lectures in the Philosophy of World History*, trans. H. B. Nisbet (Cambridge: Cambridge University Press, 1975).

39. Tseng Kung, "Wang Tzu-chih wen-chi hsü," in *CSW*, vol. 29, 1252 (22), pp. 349–350.

40. For a lengthy discussion, see my "Fan-lun chin-tai Chung-kuo shih-hsüeh te fa-chan yu i-i: fu-lun ts'ung pi-chi, cha-chi tao she-hui shih," in my *Tu-shih te lo-ch'ü* (Taipei: Yun-ch'en, 1991), pp. 180–224.

41. Scholars point out that "miscellaneous notes" works appeared before the Sung, but the awareness of them as a new genre of writing appeared only in the Sung, and this is reflected by the fact that Sung Ching coined the name for it.

42. According to the painstaking studies of Ta-hsin in his *Shih-ch'i shih shang-ch'üeh*. See also Denis Twitchett, *The Writings of Official Historiography under the T'ang* (Cambridge: Cambridge University Press, 1986).

43. J. B. Brumfit, *Voltaire, Historian* (Oxford: Oxford University Press, 1958), pp. 100–101, 104–11.

44. Denys Hay, *Annalists and Historians*, pp. 42, 58–59; Hay refutes R. L. Poole's contention, possibly inspired by Isidore of Seville, that annalists and chroniclers were predecessors of, but not, historians. Hay argues that medieval chroniclers were historians in their own right. However, he does make the point that there was a transformation from annals to chronicles, of which Froissart's famous work is an excellent example. Hay makes little emphasis on narrative cohesiveness. See also Ernst Breisach, *Historiography, Ancient, Medieval, and Modern*, pp. 144–52. For John of Froisssart, see later.

45. Yang Wan-li, *Ch'eng-chai chi*, ed. Wen-yuan ke Ssu-k'u ch'uan-shu (Taipei: Shang-wu, 1986), 79/12b. Yang used "yuan" (source, spring, origin): "The malaise of the dynasties is different, because their *yuan* are different. . . . When the *yuan* of the dynasty's malaise is known, then there is a way to cure them."

46. Johan Huiginza, *The Waning of the Middle Ages* (New York: Doubleday, 1959), 68–69, 98–99, 236, where Huiginza criticized Froissart's historiography and ideas of chivalry. But Huiginza also praised Froissart's reliability in factual presentation (35, 103, 109, 184, 248, passim, but also 236) and him as epitome of late medieval fondness for aphorism, proverbs, etc. (208, 230, passim). See also Hay, *Annalists and Historians*, pp. 75–77. For a recent study on Froissart, which also deals with the issue between chronicle and history, see Peter F. Ainsworth, *Jean Froissart and the Fabric of History: Truth, Myth, and Fiction in the* Chroniques (New York: Oxford University Press, 1990).

47. The expression and technique of using "earlier" (*hsien-shih*) of course had been employed broadly by Ssu-ma Ch'ien in the first century B.C. However, by the eleventh century, especially in the great annalist work of Ssu-ma Kuang, "earlier" was used sparingly, mostly when a event could not be dated, or when a complex of historical development comprising of several interrelated events had to be mentioned to introduce the readers to the "sudden" appearance of a major event. In both cases, "earlier" does carry the connotation of causal relationship and its use suggested that the authors had some rudimentary awareness of causal relations. But Ssu-ma Kuang for one appeared to wish that he did not have to use it.

48. Yang Chung-liang (1241–71) composed a *T'ung-chien ch'ang-pien chi-shih pen-mo* and published it in 1253, but this work was even less circulated and was not printed between late fifteenth and late nineteenth centuries.

49. P'u Ch'i-lung ed., [Liu Chih-chi,] *Shih-t'ung t'ung-shih*, 13: 379–95; 14, 397–415. These essays are entitled "Questioning the Ancients" and "Doubting the Classics."

50. I am using "common sense" here with caveat, fully aware that even "common sense" changes with times. I refrain from using "reason" or "rationality," both because these words have important connotations and because Sung thinkers were not formulating their historical criticism employing real "rational" principles. I am therefore using the term to mean something between what is as fundamentally certain as positivist "rationality" and what is accepted in the time concerned. A "common sense rationalism" is not an oxymoron, and was occasionally invoked by eighteenth-century thinkers such as Moses Mendelssohn to defend Plato's ideas like "God," "soul," or "love," which were considered as immaterial by such as Condillac. See Ernest Cassirer, *The Philosophy of the Enlightenment* (Boston: Beacon, 1955), pp. 240–42, and Ernst M. Manasse, "Platonism since the Enlightenment," in Philip P. Wiener, ed., *Dictionary of the History of Ideas* (New York: Charles Scribner's Sons, 1973), vol. 3, pp. 515–25. A moral "common sense" theory is a widely accepted foundation in moral philosophy. I am also indebted to G. E. Moore's "commonsensical" position (which Russell felt was inadequate) on the epistemological certainty of common sense. See G. E. Moore, *Philosophical Papers* (London and New York: McMillan, 1959).

51. Remarkably, Ssu-ma's failure to mention this "edifying" act was already noticed by Ch'ao Kung-wu (?–1171). See Ch'en Ch'ien-chün, "Lun *Tzu-chih t'ung-chien*" in Wu Tse, ed., *Chung-kuo shih-hsüeh shih lun-chi* (Shang-hai: Jen-min, 1980), vol. 2, 235–56.

52. Ssu-ma Ch'ien: *Shih-chi* (Hong Kong: Chung-hua, 1969 reprint of Beijing Chung-hua 1962 punctuated ed.), 69: 2262.

53. Ibid.

54. Ts'en Chung-mien, *T'ung-chien Sui, T'ang chi pi-shih chih-i* (Peking: Chung-hua, 1964), pp. 196–202.

55. For more discussion how Ssu-ma Kuang assigned causes, see Ch'en Ch'ien-chün, "Lun *Tzu-chih t'ung-chien*."

56. Ssu-ma Kuang, while aware of the need to be careful about assignment of causal comments, did not systematically articulate on the distinction between secularized, secondary causes and the "first or primary cause." In short, his method epitomized the Northern Sung tradition of a merely tentative awareness of a secondary causal nexus.

57. There are few studies on Chu Hsi's textual criticism. It is clear, though, that Chu Hsi, practicing divination and a believer in *feng-shui* geomancy notwithstanding, employed rational principles in interpreting the classics. Some of his iconoclastic interpretations were deemed embarrassing by his disciples and followers, but these interpretations reflect his "commonsensical" judgment on what could be accepted as "true" in his times. See Lin Ch'ing-chang, "Chu-tzu tui ch'uan-t'ung ching-shuo te t'ai-tu: i Chu-tzu *Shih-ching chu shu* wei-li," in Chung Ts'ai-chün, ed., *Kuo-chi Chu-tzu hsüeh hui-i lun-wen chi* (Taipei: Academia Sinica, 1993), pp. 183–202. See also Lin Li-chen, "Chu Hsi lun *I-hsiang* yü *I-li*," in ibid., pp. 153–82. Lin's interpretation is confirmed by Chou Yü-t'ung's more straightforward and critical study of the same problem in Chou's "Chu Hsi chih ching-hsüeh," in his *Chou Yu-t'ung ching-hsüeh-shih lun-chu hsüan-chi*, ed. Chu Wei-cheng (Shang-hai: Jen-min, 1983). I believe that the traditional emphasis on Chu Hsi's so-called "i-li" (meaning and principle) approach to classical learning has obscured the importance of critical scholarship (*pien-wei*) in Chu Hsi's methodology.

58. Franklin L. van Baumer, *Religion and the Rise of Skepticism* (New York: Harcourt, Brace, 1969). See also a more recent challenging study in Peter Hulme and Ludmilla Jordanova, eds., *The Enlightenment and Its Shadows* (London and New York: Routledge, 1990), pp. 16–24. The latter clearly shows how availability of new information forced people to search for new ideas, although the "enlightenment" had its shadows. See also Hayden White, "The Forms of Wildness: Archaeology of an Idea," in Edward Dudley and Maximilian Novak, eds. *The Wild Man Within: An Image in Western Thought from the Renaissance to Romanticism* (Pittsburgh: University of Pittsburgh Press, 1972), pp. 3–38.

59. Ting Ch'uan-ching, *Sung-jen i-shih hui-pien* (Peking: Chung-hua, 1981), 10: 490.

60. Both Harry E. Barnes and Breisach argue for the importance of Geographic Discovery in broadening the scope of historical writing. Breisach placed an even greater emphasis on how Christianity-centered "universal history" was brought down by new knowledge.

61. James Hargett, "Song Dynasty (960–1279) Local Gazetteers and Their Place in the History of *Difangzhi* Writing in China," *Harvard Journal of Asiatic Studies*, 56 (1996): 405–42.

62. *Yuan-ho chün-hsien t'u-chih* of the eighth century contains limited listings of tributory commodities (*kung-fu*), while Yüeh Shih's *Huan-yu chi* (pub. 980) includes detailed records of local products (*t'u-ch'an*).

63. I am mainly speculating here, but it should not be difficult to document the development in this area. See also Elizabeth Eisenstein on publication of various "books of nature" and their influence on the worldview of people around the Reformation times: *Printing Technology as an Agent for Change* (Cambridge: Cambridge University Press, 1979), pp. 453–88.

64. Sun Fu's contribution is chiefly in imaginative reading of the *Spring and Autumn Annals*. See Bol, *"This Culture of Ours,"* pp. 183–84. See also Mou Jen-sun, "Liang-Sung *Ch'ung-ch'iu* hsueh te chu-liu," in his *Chu-shih chai ts'ung-kao* (Hong Kong: Hsin-ya, 1959), pp. 141–61.

65. For a brief discussion on the massive compilation and publication projects in T'ai-tsung's time (976–97), see Bol, *"This Culture of Ours,"* pp. 151–55, and especially John W. Haeger, "'The Significance of Confusion': The Origins of the *T'ai-p'ing yü-lan*," *Journal of the American Oriental Society*, 88 (1968): 401–10. See also Kuo Po-kung, *Sung ssu-ta shu k'ao* (Taipei: Shang-wu, 1967, reprint of Shang-hai: Shang-wu, 1940 ed.)

66. Ou-yang Hsiu (in his *New T'ang History*) rejected Liu Hsu's classification scheme for books (in Liu's *Old T'ang History*).

67. For a discussion on the *lei-shu*, see Hoyt Tillman, "Encyclopedias, Polymaths, and *Tao-hsüeh* Confucians: Preliminary Reflections with Special Reference to Chang Ju-yü," *Journal of Sung-Yuan Studies*, no. 22 (1990–92): 89–108. See also Hu Tao-ching, *Chung-kuo ku-tai te lei-shu* (Peking: Chung-hua, 1982), pp. 1–14.

68. M.-D. Chanu, *Nature, Man and Society in the Twelfth Century* (Chicago: University of Chicago Press, 1968), p. 116.

69. *CSW*, vol. 22, 921 (4): 55–56. See also 923 (6): 104.

70. For "expediency," see also Conrad Schirokauer's article cited in note 86 below.

71. The problem with Su Hsün's reasoning is that the tragic sense of historical fatalism lead him to think that therefore history somewhat is pre-determined or shows regularity that can be detected. Obviously, the lack of a Judeo-Christian (more Christian) idea of providence prevented him from being able to make the distinction as St. Augustine did on fate and providence. Since history is predictably tragic, then *shih*[a] becomes understandable or comprehensible. In Western reasoning, the defining character of "fate" is its unpredictability. In that sense, *shih*[a] is different from fate.

72. Su Ch'e uses *shih*[a] almost regularly, following his father's usage. While sharing his father's morally realist attitude, Su Ch'e, however, chose to argue that moral government ultimately would prevail over malicious historical circumstances or contingencies. His article, entitled, "Historical *shih*[a] Is No Match for 'Virtue' (*te*)," *CSW*, 47, 2094 (58): 495-96.} is a good example.

73. *CSW*, vol. 19, 1259 (29): 449–50.

74. For an interesting discussion on the idea of *shih*[a] from a philosophical viewpoint, see Chou Tun-i, "T'ung-shu" (ch. 27), in Chou Wen-ying, ed., *Chou Tun-i ch'uan-shu* (Nan-ch'ang: Chiang-hsi chiao-yü, 1993), 3:150–51. Briefly speaking, Chou Tun-i thinks that the rise and fall of dynasties was the result of historical *shih*[a]. If the *shih*[a] is beyond human effort to forestall, then this is heavenly mandate (*ming*). One may wish to understand heavenly mandate here as "fate" in the Western thinking.

75. For an interesting analysis on Ranke's idea of "inner interconnectedness" (innere Zusammenhang), see Friedrich Meinecke, *Historism*, trans. E. Anderson (London: Routledge & Kegan Paul, 1975), pp. 501–03. See also J. B. Black, *The Art of History* (London: Methuen, 1926), pp. 99–100.

76. Ssu-ma's memorials relevant to the discussion here are found in *CSW*, vol. 27, 1174 (3): 508–9; 1175 (4): 517–18, 523. See also vol. 28, 1217 (46): 471. For Shen-tsung's edict, see Chang Yü, *Hsin-chiao Tzu-chih t'ung-chien chu* (Taipei: Shih-chieh, 1962), vol. 1, pp. 33–34. (This edict-preface is found in various editions of Ssu-ma's *T'ung-chien*.) Most of these documents are abridged and translated in E. G. Pulleyblank, "Chinese Historical Criticism: Liu Chih-chi and Ssu-ma Kuang," in W. G. Beasley and E. G. Pulleyblank, eds., *Historians of China and Japan* (Cambridge: Cambridge University Press, 1961), pp. 135–66, which remains the best English article on Ssu-ma's historical criticism.

77. Li Ching-te, ed., *Chu-tzu yü-lei*, 10:187. Chu Hsi says that Ssu-ma's citing Hsün-tzu on *t'ung* is in one of Ssu-ma's letters. I have not been able to track down this letter in Ssu-ma's collected works.

78. For Cheng Ch'iao, see my "History, Erudition and Good Government: Statecraft and Encyclopedic Historical Thinking in Cheng Ch'iao (1104–1162)," in my (ed.) *Imagining Multiplicity: Historical Thinking and Historiography in Sung China* (in preparation).

79. Wu Huai-ch'i, *Sung-tai shih-hsüeh ssu-hsiang shih* (Ho-fei, An-hui: Huang-shan, 1992), pp. 138–61; Wu Huai-ch'i also published several articles in the 1980s specifically on Cheng Ch'iao's *Comprehensive Records* in the journal *Shih-hsüeh shih yen-chiu*.

80. Breisach, *Historiography, Ancient, Medieval, and Modern*, p. 194; Harry E. Barnes, *A History of Historical Writing* (New York: Dover, 1963), pp. 237–42.

81. See my Chinese "Fan-lun chi-tai Chung-kuo shih-hsueh te fa-chan yu i-i: fu-lun ts'ung pi-chi, cha-chi tau she-hui shih," in my *Tu-shih te lo-ch'ü* (Taipei: Yün-ch'en,

1991), pp. 180–224. Hu Shih had suggested the possible influence Jesuit missionaries might have had on China's critical scholarship after the arrival of the missionaries.

82. Arnold Momigliano, "Gibbon's Contribution to Historical Method," in his *Studies in Historiography* (New York: Harper & Row, 1966), pp. 40–55.

83. Hok Lam Chan, "'Comprehensiveness' (*T'ung*) and 'Change' (*Pien*) in Ma Tuan-lin's Historical Thought," in Hok-lam Chan and Wm. Theodore de Bary, eds., *Yuan Thought: Chinese Thought and Religion under the Mongols* (New York: Columbia University Press, 1982), pp. 27–87; Chinese bibliographers have traditionally grouped Ma's *Wen-hsien t'ung-k'ao* (*General/Comprehensive Studies of [Historical] Records*) with Tu Yu's *T'ung-tien* (*Comprehensive Compendium*) and Cheng Ch'iao's *T'ung-chih* as belonging to the same so-called *cheng-shu* (Political/statecraft works) category. Recent interpreters, furthering this idea, have argued that an evolutionary or even progressive view of history was emerging in such works. See Yin Ta, *Chung-kuo shih-hsueh fa-chan shih* (K'ai-feng: Chung-chou, 1985), pp. 179–98. It appears that Hu Hung and Lo Pi of the Sung also held similar evolutionary ideas. For the two, see below.

84. F. M. Cornford, *Thucidides Mythistoricus* (London: Routledge & Kegan Paul, 1965, reprint of 1907 Arnold ed.), pp. 1–14.

85. The renewed interest in the idea of *pao* (retribution; reciprocity) in the Sung times could be understood in the context of neo-Confucian search for a new set of moral causality.

86. Nevertheless, Chu Hsi did not share everything Ssu-ma Kuang advocated, especially the idea of *cheng-t'ung* (legitimate succession).

87. Chu Hsi rarely talked about the idea of *shih*[a].

88. For Chu Hsi's historical thinking, see Conrad Schirokauer, "Chu Hsi's Sense of History," in his *Ordering the World*, pp. 193–220. See also Chün-chieh Huang, "Chu-tzu tui Chung-kuo li-shih te chieh-shih," in Chung Ts'ai-chün, ed., *Kuo-chi Chu-tzu hsueh hui-i lun-wen chi*, vol. 2, pp. 1083–1114.

89. The authorship of *Kang-mu* has been a subject of dispute. John W. Haeger has argued that Chu Hsi played a "limited" role. Haeger's opinion can be traced back to Ch'uan Tsu-wang, whose *Sung, Yuan hsüeh-an* has been influential on this matter. Chin Yü-fu, on the other hand, thinks that the authorship should nonetheless be attributed to Chu Hsi. It is Ch'ien Mu whose careful reconstruction of Chu Hsi's many remarks on the *Kang-mu* that firmly establishes that Chu Hsi completed a draft of only about one third of the final product. The present edition of *Kang-mu* is different from Chu's original manuscript, although a large part of the present version, mainly compiled by Chao Shih-yuan, met with Chu Hsi's approval. Ch'ien also refutes Ch'uan Tsu-wang's claim that the present version of Chu Hsi's "editorial guidelines" (*fan-li*) was not Chu Hsi's original version. Ch'ien Mu therefore considers that *Kang-mu* remains a reliable source for studying Chu Hsi's historical thinking, and that Chu Hsi of course was a great historian. For Haeger, see Yves Hervouet, ed., *A Sung Bibliography* (Hong Kong: The Chinese University of Hong Kong Press, 1978), pp. 75–76. For Ch'uan and Ch'ien, see Ch'ien Mu, *Chu-tzu hsin hsüeh-an* (Chengtu: Pa-shu, 1986), pp. 1676–95, especially 1690–92. For Chin, see his *Chung-kuo shih-hsüeh shih*, expanded edition, pp.188–89.

6. Turning Points in Islamic Historical Practice

R. Stephen Humphreys

"Turning point" is not a formal concept but a metaphor; it suggests to us a moment, a particular place, when we cease to go along the same road we have been following and instead head off in some different direction. It is fair to ask how much this metaphor really contributes to our understanding of the development of historical writing among the peoples of medieval Islam. To start with, it embodies the very bold premise that the vast medieval Islamic world can be taken as a bloc—this enormous realm stretching from Gibraltar to the Pamirs, over a period of nine centuries (ca. 600–1500), inhabited by a host of intermingled peoples writing in several languages and speaking in many more. It also asserts that the complex cultural and intellectual changes which have constantly if subtly reshaped the practice of historical writing (e.g., changes in the sense of what constitutes valid evidence for past events, in rhetoric and literary form, in underlying conceptions of time and causation, in religious thought and moral values) can usefully be represented as tracing a neatly drawn "line of development" with clearly marked "turns" and "shifts." Finally, it presupposes that historical writing in the medieval Islamic world represented a distinct and recognized genre—that among medieval Muslims, historiography was a body of well-defined literary practices that can be studied as a thing apart without doing undue violence to the cultural and intellectual contexts in which these practices were originally imbedded.

The proper thing, I suppose, is to denounce these and related presuppositions as pure Orientalism of the most invidious kind. But I would argue the contrary case and claim that they are quite useful so long as we recognize them for what they are. Nor do these presuppositions represent the imposition of modern Western concepts and categories on another culture; to a perhaps surprising degree, they reflect and are grounded in the self-understanding of medieval Muslims. To take the first point, medieval Muslim commentators were highly aware of the diversity of their world and of its ethnic, regional, cultural, and doctrinal cleavages. But they also felt themselves part of a single Muslim community, and they believed that they shared a cohesive and integrated high culture, especially in the realm of the religious sciences, such that scholars in Fez and Cordova were in an active dialogue (admittedly at long distance and with considerable delays) with those in Nishapur and Bukhara. Even the bifurcation of this unified high culture into distinct Persian and Arabic realms after the tenth century only blurred the old sense of unity; it never effaced it.

As to historiography (the third presupposition alluded to above), it is true that it never became a systematic science or even a subject of formal academic study among medieval Muslims, though there were two serious efforts (by Abu Ja'far al-Tabari [838–923] and Ibn Khaldun [1332–1406]) to make it just that. History was always a more or less self-taught subject, which one learned by copying existing works and imitating his predecessors. Moreover, it was usually written by amateurs, by people who had been trained as lawyers or bureaucrats, though here and there we find a few official court chroniclers hired to keep the annals and vaunt the virtues of the reigning dynasty. Even so, historiography emerged very early on—not later than the middle of the second Islamic century—as a recognized category of knowledge and genre of writing, under the names *akhbar* ("narratives, reports of events") and *ta'rikh* ("dating," hence "chronicle"). By the middle of the third Islamic century, there was already a mass of material by these names. Organized in many disparate ways, as long or short narratives, biography, date-lists, anthologies, this material was widely recognized as belonging to the same broad genre, and as having its own experts and exponents. In short, historiography represented a very loosely defined but surprisingly coherent and persistent set of ideas and practices; these ideas and practices were widely diffused—indeed, pervasive—among the literate classes (in particular bureaucrats and religious scholars), but they were transmitted only in highly informal, personalized, *ad hoc* ways.

That brings us to the second presupposition—viz., that we are discussing an intellectual-literary tradition that can be understood as developing along a firmly drawn line, with clearly identifiable shifts of direction marking critical changes within that tradition. I will in fact lay out a schema of this kind in the following pages. But in doing so, I will have to abandon the comforting idea that I am only adhering to the self-understanding of medieval Islamic culture. In fact, medieval Muslims did have a story to tell about their past, a complex but unmistakably linear narrative reaching from the life of Muhammad, sometimes even from Adam, down to their own times and (at least implicitly and occasionally explicitly) far into the future, even until the Last Day. However, they never show any real awareness of change and development in the literary works which embodied this narrative. So far as I can see, they regarded the writing of history as a cumulative act, as the aggregation of knowledge about the past. New works simply added to or corrected the existing record. People were certainly acutely aware of differences in quality between historians, not to mention the political and ideological agendas imbedded in their works. But historiography was not prestigious enough either as a literary genre or as a form of scientific knowledge for anyone to examine it as a self-contained tradition with a history of its own.[1] So, when I talk about the history of Muslim historiography, that does represent very much an anachronistic—i.e., a modern and Western—perspective on the subject.

If we are to understand the history of Muslim historiography as a sort of linear process, it would make good sense to construct a continuous narrative, identifying as we go the points where the plot suddenly shifted. However, that is hardly possible within the confines of a brief paper. Instead, I will rather focus on the "turning points" themselves. These may seem arbitrarily chosen (or constructed if you prefer), but they are in fact imbedded in a latent narrative which serves as the (mostly) unspoken context of my analysis. Even this strategy is hardly feasible without sharply narrowing the plot of the story. Thus I will be focusing exclusively on chronologically organized narrative works rather than the immense biographical literature produced by medieval Muslims, even though biography was explicitly categorized by them as a genre of historical writing and was largely composed by the very same individuals who wrote the chronicles.

If it seems odd to begin a story with a turning point, this one at least opens with a major cultural shift—viz., with the very emergence of historical writing among a people (the newly Islamized Arabs) whose previous, largely oral literature reflected only a limited and inchoate historical consciousness. The emergence of historical writing seems to have occurred late in the first Islamic century (the early 700s C.E.), and it was crystallized half a century later in the famous biography of the Prophet of Ibn Ishaq (d. 768). This new historical awareness was rooted in a deeply felt need to explain the triumph and trauma of Islam's first century, and as it emerged, it came to be framed within a rather stable interpretive paradigm, which I have elsewhere termed a paradigm of Covenant–Betrayal–Redemption.[2]

This emerging historical consciousness among Muslim Arabs of course embodied a radically new understanding of themselves and their place in the world. The nomadic and oasis peoples of West Arabia, where Islam began, were of course well acquainted with the impressive ancient monuments of Yemen and northwest Arabia, and their knowledge of these was enshrined in a host of folkloric tales. But they did not connect these vestiges of the Peninsula's earlier civilizations with their own societies in any direct way. Their sense of their own immediate past was embodied in three forms: genealogies of tribes and clans, tribal poetry, and prose narratives of heroic deeds (the *ayyam al-'arab*, "battle-days of the Arabs"). These three were formally very different from one another, but morally and conceptually they were intimately intertwined.

Genealogies explained the constantly shifting alliances and conflicts between one lineage group and another. Genealogy was a remarkably plastic form of knowledge: as patterns of alliance and conflict changed, so did the lines of descent by which different groups explained how they were related to one another.[3] Genealogy provided a framework for poetry and battle narratives; it allowed an audience to know how different groups mentioned in these "texts" (which were purely oral at this stage) were connected to one another, and it gave a certain relative chronology, in that events could be linked to this or that generation. However, events were in a real sense time-less. When the poets and spokesmen of the tribes declaimed their own hero-ic deeds or the failings and cowardice of their enemies, the actions they recounted were conceived and presented as moral exempla, not as links in a continuous narrative or as part of a historical process. That is, these acts and events embodied the vicissitudes of human fortune, not patterns of change and development. ¡

The Qur'an added a new frame of reference, by linking the present tri-als and triumphs of the Believers to the sacred events recounted in the Bible. But the Qur'anic understanding of human history is cyclical rather than lin-ear.[4] In its scores of narratives about the ancient prophets (to whom Muhammad is direct heir), the Qur'an presents the following fixed pattern: God sees that a particular people has forgotten him and his commandments, and in his mercy he sends a prophet to recall that people to obedience. The prophet comes with a warning—in essence, this is your last chance before God sends down his terrible judgment against you for your false gods and sinful conduct. But the great majority of peoples scornfully dismiss the prophets sent to them, and then they are abruptly annihilated by flood, pesti-lence, or some other affliction. A very few—most notably Jews and Christians—do accept their prophets and are saved, but even they soon enough corrupt the message brought by their prophets and fall into sin—though not so far that God has (as yet) utterly lost patience with them. In short, God offers every people a Covenant; they reject or accept this Covenant, and they suffer or prosper accordingly.

None of these things—genealogy, poetry and battle narratives, or the Qur'an—necessarily entails a fully developed historical consciousness, though each was a crucial element in such a consciousness. Some further cat-alyst was required, and that catalyst was the astonishing transformation of the Muslim community immediately after Muhammad's death in 632: the decision to maintain his mission by naming a successor (the caliph), the con-quests of Arabia (632–34) and then much of the Middle East (634–51), a long period of endemic bitter civil war within the Muslim community, even as Muslim armies continued their expansion across North Africa and into Central Asia.[5] These immense convulsions could not be adequately addressed within the traditional genres of genealogy, poetry, and battle-narrative, nor even by the paradigmatic prophet-stories of the Qur'an. In particular, Muslims had to make sense of the almost irresolvable conflict between tragedy and triumphalism which these events embodied. Thus we find, per-haps as early as the 680s and certainly by 700, an effort by spokesmen for every religio-political and tribal faction within a badly fragmented commu-nity to collect materials of all kinds relative to the crucial events of Islam's early decades. The motive for this collection was of course not scholarly but polemical: the object was to demonstrate the rightness of one's own cause and the falsity of his opponents'. It is far from clear how long it took for these early collections to be shaped, to settle on an agreed-upon core of key events and actors, and to yield a coherent narrative line. I will here just assert that I am confident that this had come about by the 710s or 720s. Certainly the basic plot lines which govern the competing narratives of the opposing factions (and these factions agree on the central events and actors if on little else) are clearly visible in a number of sermons and letters from these decades or slightly later.[6]

All these narratives share the same master narrative—we might also say, they embody the same explanatory myth—which runs as follows: God had offered the Muslims a covenant through the mission of his chosen prophet Muhammad, the Muslims had embraced this covenant and held on to it even during the discord and rebellion which followed Muhammad's death, and therefore they had been rewarded by God as no people before them had ever been. But at a tragic juncture early on they had betrayed this covenant and fallen into generation upon generation of bitter civil strife, from which they seemed utterly impotent to extricate themselves.[7] This story of Covenant and Betrayal raised a host of questions, which every faction answered in its own way. Had all Muslims violated the covenant or had some remained faithful? If some were still faithful, who were they? What was the incident which marked the breaking of the covenant? Was the Community's act of betrayal final and irreparable, or might it yet hope for redemption? And if redemption was to come, by whose hands and in what form?

The rapidly developing historical consciousness of Islamic culture ultimately issued in the formation of a definitive canon of narratives recounting the Community's early history, with a particular focus on its first century. This canon was solidly in place by ca. 825, the end of the second Islamic century, and it was given its final form—the form in which it was preserved throughout the Islamic middle ages and has come down to us—in the digests and great synthetic compilations of the late ninth and early tenth centuries, composed by Ibn Qutayba (d. 889), Baladhuri (d. 892), Dinawari (d. 895), Ya'qubi (d. 897), Mas'udi (d. 956), and (most massively and systematically) Abu Ja'far al-Tabari (d. 923).[8] The formation of this canon was driven by the same cultural and religious needs that had impelled the formation of a historical consciousness and the narratives which embodied it, but also by an urgent new need to explain the significance of the Abbasid Revolution (747–50) for the Community of Believers.

To speak briefly if not cryptically, the Abbasids (who were near kinsmen but not lineal descendants of the Prophet) seized power from the reigning Umayyad dynasty with a promise to establish government in strict accord with the word of God (the Qur'an) and the teaching and practice (the Sunna) of Muhammad—in effect, a messianic promise to restore the prophetic community of Muhammad. With their accession to power, the Abbasids indeed proclaimed, almost in so many words, that they had restored the Muslim Community's covenant with God. Promises are easier to make than to keep, obviously, and even among the original partisans of the Abbasids there were many who felt that the regime fell woefully (and intolerably) short of the mark. Others believed that the Abbasids might not be the best possible government, but at least they were a government; after the violence and disruption of the last decades, they were willing to settle for law and order. In the end a majority of Muslims adopted a middle position;

they argued that the Abbasids were far from restoring the ideal community created by the Prophet, but they did meet reasonable criteria for Islamic government, and thus merited the loyalty and obedience of all Muslims.

In a very real sense, ninth- and early tenth-century historical writing in the Islamic world represents an effort to come to terms with the Abbasid Revolution and the Abbasid dynasty. In the starkest terms, historians had to decide whether the Abbasid caliphate represented a real redemption of the Muslim covenant with God, or simply a continuation of the covenant betrayed. There was in fact a third alternative—viz., that the Community was not synonymous with its rulers, that its "state of grace" did not depend on those who had (rightfully or tyrannically) seized the reins of government, but rather on its own fidelity to God's commandments. In the end this alternative largely resolved the crisis of redemption, but it had only begun to emerge during the ninth century and would remain inchoate and sketchily articulated for another four centuries.

What we have described so far is of course a continuous albeit exceedingly complex and involuted process; it can hardly be portrayed as a turning point in any conventional sense. But soon after the definitive fixing of the grand narrative and the canonical narratives of early Islamic history, we do in fact find such a turning point, a real shift in the way history was thought about and written. This is the rise of a historiography focused on recent and contemporary political events.[9] The new political history dealt most fully with the ruler, his court and military affairs, but sometimes it also took in a broader spectrum of actors, especially in regions (like tenth-century Iran or early twelfth-century Syria) where states were small and weak, and their very survival depended on negotiating with local elites. This kind of history was pragmatic in intent—it did not meditate on the origins of the community and the salvational import of the vicissitudes which it had suffered, but instead asked how dynasties gained, kept, and lost power. At the same time, the new history did not lose sight of Islamic criteria of rulership, or the sense that one was still telling the continually unfolding story of Muslim peoples, even as it largely abandoned the underlying myths and ideological concerns of early historiography as no longer terribly relevant or even intelligible.

As with the earlier phases of Islamic historiography, this sea change in the nature of historical writing was a response to political crisis. In the late ninth and early tenth centuries, the Abbasid caliphs progressively lost the power to enforce their authority over the provinces of the Islamic empire, even to impose their will on their own soldiers and officials inside the caliphal palace. Political authority within the community of Muslims was soon irrevocably fragmented among a host of regional warlords, and the Abbasid caliphs became at best symbols of the ideal historical unity of the Community—a kind of visible, deeply nostalgic reminder of what the Prophet had intended and had once existed.[10]

The new political history had a long and productive life; major works in this intellectual tradition were still being produced in the early nineteenth century, though their formal characteristics were very different by that time. These works dealt with a wide array of situations from a variety of perspectives. There were universal chronicles beginning with the life of the prophet or even earlier, and coming down year by year to the present. Such chronicles claimed to cover events across the entire Islamic world (lands and peoples outside the political reach of Islam were almost always excluded), and a very few succeeded in some measure.[11] In contrast, local or regional chronicles might have a similar chronological reach, but they confined their attention to a single region, usually a city and its hinterland. In contrast to the bulky universal chronicles, which usually focus almost entirely on rulers and armies, such local chronicles give us a view of politics which encompasses urban elites and even popular groups. On an intermediate scale, there are any number of dynastic histories, which examine the deeds and fate of a particular ruling family.

The authors of these works belonged predominantly to two groups: religious scholars (*'ulama'*) and bureaucrats. Obviously (as in medieval and early modern Europe) the lines between these two professions were not always clear-cut; plenty of scholars spent part of their careers as chancery scribes or advisors to rulers, and a fair number of bureaucrats found it expedient to retire to the study of sacred texts from time to time. Still, one can overstate the degree of this intermingling; the mosque and the palace did yield quite distinct perspectives on events. It is perhaps more surprising that few bureaucratic authors produced their works to order, as empty panegyric; as a group, they were relatively independent and sometimes severely critical in their accounts of the dynasties they served.

If one does not mind the thought of two nearly simultaneous turning points—or perhaps better, the emergence of a major subplot just at the point where the main story diverges from its old path—the emergence of Islamic historical writing in Persian in the late tenth century would mark another turning point. The use of Persian in historical writing did not merely represent the use of a new language as a vehicle for themes and topics already current in Arabic. On the contrary, it connected historical writing in Persian-speaking lands directly with the political values and epic traditions of pre-Islamic Iran. These values and traditions had already put their imprint on the court culture of ninth-century Baghdad, but by the tenth century they were being actively promoted by the autonomous warlord states that were springing up throughout the Iranian plateau. Persian-language historical writing would quickly develop its own characteristic rhetoric, its way of telling stories and connecting them to one another, its style of political and ethical analysis.[12]

One key difference between the Arabic and Persian-language traditions seems a formal one, but like many "merely formal" differences it is far more than that. The narratives of events in Arabic-language chronicles tend to be organized in strict chronological order, to the degree that some historians (not all) will slice a complex event into short chunks, so that each can be placed in the appropriate chronological pigeonhole.[13] Persian-language works focus on maintaining a unified narrative line and are rather more casual about dating; it is often hard to tell just when even major events occurred, and sometimes even the proper sequence of events is left ambiguous. There was some translation of Arabic historical texts into Persian and vice versa, and almost all Persian-language historians were excellent Arabists (although the converse is not the case). Even so, Arabic and Persian historiography inhabited two distinct if intimately related worlds.

To this point, I have linked the key shifts in Islamic historiography with major political crises: the great conquests and the struggle over the caliphate in the seventh century, the Abbasid Revolution in the mid-eighth century, the dissolution of caliphal power and authority in the late ninth and early tenth centuries. Each of these crises compelled historians, who after all dealt primarily with public events, to rethink the purposes and methods of their craft. Since historians were either men of religion or men of the regime, they were every day in the thick of the political conflicts and theological brawls that wracked their world. Changes in the political world (in a broad sense) inevitably entailed changes in the kind of history they could write.

In this light, it is intriguing that the changes in historical writing brought about by the great cataclysm of the thirteenth century, the Mongol invasions, are subtle, elusive, and hard to articulate with any confidence. Muslim historians hardly passed over the Mongols in silence; works of great originality and power were written in response to them, but they showed no substantial innovations in method and structure.[14] Muslim historians seem to have felt that they already possessed the conceptual and rhetorical tools to deal with the new world brought about by the Mongols.

In the Persian-speaking lands, however, we can detect some new elements. First, there is a much more emphatic insistence on what was admittedly an old idea, the notion that kingship or empire was heaven-bestowed, that it was literally a Divine mandate given now to this ruler and now to that in an inscrutable manner that defied rational analysis and explanation. Second, among the Mongol and post-Mongol dynasties of Iran and Central Asia, there was a strongly held belief that legitimacy depended on lineal descent from Chingiz Khan. Inevitably this belief was integrated within the court-centered histories composed by Iranian historians in the fourteenth and fifteenth centuries. Doubtless the irony of grounding the right to govern a Muslim people on a ruler's descent from a brutal pagan conqueror did not escape these writers, but they prudently do not call attention to it.

It may be that the revival of "universal history" (e.g., chronicles stretching from Adam to the present) among Persian-speaking historians owes something to the new world order which emerged from the Mongol conquests. It is almost a certainty that the vast history compiled (or perhaps more accurately supervised) by Rashid al-Din, the vizier of the Mongol khanate of Iran and Anatolia, could only have been conceived and written within the world empire of the Mongols.[15] Rashid al-Din's *Jami 'al-tawarikh* was surely the first (and for many centuries remained the only) true world history. If it is an encyclopedic work rather than an integrated synthesis, that is hardly a significant criticism. As a senior minister in the Mongol Empire, Rashid al-Din could command access to accounts of almost every people in Eurasia, including the usually ignored Franks, and he had these materials digested into a rather direct, unadorned Persian. But just as Rashid al-Din had no predecessors in the Muslim world (or anywhere else, for that matter) he had no successors. His work remained a gigantic, widely known, but lonely monument.

A second great crisis, the Black Death and the subsequent endemic plague cycles of the fourteenth century, likewise evoked no reshaping of historians' agendas, at least not immediately, but it is possible that that there was an indirect long-term impact in one corner (a large corner, admittedly) of the Muslim world. The famous *Muqaddima* to Ibn Khaldun's *Kitab al-'Ibar* (first drafted in the 1370s, then more or less continually worked over in the 1380s and 1390s) is a massive survey and analysis of almost everything that needs to go into a historian's workshop—a critique of historical knowledge, an examination of the dynamics of political change, a typology of political power, the basic structures of urban societies and economies, the nature of knowledge, and more. With the *Muqaddima*, he enormously broadened the perspectives that a historian should bring to his task. Whether Ibn Khaldun actually followed his own program in the *Kitab al-'Ibar* is hard to say, because hardly anyone has made a serious study of this work as a whole. But it was widely copied and read, and clearly Ibn Khaldun had a substantial impact on the historiography of fifteenth-century Cairo, which is far more explicitly analytical, far more alert to economic events and social conflicts outside the traditional precincts of palace and citadel than any earlier Muslim historical writing.

The traditional explanation of this shift in focus (which was of course not as abrupt or complete as I have implied here) has simply been to link it to the special genius of Ibn Khaldun and his influence on his contemporaries and students (especially Taqi al-Din al-Maqrizi [1363–1442] whose enormous *oeuvre* was clearly intended to realize the historiographic program laid down by Ibn Khaldun). Ibn Khaldun is usually said to have been responding to the political turmoil of his native North Africa, in which he had been intimately involved as a would-be statesman, and which suggested to him the underlying forces which governed the rise and fall of dynasties. However, Ibn Khaldun also lived in a world devastated by the plague from his youth on—the plague was indeed an integral element of the recurrent political, economic, and social crises of his times, both in North Africa and Egypt—and even though he has little to say about it, one can surmise that its presence did much to sharpen his awareness of the issues he discusses. Whatever the case with Ibn Khaldun, it is incontestable that his most productive disciple, Maqrizi, was explicitly and deeply affected by the presence of the plague (he wrote an important treatise on it) and its economic and political effects on Egyptian life. Just as importantly, Maqrizi's new focus informs the works of his own successors such as Ibn Taghribirdi and Ibn Iyas.

It seems advisable to break off at the beginning of the sixteenth century, though obviously the traditions of Islamic historical writing continued unbroken for three centuries more, until the complex crises in thought and culture caused by the intrusion of Europe into every nook and cranny of life in the mid-nineteenth century. Islamic historiographic traditions were hardly stagnant, and Ottoman historical writing in particular has come to be recognized for its richness and variety as well as its political realism and capacity for self-criticism. But this very richness and complexity makes it difficult to continue within the limits of a conference paper. *A fortiori*, the rise of modern historical scholarship in the Muslim world—a process which has been sketched but never studied carefully—presents opportunities and challenges which must await another occasion.[16]

References

1. The contrast with poetry, so meticulously analyzed line by line by generations of commentators and grammarians, is instructive. Jurisprudence (*fiqh*) is another highly self-conscious tradition, where earlier texts were constantly scrutinized and sifted and integrated into contemporary arguments.

2. R. S. Humphreys, "Qur'anic Myth and Narrative Structure in Early Islamic Historiography," in F. M. Clover and R. S. Humphreys, eds., *Tradition and Innovation in Late Antiquity* (Madison, WI: University of Wisconsin Press, 1989), pp. 271–90. Since this paper was published, my thinking on certain points has changed: e.g., I now believe that Tabari himself accepted Sayf ibn ʿUmar's account and used it to criticize the better-known one of Waqidi, not vice-versa (p. 280); I have also come to regard Tabari not as hopeful but as deeply pessimistic (p. 281). Even so, the paper's principal thesis still seems valid.

3. This phenomenon is widely recognized in modern ethnographic studies of Arab nomads. See Emrys Peters, "Proliferation of Segments," in his *The Bedouin of Cyrenaica: Studies in Personal and Corporate Power* (Cambridge, UK: Cambridge University Press, 1990), pp. 84–111. Some medieval writers were also aware of it; Ibn Khaldun in particular comes close to the modern understanding of the problem of lineage and genealogy: *The Muqaddimah: An Introduction to History* (transl. F. Rosenthal; rev. ed.; 3 vols., Princeton, NJ: Princeton University Press for the Bollingen Foundation, 1967), pp. 264–68.

4. Tarif Khalidi, *Arabic Historical Thought in the Classical Period* (Cambridge, UK: Cambridge University Press, 1994), pp. 8–13.

5. Khalidi, *Arabic Historical Thought*, p. 14; Humphreys, "Qur'anic Myth," p. 278.

6. Humphreys, "Ta'rikh," *Encyclopaedia of Islam* (new edition; 10 vols., in progress; Leiden: E. J. Brill, 1954–), vol. 10, pp. 274–75, explores these issues briefly. For a survey and assessment of the older literature on these issues: Humphreys, *Islamic History: A Framework for Inquiry* (Princeton, NJ: Princeton University Press, 1991), pp. 86–87. From a somewhat different perspective: Khalidi, *Arabic Historical Thought*, 17–34. Finally, F. M. Donner, *Narratives of Islamic Origins: The Beginnings of Islamic Historical Writing* (Princeton, NJ: Darwin Press, 1998), for a full and well balanced (though of course sharply contested) analysis, with an exhaustive bibliography.

7. See n. 2 above.

8. The most convenient source for each of these authors is the *Encyclopaedia of Islam*, new edition, eds. H. A. R. Gibb et al. (Leiden: Brill, 1960). On Tabari consult F. Rosenthal's introduction to Vol. 1 of *The History of al-Tabari* (gen. ed., Ehsan Yarshater; 38 vols.; Albany, NY: State University of New York Press, 1982–99). Tabari's principal field of study was Qur'anic exegesis; on this aspect of his work see Claude Gilliot, *Exégèse, langue, et théologie en Islam: L'exégèse coranique de Tabari* (Paris: J. Vrin, 1990). On Masʿudi, see Tarif Khalidi, *Islamic Historiography: The Histories of Masʿudi* (Albany, NY: State University of New York Press, 1975), and Ahmed Shboul, *Al-Masʿudi and His World: A Muslim Humanist's Interest in Non-*

Muslims (London: Ithaca, 1979). On Ibn Qutayba, Gérard Lecomte, *Ibn Qutayba: L'homme, son oeuvre, ses idées* (Damascus: Institut Français de Damas, 1965). On the other authors mentioned here we still await serious studies.

9. See Khalidi, *Arabic Historical Thought*, 84, 170–76; Humphreys, *Islamic History*, 128–47;Humphreys, "Ta'rikh," *Encyclopaedia of Islam*, vol. 10, p. 276.

10. Khalidi (*Arabic Historical Thought*, chs. 3–4) connects this shift in historical thought and practice to two rising intellectual trends in the ninth century, *adab* and *hikma*, both of which owed much of their impact on Islamic culture to the active patronage of the Abbasid court. This is undeniably an important dimension of the problem, but I do not believe that it contradicts my own interpretation. The new curiosity about all things human (*adab*) and the concomitant study, absorption, and creative adaptation of the Greek and Indo-Iranian philosophic and scientific tradition (*hikma*), certainly did provide historians with new perspectives and tools for dealing with contemporary history. Ironically, these perspectives and tools had little impact on the way early Islamic history was understood; the first century or so remained *tempora sacra*, to be handled within the traditional Covenant–Betrayal–Redemption paradigm.

11. The greatest achievement of this kind was certainly the *Complete History (al-Kamil fi al-ta'rikh)* of ʿIzz al-Din ibn al-Athir of Mosul (1160–1233), whose work is unrivalled in the breadth and richness of its sources, its chronological and geographical range and balance, its clarity of language and organization, and its political astuteness.

12. Humphreys, *Encyclopaedia of Islam*, vol. 10, p. 276, and *Islamic History*, pp. 129ff. The Persian historiographic tradition still lacks a good general study; a concise overview is given by Anne K. S. Lambton, "Ta'rikh," *Encyclopaedia of Islam*, vol. 10, pp. 286–90.

13. Tabari strove to be particularly systematic and rigorous about this; no doubt his immense prestige did much to shape the practice of later historians. On the development of chronology in early Islamic historiography, see Donner, *Narratives of Islamic Origins*, pp. 230–48.

14. The finest is no doubt the *History of the World-Conqueror (Ta'rikh-e Jihangusha)* of Ata-Malik Juvayni (1226–83), fortunately available in a meticulous and literate translation by John A. Boyle (2 vols.; Manchester: Manchester University Press, 1958). On the Arabic-language side, I know nothing really comparable apart from the remarkable discursus penned by Ibn al-Athir at the time of the first Mongol incursions ca. 1220, but he died before the full impact of the Mongol invasions was felt.

15. On Rashid al-Din Tabib (1247–1318) and his *Collected Histories (Jamiʿ al-tawarikh)*, see D. O. Morgan's entry in *Encyclopaedia of Islam*, vol. 8, pp. 443–44, and Lambton, "Ta'rikh," p. 289. Portions of this great chronicle have been translated into Western languages, but the work as a whole has never received the study which it clearly merits.

16. The literature on this topic can be referenced via Humphreys, "Historiography," in the *Oxford Dictionary of the Modern Islamic World* (gen. ed., John L. Esposito; 4 vols.; New York: Oxford University Press, 1995), vol. 2, pp. 114–20.

7. The Historicization of Classical Learning in Ming-Ch'ing China

Benjamin A. Elman[1]

In the middle of the Ch'ing dynasty (1644–1911), the Che-chiang literatus Chang Hsueh-ch'eng (1738–1801) enunciated what became one of the most commented upon slogans in late nineteenth and early twentieth century Chinese intellectual circles: "The Six Classics are all Histories" (*liu-ching chieh shih yeh*).[2] Since the Han dynasties, the Classics had been referred to as the "sagely Classics" (*sheng-ching*). Together with the Four Books, which became canonical in Sung (960–1280) and Yuan (1280–1368)) times, the Classics became the basis for a classical education in late imperial schools and at home. To become an official, study of the five surviving Classics and Four Books was obligatory, and the importance of the former increased after 1787, when the classical specialization requirement was dropped on civil examinations in favor of mastery of all the Classics (see below). History was always prominent in literati learning, but it was customarily considered a subordinate field to the Classics in the "Four Divisions" (*Ssu-pu*, i.e., Classics, History, Philosophy, and Literature) of official knowledge, as exemplified in the catalog of the 1780s Imperial Library shown in table 1.[3]

Before Chang Hsueh-ch'eng, history usually provided markers for sagely moral actions and exemplifications of classical learning or their betrayal. We will see this more clearly below in the case of Chu Hsi (1130–1200), the Sung champion of *Tao-hsueh* (lit., "Learning of the Way," or "Neo-Confucianism"). Wang Yang-ming (1472–1528), although a Ming dynasty (1368–1644) critic of Chu Hsi, nevertheless held to the *Tao-hsueh* view that: "History deals with events while a Classic deals with the Way." Even for Wang, however, there was no clear break between them: "Events equal the Way; the Way equals events." Wang concluded: "The *Spring and Autumn Annals* was also a Classic, while the Five Classics were also histories."[4]

In the early Ch'ing, Ku Yen-wu (1613–82) already complained that historical studies had declined during the Sung and Ming dynasties because of excessive concern on civil examinations for literary talent. In his collected essays, Ku noted that his grandfather had been critical of Chu Hsi for basi-

CLASSICS	PHILOSOPHY	HISTORY
Change(s)	Literati/Confucians	Dynastic Histories
Documents	Military Strategists	Annals
Poetry	Legalists	Topical Records
Rituals	Agriculturalists	Unofficial Histories
Spring & Autumn Annals	Medicine	Miscellaneous Histories
Filial Piety	Astronomy & Mathematics	Official Documents
General Works	Calculating Arts	Biographies
Four Books	Arts	Historical Records
Music	Repertories of Science	Contemporary Records
Philology	Miscellaneous Writers	Chronography
	Encyclopedias	Geography
LITERATURE	Novels	Official Registers
Elegies of Ch'u	Buddhism	Institutions
Individual Collections	Taoism	Bibliographies
General Anthologies		Historical Records
Literary Criticism		Contemporary Records
Songs & Drama		Chronography
		Geography
		Official Registers
		Institutions
		Bibliographies & Epigraphy
		Historical Criticism

Table 1. Forty-four subdivisions of the *Ssu-ku ch'iian-shu* (Complete collection in the Imperial Four Treasuries).

cally just changing Ssu-ma Kuang's (1019–86) *Comprehensive Mirror of History* (*Tzu-chih t'ung-chien*) into a condensed version known as the *T'ung-chien kang-mu* (Condensation of the comprehensive mirror),[5] an issue that we will take up again below. Ku urged restoration of T'ang-dynasty style examination essays devoted solely to history.[6] By Chang Hsueh-ch'eng's time a century later, the preeminent position of the Classics in literati learning was further diminished. Other late-eighteenth-century literati-scholars such as Ch'ien Ta-hsin (1728–1804), Wang Ming-sheng (1722–98), and Chao I (1727–1814), among others, also stressed historical research and were more eminent than Chang Hsueh-ch'eng. Like Chang, they remained predominantly classicists (*ching-hsueh-chia*) and never framed their scholarly identities purely as historians (*li-shih-chia*). Nevertheless, they also attempted to restore historical studies (*shih-hsueh*) at the top of what counted for literati learning.[7]

Chang Hsueh-ch'eng's late-eighteenth-century slogan, which became more famous a century later when late-nineteenth-century German style historicism became de rigueur in Republican China, reflected the changing intellectual trajectories between classical studies and historical studies among literati elites. During the late Ch'ing, historical studies gradually replaced classical studies as the dominant framework for scholarly research. In the early twentieth century, the eclipse of classical studies was complete among modern Chinese intellectuals, the heirs of Ch'ing literati historiography. Ku Chieh-kang (1893–1980) and others who participated in the *Ku-shih-pien* debates concerning ancient Chinese history in the 1920s made the Classics the object of historical study, not the premise for historical studies.[8]

We should be careful, however, not to overstate the functional connection between Ch'ing scholars and modern historiography in China. In terms of 1) applying new empirical methods of source criticism, 2) historicizing the Classics, and 3) in searching for a wider range of source materials for history, scholars such as Chang Hsueh-ch'eng resembled the German historicists in the minds of their twentieth-century interpreters, such as Liang Ch'i-ch'ao (1879–1929) and Hu Shih 1891–1962). But in the end, Chang et al. resemble their European Enlightenment contemporaries more than modern "scientific" historians. The historicization of sources in Ch'ing China did not yet equal the "objective" premises of German historicism because Chinese literati did not yet dissolve the Classics fully into the Histories. Disenchantment with the Classics was not yet widely heralded in the eighteenth century. History was important, but the Classics were still Classics. Under the influence of German historicism in modern China, however, the Classics are no longer the Classics. They have been desacralized.[9]

In the eighteenth century, for example, the perennial relationship between classical and historical studies remained an important consideration among orthodox literati. But with the rise in status of historical studies almost to parity with classical studies, the demarcation between the universality of the Classics and the particularity of the Dynastic Histories was again called into question. Such doubts penetrated the imperial civil service examinations. The noted evidential research scholar Lu Wen-ch'ao (1717–96), while serving as a senior examination official at the 1767 Hu-nan provincial examination, prepared one of the five policy questions in which he pointedly asked the *chü-jen* (lit., "raised men," i.e., provincial graduates) degree candidates to reconsider the relationship between the Classics and Histories: "The Histories have different uses from the Classics, but they derive from the same sources. The *Documents Classic* and *Spring and Autumn Annals* are the historical records of the sages, which have become Classics. Later ages honored the latter and divided [the Histories and Classics] into two genres. Can you grasp [how this happened] and then explain it?"[10]

Others went even further when they claimed that there was no difference between the Classics and Dynastic Histories. This artificial division of genres, Ch'ien Ta-hsin contended, had not existed in the classical era. Rather, the demarcation of genres had been first used in the *ssu-pu* (four divisions) system of classification after the fall of the Later Han (A.D. 25–220) dynasty, when the Classics for the first time were demarcated from History, Philosophy, and Literature. On these grounds, Ch'ien rejected the priority given the Classics over History and concluded that both were essential historical sources for retrieving from antiquity the wisdom of the sages. Placed in its own proper historical context, then, Chang Hsueh-ch'eng's often-cited claim that "the Six Classics are all Histories" reflected the growing historicization of literati learning in the eighteenth century.[11]

This process of historicization of course had its roots, as in the case of Wang Yang-ming above, in earlier trends of literati learning. Indeed, since the T'ang (618–907) and Sung dynasties, the court and the government had prioritized historical studies within the bureaucracy, in the education of the ruler and his princes, and in the civil examination curriculum. A "History Office" (*Shih-kuan*) had been part of the imperial government since the Han dynasties (206 B.C.–A.D. 220). During the T'ang, this office had increased prestige because it was the venue for the collection of documents that were used to produce dynastic histories for each reign period, the "Veritable Records" (*Shih-lu*). Such documents were also used by succeeding dynasties to officialize the history of their immediate predecessor.[12]

During the Sung, "imperial lectures" (*ching-yen*) by senior literati-officials were instituted to create a bond of shared values and modes of policy analysis between the ruler, his princes, and the court's most senior advisors. Robert Hartwell notes that the Northern Sung (960–1126) reform debates began this way. Hartwell adds that the role of history in these lectures carried over to Sung civil service examinations as a pedagogical device to encourage candidates to learn what the dynasty deemed desirable. The incorporation of history as a topic for the Sung civil examinations occurred mainly through the "policy questions" (*shih-wu ts'e*), which during the Northern and Southern Sung were an important part of both the classical and literary tracks to the prestigious *chin-shih* (literatus presented to the emperor for appointment) degree. Hartwell contends that through both the "imperial lectures" and the "policy questions" the Northern Sung government in particular was imbued with an "historical-analogistic attitude" toward solving economic, political, and social problems, although the didacticism of Sung historiography remained intact.[13]

I. History and Policy Questions

Beginning in the Yuan dynasty, when poetry and rhyme-prose were partially eliminated from the civil examinations because of their alleged frivolity, a process that was completed during the early Ming, essays on the Four Books and Five Classics became the mainstay of the late imperial examinations to test classical models for world-ordering.[14] The policy question was retained to test "classical and historical knowledge to be applied in contemporary affairs." Although subordinate to the Four Books and Five Classics over the long run, policy questions were frequently deemed essential and thus highly prized by examiners and scholars as markers of the confluence between classical theory, historical events, and practical affairs.[15]

The prestige of policy questions increased during the late Ming Chia-ching (1522–66) and Wan-li (1573–1620) reigns, when policy answers often reached over 3500 characters per answer.[16] During this period, two compilations of outstanding policy questions and answers were undertaken. The first, completed in 1604, was entitled *Huang-Ming ts'e-heng* (Balancing of civil policy examination essays during the Ming dynasty).[17] Arranged by reign period and topic, it contained samples of metropolitan and provincial policy questions between 1504 and 1604. The collection was later enlarged in 1633 to include questions from sessions two and three of the civil examinations from 1504 to 1631 under the title *Huang-Ming hsiang-hui-shih erh-san-ch'ang ch'eng-wen hsuan* (Selection of model examination essays from the second and third sessions of the provincial and metropolitan civil examinations during the Ming dynasty).[18]

During the early reigns of the Ch'ing dynasty, Manchu emperors, like their Ming predecessors, continually criticized examiners and candidates alike for relegating policy questions to relative obscurity. The Yung-cheng (r. 1723–35) and Ch'ien-lung (r. 1736–95) emperors frequently lamented the overly literary focus in examination essays and tried to encourage attention to more practical matters.[19] In fact, a review of the 1760 provincial examinations by the Hanlin Academy revealed that in Shan-hsi, examiners had not even graded the policy questions from session three. The academicians speculated that other provinces might be guilty of similar lapses.[20] Such concerns were transmitted by examiners in the examinations themselves. The Hanlin academician Wu Sheng-ch'in (1729–1803), for instance, headed the staffs of several provincial examinations during the Ch'ien-lung reign. In 1771, he prepared a policy question for the Hu-pei provincial examination in which he asked candidates to review the history of policy questions on civil examinations and to assess the length of such questions. How examiners were using policy questions to reflect their own views was becoming problematical, and attention no longer focused on the poor quality of the graduates' answers alone.[21]

For our purposes here, the decline in importance of policy questions during the Ming and Ch'ing dynasties curiously was compensated for when examiners used the third session of both provincial and metropolitan civil examinations to express their own views in a series of relatively long essay questions on a wide range of classical, historical, and practical topics. The examiners' questions represent important historical artifacts for Ming and Ch'ing official views about history that are as interesting culturally as the policy answers by the candidates. As answers by candidates grew shorter, the policy questions by the examiners grew in length. Consequently, the policy question, because it permitted examiners to lead candidates into a variety of directions, informs us of their central intellectual concerns within changing historical contexts.

We are fortunate, for example, in having complete records that allow us to reconstruct the range of policy questions prepared by examiners in Ying-t'ien prefecture during the Ming dynasty and in Che-chiang province during the Ch'ing dynasty. For Ying-t'ien provincial examinations, we have complete records covering questions for forty-seven provincial examinations over the 126 years from 1474 to 1600. On Che-chiang provincial examinations we have complete lists of policy questions for ninety-two examinations covering 213 years from 1646 to 1859. The range and probability of policy questions during the Ming and Ch'ing in these two southern regions is summarized in Tables 2 and 3 that follow.

Rank Probability	Topic	% of Total	Selection in %
1	Learning/Selection	9.6	43.4
2	Tao-hsueh	8.3	37.5
3	Ming rulers	7.4	33.5
4	World-ordering	7.0	31.6
5	Economy/Statecraft	5.7	25.8
6	Ruler-official	5.2	23.5
7	National defense	4.3	19.4
7	Classical studies	4.3	19.4
9	Law	3.5	15.8
9	Military matters	3.5	15.8
11	Literature/Poetry	3.0	13.6
11	Natural Studies	3.0	13.6
13	History	2.6	11.8
13	Agriculture	2.6	11.8
13	Customs/Values	2.6	11.8

Table 2. Ming Dynasty Policy Questions Classified by Topic: Ying-t'ien Prefecture, 1474-1600, 230 questions, top 15 ranks only.

SOURCE: *Nan-kuo hsien-shu* (Record of civil examination success in the Southern Capital Region). Compiled by Chang Ch'ao-jui Ca. 1600 edition.

NOTE: The probability for each policy question is calculated based on the assumption that each of the five selections is mutually independent. If the selection of five questions were mutually dependent, then the probability for each type would be slightly higher. Most "topics" above and below are based on actual Chinese categories. I have added a few, such as "natural studies," which are based on combining categories, such as "astrology," "calendrical studies," and "mathematical harmonics." In the case of "classical studies" versus "philology," which of course are overlapping fields, I have separated them to show the increasing importance of the latter in Ch'ing times.

Rank Probability	Topic	% of Total	Selection in %
1	Classical Studies	14.1	63.7
2	Learning/Selection	10.7	48.4
3	Economy/Statecraft	9.6	43.4
4	World-ordering	7.8	35.3
5	History	7.4	33.4
6	Tao-hsueh	6.1	27.6
7	Literature/Poetry	5.1	23.1
7	Local governance	5.1	23.1
9	Philology	4.2	18.9
10	National defense	3.8	17.2
11	Law	3.1	14.0
11	Literati training	3.1	14.0
13	Agriculture	2.7	12.2
13	Military matters	2.7	12.2
15	People's livelihood	2.2	9.9

Table 3. Ch'ing Dynasty Policy Questions Classified by Topic: Che-chiang Province, 1646–1859, 460 questions, top 15 ranks only.

SOURCE: *Pen-ch'ao Che-wei san-ch'ang ch'üan-t'i pei-k'ao* (Complete listing of all questions from the three sessions of the Che-chiang provincial civil examinations during the Ch'ing dynasty). Compiled ca. 1860.

While these results can be read in different ways, they reveal two histor-ical trends. First, classical studies increased in frequency (from 4.3% to 14.1%) and in probability (from 19.4% to 63.7%) as policy questions from the Ming to the Ch'ing, ranking seventh overall in Ming Ying-t'ien and first in Ch'ing Che-chiang. Slipping noticably in frequency of occurrence and probability from the Ming to Ch'ing were questions concerning "Learning of the Way," which moved from second to sixth. By the eighteenth century, both classical and historical studies had eclipsed *Tao-hsueh* as topics for poli-cy questions, a finding that should not surprise us when we take into account the popularity of Han Learning and *k'ao-cheng* ("evidential research") during the Ch'ien-lung and Chia-ch'ing (1796–1820) reigns.[22]

Secondly, questions on history in the third session of the examinations had moved from thirteenth in frequency (2.6%) and probability (11.8%) in Ying-t'ien during the Ming dynasty to fifth in Che-chiang (7.4% in frequen-cy; 33.4% probability) during the Ch'ing. Moreover, 73% of the history questions on the Che-chiang examinations were prepared from 1777 on, thus paralleling the late-eighteenth-century rise in popularity of historical studies among literati such as Chang Hsueh-ch'eng. In other words, of the thirty-three policy questions devoted to history in the Che-chiang examina-tions for which we have records during the Ch'ing dynasty, only nine were asked between 1646 and 1777 (131 years); twenty-four were asked between 1777 and 1859 (82 years), when the records stop because of the Taiping Rebellion. Indeed, history questions rank a close second in frequency, after classical studies, for the period 1777–1859.

We should qualify our initial findings, however, due to the fact we have complete evidence from only two adjacent provinces in the Yangtzu delta, and because we are only counting the questions given on the third and last session of the provincial examinations. To the first qualification, we can add that even if Chiang-su and Che-chiang provinces may not be representative of all other provinces, they are representative of the wealthiest provinces in south and southeast China, such as Fu-chien and Kuang-tung, where the fre-quency of elite families possessing the financial and cultural resources required to prepare students for the civil examinations exceeded provinces in North China and elsewhere.

Concerning the second qualification, we should reiterate that after 1475 policy questions were unquestionably considered less important than the 8-legged essays on the Four Books for the provincial and metropolitan civil examinations. Consequently, even as the nature of the policy questions on session three changed, "Learning of the Way" remained the core curriculum of the first session. Both examiners and students knew very well that ques-tions on the first session were the key to the final ranking of graduates. Examiners, nevertheless, framed long policy questions to express their classi-cal and historical views and to solicit opinion about problems of the day.

The scholar-official and Han Learning advocate Sun Hsing-yen (1753–1818), for example, recommended early in the nineteenth century that the five topics for provincial and metropolitan policy questions be set so that "practical learning" (*shih-hsueh*), a code for "evidential research" in the late eighteenth century, would prevail among degree candidates. Sun advocated a series of policy questions that would stress literati techniques for governance (*ju-shu*), classical studies, ancient pre-Han learning (*chu-tzu pai-chia*), local geography, and material resources.[23] By the nineteenth century, the evolution of policy questions, both in terms of format and content had evolved into a fluid but still discernable pattern. Based on these results, we can arrive at the following arrangment for the five policy questions on provincial examinations in the late Ch'ing: 1) classical studies, 2) historical studies, 3) literature, 4) institutions and economy, and 5) local geography. This order was not obligatory, nor were these five types of questions always included, but my reading of nineteenth-century provincial policy questions and answers shows these terms and this order to be generally in use. Moreover, historical and institutional questions remained a dominant concern among examiners preparing the policy questions for session three. And with hindsight we know that as Han Learning classicism became the dominant scholarly discourse in the eighteenth century, it brought in its wake a reemphasis on historical studies and the genres of historical writing, which as we will see below were also reflected in changes in the Ch'ing examination curriculum.

II. History in Ming and Ch'ing Civil Service Policy Questions

The changing role of historical knowledge vis-à-vis classical studies is for the most part confirmed when we examine the nature of the history questions and answers found in the civil service examinations during the Ming and Ch'ing dynasties. Based on Tables 2 and 3 above, we can generally conclude that late-imperial examiners who prepared the policy questions devoted a substantial proportion of them to the study of history, a trend that increased under Ch'ing rule. In addition, most policy questions that did not take history as an object of scholarly focus presumed that candidates would prepare an historical account on whatever topic was asked, whether dealing with institutions, Classics, flood control, local governance, etc.

In addition, two of the Five Classics (the *Documents Classic* and the *Spring and Autumn Annals*) were essentially historical in format and content. Because candidates before 1787 chose to specialize on either the *Documents* or the *Annals* in relatively large numbers (25–27%), we can conclude that history was also an important part of the first session of the civil examinations, even while the frequency of policy questions focusing on history was increasing from the Ming to the Ch'ing. Around 20% chose the *Documents Classic*, and another 6–7% usually selected the *Spring and Autumn Annals* for their specialization. Consequently, about one-quarter of the provincial examination graduates chose a Classic dealing with history for their specialization, which was roughly equivalent to the number who chose the metaphysics and cosmology of the *Change(s) Classic* (30–35%) or the literature of the *Poetry Classic* (30–35%).[24]

Below we will address those policy questions on provincial examinations that focused on history as a discipline and historiography as a scholarly problem. But we should keep in mind that few policy questions remained untouched by the overall literati concern for discerning moral truth and explaining historical change. Moral philosophy and history were virtually inseparable in the policy questions. The issue for examiners was the relationship between moral philosophy and history and the relative priority one might take over the other. Here, we will see that during the Ming and Ch'ing literati weighed this balance differently.

TAO-HSUEH HISTORY IN 1516 CHE-CHIANG POLICY QUESTIONS

As the third policy question on session three of the 1516 Che-chiang provincial examination, the one on history followed two earlier questions, the first on the sage-kings model of rulership, and the second on the "orthodox transmission of the Way" (*tao-t'ung*) and the role of the mind (*hsin-fa*) in the emperor's personal cultivation. We will first examine the question on history and then compare it with the other policy questions prepared in 1516 to further elaborate on the nature of historical knowledge required in the Che-chiang provincial examination. It is unclear how representative the 1516 policy question was. In the 1489 Shan-tung provincial examination, for example, a policy question on history there did not raise any of the *tao-hsueh* issues we will discuss below, whereas one policy question on the 1489 Hu-kuang provincial examination did raise the Sung roles of Ssu-ma Kuang and Chu Hsi as historians in determining dynastic legitimacy, as did a policy question in the 1502 metropolitan examination.[25]

The examiners' 1516 question (of some 345 characters) on history opened by defining the chief genres that made up history: "Chu Wen-kung [Hsi] has said that the forms of ancient history can best be seen in the *Documents* [Classic] and the *Spring and Autumn Annals*. The *Annals* is a chronicle that comprehensively reveals the chronology of events. The *Documents* records each matter separately in order to grasp its beginning and end."[26] History was divided according to the longstanding distinction between pure chronologies (*pien-nien*), that is "annalistic history," which used the *Annals* as their model, and topical accounts (*chi-chuan*, lit., "imperial annals and official biographies") that were based on the *Documents Classic*.

Hence, lurking within the assumptions that the examiners presented in their question was the view that historical studies could be approached in terms of pure chronology (i.e., in an annalistic format) or discrete topics (i.e., in a topical or biographical format). "Process vs. structure" is an overly modern interpretation of how Ming literati viewed the genres of historiography, but it is clear that in Ming times, scholars and candidates thought about history in light of the nature of change and the role of continuity.[27]

For the 1516 examiners, both Ssu-ma Ch'ien's (145–90? B.C.) *Records of the Grand Historian* (*Shih-chi*) and Pan Ku's (A.D. 32–92) *History of the Former Han Dynasty* (*Han-shu*) represented outstanding historical works, but because neither followed exactly the classical genres of *pien-nien* or *chi-chuan* that had preceded them they were criticized by later generations. Implicitly, the examiners suggested that Han historians had not lived up to classical models. This suggestion became explicit when the examiners described how some considered the *San-kuo-chih* (History of the Three States period, A.D. 220–80) that followed the Han histories as "the betrayer of the *Spring and Autumn Annals*." Candidates were asked to identify the author of the latter and discuss whether or not such charges were right.[28]

Next the examiners brought up T'ang through Sung dynasty histories, criticism of which candidates were also asked to evaluate. Actually, these questions turned out to be simply a prelude to what the examiners were really getting at in their question, for they then turned to Ssu-ma Kuang's *Comprehensive Mirror of History* and Chu Hsi's condensed version known as the *Condensation of the Comprehensive Mirror* as historical works. Ssu-ma Kuang's work was likened to the *Tso chuan* (Tso's Commentary to the *Spring and Autumn Annals*), while Chu Hsi's condensation was said by some "to have gotten the essential meaning of the *Annals*."

In closing, the examiners brought up for evaluation Hu An-kuo (1074–1138), who had written an authoritative commentary to the *Annals* during the Northern Sung, which was part of the examination curriculum from 1313 until 1793. The examiners also cited prominently later historians who had filled in lacuna in the *Comprehensive Mirror*, such as Chin Lü-hsiang (1232–1303). They asked candidates to elaborate on Hu An-kuo's claim that the *Annals* was an "important canon on the transmission of the mind" (*ch'uan-hsin yao-tien*). Finally, the examiners asked: "Today in order to produce outstanding history that aspires to the sages' important canon on the transmission of the mind [that is, the *Annals*], what should those whose minds are set on history follow?"[29]

In effect, the examiners had dissolved a question on history into a classical framework that equated Confucius' *Spring and Autumn Annals* with Sung "Learning of the Way" stress on the "transmission of the mind." Moreover, Han and post-Han histories were criticized, while Sung histories were praised. Just as Han and T'ang literati had failed to transmit the essential moral teachings of the sages, i.e., the *tao-t'ung*, they had also failed in their histories to transmit the proper legacy of Confucius' *Annals*. History served moral philosophy, and Chu Hsi became the historian who had best captured the legacy of the *Annals*.

It did not matter to the examiners that Chu Hsi had at times belittled the *Annals* as an irrelevant record of ancient facts and details. Nor were they deterred by the fact, frequently pointed out by later *k'ao-cheng* scholars, that the terms usually associated with Sung dynasty theories of the mind did not occur anywhere in the *Annals* but were derived from the Four Books as well as Buddhist and Taoist sources. Moreover, according to some accounts, Chu Hsi had only compiled a brief "*T'ung-chien t'i-yao*" (Essentials of the *Comprehensive Mirror*), in which he set the overall guidelines for his followers to compile the detailed *Kang-mu*. As in the case of the *Chia-li* (Family rituals) and *Hsiao-hsueh* (Elementary education), during the Ming dynasty Chu Hsi received credit for works such as the *Kang-mu*, which were substantially completed by his later followers.[30]

The best policy answer to the history question was written (in about 960 characters) by Kung Hui, a student from the Yü-yao county school who had specialized on the *Poetry Classic* and ranked second overall on the 1516 provincial examination. Over 2200 candidates had competed for the 90 places on the Che-chiang provincial *chü-jen* quota, a ratio of 24 to 1. Of those who passed, 34.4% had concentrated on the *Change Classic*, 17.8% on the *Documents*, 34.4% on the *Poetry*, 7.8% on the *Annals*, and only 6.6% on the *Rites Classic*. Kung Hui was an example, then, of a typical candidate who, although he had not chosen to specialize on one of the historical Classics, still had enough general knowledge of them to compose the best history policy answer.

One of the associate examiners commented that "in testing candidates on history one wanted to ascertain the breadth of their knowledge." One of the two chief examiners noted that this candidate "recorded his knowledge broadly and in harmony; his argumentation was precise and correct [such that it was clear that] he was one who was well-versed in historical studies." Consequently, the best students studied history, regardless of what Classic they had chosen to specialize on and regardless of how well they had mastered 8-legged essays on the Four Books.[31]

First, Kung Hui enunciated the underlying principles governing history using a circular argument: "If first one takes the public good of the empire (*t'ien-hsia chih kung*) to write history, then one's writings will be transmitted. If first one takes the public good of the empire to criticize history, then the debate will be settled. History is defined as the measure of right and wrong; it is the great model for making the empire serve the public good." These principles gave history an important role in assessing the present in light of the past. Moreover, Kung's essay stressed at the outset that the *Documents* and *Annals*, the first compiled by and the second written by Confucius, represented the greatest public good imaginable: "Therefore, we can say that the *Documents* is a history included as a Classic. The *Annals* is a Classic included as a history. Later historians all have been classified according to the authority of the *Documents* and *Annals*."[32]

When measuring Ssu-ma Ch'ien's *Shih-chi* and Pan Ku's *Han-shu* against these orthodox standards, Kung found that because both had given priority to the Taoist teachings of the Yellow Emperor and Lao-tzu and relegated the Six Classics, their works had immoral implications. Similarly, Ch'en Shou's (233–297 A.D.) *San-kuo-chih* had failed to measure properly the political legitimacy (*cheng-t'ung*) of the competing dynasties, thus bequeathing moral confusion to posterity and deserving the epithet of "the betrayer of the *Spring and Autumn Annals*."[33]

Coming to the Sung historical works by Ssu-ma Kuang and Chu Hsi, prominently identified by the examiners, Kung Hui's essay described how both had been composed to continue Confucius' *Annals* for the 1362 years (403 B.C. to 959 A.D.) up to the Northern Sung. Moreover, because Chu Hsi had faithfully modelled his condensed history on the moral principles of the *Annals*, Chu deserved to be known as the successor to Confucius as model historian. Chu Hsi's predecessor Hu An-kuo had correctly perceived that the "praise and blame" (*pao-pien*) judgments in the *Annals* were equivalent to the heavenly principles and that, accordingly, the *Annals* was indeed an "important canon on the transmission of the mind." In choosing the best models for writing history, Kung Hui contended that Chu Hsi, after Confucius, was the "Grand Historian," not Ssu-ma Ch'ien.[34]

It is intriguing that Chu Hsi, whom we normally associate with the "Learning of the Way" moral and philosophic orthodoxy of late imperial times, was also considered by the 1516 examiners to have been equally important as a historian. But this surprise is lessened by the fact that the sort of history the examiners were testing candidates on was more akin to what we would today call "moralizing historiography." The historiographic differences between narrative and topical history initially raised in the question were relegated to the background.

We will see in later policy questions on history that the division of history into two different genres would itself become the issue, not just whether both genres served as "mirrors" for moral and political governance. In the 1516 history question, the only "Histories" that really mattered were "Classics." Thus, the *Shih-chi* and *Han-shu* were mere histories reflecting their time; the *Annals* and *Kang-mu* were Histories for the ages. In the 1516 provincial examination, the examiners in Che-chiang were still a long way from granting historical studies an independent status equal to classical studies. The Classics were still sacred and paramount, a position that does reflect Ming literati thought.

If we compare the history policy question to the second policy question immediately preceding it, which focused on the issue of the "orthodox transmission of the Way" and the role of the "transmission of the mind" in enabling the moral mind (*tao-hsin*) to reach its goals of "absolute refinement, singleness of purpose, and allegiance to the mean" (*ching-i chih-chung*), we find similarities in the content and phraseology of the two policy questions. One was devoted to "Learning of the Way;" the other to history. Yet, because history was dissolved by the examiners into *tao-hsueh*, both questions wound up reflecting similar moral and philosophic concerns. The examiners stressed in their second policy question, for example, that spiritual and mental subtlety were the keys to unraveling the ties between individual self-cultivation of the moral mind and public mastery of the comprehensive handles of government. Study of human nature and principle were presented as the Sung dynasty reconstruction of the mind set of the sage-king Yao who passed on the lesson of the middle way of governance to his chosen successor Shun.[35]

We complete our discussion of the 1516 civil examination by also looking at the first policy question on rulership, since this was, in the eyes of the examiners, the most important question. It was standard in a Ming dynasty civil service examination that the political authority of the ruler should be confirmed in the manner policy questions were presented. The first policy question, for example, asked students to comment on the way the sagely two emperors and three kings of antiquity took upon themselves the concerns of the empire. The question stressed that such concerns could be seen in the present ruler's own mindful efforts to cultivate his virtue, which was based on his seriousness of purpose.

The examiners noted that these ideals had been realized in antiquity, but in subsequent dynasties, such as the Sung, few emperors had lived up to them. Earlier T'ang dynasty rulers had been especially negligent in their duties, the examiners pointed out. The rhetorical flourish at the end of their question, which took the form of an historical narrative of the early Ming dynasty, quickly dispelled any likehood that the examiner's impartial political criticism would be directed at the present dynasty as well:

> Our nation has endured for some 100 years from the Hung-hsi [r. 1425] to Hung-chih [r. 1488–1505] reigns. Five imperial ances-tors have successively embodied the realm, and all have preserved seriousness of purpose and imperial majesty. None has been remiss in his concerns for the empire, nor have any failed to preserve and protect the law-models of their predecessors. It is likely that they have matched the [achievements of the] Three Dynasties [of antiquity] in recreating for today the glorious peace and prosper-ity [of yore].[36]

In asking students, who of course "were more filial and respectful of their ruler than even the examiners," for their opinions, they had successful-ly narrowed the terms of reply for this policy essay to a literary form of an oath of allegiance to the dynasty. Renowned in later literati-inspired accounts for his alleged profligacy, dabbling in esoteric Buddhism, and lechery, how-ever, the Cheng-te emperor (r. 1506–21) seemed an unlikely candidate for such pompous praise. His reign was dominated by powerful eunuchs such as Liu Chin (d. 1510), against whom literati such as Wang Yang-ming had unsuccessfully mobilized. Wang was jailed, beaten, and exiled in 1506 for his efforts. Eunuch cliques thereafter remained a powerful element in court pol-itics.[37]

Moreover, Wang Yang-ming was a native son of Che-chiang province, who had resided most of his life in Shao-hsing, and passed the provincial examination in Hang-chou in 1492. Both the provincial examiners and local candidates for the 1516 Che-chiang examinations likely were aware of how far the first policy question overpraising Ming emperors had strayed from reality. Was the inflated rhetoric a form of disguised criticism? If so, then under the circumstances in 1516 the stakes were very high. Punishment awaited anyone caught at even veiled criticism of his imperial majesty. Judging by the top answer to the first policy question prepared by Chang Huai (1486–1561), also from Yü-yao county and a specialist in the *Change*, for which the examiners spared no praise, no examination candidate dared to read into the question any explicit suggestion of contemporary imperial impropriety. Certainly not the number one ranked *chü-jen*, as Chang turned out to be.[38]

In summary, then, Chang Huai's carefully crafted opening policy essay typified the expectations that students fulfilled in the first three 1516 policy answers. The student's job in the first question was to affirm in the clearest terms possible his personal loyalty to the political system devised by the

ancients and replicated in the present. In the second, the student acknowledged his commitment to the moral philosophy of the "Tao Learning"
orthodoxy. For the third, the student followed the examiners' lead in linking
historical studies to imperial orthodoxy. The first three policy questions and
answers in the Che-chiang proceedings were in essence a ritualized exchange
of orthodox political, classical, and historical beliefs that legitimated the
dynasty and extracted a written oath of loyalty from the student. Given this
ceremonial duet between the examiner, appealing to imperial majesty, and
the student, affirming that majesty, political criticism was best left implicit.
The function of the history policy question was to affirm the classical under-
pinnings of imperial orthodoxy. If the ruler was presented in the questions as
both sage to his subjects and teacher to his examination candidates, Chu Hsi
was both moral philosopher and historian without compare.

MORALIZING HISTORIOGRAPHY IN 1594 FU-CHIEN POLICY QUESTIONS

In the 1594 provincial examinations, examiners in Fu-chien province
prepared a policy question on *shih-hsueh*, whose answer in over 3000 characters was selected for inclusion in the *Huang-Ming ts'e-heng*. Unfortunately,
we have no information concerning the examiners or the student who composed the policy answer. Nevertheless, this question and answer both show
continuity and consistency with the 1516 policy question just discussed, suggesting perhaps that it was selected as a model essay for the *Huang-Ming ts'e-
heng* because of its impeccable orthodoxy. In addition to Fu-chien, similar
policy questions on history were also prepared for other 1594 provincial
examinations, including those in Shun-t'ien, Shen-hsi, and Ssu-ch'uan.[39]
    As the third policy question in Fu-chien, the 1594 history question was
preceded by two questions, one on the proper use of talented men for governance (*yung-jen*) and the other on ways to end natural disasters (*mi-tsai*).
It was then followed by a fourth question on the equal-field system as a basis
for military organization and a fifth on dealing with Japanese pirates. It is
interesting that not a single policy question was framed in terms of *tao-hsueh*
or classical studies. In fact, all five of the policy questions in Fu-chien dealt
directly or indirectly with the historical aspects of contemporary issues.
    The policy question on history opened by broaching the difference
between annalistic and topical history and then asked candidates to "point
out the strengths and weaknesses of the two genres." Ssu-ma Ch'ien was
brought up as the historian who had led the change in ancient historiography from chronicles to topical histories. So much so, the examiners noted,
that Ssu-ma Ch'ien's favored genre had become "orthodox history," while
chronicles in the style of the *Annals* had virtually died out. Candidates were
asked to comment on the aftereffects of this reversal in historical genres.
    Revival of annalistic history by Ssu-ma Kuang, according to the exam-
iners, had reversed the earlier trend that had favored topical histories. What
advantages did Ssu-ma Kuang's *pien-nien*, the examiners asked, have over
Ssu-ma Ch'ien's *chi-chuan*? Finally, the candidates had to discuss what
improvements Chu Hsi had brought to Ssu-ma Kuang's *Comprehensive*

Mirror? As an afterthought, or so it may have seemed, the examiners ended by writing that although the chronicles were the most ancient form of historiography, there were many "who today groundlessly contend that besides [Ssu]-ma Ch'ien's [*Shih-chi*] there is no history." The intent behind the 1594 policy question on history was to debunk Ssu-ma Ch'ien as the "Grand Historian." Ssu-ma Ch'ien, for all of his strengths using the *chi-chuan* genre, was taken to task by the examiners and candidates for his moral heterodoxy and his fascination with historical persons of questionable repute.[40]

The policy answer opened by embellishing on the importance of history for the ruler. The ruler had the power to demote the unworthy and promote the worthy, but he relied on history to weigh right and wrong. While the ruler's power had limits, the rights and wrongs of history extended in all directions and provided the ruler with a guide for his policies. "History contained both words and meanings. Meanings harbored both right and wrong." All good historians can use vivid and flowery language to write history, but the words were insufficient in and of themselves. Only sages could capture the "pattern of meanings" (*i-fa*) and "scales" (*ch'üan-heng*) of right and wrong revealed through words.[41]

As in the policy question of 1516, a clear distinction was made between historical Classics and mere histories. Sages, according to the 1594 policy answer, had enunciated the principles of history in three Classics: 1) the *Documents*, 2) the *Poetry*, and 3) the *Annals*. The first contained the directives and instructions of the sage kings, but was incomplete. The second supplemented the *Documents* with the songs and chants of ancient people that had reversed trends in immorality. Confucius' explication of the rights and wrongs of history in his account of the history of the state of Lu in the *Annals* had captured the "methods of the mind" (*hsin-fa*) of the sage-kings.[42]

Although not yet explicitly stated, the author of the answer had placed Confucius' chronicles on a higher historical plane than mere histories, such as Ssu-ma Ch'ien's topical history. The answer then praised Tso Ch'iu-ming, who had aided Confucius by compiling an authoritative commentary to the *Annals* that enabled later ages to grasp the "affairs" (*shih*) and "meanings" (*i*) encoded in the chronicle of events. Tso therefore was the "loyal official of the 'uncrowned king' and the drummer who spread the word of the 'Unicorn Classic.'" The *Annals*, as annalistic history, exemplified the most ancient ideal of historiography.[43]

According to the candidate, this ancient historiographical tradition had been overturned when Ssu-ma Ch'ien created the topical history as an alternative to the chronicle. In so doing, Ssu-ma Ch'ien's *Shih-chi* had become the model for orthodox history from the Han dynasty onwards. Following the lead of the examiners, the student answer rejected this tradition by pointing out that Ssu-ma Ch'ien himself had been guilty of heterodoxy when he granted the Yellow Emperor and Lao-tzu intellectual priority over Han literati loyal to Confucius and the Six Classics. In addition, he had included in his history accounts of immoral adventurers and tricksters that served to delude rather than edify his readers. The rights and wrongs of history were no longer apparent. More importantly, however, this genre of history had focused on the strengths and weaknesses of individuals and delineated the ins and outs of historical events without correctly divining the reasons for the rise and fall of the dynasty (*kuo-yun*).[44]

After the Former Han dynasty, the essay continued, historians such as Pan Ku and Ch'en Shou had emulated Ssu-ma Ch'ien. Annalistic history had almost disappeared, but there had been some who had kept the genre alive by producing limited chronicles based on a single dynasty—enough so that the author of the policy answer rejected claims made by earlier literati that "after [Tso] Ch'iu-ming there was no history." Nonetheless, it was not until Ssu-ma Kuang completed his *Comprehensive Mirror* in the eleventh century that the *pien-nien* genre revived, thereby illuminating the history of sixteen dynasties over 1362 years and earning Chu Hsi's praise for being the most important history since the Han dynasties.[45]

Though Ssu-ma Kuang had followed the model of Confucius' *Annals*, his massive historical compilation had, however, confused the vital historical issue of the political legitimacy of dynasties during the periods of disunity before the rise of the Han dynasty. The policy answer noted that such oversight, according to some, demonstrated that Ssu-ma Kuang was morally deficient in his historical analysis and was unclear about the difference between a legitimate king (the Chou dynastic ruler) and illegitimate usurpers (*wang-pa chih pien*).

Accordingly, the historian who saved the *Comprehensive Mirror* from its flaws was Chu Hsi. With a penetrating understanding of the classical principles of political legitimacy bequeathed by Confucius' *Annals*, Chu Hsi prepared guidelines (*fan-li*) for the *Kang-mu* condensation of Ssu-ma Kuang's work that eventually made it into a textbook of political ethics replete with *Annals*-like "praise and blame" historiography: "I dare to say that Ssu-ma Kuang used the methods of the *Annals* and at times captured its intent. Chu Hsi got the [full] intent of the *Annals* and also was marvelous in employing its methods. Since the 'Unicorn Classic,' this is the only compilation that counts."[46]

The essay ended by giving a brief account of historiography after the Sung dynasties. Later historians had produced continuations to the *Comprehensive Mirror* that kept it up to date and carried it further back in time. Moreover, during the Ch'eng-hua reign (1465–87) the emperor authorized an imperial supplement that included the Sung and Yuan dynasties and brought the *Comprehensive Mirror* up to 1367. The model for the twenty-two dynastic histories up to the Ming remained the *Annals*, but the essay reached a conciliatory conclusion concerning the two genres of annalistic versus topical histories. According to the candidate, the distinction was a product of Ssu-ma Ch'ien's misguided historiography. Previously the two genres had been unified. Consequently, "it was wrong to honor topical history at the expense of annalistic history. But it was equally mistaken to prepare annalistic history and overlook topical history." What was required of contemporary historians was for them to reunite the two genres and recapture the classical model for historiography that preceded Ssu-ma Ch'ien.[47]

Overall, the 1516 and 1594 policy answers resonated. Ssu-ma Ch'ien and his topical historiography were attacked on moral grounds. The *chi-*

chuan genre of historiography placed a premium on style and language, but its authors had missed the forest for the trees. Uninformed by moral vision, historical events became meaningless. Although separated by seventy-eight years, both policy essays stressed that moralizing historiography was the key. And both answers contended that after Confucius only Chu Hsi had recaptured the *cheng-t'ung* of the rise and fall of dynasties. "Political legitimacy" was the historical correlate to the "orthodox transmission of the Way" (*tao-t'ung*), which Tao Learning, leaping over T'ang and Han literati, traced back to Confucius and Mencius. In both philosophy and history, then, literati after the Han had lost their way. Not until the Sung was the moral vision of antiquity restored in classical and historical studies. As a continuator of the Sung vision, the Ming confirmed through such questions and answers that the Sung legacy remained orthodox.[48]

THE REASSERTION OF HAN DYNASTY STYLE HISTORY IN 1654 AND 1685

As we turn now to early Ch'ing policy questions on history, we should recall our earlier discussion of the changing trajectories of historical vis-à-vis classical studies in the eighteenth century. In mid- and late Ch'ing policy questions on history, the earlier focus on *tao-hsueh* historiography increasingly receded into the background and moralizing historiography became less important. In the process, Ssu-ma Ch'ien and Pan Ku reemerged as historical models who exemplified the best Han models of historiography. Just as Ch'ing dynasty Han Learning classicists stressed Han dynasty classical studies over now suspect Sung and Ming Tao Learning, so too eighteenth- and nineteenth-century Han Learning historians emphasized Ssu-ma Ch'ien and Pan Ku, rather than Chu Hsi, as exemplary historians.[49]

In the 1654 Kuang-tung provincial examination, for instance, the second policy question addressed the relationship between the Classics and the Dynastic Histories. We know that over 2600 candidates took this examination, of whom only 86 (3.6%) passed. Of the latter, 25.8% specialized on the *Change Classic*, 17.2% on the *Documents*, 43% on the *Poetry*, 6.5% on the *Annals*, and 7.5% on the *Record of Rites*. As estimated above, we find that roughly 25% of the graduates and candidates mastered one of the historical Classics in their preparations for the Kuang-tung provincial examination of 1654. In addition, all students had to answer the policy question raising the issue of the boundaries between historical and classical studies.[50]

In his introduction to the official record of the examination proceedings, the chief examiner Chang Feng-pao, a 1643 *chin-shih* from T'ien-chin, noted that during the Ming dynasty Kuang-tung had produced an outstanding scholar of *tao-hsueh* in Ch'en Hsien-chang (1428–1500) and a historian of major stature in Ch'en Chien (1497–1567), suggesting the centrality of classical and historical studies among literati scholars there. Ch'en Chien had passed the Kuang-tung provincial examination in 1528 but failed twice in the metropolitan examinations. Ironically, his annalistic history of the Ming dynasty up to 1521, entitled *Huang-Ming t'ung-chi* (Comprehensive records of the Ming dynasty), first published in 1555 and in several later editions, became a handy reference book for examination candidates. In this vein, we should add that all five of the policy questions prepared by Chang Feng-pao and his associates assumed a historical understanding of various policy matters: 1) education for the present young ruler, 2) classics and histories, 3) creating and employing talented men, 4) military structure and agricultural labor, and 5) the need for reform to keep pace with change. As in 1594, we again find no policy question directly questioning students about "Learning of the Way."[51]

The 1654 policy question was quite different from the earlier Ming dynasty questions we looked at. Students were asked to discuss in detail the "origins and development" (*yuan-liu*) of the Classics and the "core and branches" (*pen-mo*) of the Histories. Candidates had to delineate the evolutionary pattern of the Classics from six in number originally to thirteen by the Sung dynasty. This completed they were then asked to take up the evolution of historical writing from Tso Ch'iu-ming to Ssu-ma Ch'ien and Pan Ku. Historical and classical studies in effect stood on equal ground, as the examiners noted: "Earlier literati have said that classical studies focused on matters of the mind (*hsin-shu*); historical studies have stressed actual achievements (*shih-kung*)." Ssu-ma Kuang and Chu Hsi were no longer the focus of attention.[52]

Chosen as the best policy answer for this question was Ch'en I-hsiung's essay in some 2300 characters. The examiners rated it as "penetrating," "comprehensive," and "elegant," suggesting that they valued both historical knowledge and narrative style. The policy essay opened with the usual general discussion of the importance of history that we have seen in earlier policy answers, but Ch'en noted that the Classics and the Histories taken together represented the proper standard for public well-being: "The Classics are the stars, planets, sun, and moon in the human realm; the Histories are the lofty peaks and the Yangtzu and Yellow rivers of our human realm." By "advancing our knowledge through the investigation of things" (*chih-chih ko-wu*) one could master the Classics. The *Spring and Autumn Annals* should be mastered for it contained the "rights and wrongs" essential for public well-being.[53]

Classical studies were still the provenance of Tao Learning, as the appeal to the doctrine of *ko-wu* demonstrates. Similarly, the *Annals* remained the core of the orthodox moralizing historiography. In this regard, Ch'en's essay was in essential agreement with his Ming predecessors. Moreover, Ch'en contended that while historical circumstances changed, the principles underlying those changes remained eternal, a reassuring theme in a time of dynastic change. The Classics already contained the essentials of the Histories, while the Histories were based on the unified vision informing classical studies. This vision, however, had been lost during the period of disunity after the fall of the Later Han dynasty and not recovered until the great *tao-hsueh* masters of the Sung, best represented by the "original meanings" (*pen-i*) elucidated by Chu Hsi.[54]

In theory, Ch'en I-hsiung's essay diverged very little from earlier essays that dissolved history into the classical philosophy of "Learning of the Way."

But in practice, there were some important differences. First of all, Ch'en was forced by the examiners to detail Han and T'ang dynasty vicissitudes in classical and historical studies, which had been undervalued during the Ming. More importantly, however, Ch'en's essay, although it prominently displayed Confucius' *Annals*, made no significant mention of Ssu-ma Kuang's *Comprehensive Mirror* or of Chu Hsi's condensation, which some Ming examiners and candidates had prioritized as the model for orthodox historiography. The Chu Hsi that appeared in Ch'en's 1654 policy essay was circumscribed. Chu was hailed for his classical studies but ignored for his history. In effect, the question on classical and historical studies revealed a rudimentary but still noticeable distance that the examiners had placed between the two disciplines. Thereafter, Chu Hsi "the historian" receded from Ch'ing policy questions.[55]

In concluding remarks, Ch'en emphasized that historians should base themselves on the "methods of the mind" (*hsin-fa*) of the *Annals*, but this was more formulaic than substantive. In Ming essays, those "methods" had been articulated in light of Ssu-ma Kuang's and Chu Hsi's revitalization of the genre of annalistic history as a textbook for political ethics. Without the latter guidelines, or the earlier premeditated attacks on Han and post-Han historians for their heterodox views, Ch'en's use of the stock terminology of the "Learning of the Way" had lost some of its normative power. His answer had lost the self-righteous conviction that informed Ming essays.[56]

For comparative purposes we can refer to the 1685 metropolitan examination. By this time the K'ang-hsi emperor (r. 1662–1722) had established an office to compile the history of the Ming dynasty, which likely affected thinking about historiographical formats. As part of the 1685 examination, the second policy question also tested candidates on the distinction between classical and historical studies. As in 1654, the examiners asked candidates to describe in detail the evolution of the Thirteen Classics and Twenty-one Dynastic Histories. Along the way the examiners expressed what was then a common position among Ch'ing literati concerning the provenance of the Histories: "The *Annals* is a Classic of history; [Ssu-ma] Ch'ien and [Pan] Ku are the patriarchs of history." The late Ming exclusion of Han historians from the lineage of orthodox historiography was effectively over.[57]

What concerned the examiners was not the disjunction between annalistic and topical history. Rather they asked students to discuss how orthodox history (*cheng-shih*) had rightly been modeled on the histories by Ssu-ma Ch'ien and Pan Ku. Han and post-Han dynastic historians were now offered to candidates as respectable scholars. This relative openness, when compared to the relatively "closed" Ming policy questions on history, allowed graduates such as Chin Chü-ching, whose essay was selected as the best policy answer for the 1685 question on classical and historical studies, to itemize the Twenty-one Dynastic Histories as individual works. He thereby could exclude such comprehensive histories as Ssu-ma Kuang's *Tzu-chih t'ung-chien* from mention. Chin's model essay also criticized individual histories by T'ang scholars such as Liu Chih-chi (661–721) (conspicuously missing in the 1516 and 1594 and most Ming policy questions), but the aim of such criticism was not to exclude the dynastic histories from consideration. Rather, the criticism was meant simply to correct or reconsider earlier accounts.[58]

Chu Hsi was discussed in light of the Classics and not the Histories. Both the examiners and Chin Chü-ching made clear that the distinction between annalistic and topical histories was part of the classical legacy itself and not the invention of Ssu-ma Ch'ien. As Chin noted at the outset of his prized essay, "Ancient histories were also Classics. The *Documents Classic* followed the genre of topically recording [history]. The *Annals* followed the genre of chronicling events." In the process, dynastic history had evolved into the accepted form for "dynastic history" (*kuo-shih*). Unlike the Ming views of historiography we have analyzed, the Ch'ing examiners did not think that chronicles should take precedence, as Ssu-ma Kuang and Chu Hsi had wanted it, over topical histories. In the early Ch'ing, the genre of *chi-chuan* was preferred over *pien-nien*.[59]

The 1685 metropolitan examination question on history had also gone one step further than the 1658 Kuang-tung policy question by dropping all mention of the *tao-hsueh* "methods of the mind" that were still part of the 1658 question and answer on history. Instead, the 1685 examiners gave the "doctrines of the mind" (*hsin-hsueh*) prominence of place in the first policy question devoted solely to the "orthodox transmission of the Way." There, separate from questions of history, *tao-hsueh* orthodoxy still held sway in moral philosophy.

In the policy question on classical and historical studies, however, the scope of "Learning of the Way" had been curtailed. There had been a clear diminution of Chu Hsi as a historian, which was corroborated by Ku Yen-wu's grandfather's late Ming critique of the *Condensation of the Comprehensive Mirror*. No longer was history automatically reduced to the Classics. No longer was historiography simply a question of the proper moralizing historiography. But neither were any of the Classics themselves yet reduced to history. Nor were the historical Classics denied their priority. Changes were brewing, but another century would pass before late eighteenth century literati such as Chang Hsueh-ch'eng would begin to gainsay the priority of the Classics and dissolve classicism into historical studies. Overall, Ch'ing dynasty policy questions on history increasingly reflected the views the examiners enunciated in 1685.[60]

III. The Historicization of Classical Learning in Ch'ing Policy Questions

In the seventeenth and eighteenth centuries, the Classics and Dynastic Histories were carefully scrutinized by a growing community of textual scholars in Yangtzu delta urban centers.[61] The slow but steady emergence of evidential research studies (*k'ao-cheng-hsueh*) in the delta as a self-conscious field of academic discourse was predicated on the centrality of philological research to: 1) determine the authenticity of classical and historical texts, 2) unravel the etymologies of ancient classical terms, 3) reconstruct the phonology of ancient Chinese, and 4) clarify the paleography of Chinese characters. These trends began in the late Ming, but climaxed under the Ch'ing. All of these philological techniques had important historical components.

Evidential scholars favored a return to the most ancient sources available, usually from the Han and T'ang dynasties, to reconstruct the classical tradition. Because the Han was closer in time to the actual compilation of the Classics, Ch'ing scholars increasingly utilized Han works (here called "Han Learning") to reevaluate the Classics. Frequently, this change in emphasis also entailed a rejection of Sung sources (here called "Sung Learning") to study the Classics because the latter were separated by over 1500 years from the classical era, and because many Ch'ing scholars were convinced that the Tao Learning schools of Chu Hsi and Wang Yang-ming had unwittingly incorporated heterodox Taoist and Buddhist doctrines and theories into the literati canon.[62]

THE OLD TEXT *DOCUMENTS* CONTROVERSY

As a representative example of the growing historicization in Ch'ing evidential studies, many *k'ao-cheng* scholars claimed, for instance, that the Old Text portions of the *Documents Classic* (also called in English the "Book of History") were forgeries from the third century A.D., and not the authentic historical records of the sage-kings of antiquity. This textual controversy became a *cause célèbre* among Han Learning scholars, at the same time that the civil examination system used Old Text passages on the "human mind and the mind of the Way" (*jen-hsin tao-hsin*) to test candidates' knowledge of the Sung Learning orthodoxy. Students were expected to memorize the Ch'eng-Chu position on the Classics and elaborate on it for imperial examiners, but even the latter increasingly recognized that many orthodox views were philologically suspect and thus historically questionable.[63]

Since the Sung dynasty, doubts had been expressed concerning the historical provenance of the Old Text chapters of the *Documents*, but it was not until Yen Jo-chü's (1636–1704) research and the definitive conclusions he drew in his unpublished but widely distributed manuscript entitled *Evidential Analysis of the Old Text Documents* (*Shang-shu ku-wen shu-cheng*) that the question was considered settled.[64] Based on Yen's demonstrations that the Old Text portion was not historically authentic, some officials sent memorials to the throne in the 1690s and again in the 1740s calling for elimination of the Old Text chapters from the official text used in the civil examinations. Each time the proposals were set aside.

Hui Tung (1697–1758), the doyen of Han Learning in Su-chou, had renewed Yen Jo-chü's attack on the Old Text chapters in the 1740s. Hui noted that it had taken several centuries for suspicions concerning the Old Text *Documents* to lead anywhere conclusive. Hui Tung's Han Learning followers continued research on the Old Text chapters, picking up where their mentor had left off. Ch'ang-chou's Sun Hsing-yen, with his definitive study of the variances between the Old and New Text Documents brought to com-

pletion the attack on the spurious Old Text chapters.[65] The Han Learning
threat to the historicity of the orthodox Old Text Classics threatened the
shared historical consensus enshrined since the early Ming in the civil examination curriculum. Many refused to accept the historical implications of the
textual findings of evidential research scholars.

For example, Chuang Ts'un-yü (1719–88), a Hanlin academician and
Grand Secretary frequently assigned to supervise provincial examinations,
and later a leader in the reemergence of New Text classicism in Ch'ang-chou
prefecture, noted while serving as a court secretary to the Ch'ien-lung emper-
or in the 1740s that if the long accepted Old Text chapter known as the
"Counsels of Yü the Great" were impugned, then the cardinal doctrine of the
"human mind and mind of the Tao," as well as Kao Yao's ministerial legal
injunction to Emperor Shun, which stated "rather than put to death an innocent person, you [Shun] would rather run the risk of irregularity," would be
subverted. These were teachings, Chuang contended, that depended on their
historical authenticity for their classical sanctions. Accordingly, on ideological grounds, Chuang Ts'un-yü attempted to set limits to the accruing k'ao-
cheng research in the Han Learning mainstream by insulating the classics
from such historical criticism.[66]

Moreover, the provincial and metropolitan examinations continued to
cite the passage on the human and mind of the Tao from the Old Text
"Counsels of Yü the Great" with no indication of the philological controversy surrounding its historical authenticity. Examiners and students faithfully recapitulated the Ch'eng-Chu interpretation of the transmission of the
mind of the sage-kings as bonafide historical events. However, in the eighteenth century, policy questions on session three of the provincial and metropolitan examinations became a venue for the philological analysis and historicization of the Classics, unlike the Ming when such questions and
answers were usually linked to statecraft and had not yet become critical of
the textual basis of the Ch'eng-Chu orthodoxy.

Classical predispositions began to change in the late eighteenth century,
when provincial and metropolitan examiners at times tested technical k'ao-
cheng topics previously outside the civil curriculum. In chronological terms,
however, policy questions based on Han Learning crested in the nineteenth
century, a generation after its intellectual triumph among southern literati
during the last twenty years of the Ch'ien-lung reign. In the 1810 Chiang-
nan provincial examination for candidates from An-hui and Chiang-su, for
instance, the first of the third session's policy questions straightforwardly
raised the issue of the historical authenticity of portions of the *Documents
Classics*.

The examiners opened their query by raising the debate concerning the
relation of the "Preface" ("Hsu") to the original hundred-chapter version of
the *Documents*, which had long been attributed to Confucius. The examiners
asked: "Why hadn't the preface been included in the [original] listing of the
hundred chapters?" Next, candidates were asked to explain why during the
Former Han dynasty there were discrepancies over how many chapters (28
or 29) of the New Text version of the *Documents* text had survived the Ch'in

"burning of the books" policy. Following this, the candidates were required to explicate the perplexing circumstances whereby K'ung An-kuo (156–74? B.C.), a descendent of Confucius and a Han Erudite of the Classics, had prepared his own "Preface" for a version of the *Documents* that added 29 more Old Text chapters from a recently discovered text of the Documents to the earlier New Text version. "Why," the examiners asked, "had 59 chapters been listed for this version when there should have been only 58?"

After dealing with Former Han sources, the examiners turned to the Later Han dynasty classicist Cheng Hsuan (130–200), the "patron-saint" of Ch'ing dynasty Han Learning, whose scholia listed the 100 chapters in the original but lost *Documents* in a different order from K'ung An-kuo's version. "Why this discrepancy?" the candidates were asked. Subsequently, issues related to T'ang and Sung handling of the *Documents* text were raised. Why had K'ung Ying-ta (574–648), then in charge of T'ang efforts to settle on authoritative texts for the classical examination curriculum, labeled a third version of the *Documents* from the Han dynasty a forgery? Why had Chu Hsi voiced suspicions concerning the unusual phraseology (for Han dynasty writings) of K'ung An-kuo's commentary and preface to the *Documents*?[67]

The organization and content of this query reveal the degree to which the philological discoveries associated with Han Learning and evidential research had begun to filter into the civil examination system and historicize even a Classic of "History." Although still a test of cultural and political loyalty, whereby the Ch'ing reign was praised by the examiners for its nourishing of classical studies, this exploration of the textual vicissitudes surrounding the *Documents Classics* required precise information that would demonstrate to the examiners that the candidate was aware of the historical controversy surrounding this particular Classic. Rather than a test of cultural orthodoxy, however, the question raised potentially corrosive issues that could challenge historical reliability of orthodox "truths." One of the key Old Text chapters now thought by many literati to be a forgery was the "Ta Yü mo," which contained classical lessons on the basis of which the theories of "orthodox statecraft" and "orthodox transmission of the Way" had been constructed.[68]

Such textual concerns might be considered unique to the Yangtzu delta because the academic community there had been pioneers in reviving Han Learning concerns and appropriating *k'ao-cheng* research techniques for classical and historical studies. On the contrary, however, changes in civil examination questioning were occurring empire-wide, principally as a result of the Ch'ing appointments of provincial examiners, who frequently came from the Yangtzu delta and thus were conversant with the latest research findings of classical scholars there. Yangtzu delta scholars had long been the most successful on the metropolitan and palace examinations in Peking and thus were the most likely to gain appointment to the Hanlin Academy and the Ministry of Rites. Most who served as provincial examination officials were chosen from the latter two overlapping institutions in the metropolitan bureaucracy. Examinations held in the culturally peripheral provinces of Shan-tung in the north, Ssu-ch'uan in the southwest, and Shan-hsi in the northwest all reveal the magnitude and scope of the scholarly changes promoted by literati examiners that were appearing after 1750.[69]

As might be expected of a dynasty that used Sung *tao-hsueh* rhetoric to defend its cultural legitimacy, changes in policy questions for the metropolitan and palace examinations were slower in coming than in their provincial counterparts. Here, we are witness to dynamic intellectual changes that began in the urban centers of the Yangtzu delta and first influenced local provincial examinations before these new developments filtered up into the capital selection process. Ch'ing currents of classical and historical scholarship were ascending the examination ladder on the strength of those Han Learning and *k'ao-cheng* scholars who as examiners were themselves moving up the civil service ladder of success.

As we have seen above, the 1685 metropolitan examination was administered by officials who prepared questions that required mastery of Sung moral and political theory. Although classical issues dealing with texts and their transmission were tested, the overall Sung Learning mind set did not change. In the metropolitan examination of 1730, for instance, the 1685 question on the "human mind and the mind of the Tao" was repeated almost verbatim. In 1737, the question appeared again. In the metropolitan examinations of 1739, 1742, 1748, 1751, and 1752, the first policy question for each characteristically dealt with the topic of "orthodox statecraft" and the "orthodox transmission of the Way."[70] Examiners in Peking seemed intent on making sure that students got the message: the doctrine of "mental discipline," which enabled students to "grasp the fundamentals of moral principles," was the sine qua non for discussing the "methods of governance of the [Three] Emperors and [Five] Kings."[71]

Although questions dealing with textual aspects of the Classics were presented in some of these metropolitan examinations, the mind set the examiners sought to reproduce among the candidates was decidedly in favor of the Sung Learning orthodoxy. This was so much so that in the 1754 metropolitan examination, which became famous as the examination passed by five of the greatest Han Learning scholars of the late eighteenth century (Ch'ien Ta-hsin; Chi Yun; Wang Ch'ang, 1725–1807; Wang Ming-sheng; and Chu Yun, 1729–81), only one of the policy questions dealt with textual issues at all. The first policy question in fact required an orthodox restatement of the premises of the Ch'eng-Chu "school of principle," which the Han Learning scholars-to-be, three of whom would also be distinguished historians, would later attack as "empty and unverifiable" rhetoric (*k'ung-t'an*).[72]

Ch'ien Ta-hsin's 1754 examination essay for the second policy question, which dealt with textual issues concerning the transmission of the Four Books and Five Classics, was selected as the most outstanding answer to the question. Although the examiners had stressed the importance of Chu Hsi's place in classical studies, particularly with regard to arranging the proper order of chapters in the *Great Learning* (one of the Four Books), their question did address technical issues surrounding the Four Books. Ch'ien Ta-hsin's extremely long model answer (indicating that unlike most other candidates in the mid-eighteenth century he took this policy question on session three seriously) deftly maneuvered through the historical complexities of the classical issues.

Without directly impugning the Sung Learning orthodoxy, Ch'ien pointed out that the Four Books were never referred to as the "Four Books" until the Sung dynasty, when Chu Hsi and his followers had brought the *Analects*, the *Mencius*, *Great Learning*, and *Doctrine of the Mean* together as a special repository of classical teachings. Although the Four Books had since 1384 taken precedence over the Five Classics, Ch'ien Ta-hsin noted that originally the Four Books had been secondary to and a historical derivative of the Five Classics. According to Ch'ien, "the six Classics were all definitively compiled by the sages," thus suggesting that the later Four Books had less classical authority because they were only authorized by recent Sung literati. In his essay, Ch'ien also raised doubts concerning the historical authenticity of the Old Text portions of the *Documents Classic*.[73]

Policy questions dealing with the historicity of the classical Canon increasingly moved from obligatory requests of candidates to reproduce Sung Ch'eng-Chu moral discourse to tests of their mastery of classical and historical information. In the 1766 metropolitan examination, for example, candidates were asked a policy question requiring mastery of the Han Learning field of phonology. The examiners pointed out in their question that "because the Han was not very far separated historically from antiquity," the initials and finals (*sheng-yun*) in Han versions of the *Poetry Classic* were likely to be the most accurate ancient pronunciations available. The intertwined histories of classical language and literati thought were being addressed.[74]

Later policy questions prepared during the 1793 and 1823 metropolitan examinations reveal the degree to which Ch'ing classical and historical studies were penetrating the civil examination process. In 1793, students were asked to deal with the controversies surrounding the three orthodox commentaries to Confucius' *Spring and Autumn Annals*, particularly the debate over the reliability of the more historical *Tso chuan*, whose author Tso Ch'iu-ming (see above) had been regarded as one of Confucius' direct disciples, although this Old Text claim had been challenged by eighteenth-century New Text scholars. In 1792, for instance, Chi Yün had memorialized the throne concerning the various commentaries to the *Annals*, which had included the Sung Hu An-kuo *tao-hsueh* commentary as one of four required commentaries in dynastic schools since the Ming dynasty. Chi requested that this Sung commentary should be removed from the school curriculum because of its more than 1500 year distance from the date of the Classic itself. Chi's request was granted, which symbolized the victory of Han Learning views of both the Classics and Histories at court. Thereafter only the three Han commentaries were regarded as orthodox, and the Hu commentary fell into oblivion.[75] Later, as chief examiner for the 1796 metropolitan examination, Chi Yün wrote in his preface to the final report that the civil examiners "should make Sung Learning the main line of [doctrinal] transmission but where it was lacking they should supplement it [historically] with Han Learning."[76]

Earlier in 1758 the Hu commentary on the *Annals* had already been attacked as arbitrary. In its place, Han Learning scholars, following Ku Yen-wu's lead, recommended that Tu Yü's (222–84) more historically nuanced commentary to the *Tso chuan* should be used to "recover ancient studies."[77] In addition to removing one of the Sung dynasty commentaries to the Five Classics, Han Learning scholar-officials such as Hung Liang-chi (1746–1809) stressed Han masters for each Classic, thus seeking to restore the teacher-disciple eruditional model (*chia-fa*) of learning during the early empire and replace the mind-to-mind *tao-t'ung* transmission associated with Tao Learning. Hung regarded Confucius, not Chu Hsi, as the model example for *chia-fa* learning.[78]

In addition, Ch'ing literati in the late eighteenth century attacked the early Ming *Ta-ch'üan* (Great Collection) trilogy, which the Yung-lo emperor (r. 1402–25) had established as the key repository of Sung-Yüan classical commentaries required in the civil examinations for the Four Books and Five Classics.[79] Sun Hsing-yen, for instance, drafted a memorial to the emperor requesting that the Han-T'ang scholia in the *Shih-san ching chu-shu* (Scholia for the Thirteen Classics), compiled in the Sung, replace the *Ta-ch'üan* trilogy, which, according to Sun, had elided the true historical face of antiquity: "In the [current] atmosphere inside examination compounds, all that matters is the rise and fall of human talent. If we compel everyone to read the scholia, then the literati will all master the Classics. If the Classics are mastered, then they will also master the dynasty's rules and regulations. The meaning of the Classics will then be translated into useful knowledge."[80]

Although eighteenth-century evidential scholars in the Yangtzu delta were somewhat insulated from the civil examination system by their specialized work as researchers, historians, compilers, and teachers,[81] their classical and historical views had become mainstream in the late eighteenth and early nineteenth centuries. Many were successful in the changing format of the provincial and metropolitan examinations, which after 1756 and 1787 favored the erudition of *k'ao-cheng* scholars.[82] In addition to the authenticity of the Old Text *Documents*, mid-Ch'ing examiners also raised other important historical cum textual puzzles. In the 1795 Hu-nan provincial examination, for instance, the second policy question honed in on the delicate issue of the late Ming appearance of an "ancient version of the Great Learning" (*ku-pen ta-hsueh*), which reopened the Wang Yang-ming claim that Chu Hsi had manipulated the original text in Sung times to validate his interpretation of the "investigation of things" as its key passage.[83]

The 1823 metropolitan examination, for which the distinguished *k'ao-cheng* scholar Wang Yin-chih (1766–1834) served as examiner, included three policy questions that queried students about the historicization of classical studies. In the first, examiners asked candidates about the historical transmission of the Classics. The model answer by Chou K'ai-ch'i, who finished 56th in the metropolitan examination but moved up to third in the palace examination, focused on the role Cheng Hsuan had played during the Later Han dynasty as the key transmitter of the meaning of the Classics to posterity.

For the second policy question, students were asked to describe the origins, evolution, and content of lectures to the emperor by prominent literati since the Han dynasties. Again, the best essay was by Chou K'ai-ch'i. The third policy question tested the role of literati in the imperial system. In his prize essay, Lin Chao-t'ang (n.d.), twenty-sixth on the metropolitan but *optimus* for the palace examination, noted how emperors had variously promoted the teachings of notable literati. Lin described how in 1242 the Ch'eng-Chu school was patronized, whereas Ming T'ai-tsu (r. 1368–98) had for a time promoted the teachings of the Former Han literatus Tung Chung-shu (179?–104 B.C.), who had advised Emperor Wu.[84]

A Han Learning bent to policy questions was solidified in session three of the 1847 and 1852 metropolitan examinations. Prize essays for the initial policy questions by Hsu P'eng-shou, first on the 1847 metropolitan examinations, covered the fields of classical studies, with an emphasis on historical etymology in the first question, and poetic rhymes and cadences in the second. In 1852, examiners who prepared the first policy question for session three asked students to present evidence (*cheng*) concerning textual issues related to the Classics. In his prize essay, Hsu Ho-ch'ing, who was ranked in the third tier of graduates after the palace examination, summarized the contributions made by earlier Han and T'ang literati to the study of the Classics. In a closing rhetorical flourish, however, Hsu revelled in the historical "research" (*yen-chiu*) for "mastering the Classics" (*ch'iung-ching*) by Ch'ing scholars, which candidates should emulate.[85]

Consequently, policy questions during the late eighteenth and early nineteenth centuries increasingly reflected the changing intellectual context within which the imperial civil service examinations were administered. Although the quotations from the Four Books and Five Classics presented during sessions one and two of the metropolitan examinations remained, for the most part, unchanged in content and governed by orthodox Ch'eng-Chu interpretations (there were stylistic developments as the length of 8-legged essays increased, however), Han Learning trends in historical studies and textual cum historical issues had successfully penetrated both provincial and metropolitan examinations through the policy questions.

IV. *K'ao-cheng* Historiography

Erudition and searching criticism were expected by the mid-Ch'ing literati community of those who pieced together chronology, topography, institutions, rituals, and astronomy in their textual research. In the growing importance attached to epigraphical evidence by evidential scholars, for instance, we can also discern a reform of historical method in the eighteenth century. In addition to references to other scholars and the reworking of historical sources, the citing of bronze and stone epigraphical and archaeological evidence became a major element in *k'ao-cheng* scholarship. Inscriptions on bronze and stone were the two major subjects of study in Chinese archaeology before the discovery of writings on bones and shells, pottery and clay, and bamboo and wood at the end of the nineteenth century.[86]

EPIGRAPHY AND HISTORICAL RESEARCH

Epigraphy (*chin-shih-hsueh*) had developed as a special field of study in the eleventh century. Ou-yang Hsiu's (1007–72) *Chi-ku lu* (Record of collecting relics), printed in 1061, touched off a remarkable series of works during the Northern Sung that focused on the art of epigraphical copying and collecting. R. C. Rudolph points out that Sung scholars had progressed beyond collecting curiosities and were actively engaged in research concerned with identification, etymology, dating, and interpretation of findings.[87]

During the Ming dynasty, an interest in ancient artifacts as curiosities was evident, but as in so many other fields, the Northern Sung concern for exact scholarship was not continued. Ming collectors were mainly concerned with aesthetic elements of color and shape in their antique collections. No extensive archaeological fieldwork was attempted, with few works on paleographical study. An exception to this tendency, Ts'ao Chao's (fl. 1387–99) *Ko-ku yao-lun* (Essential criteria of antiquities) was one of the earliest comprehensive and systematic treatises on Chinese art and archaeology. Apart from the traditional subjects of calligraphy, painting, zithers, stones, jades, bronzes, and ink-slabs, Ts'ao Chao included discussions of ceramics and lacquer, as well as foreign items. Wang Tso (ca. 1427) made additions to Ts'ao's collection by including findings from the Cheng Ho (1371–1433) expeditions, but he also broke new ground by adding subjects such as imperial seals, iron tallies, official costumes, and palace architecture.[88]

Ch'ing scholars rejected the preponderantly aesthetic criteria employed by most Ming collectors and instead kept records of their journeys and findings. As in the Sung, such accounts generally included complete descriptions of important temples, tombs, monuments, and other objects studied. These recordings gave specific locations of discoveries, and frequently transcriptions of epigraphical findings were appended. The scale of collecting also increased dramatically. More than three thousand ancient bronze items were recorded during the Ch'ing compared with 643 during the Sung. In comparison with some twenty known Sung catalogs, there were upwards of five hundred such compilations during the Ch'ing.[89]

Ku Yen-wu was one of the pioneers in the use of bronze and stone relics for research purposes. In the preface to his *Ch'iu-ku lu* (Record of the search for antiquities), Ku wrote: "Then when I read Ou-yang Hsiu's *Chi-ku lu* I realized that many of the events recorded in these inscriptions are verified by works of history so that, far from being merely bits of high-flown rhetoric, they are of actual use in supplementing and correcting the histories." Yen Jo-chü also used the extensive relics to correct errors he discovered in the Classics and Histories. Seventeenth-century scholars such as Yao Chi-heng (1647–1715?) and Chu I-tsun (1629–1709) maintained large collections of relics and rubbings in their libraries. In addition, Chu I-tsun in 1687 completed a well-known history of Peking and its environs in which he described its archaeological and historical sites of interest.[90]

Interest in epigraphy peaked during the late eighteenth and early nineteenth centuries. Pi Yüan (1730–97) was credited with epigraphical collections compiled in Shen-hsi in 1781 and Ho-nan in 1787 under his direction. Weng Fang-kang (1733–1818) also was an authority on bronze and stone inscriptions. His well-known *Liang-Han chin-shih chi* (Record of bronze and stone epigraphy in the Former and Later Han) was printed in 1789. While serving as director of education in Kuang-tung from 1764–71, Weng had already described many ancient and contemporary inscriptions from that province in a work entitled *Yüeh-tung chin-shih lüeh* (Treatise on bronze and stone epigraphy in eastern Kwangtung).[91]

Ch'ien Ta-hsin, who also applied epigraphy to his historical research, noted:

> For the most part, writings on bamboo and silk deteriorated rapidly over time. In the process of recopying [these writings] by hand over and over again, their original appearance was lost. Only bronze and stone inscriptions survive from hundreds and thousands of years ago. In them, we see the real appearance of the ancients. Both the writings [of this type] and the affairs [described in them] are reliable and verifiable. Therefore, they are prized.[92]

Epigraphy received greater attention from *k'ao-cheng* historians because they were committed to the use of bronze and stone inscriptional evidence to verify the Dynastic Histories.

WIDER AND MORE CRITICAL USE OF WRITTEN SOURCES

A pioneer in applying Han Learning techniques to historical research, Wang Ming-sheng, for example, contended that the historian should take into account all possible sources available to him. For Wang's research on the Dynastic Histories, such sources included the pre-Han masters (*chu-tzu*), fiction, poetry, random jottings, literary collections, gazetteers, and writings of the Buddhists and Taoists.[93] Yü Ying-shih has indicated that Chang Hsüeh-ch'eng, despite his dissatisfaction with the lack of synthesis in *k'ao-cheng* historiography, was also committed to a critical evaluation and use of sources, which he then employed to give a more comprehensive picture of the past.[94] Tu Wei-yun has described in considerable detail the emergence of specialized *kao-cheng* historiography in the latter half of the eighteenth century. The efforts of Wang Ming-sheng, Ch'ien Ta-hsin, and Chao I placed the historical disciplines in China on a firm base of impartial inquiry. The credo of Ch'ing historiographic scholarship was enunciated by Wang Ming-sheng in the 1787 introduction to his study of the Dynastic Histories:

> Historical facts and clues reveal what [should be] praised and what [should be] deplored. Readers of the Histories ideally should not

force the words and arbitrargy draw out [notions of] praise and blame. They must consider the reality to which all facts and clues point. . . . Then they can proceed to record all the variations [of the facts that they can find]. When the discrepancies are analyzed one by one, and there is no [remaining] doubt, then after proceeding in this manner they can praise or blame and [still] remain sensitive in such judgments to fair discussions of the empire. . . . Generally the way of scholarship should be sought in facts and not in empty [speculation]. Discussions of praise and blame are merely empty words. The writing of history is the recording of the facts. Overall the goal is simply to ascertain the truth. Besides the facts, what more can one ask for?[95]

In complete agreement with Wang Ming-sheng's assessment, Ch'ien Ta-hsin also maintained that historical facts themselves should reveal whom to praise and whom to blame. According to Ch'ien, the process of laying blame should be analogous to the deliberations involved in deciding court cases. There must be no forced or self-serving use of the historical evidence to support political and dynastic prejudices. In his use of sources, Ch'ien emphasized the most ancient account of an event to correct the accounts that appeared later.[96]

One of the most prominent features of *k'ao-cheng* historiography was the use of *jen-wu piao* (tabulation of personages), supplemental tables, and factual supplements to make the Dynastic Histories more accessible as research tools. Ku Tung-kao's (1679–1759) *Ch'un-ch'iu ta-shih piao* (Tables of major events in the Spring and Autumn period, 722–481 B.C.), printed in 1748, served as a model for the collection of chronological, geographical, genealogical, and economic information concerning the pre-Ch'in and Han period. Arranged in tabular form under fifty topics, Ku's tables included supplementary notes by other scholars after each topic whenever there was an element of dispute or doubt. Also attached were maps that included explanations in which the ancient and present forms of place-names were given.[97]

Ch'ien Ta-hsin, Sun Hsing-yen, Hung Liang-chi (1746–1809), Hang Shih-chün (1696–1773), and Ch'üan Tsu-wang (1705–55)—all major figures in Ch'ing historiography—completed important works in these areas in the eighteenth century. In particular, stress was placed on making the *Han-shu* (History of the Former Han) and the *Hou Han-shu* (History of the Later Han) more accessible and accurate. Similarly, Chang Hsueh-ch'eng adamantly insisted that historical writing should include documentation devices that would describe the institutional forms and workings of local government, as well as *jen-wu piao* to facilitate reference.[98]

The use of notation books (*cha-chi ts'e-tzu*) and inductive methods by evidential scholars indicated that they had rediscovered a rigorous methodology to apply to historiography. Their analysis of historical sources, correction of anachronisms, revision of texts, and addition of commentary and supplements represented a direct application of methods that had first been used in classical and literary research. Wang Ming-sheng and Ch'ien Ta-hsin made significant contributions to both classical studies and history. Historians focused on resolving textual puzzles or on elucidating ritual and institutional terminology. Chao I, for example, extended his historical inquiry to include topical discussions of such subjects as epigraphical discoveries during the Sung, Ming academics, and Ming institutional weaknesses.[99]

On the other hand, Wang Ming-sheng argued that there remained a difference between the Classics and the Histories: "In ordering the Classics, one absolutely never dares to deny the Classics, whereas in history . . . if there are errors, there should be nothing to stop you from criticizing those errors. Herein lies the difference." Yet Wang relegated this difference to only minor status: "The important consideration, however, is that, although there exists a small difference between them, in general they both reveal a commitment to deal with concrete matters. This [goal] unites them." Ch'ien Ta-hsin went even further, as we have seen above, in his claim that there was no difference between the Classics and the Histories. Ch'ien Ta-hsin rejected the priority given to the Classics vis-à-vis the Histories as the means to reconstruct the classical tradition. Both Wang and Ch'ien were indirectly criticizing classical scholars such as Hui Tung, who worked only on the three Han histories (*Shih-chi*, *Han-shu*, *Hou Han-shu*), and Tai Chen, who had focused his research solely on the Classics, for overlooking the value of all the Histories.[100]

RECOVERY OF THE PRE-HAN MASTERS

Textual recovery, collation, and reconstruction occasioned the revival of unorthodox and non-standard texts overlooked for centuries. The reasoning that led Ch'ing scholars back to the Later and Former Han dynasties as sources for the beginnings of the classical tradition also led eighteenth-century scholars back to the pre-Han masters (*chu-tzu*) and their texts from the Warring States period (403–221 B.C.). Seventeenth-century scholars had emphasized use of pre-Han philosophical texts to explicate the Classics, but the full implications of this approach were not worked out until the eighteenth century when Later Han dynasty sources were left behind in favor of Former Han and pre-Han texts. The revival of the *Mo-tzu*, *Hsun-tzu*, and *Kung-yang* texts in particular presented serious threats to the classicism in Later Han sources.

Wang Chung (1745–94) and Chang Hsueh-ch'eng, although usually antagonists, each played a key role in challenging Confucius' supreme position at the heart of the classical culture. A native of Yang-chou, Wang Chung was an admirer of Ku Yen-wu, Yen Jo-chü, Hu Wei, Mei Wen-ting (1633–1721), Hui Tung, and Tai Chen, whom he regarded as the six greatest scholars of the Ch'ing dynasty. Initially, Wang was interested in the Hsun-tzu text, and he reconstructed Hsun-tzu's forgotten but important role in classical scholarship during the Warring States period. In addition, Wang Chung initiated a revival of the *Mo-tzu* text at a time when the natural studies in Mohist thought had begun to attract the attention of several *k'ao-cheng* scholars, who saw affinities between the recently introduced Jesuit *scientia* and ancient Chinese learning.[101]

In 1780 and 1783 prefaces for Pi Yüan's edition of the *Mo-tzu*, collated by Sun Hsing-yen, and others, Wang Chung defended Mohism from charges of heterodoxy by linking Mohism and Confucius' followers as related movements during the Warring States period. He also placed Mo-tzu on the same footing with Confucius. What attracted Wang Chung's interest was the statecraft and technical expertise included in Mohist writings. Weng Fang-kang, on the other hand, found Wang's perspective infuriating: "Moreover, [Wang Chung] dares to say that Mencius libeled Mo-tzu in Mencius' accusation that [the Mohist doctrine of] universal love knows no [respect for] the father.' Without question this makes him [Wang] a criminal who [goes against] the orthodox teachings."[102]

It is intriguing that revival of the *Hsün-tzu* and *Mo-tzu* texts would arouse such emotional responses. Later, Fang Tung-shu, defender of the Ch'eng-Chu orthodoxy, took dead aim at those Han-Learning scholars who were returning to the pre-Han masters. He rejected, for example, Ch'ien Ta-hsin's insinuation that Hsün-tzu had been closer to Confucius' actual teachings than Mencius had been. It was clear that *k'ao-cheng* scholars were daring to reconsider the Hsün-tzu versus Mencius debate, which had been dormant for so long. To take Hsün-tzu's side after all was to attack Sung Learning and its reliance on Mencius. Fang Tung-shu also attacked Wang Chung for his use of the *Mo-tzu*.[103]

Chang Hsüeh-ch'eng located in pre-Han and Former Han sources evidence to show that Confucius was simply the most important of many Warring States philosophers. Confucius' teachings had been only one school among others, and Confucius' role had been limited to transmitting the teachings enunciated by the Duke of Chou centuries before. Chang's research on the pre-Han masters paralleled Wang Chung's efforts to reconstruct currents of thought in the Warring States period. Chang's historical research was part of the retrospective progression of research in evidential scholarship.

Chang's discussion of the different roles played by Confucius and the Duke of Chou revived debates concerning the priority of the *Rituals of Chou* (associated with the Duke of Chou) over the *Spring and Autumn Annals* (associated with Confucius). Such debates had taken place in connection with earlier imperial reform efforts, for example, during Wang Mang's brief reign (A.D. 9–23) and during Wang An-shih's (1021–86) reform program initiated in 1069. The question of who was the major figure in the origin of the literati tradition reflected the growing rejection in the eighteenth century of the *Tao-hsüeh* view of the "orthodox transmission of the Tao" (*Tao-t'ung*), which since the Sung dynasty stressed Confucius and Mencius. According to Chang Hsüeh-ch'eng, the Duke of Chou, not Confucius, had been the last of the world-ordering sages.[104]

Revival of the unorthodox *Kung-yang Commentary* to Confucius' *Spring and Autumn Annals* by the Ch'ang-chou scholars indicates that opposing views concerning the nature of the historical Confucius and the literati tradition were taking shape during the eighteenth century. The revival of interest in the pre-Han masters among Ch'ing Old Text scholars was accompanied by a revival in the *Kung-yang* emphasis on Confucius' central role in the formation of the classical orthodoxy. According to the New Text tradition, Confucius and not the Duke of Chou had been the central figure. From this point of view, Confucius had brought together earlier strands of the tradition and forged the literati vision in a time of war and decline. For the Ch'ang-chou scholars, the *Kung-yang Commentary* was the central text that elucidated Confucius' intentions in composing the *Annals* and compiling the Five Classics.[105]

ESTABLISHING THE HSUEH-AN GENRE

Intellectual and cultural history also remained important areas of historical scholarship, particularly among Eastern Che-chiang scholars (*Che-tung*). Huang Tsung-hsi's (1610–95) *Ming-ju hsueh-an* (Studies of Ming scholars), completed in 1676, marked the formal emergence of the "studies in scholarship" (*hsueh-an*) genre as an important form of comprehensive analysis and incisive synthesis, according to schools, of the classical scholarship associated with a particular period of time, which as Tom Wilson and Ch'en Tsu-wu have shown built on earlier biographical collections, *Tao-t'ung* traditions, and accounts of school lineages.

Huang's account included discussions and citations of two hundred Ming literati. The *Sung-Yuan hsueh-an* (Studies of Sung and Yuan scholars), begun by Huang Tsung-hsi but completed by his son Huang Po-chia (b. 1643) and Ch'üan Tsu-wang, was another important contribution to China's intellectual history and to the analysis of the proliferation of literati schools of learning before the Ming dynasty. As a result of these two pioneering works, the *hsueh-an* became established as the superior narrative form for dealing with classical history and tracing the development of lines of thought in that tradition. This form of intellectual history stressed lines of discipleship, that is, transmission, within schools of thought. The *Sung-Yuan hsueh-an* was supplemented in a follow-up collection completed in 1841, and the *Ch'ing-ju hsueh-an* (Studies of the scholarship of Ch'ing literati) was compiled in 1928–38 by Hsu Shih-ch'ang (1855–1939) to commemorate Ch'ing classical schools of learning.[106]

In writing intellectual history, Ch'üan Tsu-wang in particular was committed to a recovery and preservation of materials concerning southern scholars who had lived during the tragic Ming-Ch'ing transition period, when the Ming dynasty fell to the Manchus. Ch'üan was following in the tradition of the seventeenth-century Che-tung scholar Wan Ssu-t'ung (1638–1702), who tirelessly gathered materials on Ming martyrs. Reflecting a continued interest in the traumatic effects of the Ming collapse, Ch'üan attempted to record for posterity the tragic lives of the Ming loyalists whose heroic deeds he thought were being forgotten in the eighteenth century. Ch'üan 's efforts to revive the scholarship of the seventeenth century were closely connected to his perception of late Ming history as an important record of martyrdom, which he wished to see included in the official *Ming History*.[107]

Anthologies of biographies also paralleled the *hsueh-an* collections and were another important form of intellectual history in the eighteenth century, which of course had roots in earlier dynasties. Ch'ien Ta-hsin's biographies of eleven major figures in Ch'ing scholarship, for example, which included biographies of Yen Jo-chü, Hu Wei, Hui Tung, and Tai Chen, represented this form by focusing on the classical giants in Ch'ing intellectual history. Chiang Fan (1761–1831) later made use of Ch'ien's biographies in his controversial account of the Han Learning school during the Ch'ing dynasty entitled *Kuo-ch'ao Han-hsueh shih-ch'eng chi* (Record of Han Learning masters in the Ch'ing dynasty). Chiang also compiled a work entitled *Kuo-ch'ao Sung-hsueh yuan-yuan chi* (Record of the origins of Sung Learning during the Ch'ing dynasty), in which he divided the history of Ch'ing Sung Learning into northern and southern schools.[108]

Chang Hsueh-ch'eng's own interest in the nature and requirements of historical writing led him to favor the comprehensive history (*t'ung-shih*) genre as the most acceptable form for adequate coverage of the intellectual and cultural history of China. Relying on Cheng Ch'iao's (1104–60) historiographic principles, Chang's notions of cultural history drew on an evolutionary view of political and cultural institutions.[109] In an effort to explain texts by relating them to their historical background, Chang was committed to an interpretation rooted in exhaustive bibliography and precise scholarship. He went further than other *k'ao-cheng* historians in his effort to mold historical materials into a synthetic and well-rounded whole. Chang's *Wen-shih t'ung-i* (General meaning of literature and history) was an attempt to reconstruct the successive stages of the literati classical and historical tradition, before there had been any efforts at conventional, that is, orthodox, explanation of the tradition. History, he felt, had become imprisoned by the artificial rules used in the official histories, which were the product of the collaboration of scholar-officials who owed their positions to the dynasty sponsoring the project. Chang's ideal of impartiality forced him to reject the stereotyped judgments that pervaded the official histories after the T'ang dynasty. The historian, according to Chang, should make a personal contribution to historical knowledge.[110]

These developments demonstrate that Chinese traditional historiography had by Ch'ing times evolved impartial premises for questioning research sources and accounts, which David Nivison revealed in his precocious 1966 study of Chang Hsueh-ch'eng. In fact, this movement in historical research was transmitted to Korea and Tokugawa Japan (1600–1867). In Japan, *k'ao-cheng* (*kôshô* in Japanese) historiography also developed into a rigorous methodology. Through the efforts of Shigeno Yasutsugu (1827–1910), among others, Japanese historians in the nineteenth century learned to apply the methods of German Rankean history by relying on their earlier experience with evidential research.[111]

CONCLUSION

In closing, we can refocus on the Imperial Library bibliography, whose categories and sub-categories in the 1780s were summarized in Table 1 above. It was compiled after an empire-wide search for rare books and man-uscripts to include in the four branches of the archives in the Forbidden Palace in Peking. The imperially chosen editors summed up their efforts in light of Ch'ing dynasty developments in historiography. They noted in their introductory remarks on the massive "History Section" (*Shih-pu tsung-hsu*) that not only was "writing history a contribution to evidential research," but also "reading history was a contribution to *k'ao-cheng*." In their view, the airy debates and useless discussions of Sung and Ming literati could have been ameliorated by reference to the fifteen precise categories of history books included in the Imperial Library and the wisdom and information therein:

> Without historical records, even the sages would have been unable to compile the *Spring and Autumn Annals*. Without knowing those historical records, even had the sages read the *Annals*, they would not have understood the reasons underlying whom to praise and whom to blame. Literati like to make great statements emotively saying they can "get rid of the commentaries to seek the Classics." This kind of talk cannot be comprehensive.[112]

By 1800, then, historical studies had become the antidote to what was perceived as airy reflection about moral verities. Chang Hsueh-ch'eng's claim that "the Six Classics are all Histories" was less influential in his own time precisely because it was part of the sea change in literati views of the rela-tionship between the Classics and History that climaxed in the late eigh-teenth century. We should recall that Chang went on to write: "The ancients never departed from [concrete] affairs to discuss [moral] principles. The Six Classics are all the governmental regulations of the early kings."[113] The rela-tionship between moral philosophy and history, and the relative priority between them, had been reversed by 1800. Late Ch'ing literati weighted this creative tension in favor of history.

Although evidential scholars proposed changes in historical research, they reaffirmed the role of classical ideals in the present. For them, classical learning remained the starting point and unquestioned constituent for new beliefs and patterns of historical research. New Text classicists appealed to a radical reconstruction of the past to authorize the present and prepare for the future. They had not yet reached a concept of objectivity in the modern sense or demonstrated a full understanding of what German professional histori-ans called "historicism," but evidential styles of empirical research and New Text notions of historical change and advocacy for practical adjustment of institutions to changing times were important stepping stones to a histori-cized vision of political and cultural transformation. It is impossible to think of Ku Chieh-kang and China's "New History" in a modernist vacuum. Many of his building blocks came from Ch'ing evidential research, and with them, he and others in the May 4th era adapted modern European views to unravel the facts posing as truths in imperial history.

The historical and philological consequences of evidential research thus contributed to the emergence, in the decades of the late Ch'ing and early Republic, 1890–1930, of a virulent form of cultural and historical iconoclasm and revolution that saw its roots, and hence its legitimation, in such studies. But such perspectives misrepresent the actual motives that Ch'ing scholars clearly laid out in their own writings. In the end, the scholarly intentions and cultural consequences of Ch'ing dynasty evidential research are analytically distinct. Too often we have read the twentieth-century historicist consequences of evidential research anachronistically into the classical intentions of literati-scholars writing during the seventeenth and eighteenth centuries. Such a procedure has incorrectly turned scholars such as Chang Hsueh-ch'eng, Wang Ming-sheng, and Ch'ien Ta-hsin into a sort of modern historicist that they never were. They remained committed to classical ideals.

References

1. I greatly benefited from discussions at the conference with Professor Jörn Rüsen, who commented formally on my paper, concerning the scope and limits of comparative historiography and the interpretive dangers in applying the teleology of Western modernism to traditional and modern Chinese historiography uncritically.

2. See Chang, *Wen-shih t'ung-i* (General Account Of literature and history) (Taipei: Han-shan ch'u-pan-she, 1973), 1.1. For discussion, see Yü Ying-shih, *Lun Tai Chen yü Chang Hsueh-ch'eng* (On Tai Chen and Chang Hsueh-ch'eng) (Hong Kong, Lung-men shu-tien, 1976), pp. 45–53. See also Shimada Kenji, "Rekishi teki risei hihan—'Rikkei minna shi' no setsu" (Criticism of historical reason—The theory that 'the Six Classics are all Histories'), *Iwanami kôza: tetsugaku* (1969):123–157.

3. See also my *A Cultural History of Civil Examinations in Late Imperial China* (Berkeley: University of California Press, 2000), pp. 563-68.

4. See Wang Yang-ming, *Ch'uan-hsi lu* (Record of transmitted cultivation), in *Wang Yang-ming ch'üan-chi* (Complete works of Wang Yang-ming) (Taipei: K'ao-cheng ch'u-pan-she, 1973), p. 8 (#13). I have modified the translation found in Wing-tsit Chan, tr., *Instructions for Practical Living and other Neo-Confucian Writings by Wang Yang-ming* (New York, Columbia University, Press, 1963), p. 23.

5. See Ku Yen-wu, *Ku T'ing-lin shih-wen-chi* (Collection of Ku Yen-wu's poetry and essays) (Hong Kong: Chung-hua Bookstore, 1976), 2.32–33.

6. Ku Yen-wu, "San-ch'ang" (The three examination sessions), in *Jih-chih lu chi-shih* (Record of knowledge gained day by day, collected notes) (Taipei: Shih-chieh Bookstore, 1962), 16.385–86, and "Shih-hsueh" (Historical studies), in ibid., 16.391–92. For discussion, see Inoue Susumu, "Rikkyô mina shi setsu no keifu" (The descent of the thesis that the "Six Classics are all Histories"), in Ono Kazuko, ed., *Mimmatsu Shinsho no shakai to bunka* (Late-Ming early-Ch'ing society and culture) (Kyoto: Ming-wen Press, 1996), pp. 535–85, which presents other Ming precedents.

7. On the rediscovery of Chang Hsueh-ch'eng in the early twentieth century, see Joshua Fogel, "On the 'Rediscovery' of the Chinese Past: Ts'ui Shu and Related Cases," in Fogel and William Rowe, eds. *Perspectives on a Changing China* (Boulder: Westview Press, 1979), pp. 219–35.

8. Tu Wei-yun, *Ch'ing Ch'ien-Chia shih-tai chih shih-hsueh yü shih-chia* (Historians and historical studies in the Ch'ing Ch'ien-lung and Chia-ch'ing eras) (Taipei: Wen-shih ts'ung-k'an, 1962), pp. 13–48, 99–121. See also Laurence Schneider, *Ku Chieh-kang and China's New History* (Berkeley: University of California Press, 1971), pp. 53–84.

9. See Elman, *From Philosophy To Philology: Social and Intellectual Aspects of Change in Late Imperial China* (UCLA Asian Pacific monograph, 2001), *passim*. See also Joseph Levenson, *Confucian China and Its Modern Fate: A Trilogy* (3 vols. Berkeley: University of California Press, 1969), I/90–94, and Mark Elvin, "The Collapse of Scriptural Confucianism," *Papers on Far Eastern History* 41 (1990): 45–76.

10. Lu Wen-ch'ao, *Pao-ching-t'ang wen-chi* (Collected essays from the Hall for Cherishing the Classics) (Shanghai: Commercial Press, 1937), 4.327.

11. Ch'ien Ta-hsin, "Hsu" (Preface), in *Nien-erh-shih k'ao-i* (Examination of variances in the Twenty-two Dynastic Histories) (Shanghai: Commercial Press, 1935–37), p. 1. See also the prefaces to Chao I, *Erh-shih-erh-shih cha-chi* (Notations to the Twenty-two Dynastic Histories) (reprint. Taipei: Kuang-wen Bookstore, 1974).

12. See Denis Twitchett, "The T'ang Official Historian," in *The Historian, His Readers, and the Passage of Time: The Fu Ssu-nien Memorial Lectures* (Taipei: Academia Sinica, Institute of History and Philology, 1997), pp. 57–77, and David McMullen, *State and Scholars in T'ang China* (Cambridge: Cambridge University Press, 1988), pp. 20–21. See also K. H. J. Gardner, "Standard Histories, Han to Sui," in Donald Leslie et al., eds., *Essays on the Sources for Chinese History* (Columbia: University of South Carolina Press, 1975), pp. 42–52, Yang Lien-sheng, "The Organization of Chinese Official Historiography: Principles and Methods of the Standard Histories from the T'ang Through the Ming Dynasty," in W. G. Beasley and E. G. Pulleyblank, eds., *Historians of China and Japan* (Oxford: Oxford University Press, 1961), pp. 44–59.

13. See Hartwell, "Historical-Analogism, Public Policy, and Social Science in Eleventh- and Twelfth-Century China," *American Historical Review* 76, no. 3 (June 1971): 690–727. See also Richard Davis, "Sung Historiography: Empirical Ideals and Didactic Realities," in *Proceedings of the International Symposium on Sung History* (Taipei: Chinese Culture University, 1988), pp. 109–23. On the overall achievements in Sung historiography, see Naitô Torajirô, *Shina shigakushi* (Chinese historiography) (Tokyo, 1949), pp. 241–320. Cf. Thomas Lee, *Government Education and Examinations in Sung China* (Hong Kong: Chinese University, 1982), and John Chaffee, *The Thorny Gates of Learning in Sung China* (Cambridge: Cambridge University Press, 1985. New edition, Albany: SUNY Press, 1995).

14. See Elman, *A Cultural History of Civil Examinations in Late Imperial China*, pp. 25-46.

15. Yuan dynasty policy questions can be found in Huang Chin, *Chin-hua Huang hsien-sheng wen-chi* (Collected essays of Huang Chin from Chin-hua) (Shanghai: Commercial Press, *Ssu-pu ts'ung-k'an*, 1919–37), pp. 191–200. Early Ming policy questions prepared by Su Po-heng (1329–92?) in 1385 can be found in *Huang-Ming wen-heng* (Balancing of essays from the Ming dynasty) (Shanghai: Commercial Press, *Ssu-pu ts'ung-k'an*, 1919–1937), 23.220–222. See also the 1370–71 provincial, metropolitan, and palace policy answers by the first Ming *optimus* Wu Po-tsung in the *Ssu-k'u ch'üan-shu* (Complete collection in the imperial four treasuries) (Reprint. Taipei: Commercial Press, 1983–86),1233.217–236.

16. For examples, see *Chü-yeh cheng-shih* (Correct models for examinations) (Chia-ching edition), pp. 1a–58b, which gives examples from 1529–53 policy questions, and *Ming Wan-li chih Ch'ung-chen chien hsiang-shih-lu hui-shih-lu hui-chi* (Digest of provincial and metropolitan civil examination records from the Wan-li and Ch'ung-chen reigns of the Ming dynasty) (late Ming edition).

17. *Huang-Ming ts'e-heng*, compiled by Mao Wei (Wu-hsing, 1605 edition).

18. *Huang-Ming hsiang-hui-shih erh-san-ch'ang ch'eng-wen hsuan*, compiled by Ch'en Jen-hsi (1633 *Pai-sung-t'ang* edition).

19. See *Ch'in-ting mo-k'an t'iao-li* (Imperially prescribed guidelines for the civil examination review) (1834 edition), 2.7b–13b, and 2.21b–25a.

20. See the 1760, tenth month, fifteenth day report by the Hanlin Academy, in the *Li-pu t'i-pen* (Memoranda including memorials from the Ministry of Rites), in the Ming-Ch'ing Archives, Academia Sinica, Taiwan, which indicates that only 8-legged essays on session one were graded in Shan-hsi province that year.

21. See Wu, "Ch'ien-lung san-shih-liu nien Hu-pei hsiang-shih ts'e-wen erh shou" (Two policy questions from the 1771 Hu-pei provincial examination), in *Ch'ing-tai ch'ien-ch'i chiao-yü lun-chu hsuan* (Selections of writings on education from the early Ch'ing period), edited by Li Kuo-chün, et al. (Peking: People's Education Press, 1990, 3 vols.), 3/167.

22. See my "The Unravelling of Neo-Confucianism: From Philosophy to Philology in Late Imperial China," *Tsing Hua Journal of Chinese Studies*, n.s. 15 (1983): 67–89.

23. See Sun Hsing-yen, "Kuan-feng shih-shih ts'e-wen wu-t'iao yu-hsu" (Preface for observations on trends in five policy questions for testing literati), in *Ch'ing-tai ch'ien-ch'i chiao-yü lun-chu hsuan*, 3/285–86.

24. See my *A Cultural History*, pp. 627-45, "Appendix One."

25. *Che-chiang hsiang-shih lu,*, 1516: 5/2643–2830, in *Ming-tai teng-k'o-lu hui-pien*, Vol. 5. See also *Shan-tung hsiang-shih lu*, 1489: 2/1370–72 (question), 2/1460–67 (answer), *Hu-kuang hsiang-shih lu*, 1489: 2/1531–33 (question), 2/1628–33 (answer), and *Hui-shih lu*, 1502: 5/2236–38 (question), 5/2361–70 (answer), all in *Ming-tai teng-k'o lu hui-pien*, Vols. 2–5. On Ssu-ma Kuang's (1019–86) views of history, see Peter Bol, *"This Culture of Ours": Intellectual Transitions in T'ang and Sung China* (Stanford: Stanford University Press, 1992), pp. 233–46.

26. *Che-chiang hsiang-shih lu*, 1516: 5/2681.

27. Political institutions, social family histories, and economic processes described in Chinese topical histories were never presented in purely structural terms and still stressed the role of human agency in historical change.

28. *Che-chiang hsiang-shih lu*, 1516: 5/2682. The Han histories as examinable texts had been the mainstay of the T'ang civil examination questions on history, thus putting these Ming examiners at odds with their T'ang predecessors; see McMullen, *State and Scholars in T'ang China*, pp. 197–99.

29. *Che-chiang hsiang-shih lu*, 1516: 5/2682-4.

30. See *Chu Wen-kung wen-chi, hsu chi* (Continuation to the collected essays of Chu Hsi) (Shanghai: Commercial Press, Ssu-pu ts'ung-k'an edition, 1934–35), 2.6b. On Chu's limited role in compiling the *Kang-mu*, see Sung Lien §º ¾ü, *Sung Wen-hsien kung ch'üan-chi* (Shanghai: Chung-hua Bookstore, Ssu-pu pei-yao edition, 1927–37), 12.14b–15a. See also Patricia Ebrey, *Confucianism and Family Rituals in Imperial China: A Social History of Writing About Rules* (Princeton: Princeton University Press, 1991), pp. 102–44, 167–87, and M. Theresa Kelleher, "Back to Basics: Chu Hsi's *Elementary Learning* (*Hsiao-hsueh*), in Wm. Theodore de Bary and John Chaffee, eds., *Neo-Confucian Education: The Formative Stage* (Berkeley: University of California Press, 1989, pp. 221–24.

31. *Che-chiang hsiang-shih lu*, 1516: 5/2794–95.

32. *Che-chiang hsiang-shih lu*, 1516: 5/2795-7.

33. *Che-chiang hsiang-shih lu*, 1516: 5/2797-8.

34. *Che-chiang hsiang-shih lu*, 1516: 5/2799–2802. For discussion, see Yves

Hervouet, ed., *A Sung Bibliography* (H.K.: Chinese University Press, 1978), pp. 75-76.

35. *Che-chiang hsiang-shih lu*, 1516: 5/2679–81.

36. *Che-chiang hsiang-shih lu*, 1516: 5/2676–79.

37. *Dictionary of Ming Biography*, compiled by L. C. Goodrich, et al., eds. (2 vols. New York: Columbia University Press, 1976), pp. 308–09, 1409–10.

38. *Che-chiang hsiang-shih lu*, 1516: 5/2778–80. See also *Ming-Ch'ing chin-shih t'i-ming pei-lu so-yin* (Index to the stelae rosters of Ming and Ch'ing *chin-shih*) (Taipei: Wen-shih-che Press, 1982) , 3/2504. Curiously, however, the fourth policy question raised the issue of official remonstrance (*chien*): "the official shows his loyalty through good remonstrance; the ruler shows his sageliness by obeying [such] remonstrance." See *Che-chiang hsiang-shih lu*, 5/2684–86. This question indicates that examiners were not imperial lackeys and could use the policy questions to invoke the official's moral high ground vis-à-vis the ruler, even one like the Cheng-te emperor.

39. *Huang-Ming ts'e-heng*, "Mu-lu" (table of contents), pp. 10a–12a. The degree of continuity or consistency should not be overstated, however. For example, the history policy question that Wang Shih-chen (1526–90) answered on his Ying-t'ien provincial examination for the *chü-jen* degree in 1543, not included in *Huang-Ming ts'e-heng*, made no mention of Chu Hsi and stressed the incompatibility between the more ancient—and thus better—Han histories by Ssu-ma Ch'ien and Pan Ku and the more recent Sung histories by Ou-yang Hsiu and Ssu-ma Kuang. See Wang's policy question and answer in *Ming ching-shih wen-pien* (Essays on statecraft during the Ming dynasty), compiled by Ch'en Tzu-lung (1608–47) and others (Peking: Chung-hua Bookstore Reprint, 1962), Vol. 5, pp. 3597–99.

40. *Huang-Ming ts'e-heng*, 13.17a. See also 7.54a–59a for the policy question and answer in the 1582 Kwangtung provincial examination that focused on the *Shih-chi*.

41. *Huang-Ming ts'e-heng*, 13.17b.

42. *Huang-Ming ts'e-heng*, 13.17b.

43. *Huang-Ming ts'e-heng*, 13.18a–b. Reference to Confucius as an "uncrowned king" (*su-wang*) and the *Annals* as the "Unicorn Classic" (*Lin-ching*) derive from the *Kung-yang Commentary*, not the *Tso chuan*, which the essay in a curious way has rhetorically elided. For discussion see Elman, *Classicism, Politics, and Kinship: The Ch'ang-chou School of New Text Confucianism in Late Imperial China* (Berkeley: University of California Press, 1990), chapters 4–7.

44. *Huang-Ming ts'e-heng*, 13. 19a–b.

45. *Huang-Ming ts'e-heng*, 13.19b–22a.

46. *Huang-Ming ts'e-heng*, 13.22a–23a.

47. *Huang-Ming ts'e-heng*, 13.23a–25a.

48. Again, the resonance should not be overstated. If one compares the 1594 Fu-chien policy question and answer on history with the ones in Shun-t'ien and Shen-hsi the same year, the chief difference one finds among them is that the latter two paid more attention to the two genres of annalistic versus topical histories per se and focused much less or hardly at all on *tao-hsueh* moralizing historiography. See *Huang-Ming ts'e-heng*, 12.13a–18b, 13.83a–90a. Similarly, the 1582 policy question on history in Kuang-tung province stressed genre issues rather than moralizing history. See 7.54a.

49. See for example the *Shun-t'ien hsiang-shih-lu* (Record of the Shun-t'ien civil provincial examination), 1831: 4a–5a, pp. 64a–66b, and *Hui-shih lu* (Record of the civil metropolitan examination), 1685: 13a–15a, 74b–77a. On the latter, see further below.

50. *Kuang-tung hsiang-shih lu*, 1654: "Hsu" (Preface), pp. 1a–5a, and pp. 15a–20a of the record.

51. *Kuang-tung hsiang-shih lu* (Record of the Kuang-tung civil provincial examination), 1654: "Hsu," p. 10a, and pp. 8b–14b of the record. Cf. *Dictionary of Ming Biography*, pp. 148–51 and 153–56.

52. *Kuang-tung hsiang-shih lu*, 1654: 10a–11a.

53. *Kuang-tung hsiang-shih lu*, 1654: 61b–63b.

54. *Kuang-tung hsiang-shih lu*, 1654: 63b–64b.

55. *Kuang-tung hsiang-shih lu*, 1654: 64b–69b. Among the many that I have read, I have not seen a policy question on history during the Ch'ing that stresses Chu Hsi's contributions to historical studies the way the Ming questions and answers above did.

56. *Kuang-tung hsiang-shih lu*, 1654: 69a–70a.

57. *Hui-shih lu*, 1685: 13a–15a.

58. *Hui-shih lu*, 1685: 74a–76a.

59. *Hui-shih lu*, 1685: p. 74b.

60. *Hui-shih lu*, 1685: pp. 11a–13a.

61. See, for example, Ono Kazuko, "Shinsho no Kôkeikai ni tsuite" (On the Society for the Discussion of the Classics in the early Ch'ing), *Tôhôgaku hô*, 36 (1964): 633–661, and Lynn Struve, "The Early Ch'ing Legacy of Huang Tsung-hsi: A Reexamination," *Asia Major* 3rd series, 1,1 (1988): 83–122, which draws on a rich Japanese scholarship cited copiously in the footnotes.

62. See Elman, *From Philosophy To Philology*, Chapter 3. See also Ping-yi Chu, "Ch'eng-Chu Orthodoxy, Evidential Studies and Correlative Cosmology: Chiang Yung and Western Astronomy," *Philosophy and the History of Science: A Taiwanese Journal* 4, 2 (October 1995): 71–108.

63. See Elman, "Philosophy (*I-li*) versus Philology (*K'ao-cheng*): The (*Jen-hsin Tao-hsin*) Debate," *T'oung Pao* 59, nos. 4–5 (1983): 175–222.

64. For recent research, see Liu Jen-p'eng, "Lun Chu-tzu wei-ch'ang i ku-wen shang-shu wei-tso" (Chu Hsi never doubted the authenticity of the Old Text Documents), *Ch'ing-hua hsueh-pao* New Series, 22, 4 (December 1992): 399–430.

65. For discussion, see Elman, "Philosophy (*I-li*) Versus Philology (*K'ao-cheng*)," pp. 175–222.

66. See Elman, *Classicism, Politics, and Kinship*, chapters 3–5.

67. *Chiang-nan hsiang-shih t'i-ming lu* (Record of successful candidates in the Chiang-nan provincial examination), 1810: 9a–9b, in the archives of the No. 1 Historical Archives, Peking. For purposes of focus, I have not described other important debates, which I have done elsewhere. See for example, my "Ming Politics and Confucian Classicism: The Duke of Chou Serves King Ch'eng," in *Ming-tai ching-hsueh kuo-chi yen-t'ao hui lun-wen chi* (Taipei: Academia Sinica, 1996), pp. 93–171. I have chosen the relatively well-known and representative Old Text versus New Text *Documents* debate to summarize the changes in examination questions that were occurring in the eighteenth and nineteenth centuries.

68. For discussion, see Elman, *From Philosophy To Philology*, Chapter 2.

69. See Elman, "Changes in Confucian Civil Service Examinations from the Ming to the Ch'ing Dynasty," in Elman and Alexander Woodside, eds. *Education and Society in Late Imperial China, 1600–1900* (Berkeley: University of California Press, 1994), pp. 139–40.

70. Elman, "Changes in Confucian Civil Service Examinations from the Ming to the Ch'ing Dynasty," pp. 140–43.

71. *Hui-shih lu*, 1739: 4a–4b, 36a–38b.

72. *Hui-shih lu*, 1739: 6a–6b, 1748: 6a–7b, 1751: 6a–8a, 1754: 4a–5a.

73. *Hui-shih lu*, 1754: 39b–45b.

74. *Hui-shih lu*, 1766: 3a–4b, 50a–53b.

75. *Hui-shih lu*, 1793: 15a–17a, 46a–50, and *Huang-ch'ao hsu wen-hsien t'ung-kao* (Comprehensive survey of state documents during the Ch'ing dynasty, continuation), compiled by Liu Chin-tsao (Shanghai: Commercial Press, 1936), p. 8429. See also Elman, *Classicism, Politics, and Kinship*, chapters 5–8.

76. See Chi's preface in *Ch'ing-tai ch'ien-ch'i chiao-yü lun-chu hsuan*, 3/114–18;

77. See *Ch'ang-t'an* (Everyday discussions on the civil examinations), compiled by T'ao Fu-lü (*Ts'ung-shu chi-ch'eng ch'u-pien*. Shanghai: Commercial Press, 1936), pp. 14–15, and, for discussion, my *Classicism*, p.156–57, 166–68.

78. For Hung's views, see *Ch'ing-tai ch'ien-ch'i chiao-yü lun-chu hsuan*, 3/269.

79. See Elman, "'Where is King Ch'eng?': Civil Examinations and Confucian Ideology During the Early Ming, 1368–1415," *T'oung Pao* 79 (1993): 57–61.

80. Sun's draft memorial is in *Ch'ing-tai ch'ien-ch'i chiao-yü lun-chu hsuan*, 3/278–79.

81. See Elman, *From Philosophy To Philology*, Chapter 4, on the professionalization process.

82. On this phenomenon and how it favored Yangtzu delta scholars, see Kai-wing Chou, "Discourse, Examination, and Local Elite: The Invention of the T'ung-ch'eng School in Ch'ing China," pp. 195–205.

83. See *Hu-nan hsiang-shih lu* (Record of the Hu-nan civil provincial examination), 1795: second policy question. Cf. Daniel Gardner, *Chu Hsi and the Ta-hsueh: Neo-Confucian Reflection on the Confucian Canon* (Cambridge: Harvard University Council on East Asian Studies, 1986), pp. 27–59, a particularly fine piece of work.

84. *Hui-shih lu*, 1823: 16a–19b, 61a–72a.

85. *Hui-shih lu*, 1847: 17a–20a, 62a–70b; 1852: 17a–18a, 62a–65b. See also *Chiang-nan hsiang-shih lu*, 1894: "Hsu" (Preface), pp. 2b–3a, and "Hou-hsu" (Afterword), pp. 2a–b.

86. Tsuen-hsuin Tsien, *Written on Bamboo and Silk* (Chicago, University of Chicago Press, 1962), p. 64

87. Rudolph, "Preliminary Notes on Sung Archaeology," *Journal of Asian Studies* 22 (1963): 169–177. See also Wang Kuo-wei, "Archaeology in the Sung Dynasty," in C. H. Liu, tr., *Chinese Journal of Arts and Sciences* 6 (1927): 222–231.

88. Sir Percivel David, tr., *Chinese Connoisseurship, The Ko Ku YaoLun: The Essential Criteria of Antiquities* (London: Faber, 1971), pp. liv–lix. See also Chuang Shen, "Ming Antiquarianism, An Aesthetic Approach to Archaeology," *Journal of Oriental Studies* 8 (1970): 63–82, and Craig Clunas, *Superfluous Things: Material Culture and Social Status in Early Modern China* (Urbana: University of Illinois Press, 1991).

89. Rudolph, "Preliminary Notes," pp. 171–172, and Kwang Tsing Wu, "Scholarship, Book Production, and Libraries in China, 618–1644" (Chicago: University of Chicago Ph.D. dissertation, 1944), p. 106n.

90. Ku Yen-wu's remarks are from his "Hsu" (Introduction) to the *Ch'iu-ku lu*, p. 1a, in *T'ing-lin hsien-sheng i-shu hui-chi* (Composite collection of Ku Yen-wu's bequeathed writings) (Shanghai: Chiao-ching shan-fang, 1888).

91. See *Eminent Chinese of the Ch'ing Period*, pp. 183, 807, 857.

92. Ch'ien Ta-hsin, *Ch'ien-yen-t'ang wen-chi* (Collected essays of the Hall of Subtle Research) (8 vols. Taipei, Commercial Press, 1968), 4.367 (*chüan* 25)

93. Wang Ming-sheng, "Hsu" (Introduction), in *Shih-ch'i-shih shang-ch'üeh* (Critical studies of the seventeen dynastic histories) (reprint. Taipei: Kuang-wen Bookstore, 1960), pp. 2b–3a.

94. Yü Ying-shih, *Lun Tai Chen yü Chang Hsüeh-ch'eng*, pp. 38–39

95. Wang Ming-sheng, "Hsu," in *Shih-ch'i-shih shang-ch'üeh*, pp. 1a–2a.

96. Ch'ien Ta-hsin, *Ch'ien-yen-t'ang wen-chi*, 2.224–225 (*chüan* 16).

97. *Eminent Chinese of the Ch'ing Period*, p. 421. Tu Wei-yun, *Ching Ch'ien-Chia*, pp. 11–12, gives a comprehensive list of such supplements.

98. See Nivison, *The Life and Thought of Chang Hsüeh-cheng (1738–1801)* (Stanford, Stanford University Press, 1966), pp. 195, 216.

99. Chao I, *Erh-shih-erh-shih cha-chi*, pp. 418–419, 616, 629–658.

100. Ch'ien Ta-hsin, *Ch'ien-yen-t'ang wen-chi*, 2.224–225 (*chüan* 16).

101. Wang Chung, *Shu-hsüeh, pu-i* (Discourses on learning, supplement) (reprint. Taipei: Kuang-wen Bookstore, 1970), 5b–8a. See also my "Ts'ung ch'ien hsien-tai te ko-chih-hsüeh chih hsien-tai te k'o-hsüeh" (Transition from the pre-modern 'Chinese Sciences' to 'Modern Science' in China), *Chung-kuo hsüeh-shu* (China Scholarship) (Beijing), 2 (Spring 2000): 1-43.

102. Wang Chung, *Shu-hsüeh, nei-p'ien* (Discourses on learning, inner chapters) (reprint. Taipei: Kuang-wen Bookstore, 1970), (inner chapters) (Taipei, 1970), 3:1a–4a. See also Weng Fang-kang, *Fu-ch'u-chai wen-chi* (Collection of writings from the Studio of Return to Beginnings) (1877 edition), 15.9a.

103. See Fang Tung-shu, *Han-hsüeh shang-tui* (An assessment of Han Learning) (reprint. Taipei: Kuang-wen Bookstore, 1963), 2A.23b–24a, and 2A.32a–34a.

104. See Shimada Kenji, "Rekishi teki risei hihan," pp. 140–41, 151. See also Nivison, pp. 147–150.

105. Elman, *Classicism, Politics, and Kinship*, chapters 5–7.

106. See Wilson, *Genealogy of the Way: The Construction and Uses of the Confucian Tradition in Late Imperial China* (Stanford: Stanford University Press, 1995), *passim*, and Ch'en Tsu-wu, *Chung-kuo hsüeh-an shih* (History of the Chinese studies of scholars genre) (Taipei: Wen-chin Press, 1994), pp. 111–98. See also Tu Wei-yun, *Ch'ing Ch'ien-Chia*, pp. 5, 49–51, 59.

107. See Lynn Struve, "Ambivalence and Action: Some Frustrated Scholars of the K'ang-hsi Period," in Jonathan Spence and John Wills, eds., *From Ming to Ch'ing: Conquest, Region, and Continuity in Seventeenth-Century China* (New Haven: Yale University Press, 1979), pp. 323–65.

108. *Ch'ing-shih lieh-chuan* (Qing official biogrpahies) (Taipei: Chung-hua Bookstore, 1962), 69.38a.

109. Tu Wei-yun, *Ch'ing Ch'ien-Chia*, pp. 7, 53–58, 90–97, and David Nivison, pp. 60–64.

110. Yü Ying-shih, *Lun Tai Chen*, pp. 45–81, and Nivison, pp. 172–173, 186, 220, 227ff, 297. See also Albert Mann, "Cheng Ch'iao: An Essay in Re-evaluation," in David Buxbaum and Frederick Mote, eds., *Transition and Permanence: Chinese History and Culture* (Hong Kong: Cathay Press, 1972), pp. 23–57

111. See Nivison, *passim*, and Jiro Numata, "Shigeno Yasutsugu and the Modern Tokyo Tradition of Historical Writing," in in W. G. Beasley and E. G. Pulleyblank, eds., *Historians of China and Japan*, pp. 264–287. Cf. Elman, "Qing Learning and *Kôshôgaku* in Tokugawa Japan," paper prepared for the conference volume *Sagacious Monks and Bloodthirsty Warriors: Chinese Views of Japan in the Ming-Qing Period*, edited by Joshua Fogel, (Norwalk, CT: East Bridge, 2002), forthcoming.

112. *Ssu-k'u ch'üan-shu tsung-mu* (Catalog of the complete collection of the four treasuries), compiled by Chi Yun et al. (Taipei: I-wen Press reprint, 1974), 45.1a–3a. See also R. Kent Guy, *The Emperor's Four Treasuries: Scholars and the State in the Late Ch'ien-lung Period* (Cambridge: Harvard University Council on East Asian Studies, 1987).

113. Chang, *Wen-shih t'ung-i*, 1.1.

PART II

8. Conceptions of Scientific History in the Nineteenth-Century West

Eckhardt Fuchs

Peter Burke recently developed ten categories of Western historical thinking and discussed them from a cross-cultural perspective. He states that the specific combination of these elements characterizes the phenomenon of Western historical thinking, especially in the modern period, that differentiated it from non-Western modes.[1] Although Burke carefully eschews the assumption that there was a single and monolithic historiographical scholarship in the West, he nevertheless thinks that these general categories can become a basis for a global comparison of historiographical thinking. Applying these categories to nineteenth-century Western historiography, however, we find that they took different shapes in varying contexts. Talking about *Western* historiography one has to bear in mind that the notion "West" suggests more than the geographic land mass of Europe. It also includes those countries that owe their cultural heritage in whole or in a significant part to the European tradition, namely the "neo-European" countries grown from former "white settlement colonies" in Latin America, North America, and Australia.[2] Western historians of historiography have considered the way in which European and especially German historiography became professionalized and "scientific" as a universal model and have taken it as a comparative measure for international historiographical development. But until now, research on the history of Western historiography has been more or less bound to the four historiographical centers of the West, namely Germany, France, Great Britain, and the United States. Much less is known about the historiography in other European countries. For example, extensive research on *historicism* and positivism in Italy has not yet found its way into German or Anglo-American scholarship.[3] Studies of historical scholarship in countries like Spain, Finland, Poland, Hungry, and Russia, not to mention Argentina or Mexico, are even rare. In many of these countries at the periphery the emergence of an academic historical discipline did not begin until the end of the nineteenth century, if not the early twentieth century.[4]

In this essay I will not deal with the cultural differences and social institutions of historiographical production in the West but concentrate on epistemology and methodology in history because they played a significant role in the process of scientification of historical scholarship. The development of historiography as an academic discipline in Europe is a nineteenth-century phenomenon. The professionalization of historical studies and the re-definition of their theoretical and methodological foundations were embedded in the process of modernization and nationalization of Europe. Historians not only began to create their own institutions, but also laid down new epistemological and methodological concepts in order to establish a valid "scientific" basis for their profession. This development was characterized by intensive debates on how history could be transformed into and conducted as a "scientific" discipline. For many nineteenth-century historians this notion was a major source of controversy. The debates about the epistemological and methodological foundations of historical writing differed with regard to the country, the time, the intensity, and the results, but they all dealt with the questions of how to write history scientifically and how to create an academic discipline independent from other branches of knowledge.

Western historical scholarship in the nineteenth century was characterized by a conflict between a hermeneutic and a causal approach.[5] One can distinguish two ideal types of historical science in the nineteenth century: first, *historicism* (*Historismus*) as a conception that had its roots in the traditions of German idealistic philosophy and philology, was bound to the metaphysical doctrine of ideas (*Ideenlehre*), a hermeneutic and idiographic method, and concentrated on an event-orientated history of politics and "great men."[6] The representatives of this "science of history" (*Geschichtswissenschaft*) were mostly academic historians. Nomothetic positivism is the second conception. It drew heavily on the methodology of natural sciences and their knowledge, focused on causality in history, and sought to discover historical laws. The main subjects were social and economic history as well as history of ideas. I call this conception the same way their representatives called themselves in the last century, namely 'scientific historians." The protagonists of such a nomothetic "scientific history" were mostly non-academic, amateur historians, or scholars who belonged to other disciplines.[7]

There is a consensus among German historians of historiography that *historicism* is—with all its variations—the key term that symbolizes the genesis of modern historical scholarship in the course of the nineteenth century.[8] Some of them state that this concept, if defined as a specific mode of German historical scholarship, was the prototype of a "science of history" that spread fast beyond Germany and was adopted as a model of historical research all over the Western world.[9] There is no doubt that Germany had an immense international impact on the professionalization of history as an academic discipline and on perfecting the methods of historical research. Scientification and professionalization, however, should not be mixed. I would like to argue that *historicism* did not become the only epistemological basis for Western historical scholarship but rather that there was an amalgam of different approaches, a blending of various theories and methods that shaped international historical studies in a different manner. German *historicism* was not a universal model but rather an exception in the international development of historiography in the nineteenth century. Here I do not want to extend the *Sonderweg* thesis (a thesis that advocates a special way of German modernization that ultimately led to Hitler) into the realm of historiography. I just want to point out that the specific and unique historiographical field in Germany created a highly politicized and philosophical *historicism* that excluded other conceptions of historical sciences. With regard to the scientificity of the history discipline, I argue that the concept of history as a science was perceived rather differently by Western historians.[10] Different scholarly communities defined the scientific character of the historical discipline differently. Although German professional institutions and the idea of "science of history" were adopted by other countries, they were modified to allow variations and alternative approaches. We find, for example, that historical science in France, England, and the United States was similar, whereas in Germany, it appeared different. All concepts of historical sciences were restricted to nineteenth-century thought and must be interpreted as unique forms of historical knowledge.

I. "History of Science" in Germany

In Germany the emergence of an academic historiography began at academies and universities during the late Enlightenment. The so-called Göttingen school set early standards for teaching and writing history in the second half of the eighteenth century. That was however a rather singular phenomenon. Only the reform of the educational system after 1815 opened the way for the establishment of historical institutions at universities and of standards of historical learning. History became both a profession and an academic discipline in the following decades. By the middle of the nineteenth century there existed a firmly established methodological understanding going back to Wilhelm Humboldt, Barthold Georg Niebuhr, and Leopold von Ranke.[11] The science of history, whose ideal was objectivity and whose main aim was to develop a strictly defined methodology, was fully developed in *historicism*. Based on methodological tools of philology and a hermeneutic approach to history, German historians made the critique of sources, *(Quellenkritik)*, the basis of their research, and emancipated the writing of history from the philosophical synthesis of history in Kant and Hegel.

In Germany, academic historiography fully established its "scientific" canon around the middle of the century. *Historicism* became the tradition of German historical studies from Ranke to Mommsen and, therefore, the historiographical outlook and practice of nineteenth-century academic historians. Ever since the publication of Johann Gustav Droysen's manual *"Historik"* in 1857, *historicism* has been based on a theoretical and methodological conception, which was formulated in a sharp contrast to a nomothetic concept of historical writing.[12] Nevertheless, the academic "science of history" in the idealistic tradition became challenged by a nomothetic "scientific history." This "scientific history" was based on epistemological and methodological problems raised by natural sciences. In the 1850s and 1860s it was Auguste Comte's positivism, his theory of science, his empiricism, his social theory, and his ideas about laws in history and society that seemed to bridge the epistemological gap between the natural and social sciences, including the humanities, and gained prominence among scholars and scientists.

The crucial link between Comte's positivist philosophy and historiography was provided by the English amateur historian Henry Thomas Buckle, who published his influential *History of Civilization in England* in two volumes in 1857 and 1861.[13] Buckle's theoretical and methodological principles included a rejection of traditional historiography, which consisted largely of an assemblage of facts, a recounting of political events, and their mere description. His conception of "scientific history" differed from German historicist "science of history" in many ways: for Buckle the history of mankind was based on historical laws that can be found and explained by historians through the application of "scientific methods," such as statistics, and through the use of the latest findings of the natural sciences, such as meteorological, geological, and psychological knowledge. History was to be made "scientific" on the model of the explanatory character of natural sciences.

After the process of professionalization was complete by the middle of the nineteenth century, the historical profession in Germany showed little interest in new concepts of history, let alone a willingness to incorporate them into its practice. Buckle's definition of historical science therefore was immediately rejected by academic historians in Germany. Nonetheless, for contemporaries, Droysen's critique of Buckle in 1863 neither answered the question of the scientific character of history and other social sciences, nor solved the theoretical problem of historical laws.[14] Outside the academic historical profession there was a widespread interest in the views of Buckle and other evolutionary concepts based on the works of Charles Darwin—in particular, among social scientists, cultural historians, and educated amateur scholars. Scientific ideas, many of which did not come directly from positivism but were the expression of an intellectual consensus about a concept of science based on inductive reasoning, empirical observation, and evolutionary theories, were quickly accepted in historical and theoretical studies. The general lack of interest shown by leading historicists in the development of thinking in the natural sciences and in scientific research, and their ignorance of serious attempts to test new methods, contrasted with the high level of historical awareness revealed by scholars from other disciplines. Moreover, an important debate took place within other social sciences that went considerably further than academic historiography in relating to the natural sciences. The famous and—for German historiography—influential Lamprecht controversy at the end of the century was the high- and endpoint of these discussions among historians.[15] Eventually they led to a radical rejection of the innovative potential of other disciplines and the closure of the discipline to a wider range of historiographical and theoretical approaches. Consequently *historicism* became more one-sided in the decades to follow. Nevertheless, the concentration on the individualization of the historical process and on political history, the elevation of hermeneutics and its idiographic method into an absolute value, and a self-imposed limitation to editorial work based on textual criticism, ultimately favored an atheoretical positivism of facts. The "victory" of *historicism* in the German academic historical community in the course of the nineteenth century was not due to a more advanced stage of its scientific character but to the domination of the academic field by the historicists that led to the control of professional institutions and the marginalization and even exclusion of academic outsiders and non-academic historians from the disciplinary community.[16]

II. "Scientific History" in the West

The institutional development of professionalization in Germany was innovating, and in the course of the century, historical studies became professionalized in other countries as well. This process of professionalization—producing an academic caste that defined its subject in methodological terms—seems to be more or less similar throughout the West but occurred at different times. In England it started with the founding of chairs of history at Oxford and Cambridge in the 1860s, in France with the reform of the educational system since the 1860s, and in the United States in the last two decades of the nineteenth century. The emergence of historical institutions did not, however, mean that history became automatically "scientific"—that a consensus about a unique theoretical and methodological set and generally valid standards for historical research existed. The epistemological foundation of history was not just the result of an inner development of the discipline but of the revolution in the natural sciences since the middle of the nineteenth century and of the social sciences at its end. The intensity and the result of the debates in different countries depended on the stage of the professionalization of the discipline.

It must, therefore, be asked if the institutionalization of historical science, such as the founding of professional historical journals, the establishment of the historical seminar, and the edition of national historical sources, was really only the result of merely taking over a German "model" and not the consequence of the inner logic of the development of an academic discipline itself. In England, France, and the United States there was a much broader response among historians to the latest developments in the natural sciences than in Germany. After all, Comte's system fit in with an unlimited and optimistic belief in progress and a faith in science because of these developments. In all three countries the natural sciences were academically well established and publicly admired, and empiricism and rationalism were also prevalent in the disciplines of social sciences. Historiography was not—as it was in Germany—imbedded in a Hegelian historical theology and speculative philosophy. Debates on the scientific status of history, therefore, differed from them in Germany. The notable gap between natural sciences and humanities never existed as it did in Germany.[17]

In England positivism fast received wide attention among scientists and scholars, and the writings of Buckle proved to be catalytic for the rise of "scientific history" in the 1860s and 1870s. Buckle had died in 1861 and could not take part in the debate, but his approach was supported by a group of amateur "scientific historians" who defended the nomothetic view of history. Its members included Edward Spencer Beesly, who later became professor of history at University College London, and the journalist and historian Frederic Harrison. Despite their different views of Comte's philosophy, John Stuart Mill, John Morley, and the young historian William Lecky must also be counted as supporters of "scientific history."[18] For these "scientific historians" the epistemological aim of historiography was to discover historical laws. In their view the basis of such laws was the application of methods borrowed from the natural sciences and the selection of subjects that had nothing to do with an individualizing view of history. However, the debate about "scientific history" and the positivist concept of science soon moved away from both Comte's original definition and from Buckle's work. The triumph of Darwinism, new, anthropologically based concepts of evolution, and the narrowing down of Comte's intentions to a sectarian "positivistic society" led to a decline in positivism, rendering Buckle's theory of history less attractive in the process. However, more important was the fact that, from the 1870s onward, history began to establish itself as an academic discipline at the English universities, which resulted in a professional status for English historians.[19] This was associated with the devaluation of the amateur status of many 'men of letters,' who pursued science as a hobby, and was reflected in the way in which professionals attacked them for the shallowness and incorrectness, biased nature, and didactic purpose of their scientific work. The professionalization of history and the establishment of the 'research ideal' was tied, by the professional historians, to objective and systematized knowledge, or in other words, factual knowledge. This expert knowledge could be verified, mastered, and extended only by specialists who had acquired the requisite theoretical and methodological standards through a thorough education. History as "science of history" now brought together primary research and source criticism with a division of labor between the various historical disciplines.

The American evolutionary "scientific history" that originated and quickly gained influence after the 1870s also found its orientation in Comte, Buckle, and later Spencer. The first president of the American Historical Association, Andrew D. White, in his speech in 1885 called Buckle one of the most important historians.[20] By giving this honor to Buckle, American historians showed the intention to use concepts from the natural sciences in pursuing scientific history. The historian John Fiske was among the first who not only popularized a "scientific" history, but also based his historical writings on the discovery of historical laws. Influenced by Spencer's philosophy and Darwin's theory, Fiske did not overtake Comte's system but leaned towards evolutionary concepts. He made his idea of a "law of progress" well known in a lecture series on evolutionary theory and "positive philosophy" at Harvard University in 1869/70 before he published his major book *Outlines of Cosmic Philosophy, Based on the Doctrine of Evolution, with Criticism of the Positive Philosophy* in 1874. In contrast to England and Germany, in the

United States "scientific history" became also popular among academic historians, such as Henry Adams or Herbert Baxter Adams, who used theories and concepts of the natural sciences as the basis of their historical approaches. Influenced by Spencer, Herbert Baxter Adams of Johns Hopkins University interpreted American history as a biologically defined "organism of historic growth" and explained the specific forms of American political institutions by the so-called theory of germs.[21] Both Fiske and Baxter Adams belonged to the most popular representatives of American scientific historians in the second half of the 19th century. Of course, Americans who studied in Germany were impressed by the German method of *Quellenkritik* and the German historical seminar, but they did not copy the German conception of "science of history" nor did they copy the institutional forms of the German profession. More than in England, there was a blend of various concepts available to American historians, which made their academic field much more open and less ideologically restricted and hierarchical than that in Germany.[22]

In France the debates on the foundation of the "science of history" paralleled the German Lamprecht controversy in the 1890s. As in the United States, there existed two positions among academic scholars: the one represented by historians, such as Charles Seignobos and Charles V. Langlois, who doubted the possibility of a nomothetic historiography and argued for a reconstruction of history based simply on historical political events, and the other defined by scholars, such as Paul Lacombe, François Simiand, and Émile Durkheim, who as "scientific historians" favored the principle of causality and expressed their beliefs about the existence of historical laws. In contrast to the United States and England, there was a third group of historians who tried to mediate between these two positions in France. The arguments used by the representatives of "scientific history" originated from the writings of Comte, Spencer, and John Stuart Mill. The debate in France, therefore, was characterized by a scientism that found its roots in positivism.[23] The competition between the disciplines was not about history versus natural sciences as it was in Germany. In France it was the new empirical social sciences that, based on scientific concepts, seemed to threaten the professional historians. The interdisciplinary opening of the historical discipline toward economics, geography, and ethnology, to name just a few, undermined in their eyes the exceptional role of history in society, its cultural influence, and its academic supremacy.

So far we have seen that similar developments of professionalization, a process I cannot investigate in greater detail at this point, still allowed different modes of historical science, an overlapping of various theoretical concepts. One could ask if a look at Western historiographical peripheries reveals similar results. "Scientific history" in the form of Buckle's ideas and the "science of history" à la Ranke spread quickly into many countries. In Belgium and the Netherlands, for example, positivism received wide attention in the intellectual milieu but did not attract many historians.[24] In the discourse of Dutch historians, however, "scientific history" occupied a central position until the end of the nineteenth century. Nevertheless, it was not the nomothetic conception but rather the broad cultural and social approach and Buckle's liberal views that were well received.[25] In Belgium, which was intellectually much closer to France, a methodological debate among historians only started in connection with the writings of the German Karl Lamprecht in the 1890s. While in Germany almost the entire academic community rejected Lamprecht, the debate in Belgium was more heterogeneous, and Henri Pirenne belonged to the most famous defenders of the German cultural historian. In Russia there existed two schools in the second half of the century: the so-called *Russian historical school*, which tried to replace "ideas" by social and natural factors as the basis of their historical studies, like Comte and Spencer; and the so-called *state school*, which oriented itself toward the writings of German historicists. The methodological debates in the first two decades of the twentieth century over the relationship between natural and cultural sciences reveal, however, that Russian historians discussed similar issues compared to the centers but that there were no clear lines between the different positions, and none of them was excluded from the academic profession.[26] Poland was another entirely unique case because it did not exist as a unified country and was occupied by three different empires. But there was also an academic profession developed in the course of the nineteenth century that adopted German historical institutions and methodological standards and used the nomothetic model. While the *Krakow historical school* referred to the German concept of historical science, the historicist approach was highly criticized by the positivist *Warszaw historical school*, whose approach was based on nomothetic conceptions of positivist provenience.[27] In Romania the professionalization of history also started late, although the University of Bucharest had been founded in 1864, thirteen years before national independence. At the end of the century Alexandre D. Xenopol gained fast recognition abroad, especially in France. In his book "*Fundamental Principles of History*," published in Paris in 1899, he refused a nomothetic approach but based historical knowledge on the use of hypothesis and causal explanation.[28]

These few examples do not allow broad generalizations but they show that there was no unique conception of historical science deriving from a German "model." Historians of those countries took up the issues discussed abroad, took over ideas, and used them according to their needs. A variation of scientific concepts seemed to have existed among academic historians. Seen from an international perspective, the debates on the character of historical science at the first International Congress of Historical Science in Paris in 1900 and at the Congress of Arts and Science in St.Louis in 1904 also displayed the diversity of views that existed among historians.[29]

III. Historical Sciences in the Nineteenth Century: A Reappraisal

As I have tried to show, with the exception of Germany the concept of "scientific history" did not exist until the middle of the nineteenth century.

On the one hand, in the other three centers discussed here in more detail as well as in smaller countries, German methodical standards and historical institutions were seen as innovating developments. On the other hand, it was Comte's positivism and Buckle's work that expanded the discussion of the scientific nature of knowledge in the natural sciences to include historiography in the middle of the nineteenth century. At the end of the century the social sciences became another important factor in these debates. The process by which historiography came to be seen as a "science," however, did not proceed at the same pace in many Western countries. In France, England, and the United States the scientification of history was characterized by the dual process of professionalization that included an adoption of certain German institutions and methods on the one hand, and of an incorporation of methods and concepts of other disciplines on the other. Depending on the particular historiographical field the impact of other disciplines on the historical profession varied. In general one could say that the German "science of history" as a methodological tool was favored by university historians, while "scientific history" was promoted by non-academic historians and scholars from other disciplines. However, in France and the United States academic historians also supported a nomothetic approach.

At the end of all these debates around the turn of the century, we can observe a successful resistance of "scientific history" by most of the professional historians. But the level of this resistance varied as well. In German historical scholarship the historicist orthodoxy was unique in the complete refusal of any approach that came from outside the historicist "science of history." This holds not only true for methods and concepts used by the natural sciences but also for subjects that required a different approach. Radical new ideas, such as the concept of historical science as research raised by Max Weber in the first decades of the twentieth century, did not draw attention from historians; voices that radically critiqued an objective "history of science" such as Friedrich Nietzsche's were not heard; and social and cultural history, such as that conducted by Karl Lamprecht, was sharply rejected. In contrast, the other three countries did not completely exclude concepts from other disciplines. Their historical profession was therefore much more divided, a situation that opened ways for historiographical innovations. A major reason for this can be found first in the different phases of professionalization in these countries when these alternative concepts arose, and second in the specific philosophical traditions: Germany with its idealistic philosophy, England and the United States with their utilitarianism, and France with its rational philosophy and positivism. As the United States case indicates, the positivist scientism seems to have found much more resonance among historians because the historical discipline was only at the beginning of its professionalization around the middle of the century, and the historiographical field was not yet completely established. English historiography was confronted with positivist "scientific history" at a time when it was beginning to establish itself as an academic discipline. In other words, "scientific history" occurred in England during the early phase of the process of professionalization. Although it was criticized and condemned by the first academic historians, there was no radical rejection of the nomothetic program. The discussion between professional and positivist "scientific" historians was therefore moderate in tone; the methodological dispute was a periodic process that lasted until the turn of the century. In France the amalgam of scientific theories, the rise of social sciences, and the adherence to an event-oriented, hermeneutic approach shaped the debates on the theoretical foundations of the discipline.

On the whole, "scientific history" should not be seen as a contradiction to the "science of history." It is by no accident that some contemporary scholars wanted both strands to be united.[30] The nomothetic model of a positivist historical science provided theoretical and methodological approaches that went beyond the historicist paradigm, or at least supplemented it. Similarly, *historicism* raised issues that a nomothetic concept did not deal with. Justified criticism of one-sided interpretations of positivism and its scientific determinism, of the nomothetic concept of science, and of knowledge of laws disguised the fact that in terms of the aims and functions they assigned to historiography, their overall concept of history, and the metaphysical frame of reference they used, the two views did not materially differ, either in their objectivism, their search for a universal meaning and absolute truth, or their normative and teleological view of history. If we put both strands of historical science in the larger context of the history of historical thinking since the eighteenth century, we can observe that they reflected a specific epoch in the history of historical thinking that differed from previous and succeeding modes of scientificity. But it would be misleading to reduce the complexity of the history of historiographical thinking to a few ideal types as the representative ones. We can always see diverse sets of theoretical and methodological assumptions that were overlapping in time and space. Nevertheless, the German case seems to be an exception in the nineteenth-century discourse. The strict separation of natural and historical sciences in Germany after the 1840s indicated a major difference from other countries and even a shift from early versions of *historicism* such as that of Wilhelm von Humboldt, who in the beginning of the nineteenth century had founded his *Ideenlehre* partly on one specific form of scientism of the Enlightenment in order to create a science of humanity using organic metaphors.[31] A new era of debates on the re-definition of historical science was opened in the early twentieth century with the critique of the objectivism of "scientific history" and "history of science" by such thinkers as Max Weber, Georg Simmel, and Emile Durkheim. These debates led to a new concept of historical science that acknowledged the relativity and infinity of historical research allowing complementary theories and interpretations of the historical process to ensue.[32]

If we interpret the various modes of historical science of the nineteenth century as different but yet in many ways very similar attempts to re-define the scientific status of history and as process of disciplinary emancipation, we can see that this development was not very successful because in the process of the scientification of history, it was heavily influenced by nationalism and Eurocentrism. Historical sciences in the nineteenth century focused mostly on national history. A main social and political purpose of historiography was to offer general social norms and a scientifically authenticated and authorized historical model in order to create a national myth that placed one's own nation at the center of the historical discourse. Aimed at legitimizing political and cultural values, history was instrumentalized for national purposes.

The re-definition of the scientific character of historical studies also meant a geographic narrowing of its subject matter. During the Enlightenment the writing of world history was still part of the arsenal of historiography. However, it soon became obvious that a gulf was developing between enlightened universalism and the belief in the superiority of one's own civilization. The universalization of European historical thought in the nineteenth century coincided with a national historiography that barely took non-European peoples into account. European history was elevated to the level of world history in which the "Other" simply faded away. It was this "invention" of Europe with its unified history and culture since classical Greece that caused certain peoples and societies to be excluded from world history.[33] Notwithstanding the fact that the objective of capitalism and modernity was a universal power, Eurocentrism found its initial historiographic expression in the European national histories.

I do not see nineteenth-century historiography as an ongoing attempt of historians to find a common consensus about the scientific foundations of their discipline. Historians rather tried to adapt their standards to secure their social status against other disciplines. The notion of historical science, therefore, has changed over time, but these changes cannot be interpreted as a linear progressive development or as a process of modernization. There has never existed just one uniform scientific model of the "history of science" or "scientific history," either in Germany or anywhere else. The search for the scientific status of historical studies in the nineteenth century was a broad intellectual movement in- and outside the academic field; many varying concepts competed not only among countries but also within one country. The scientification of history that was accompanied by a professionalization led to the establishment of disciplinary institutions. Historical scholarship could emancipate itself from other disciplines, such as philology, philosophy, biology, and the social sciences. Nevertheless, there was neither a uniform definition nor a consensus about the theoretical foundations of historical science.

References

1. This western historical thinking includes categories such as progress, historical perspective, development and individualization, collective action, epistemology, explanations of reasons, objectivity, quantification, narration, and space and time. See Peter Burke, "Westliches historisches Denken in globaler Perspektive—10 Thesen," in *Westliches Geschichtsdenken: Eine interkulturelle Debatte*, ed. Jörn Rüsen (Göttingen 1999), pp. 31–52.

2. See Jürgen Osterhammel, "Sozialgeschichte im Kulturvergleich: Zu künftigen Möglichkeiten komparativer Geschichtswissenschaft," in *Geschichte und Gesellschaft* 22, 1996, p. 147f.

3. The reception of Italian historiography in Germany starts mostly with Benedetto Croce and is confined to the twentieth century. A short overview of recent Italian literature on historicism can be found in Georg G. Iggers, "Historicism: The History and Meaning of the Term," in *Journal of the History of Ideas* 56, 1995, p. 135f. For examples of a broader international approach see Otto Gerhard Oexle and Jörn Rüsen, eds., *Historismus in den Kulturwissenschaften Geschichtskonzepte, historische Einschätzungen, Grundlagenprobleme* (Cologne, Weimar, Vienna 1996), ch. 4. See also *Historismus am Ende des 20. Jahrhundert: Eine internationale Diskussion*, ed. Gunter Scholtz (Berlin, 1997).

4. As an attempt to include the international dimension see *Geschichtsdiskurs, vol. 4, Krisenbewußtsein, Katastrophenerfahrungen und Innovationen 1880–1945*, ed. Wolfgang Küttler, Jörn Rüsen, and Ernst Schulin (Frankfurt am Main 1997). In recent years history of historiography in a transcultural perspective has been established as a new project. See "Provincializing Europe: Historiography as a Transcultural Concept," in Eckhardt Fuchs and Benedikt Stuchtey, eds., *Across Cultural Borders: Historiography in Global Perspective* (Boulder 2002), 1-26; Jörn Rüsen, "Some Theoretical Approaches to Intercultural Comparative Historiography," in "Chinese Historiography in Comparative Perspective," *History and Theory* 35:4 (Theme Issue 35), 1996, pp. 5–22.

5. Burke, *Westliches historisches Denken*, p. 44.

6. On the history of and the most recent literature about the term see Georg G. Iggers, "Historicism: The History and Meaning of the Term," in *Journal of the History of Ideas* 56, 1995, pp. 129–52. See also Irmline Veit-Brause, "Eine Disziplin rekonstruiert ihre Geschichte: Geschichte der Geschichtswissenschaft in den 90er Jahren (I)," in *Neue Politische Literatur* 43, 1998, pp. 36–66. On the Anglo-American debate see Frank R. Ankersmit, "Historicism: An Attempt at Synthesis," in *History and Theory* 34, 1995, pp. 143–61 (and the discussion between Ankersmit and Georg G. Iggers, ibid., pp. 162–73).

7. Historical materialism might be seen as a part of "scientific history" since it also offered a nomothetic view of history. It had, nevertheless, very strong roots in German idealistic philosophy as well. Since this materialism hardly influenced nineteenth-century historiography, I will not include it in my essay. See Otto Gerhard Oexle, *Geschichtswissenschaft im Zeichen des Historismus: Studien zu Problemgeschichten der Moderne* (Göttingen 1996), p. 29. Materialism, however, played a more important role in Russian historiography even before the revolution of 1917.

8. In recent debates on the term historicism German historians distinguish between two meanings of the term. Whereas some historians, such as Otto Gerhard Oexle, define the term as a general mode of thinking in the nineteenth century that fundamentally changed the historical studies as well as social and cultural sciences, for others, such as Jörn Rüsen, Horst Walter Blanke, and Ulrich Muhlack, the term refers to a specific epoch of German historical scholarship. See Otto Gerhard Oexle, "Meineckes Historismus: Über Kontext und Folgen einer Definition," in Otto Gerhard Oexle and Jörn Rüsen, *Historismus in den Kulturwissenschaften*, pp. 139–99; Jörn Rüsen, *Grundzüge einer Historik*, 3 vols. (Göttingen 1983–89); Horst Walter Blanke, *Historiographiegeschichte als Historik*, (Stuttgart-Bad Cannstadt 1991); Ulrich Muhlack, *Geschichtswissenschaft im Humanismus und in der Aufklärung: Die Vorgeschichte des Historismus* (Munich 1991). See also Wolfgang Hardtwig, "Geschichtsreligion—Wissenschaft als Arbeit—Objektivität," in *Historische Zeitschrift* 252, 1991, pp. 1–32.

9. See Muhlack, *Geschichtswissenschaft im Humanismus und in der Aufklärung*, p. 10; Friedrich Jäger and Jörn Rüsen, *Geschichte des Historismus* (Munich 1992).

10. As example see the different reception of positivism in Germany, Great Britain, and the United States in Eckhardt Fuchs, "Positivism and History in the 19th Century," in *Positivisme*, ed. Andrée Despy-Meyer and Didier Devriese (Brussels 1998), pp. 147–62.

11. See D. A. Jeremy Telman, "Clio Ascendant: The Historical Profession in Nineteenth-Century Germany" (Ph.D. dissertation, Cornell University, 1993).

12. Johann Gustav Droysen, *Historik: Vorlesungen über Enzyklopädie und Methodolgie der Geschichte*, ed. Rudolf Hübner (Munich, Vienna 1937).

13. For details of Buckle's theoretical and methodological views, see Eckhardt Fuchs, *Henry Thomas Buckle: Geschichtsschreibung und Positivismus in England und Deutschland* (Leipzig 1994).

14. Johann Gustav Droysen, "Die Erhebung der Geschichte in den Rang einer Wissenschaft," in *Historische Zeitschrift* 9, 1863, pp. 1–22.

15. On the Lamprecht controversy see Blanke, *Historiographiegeschichte*, pp. 439ff. On other debates of this time see Annette Wittkau, *Historismus* (Göttingen 1992) and Fuchs, "Positivism and History in the 19th Century."

16. On the marginalization of historians in Germany see Rober Deutsch and Wolfgang Weber, "Marginalisierungsprozesse in der deutschen Geschichtswissenschaft im Zeitlater des Historismus," in *Schweizerische Zeitschrift für Geschichte*, 35, 1985, pp. 174–97. Also Wolfgang Weber, *Priester der Klio: Historisch-sozialwissenschaftliche Studien zu Herkunft und Karriere deutscher Historiker und zur Geschichte der Geschichtswissenschaft* (Frankfurt 1984).

17. See on "scientific history" in the United States, Matthias Waechter, *Die Erfindung des amerikanischen Westen: Die Geschichte der Frontier-Debatte* (Freiburg im Breisgau 1996), pp. 60ff.

18. Edward Beesly, "Mr. Kingsley on the Study of History," in *Westminster Review* 19, 1861, pp. 305-336; Frederic Harrison, "Mr. Goldwin Smith on the Study of History," in *Westminster Review* 20, 1861, pp. 293-334; John Morley, "Mr. Froude on the Science of History," in *Fortnightly Review* 2, 1867, pp. 226-237.

19. There is general agreement that William Stubbs's appointment to a professorship in modern history at Oxford in 1866 and John E. Seeley's appointment at Cambridge in 1869 marked the beginning of history becoming established as an aca-

demic discipline. On the history of historiography in England see, among others, Christopher Parker, *The English Historical Tradition since 1850* (Edinburgh 1990); Doris Goldstein, "The Professionalization of History in Britain in the Late Nineteenth and Early Twentieth Centuries," in *Storia della Storiografia* 3, 1983, pp. 3–27; Rosemary Jann, *The Art and Science of Victorian History* (Columbus 1985); John Philips Kenyon, *History Men: The Historical Profession in England since the Renaissance* (London 1983); Jürgen Osterhammel, "Epochen der britischen Geschichtsschreibung," in *Geschichtsdiskurs*, Vol. 1: *Grundlagen und Methoden der Historiographiegeschichte*, ed. Wolfgang Küttler, Jörn Rüsen, and Ernst Schulin (Frankfurt am Main 1993), pp. 157–88.

20. Andrew D. White, "On Studies in General History and the History of Civilization," in *Papers of the American Historical Association* 1, 1885, pp. 49–72.

21. See Waechter, *Die Erfindung des amerikanischen Westen*, pp. 68ff.

22. Gabriele Lingelbach, "The German Historical Discipline: A 'Model' for the United States in the Second Half of the Nineteenth Century?" in Fuchs and Stuchtey, *Across Cultural Borders*, pp. 183-204. On American historiography see Peter Novick, *That Noble Dream: The "Objectivity Question" and the American Historical Profession* (Cambridge, 1988) and Ernst Breisach, *American Progressive History: An Experiment in Modernization* (Chicago, London, 1993).

23. Lutz Raphael, "Historikerkontroversen im Spannungsfeld zwischen Berufshabitus, Fächerkonkurrenz und sozialen Deutungsmustern: Lamprecht-Streit und französischer Methodenstreit der Jahrhundertwende in vergleichender Perspektive," in *Historische Zeitschrift* 251, 1990, p. 336. On French histiorography in general see Pim den Boer, *History as a Profession: The Study of History in France, 1818–1914* (Princeton 1998).

24. P. Gérin, "La condition de l'histoire nationale en Belgique à la fin du 19e et au début du 20e siècle," in *Storia della Storiografia* 11, 1987, pp. 64–103; Kaat Wils, "Les insuffisances historiques du positivisme," in Despy-Meyer and Devriese, *Positivismes*, p. 163-85.

25. Wils, "Les insuffisances historiques," pp. 182ff.

26. Zenonas Norkus, "Historismus und Historik in Russland (1865–1933)," in Oexle and Rüsen, *Historismus in den Kulturwissenschaften*, pp. 369–86.

27. Andrzej F.Grabski, "Die polnische und die deutsche Historiographie im der zweiten Hälfte des 19. Jahrhunderts," in *Kwartalnik Historii Nauki I Techniki* 29, 1984, pp. 323–44; Jerzi Krasuski et al., eds., *Stosunki Polsko-Niemieckie w Historiografii*. Part 2. *Studia z Dziejow Historiografi Polskiej I Niemieckie* (Posen 1984).

28. Dan Berindei, "L'historiographie roumaine et la communauté oecuménique des historiens jusqu'à la première guerre mondiale," in Hartmut Bockmann and Kurt Jörgensen, eds., *Nachdenken über Geschichte: Beiträge aus der Ökumene der Historiker in memoriam Karl Dietrich Erdmann* (Neumünster 1991), pp. 241–46; Stefan Stefanescu, "L'historiographie roumaine dans le contexte international de la fin de XIXe siècle et du début du XXe," *Analele Universitatii Bucuresti: Istorie* 32, 1983, pp. 77–90.

29. See Karl-Dietrich Erdmann, *Die Ökumene der Historiker: Geschichte der Internationalen Historikerkongresse und des Comité International des Sciences Historiques* (Göttingen 1987).

30. See Fuchs, *Henry Thomas Buckle*, p. 333.

31. Peter Hanns Reill, "Science and the Construction of the Cultural Sciences in Late Enlightenment Germany: The Case of Wilhelm von Humboldt," *History and Theory* 33, 1994, pp. 345–66; "History and the Life Sciences in the Early Nineteenth Century: Wilhelm von Humboldt and Leopold von Ranke," in *Leopold von Ranke and the Shaping of the Historical Discipline*, ed. Georg G. Iggers and James M. Powell (Syracuse, NY 1990), pp. 21–35; "The History of Science, the Enlightenment and the History of 'Historical Science' in Germany," in *Geschichtswissenschaft vor 2000: Perspektiven der Historiographiegeschichte, Geschichtstheorie, Sozial- und Kulturgeschichte: Festschrift für Georg G. Iggers zum 65. Geburtstag,* ed. Konrad H. Jarausch, Jörn Rüsen, and Hans Schleier (The Hague 1991), pp. 214–31.

32. Oexle, *Geschichtswissenschaft im Zeichen des Historismus*, pp. 38ff.

33. See James M. Blaut, *The Colonizer's Model of the World: Geographical Diffusionism and Eurocentric History* (New York, London, 1993); see Eckhardt Fuchs, "Reshaping the World: Historiography from a Universal Perspective," in Larry Eugene Jones, ed., *Crossing Boundaries: The Exclusion and Inclusion of Minorities in Germany and the United States* (New York and Oxford, 2001) pp. 243-63; Andreas Pigulla, *China in der deutschen Weltgeschichtsschreibung von 18. bis zum 20. Jahrhundert* (Wiesbaden 1996); Christoph Marx, *Völker ohne Schrift und Geschichte: Zur historischen Erfassung des vorkolonialen Schwarzafrika in der deutschen Forschung des 19. und frühen 20. Jahrhunderts* (Stuttgart 1988); Jürgen Osterhammel, "'Peoples without History' in British and German Historical Thought," in Benedikt Stuchtey and Peter Wende, *British and German Historiography 1750-1950: Traditions, Perceptions, and Transfers* (Oxford 2000), pp. 265-87.

9. National Histories and World Systems: Writing Japan, France, and the United States

Christopher L. Hill

Cultural historians typically term the late nineteenth century the age of nationalism. Historians of historiography, when they have been sensitive to the eras in which historical works have been produced, no less typically see the efflorescence of "national history" during this period as a reflection of the nationalistic climate of the age. In such a view, the writing of history at this political and intellectual turning point served mainly to create a past for a new thing called the nation-state, to make this new thing old. Thus the argument is that the writing of national history naturalizes the "nation" as a form of community and thereby naturalizes the nation-state as a political organization.

The contention of this paper is that such interpretations of the practice of national history take the nation-state out of the world.[1] Certainly the argument that national history naturalizes the nation-state by giving it a history is a great advance over the perspective of national history itself, which pretends to write the history of something that exists from time immemorial. This level of critique brings into question the apparently natural status of the nation and thus also that of the nation-state, the nation's apparently organic political manifestation. The critique gives a history not to the nation and the nation-state, but to the *ideas* of nation and nation-state: they lose their status as fixed categories and are thrust into time. A question remains, however: what about the *space* that the nation-state claims for itself? Does this claiming, too, have historical determinants? The naturalizing gaze of national history operates not only in time but also in space. It devises historical legitimations for the territorial claims of specific nations, but even more importantly devises legitimations for the territoriality of the nation-state in general. This form of territoriality, in which juridical, economic, and social space are made to share the same frontiers, is essential to the temporal operations of national history. National history always is staged in a retrospectively claimed space.

The spatial claims of national history have largely escaped the type of paradigmatic critique that has revealed so clearly the politics of its operations in time. Scholars have examined specific issues, such as the status of areas around the Rhine in nineteenth century French historiography, but only since the rise of postcolonial historiography have the spatial operations of national history emerged as a general problem. These operations are geopolitical in nature, not limited to the political situation in one nation-state but rather responding to the aggregate of relations within the political and economic system of nation-states on a global scale. Indeed, by neglecting the geopolitical context in which the nation-state was established as the universal political and economic form of modernity—that is, by examining the writing of national history only in a national context—the critique of national history risks unwittingly re-naturalizing what it sets out to study. It risks naturalizing the nation as the universal category of historical writing by accepting the nation-state's claims to space.

If we examine the practice of national history in the late nineteenth century in its global geopolitical context, we can see that "national history" served not only the nation-state but more broadly served the ideological articulation of world capitalism, at a time when the market rapidly was being consolidated through the division of the world into discrete nation-states and colonies. During this period the writing of national history did naturalize the nation-state as a political and economic form. It did not do so, however, simply by creating a past for the nation. The practice of national history also articulated the relationship of that new form of territory, the nation-state, to the world. It did so by establishing a particular sort of epistemological space that I call the space of national history. This space, inside of which national history unfolds, exists in apposite relation to other such spaces: defined by its difference from them, a difference that is established through the mediation of the matrix of national-historical spaces as a whole. According to the totalizing gesture of this perspective, no territory is without its national history. If it lacks such a history then the territory properly belongs to another nation that can give it one. In this view, geopolitics thus can be understood as the sum of all separate national histories. The territory of the nation-state emerges as the common-sense division of space, not only in the present but also in the past, where the latent unity of national space awaits the national subject that will make it manifest.

Even such a cursory analysis of the spatial operations of "national history" suggests that the major challenge national history faces is to manage the relationship of national space to that of the world. The further critique of the writing of national history thus requires that we adopt a perspective broader than that of single nation-states, in order to account for the ways in which national space always is embedded in supra-national systems. In what follows, I examine the articulation of the space of national history through examples drawn from three countries that experienced what could be called spatial "upheavals" in the latter half of the nineteenth century, Japan, the United States, and France. While other examples would be possible (notably that of Germany), these three countries offer a range of positions in the world and thus suggest the ways in which the writing of national history was punctuated by global asymmetries even as it responded to the general grammar of the system of nation-states. In the case of Japan, I examine a peripheral state that only had been integrated into the capitalist market in the 1850s; in the United States, an expanding settler colony, no less peripheral at the time, that was commencing rapid industrialization, and in France a metropolitan power that just had suffered a great setback on the Continent but which soon began pouring resources into the development of an empire.

My entry into the problem is the intersection in the late nineteenth century between liberal economic thought—which in its treatment of international trade offered widely accepted arguments on the relation of one national space to another—and the rhetoric that historians and social theorists used to describe the process of national development. From this point of view, the names of my examples are Fukuzawa Yukichi, Frederick Jackson Turner, and Paul Leroy-Beaulieu. The interplay between economic liberalism and the rhetoric of national history is only one way into the issue. Considering that the period with which I am concerned saw not only the rise of nationalism and the efflux of national history but also a shift in world political economy from free-trade imperialism to formal empires, however, it seems an appropriate approach. My examples in fact indicate that the latter transition was as important a turning point in historiography as the two former.

One methodological point needs to be clarified before proceeding. The perspective of what follows is not "comparative" if comparison means juxtaposing two or more objects considered to exist *prior* to the comparison itself. This sort of comparison would seek general conclusions about the writing of national history by observing parallels and divergences among native "Japanese," "American," and "French" traditions, each assumed to have some sort of organic relationship to local religion, literature, philosophy, and the other things usually subsumed under the category of "culture." If one accepts that national history emerged to articulate the relationship of the nation-state to a supra-national system (whether or not one agrees with the details of Immanuel Wallerstein's theory, for example) then such a comparative approach clearly is inappropriate to the issue at hand. The reason is that it reproduces a central tenet of national ideology itself, namely that cultural unities called nations objectively exist and exert a determining sway over the mental lives of the subjects of nation-states. To avoid this pitfall we must examine the writing of national history in these three cases in the context of their relationship to one another, a relationship that we must recognize as mediated through geopolitics as a whole. In other words, we must approach the practice of national history from a systemic as well as a local perspective. The influence of local textual genealogies, while important, must be considered subordinate to the common problems faced by the intellectuals involved in the production of ideology, and these problems stem from the reorganization of the world into a system of nation-states. To avoid the grandiose adjective "global," I would call this approach international or transnational.

Before examining the role of the rhetoric of economic liberalism in historical writing in my three countries I want to look briefly at the use of this rhetoric within liberalism itself. The rhetorical techniques that become essential to historical writing in the late nineteenth century emerge from a style of talking about social development that proposes something called the division of labor as a model of social relations. The division of labor in turn has exchange as its basis. In this method of representing society, exchange is more than an economic activity. It is both the condition for the institution of society and the means by which it develops. As such, it becomes the fundamental mode of intersubjective relations. Consequently, anything that aids exchange between individuals (in the typical example, roads) aids the constitution and advancement of society as a whole. By the same token anything that impedes exchange (tolls) threatens society at the most fundamental level.

Such a promotion of free exchange as a social good—the idea of exchange being essential to the notion of "society" itself—appeared before liberalism in mercantilism's treatment of domestic economic policy and was prominent in the work of the physiocrats.[2] I take Adam Smith, however, as my example of this problematic for several reasons. One is the simple fact of Smith's prominence as a point of reference in economic discourse in the late nineteenth century. Another whose import will be clear later is the fundamental departure in Book One of *The Wealth of Nations* from previous considerations of the causes of economic specialization. As Pierre Rosanvallon has pointed out, Smith's innovation in this area was to posit the division of labor as the *consequence* of exchange, rather than the reverse.[3] Instead of seeing *exchange* as a necessity created by *specialization*—by a guild system, for example—Smith argued that specialization resulted from the opportunities offered by what he famously called "the propensity to truck, barter, and exchange one thing for another."[4]

With exchange thus established as the founding social act, the division of labor becomes a thoroughly dynamic way of conceiving social relations. Anything that aids intersubjective exchange deepens the division of labor, and the structural composition of society therefore is subject to positive change from moment to moment. At this point a theory of social development appears in Smith's thought—the unacknowledged philosophy of history of liberal and neoliberal economics, which could be called the "market imaginary of history." Smith observes on the one hand that the division of labor is limited by the extent of the market, and on the other that improvement and extension of networks of transportation and communication allow markets, and thus the division of labor, and thus society itself, to expand.[5] In this way Smith presents expanding trade, aided by improvements in transportation, as a mechanism for the integration of new territory into society. Smith calls such integration "civilization." We should note that in Smith's explicit statements, society inherently is something that expands. It does so by integrating new territory into its networks. The only limits to such expansion are the limitations of transportation and communication.

I would like to make clear that what is at stake here is not a straightforward "recognition" on Smith's part of the importance of the division of labor in social structures, but rather Smith's use of the division of labor as a philosophical concept for organizing social phenomena as knowledge.[6] Such an epistemological function of the division of labor is clear in Smith's famous initial proposition in *The Wealth of Nations* of a factory—specifically a pin factory—as a model for "the general business of society." The advantage of examining a small and trivial example of the division of labor, Smith says, is that it may be "placed . . . under the view of the spectator" in its entirety.[7] Smith proposes the factory as a social metaphor. The value of the metaphor for him is that it allows observation. In turn it allows *representation*: it is through metaphors such as the factory, the division of labor, and exchange that Smith renders representable the thing called society. It is such an understanding of economic liberalism as a system of rhetoric, rather than as simply a theory of economics, that I want to apply to representations of national history.

I would like to consider now the use of this sort of rhetoric in a text called *Bunmeiron no gairyaku* (*Outline of a Theory of Civilization*) published in Japan in 1875 by Fukuzawa. The appearance of *Outline of a Theory of Civilization* marked a decisive shift in Japanese historical writing, which had been dominated by Neo-Confucianism for more than two centuries, and the appearance of a new genre of historical practice, *bunmeishi* or history of civilization.

The genre emerged as an attempt to create a Japanese past for *bunmei kaika*, a slogan usually translated as "civilization and enlightenment" that designated a diffuse project among intellectuals in the 1870s to use education to make modern worker-citizens out of a populace they regarded as ignorant and dominated by custom. At the time, optimism about the possibility of rapid social change and enthusiasm for European and American learning—which had been widespread among intellectuals since the last years of the Tokugawa shogunate in the 1860s—were giving way to pessimism about the force of social habit and to concern that a vogue for superficial "Westernization" would have malign effects on the people. In the face of these changing sentiments, the genre of history of civilization elaborated a view of social change as a long-term process extending into the future and beginning in the Japanese past. After the publication of *Outline of a Theory of Civilization* in 1875, the genre continued with *Nihon kaika shōshi* (*Short History of Japanese Civilization*), published from 1877 to 1882 by Taguchi Ukichi, a laissez-faire economist and one-time translator for the Finance Ministry. The following years saw the appearance of a host of histories of civilization, but the genre began to wane with the anti-liberal reaction of the mid-1880s and was displaced decisively by Rankean academic historiography in the 1890s. Histories of civilization now are regarded dubiously as the obsolete foundation of modern Japanese historiography.

To elaborate their view of civilization as a process of endogenous, national social change, the writers of histories of civilization appropriated the work of several liberal European historians, in particular François Guizot and Thomas Buckle, of liberal political economists including J. S. Mill and Francis Wayland, and of the laissez-faire social theorist Herbert Spencer. The theoretical borrowing has been documented at great length.[8] What I am concerned with here is not the theory but the rhetoric that Fukuzawa and other intellectuals took from these Western sources. It is in the rhetoric of the genre that the liberal historical imaginary that I have associated with Adam Smith emerges as an important technique of representation.

The rhetoric of histories of civilization is dominated by a constellation of related words that appear throughout the genre. The words include *kōtsū*, communication or concourse; *tsūkō*, transit, passage; *kōeki*, trade or barter; *kōkan*, exchange or swap, and most importantly, *kōsai*, relations, communication, or intercourse. All of these terms include a Chinese character (read as *kō—majiwaru* in a Japanese reading) whose most basic meaning is mixing or association, and a second character signifying circulation or exchange in some form. What defines histories of civilization as a genre of historical knowledge is an evangelical desire to explain all aspects of society, from the economic to the intellectual and political, as manifestations of circulation, exchange, and intercourse. Fukuzawa writes in *Outline of a Theory of Civilization*:

> The nature of humankind inherently is to associate with others. . . . As those in the world associate together and people come into contact with each other, their intercourse gradually widening and their laws gradually becoming regular, human sentiment gradually moderates and knowledge gradually unfolds. In English, *bun-mei* is "civilization." It derives from the Latin *civitas* and thus means "country." Hence the word "civilization" describes the tendency toward successive improvement of human intercourse for the better, and in contrast to the independence of barbarian anarchy, means the formation of a country [*ikkoku*].[9]

While this passage clearly presents intercourse as an indiscriminate mechanism of civilization, the rhetoric of *Outline of a Theory of Civilization* and other histories of civilization in fact breaks down into two different "tropes"—on the one hand, an integrative trope of intercourse *within* a nation that recalls Adam Smith, and on the other, a differentiating trope of intercourse *between* nations. The distinction between the tropes is implicit: the texts offer no theoretical justification for the two quite different ways that they use the same constellation of words.

The first trope of integration within a nation already has raised its head in Fukuzawa's declaration that human nature is to associate in ever-widening circles. Fukuzawa also uses this trope to describe the formation of *shūron*, popular opinion, in Western countries. He writes, "Even in a remote village, people form circles and discuss public and private affairs. With these circles formed, each inevitably will have its own views. . . . This view and that view converge and change slightly, gradually merging and including more until finally the public opinion of the country is decided. . . ."[10] The state of unity that Fukuzawa describes here is achieved by overcoming barriers to communication in order to create an ever-widening space for the circulation of opinion. His insistence that a unified opinion necessarily results indicates that this trope of intercourse also implies a converging self-recognition in which one recognizes one's interest in the interests of others.

In contrast, the second differentiating trope of intercourse in the representation of history in the genre implies the recognition of sharp distinctions between self and other. Nations, not citizens, are the agents here. The shift is clear in remarks that Fukuzawa makes on international relations in the closing chapter of *Outline of a Theory of Civilization*. Fukuzawa warns that "there are only two sorts of intercourse between country and country. In peacetime, buying and selling things and fighting each other over the profit; or when it comes to it, killing each other with weapons. In other words, today's world could be called one of trade and war."[11] Fukuzawa's phrasing shows that the nature of intercourse changes entirely when it takes place between states. The expansive integration that in Fukuzawa's general theory of social development is unlimited never proceeds beyond the territory of the nation-state and is superseded by an intercourse that by definition is antagonistic.

That the nation-state provides the frontier that literally lies between these tropes is clear in Fukuzawa's explanation of the existence of *kokutai*, a word that he uses to translate J. S. Mill's term "nationality." "Nationality," Fukuzawa says,

> means that a race [*isshuzoku*][12] of people gather together and share sorrows and joys, create differences between themselves and other nations, regard each other more warmly than they regard people of other nations, strive to expend their energies for each other rather than for people of other nations, govern themselves under a single government, resent suffering the control of other governments, [and] bear their calamities and happiness themselves in independence.[13]

Such rhetoric of self and other should leave little doubt that in the liberal theory of history propounded by histories of civilization, the two irreconcilable tropes of intercourse limn a figurative national space within which nations form and achieve independence. The boundary of this space is maintained simultaneously by the activities of integrative and differentiating intercourse. The fundamental activity of exchange thus institutes society, as it does in Smith, but in Fukuzawa's text it institutes society as *national*. Social development, which it is Fukuzawa's main concern to describe, takes place in a national space that is strictly separate from other national spaces existing in differential relationship to it. Here history is solely the history of national intercourse, an inherently unifying activity, while national subjects are the universal subjects of liberal political economy given a national purpose: the realization of independence.[14]

What the market imaginary of history finally accomplishes in the Japanese genre of history of civilization, then, is the establishment *on the global periphery* of the type of internal theory of social change that had played an essential legitimating role in the expansion of the economic and political power of Europe since the sixteenth century. Scholars such as Samir Amin and Enrique Dussel have argued convincingly that the assertion in such theories that the power and wealth of Europe arose because of internal factors (such as Protestantism) which were "lacking" in other regions not only gave the imprimatur of history to metropolitan domination, but also served to justify the forcible imposition of European models of development on colonial (and more recently neocolonial) possessions. The key legitimating function of such internal paradigms was to efface the systemic factors that made European domination not only possible but at a certain point inevitable (in particular, the accumulation of capital at the metropole) and instead to blame the periphery for its own subjugation.[15] In appropriating such internal theories of social change, Fukuzawa and other writers of histories of civilization accepted what Dussel calls the "developmentalist fallacy." At the same time, however, they rearticulated these theories to represent development as a *national* project, relativizing the dominant position of Europe by insisting that the universalist pretensions of European social thought be taken at face value: Japan could and would achieve "civilization."

Two consequences must be observed before moving on to American and French examples. First, the interplay of tropes of intercourse in the genre formalizes in epistemology the organization of the world as a system of political-economic subjects known as nation-states that was being implemented at the time through the consolidation of the world market and the international state system. The nation-state becomes the universal political-economic form and the *telos* of all separate national histories. The insertion of Japan as a full, independent partner in this global political economy was to be accomplished by the project of "civilization and enlightenment." But as an extension of the same logic, histories of civilization situated enlightened Japanese intellectuals in the same relationship to the inhabitants of the archipelago as colonial administrators to their subjects. The agents of a coercive transformation of daily life to suit the needs of the nation-state, such intellectuals nonetheless were able to claim for themselves the legitimation of history and to maintain that they acted on behalf of the "nation."

The emergence of such a historiographical problematic therefore is not only an issue of the legitimation of inequities in "international" relations. It also is an issue of the production and reproduction of epistemological categories that support the enclosure and administration by nation-states of geographical areas and their populations. In the new nation-state of Japan, the genre of history of civilization was instrumental in the establishment of these categories. National history from this point of view is a category for enclosing a populace that henceforth will be the object of a civilizing process whose seeming subject is the nation rather than intellectuals and bureaucrats. Yet for all the apparent confidence of Fukuzawa and his confederates that the steamroller progress of civilization was unstoppable, the very premises of such a project dictate that any persistent internal division or heterogeneity be regarded as threatening the entire national endeavor.

Such heterogeneity in fact is the focus of the deployment of liberal economic rhetoric in the historical writing of Frederick Jackson Turner. Turner's famous 1893 essay "The Significance of the Frontier in American History" was one of the founding texts of Progressive history, the current that dominated the practice of history in the United States from the turn of the twentieth century to the Second World War.[16] While the name given to the movement was meant to indicate its political stance, not simply its enthusiasm for progress in the abstract, the national character that Turner and others attributed to progress was fundamental to their representation of history. On this point Turner had much in common with his contemporary Fukuzawa: as in Fukuzawa, Turner's early work seizes on exchange as a fundamental trope for representing social relations. The ideological challenge that Turner faced was, needless to say, greatly different. From the point of view of white intellectuals in the so-called Gilded Age, the unity of the people was the major problem facing the American settler colony. Like Fukuzawa, however, Turner approached this problem as one of space.

Like Japanese theories of civilization, social thought in the United States in Turner's era was concerned with the position of the United States in the world and with the relationship of national history to world history. The inquiry took place in the context of a long history of exceptionalism in American social thought, and specifically had to contend with the failure in the late nineteenth century of the strongly exceptionalist Jacksonian view of U.S. history. According to this view, current since the 1830s, the United States was exempt from the social ills observable in Europe because its abundance of land made possible a perpetual democracy based on a polity of small agrarian freeholders.[17] The United States would be exempt from the forces of social change because of the unique conditions that prevailed there. Underlying such a conception of U.S. society, then, was a profound antagonism toward time.

Since the 1870s this antihistorical view of the United States increasingly had been undermined by the appearance of what intellectuals euphemistically referred to as "complexity." By this they meant a host of phenomena that threatened the idealized Jacksonian nation, including industrialization—which brought with it a working class—and the influx of immigrants from Eastern and Southern Europe and Asia who looked and acted differently from the so-called "native stock" of Anglo-Germans. "Complexity" thus essentially meant social heterogeneity. Its persistence brought grudging acknowledgement that the United States was subject to the same forces that were changing Europe, and prompted efforts to view U.S. history in the light of universalistic theories based on the histories of European societies. Turner, for one, enthusiastically embraced liberal theories such as those of Achille Loria that postulated universal stages of social change.[18] Turner employed such theories to argue that the particular conditions prevailing in the expanding American settler colony were reflections of the universal.

According to the universalism that Turner espoused, all societies pass through successive economic stages as they evolve. The peculiarity of the United States was that a new instance of the universal process of social evolution began each time the frontier of settlement shifted west. Each of these separate processes of social evolution—he counted five—had a division of labor appropriate to its stage, while all were linked by the national system of circulation that pushed the frontier westward as the system expanded. Social change in the nation as a whole thus moved in step with the extension of the networks through which intercourse took place. The prominence of these networks in Turner's representation of history is clear, for example, in his declaration that

> . . . civilization in American has followed the arteries made by geology, pouring an ever richer tide through them, until at last the slender paths of aboriginal intercourse have been broadened and interwoven into the complex maze of modern commercial lines; the wilderness has been interpenetrated by lines of civilization growing ever more numerous. It is like the steady growth of a complex nervous system for the originally simple, inert continent. If one would understand why we are to-day one nation, rather than a collection of isolated states, he must study this economic and social consolidation of the country.[19]

For Turner the penetration of the territory of the nation by highways, railroads, and so forth simply makes manifest a territorial unity that up to now has been latent: the integral territory of the nation exists prior to networks that *realize* it rather than create it.

The extension of the pathways of intercourse plays a more active role in the advent of the *people* in Turner's representation of history. According to Turner the extension of the networks of circulation constantly put immigrants in contact with the frontier, which itself was renewed without cease as settlement pushed westward. Discussions of Turner's "frontier thesis" typically stop with Turner's observations on the movement of the frontier, which he considered to have "closed" in 1890. Turner's description of what happens at the frontier, however, deserves a closer reading. He writes in "The Significance of the Frontier" that

> The frontier is the line of most rapid and effective Americanization. The wilderness masters the colonist. It finds him a European in dress, industries, tools, modes of travel, and thought. . . . It strips off the garments of civilization and arrays him in the hunting shirt and moccasin. . . . Before long he has gone to planting Indian corn and plowing with a sharp stick; he shouts the war cry and takes the scalp in orthodox fashion.[20]

The label "Americanization" that Turner applies to the costume pageant that he describes taking place at the frontier was the common phrase of the era for the assimilation of immigrants. It therefore should be clear that in contrast to the common view of Turner as a historian concerned with the process of western settlement, the frontier thesis was closely engaged with contemporary alarm about the rise of so-called "complexity." In Turner's view the constant extension of networks of exchange, which transport the immigrant to an ever-fresh frontier and simultaneously knit the nation together, is essential to the reversal of such complexity. As the foundation of society, intercourse thus becomes inseparable from the genesis of the people, which takes place not in the past but in the present.

It is well known that Turner's essay gloomily predicts that with the frontier now closed such transformations of the people are impossible. The prophesy and indeed the thesis on which it was based had and have no foundation because even setting aside objections to Turner's exclusive focus on western regions, the frontier moved in more complex ways than Turner ever allowed. If we examine Turner's famous essay in light of the politics and economics of his time, however, we can see that by deploying the liberal rhetoric of intercourse Turner was able to represent the expropriation of western lands for capitalist agriculture, the rapid industrialization of the East, the reorganization of space by railroads, to wit, the vast economic change of the Gilded Age in its entirety, as a movement of "Americanization" in which the nation realizes its true character. Despite the fact that the phenomena Turner cites in the essay are economic ones, economics drops into the background and plays a minor role in what essentially is a drama of national awakening.

Although ostensibly concerned with the formation of citizens, what the drama of Americanization in Turner's early work naturalizes is the movement of capital. By attributing a national and indeed even popular quality to the expansion of the networks of capital, Turner claims—in the name of the "nation"—the territory of the nation-state as a space of free capitalist circulation. Obstacles to such free circulation appear in Turner's representation of history as threats to the integrity of the national space and thus to the life of the nation itself. Yet the major threat that Turner isolates in his essay is not, for example, the unequal relationship of the agricultural regions of the American South and West to the industrial and financial centers of the East, but rather the presence of unassimilated immigrants. The immigrant, indeed, emerges as a figure for the resistance to capitalism typified at the time by the Populist movement and labor agitation. Turner's national history, in contrast, posits the elimination of all such resistance as part of a positive narrative of unification and national rising.[21]

A comparison to Fukuzawa helps to illustrate what Turner accomplishes for national ideology in the United States. The genre of history of civilization articulated a position for the new Japanese nation-state in a radically changed world by outlining a space within which the nation would achieve unity and advance toward civilization. Although there were great regional differences within the new Japanese state, and although the status of the land and inhabitants of border areas such as Hokkaido and Okinawa was far from clear, myths such as the continuity of imperial rule gave the writers of these histories the means to assert that both the people and the territory of Japan were one and needed only to be made to advance through policies of "civilization and enlightenment." Turner, in contrast, wrote in a settler colony that always had been populated by immigrants, whose borders had not been stable since its establishment, and whose regions had deeply differing political and economic interests. In his case the ideological problem was not to create a history that explained the relationship of the nation to the "civilized" states of Europe but to create a history that posited the conditions for the unification of the nation itself in both territory and populace. The frontier, as an ur-site of intercourse, served this purpose. In the United States the rhetoric of economic liberalism deployed in historical writing thus served greatly different ideological needs, even if the ultimate goal remained to represent national history as the genesis and growth of the people.[22]

Domestic politics and geopolitical position similarly inflected the ways in which the general tactic of representation that I call the market imaginary of history was used in debates on the state of the French nation in the 1870s, the third of my examples. Here at the industrialized center of the world economy tropes of intercourse, exchange, and circulation became privileged means for advancing arguments not on national genesis but on national regeneration. The preeminent work of colonialist propaganda in the early decades of the French Third Republic, *De la colonisation chez les peuples modernes* (*On Colonization among Modern Peoples*) illustrates such a local focus on rebirth at the same time that it allows us to further examine the problem of frontiers in the establishment of national-historical space. Published in 1874 by Paul Leroy-Beaulieu, a young man soon to become the era's foremost liberal economist, this massive study of European colonialism was the touchstone of Jules Ferry's program for colonial expansion.[23] Analysis of the narrative of social development that Leroy-Beaulieu offers in it suggests an essential instability in the spatial suppositions of national history that is remedied only by the proposition of colonies as a type of supplemental historical space.

On Colonization was written in the wake of the founding traumas of the Third Republic, the defeat to Prussia in 1870 and the rise and suppression of the Commune in 1871. As a number of cultural historians have shown, the double shock of defeat abroad and civil war at home fostered a widespread meditation on national decadence and a reassessment of the course of French history since 1789.[24] A concern to find the means of national renewal surfaced at the same time. While statements of the diagnosis and the cure ranged widely, including jeremiads that France was suffering divine retribution, a strong current of opinion held that the Defeat and the loss of Alsace and part of Lorraine had created a problem of closed space: blocked and dismembered on its eastern frontier, France had been thrown back on itself and was degenerating as a result. Essentially, the source of French ills in this view was a deficiency in national space. *Revanchisme*, the determination to retake Alsace-Lorraine and punish Bismarck's Empire, was one response to such a conclusion. Another proposed remedy, disputed by Continentalists but embraced by many others with enthusiasm, was colonization. Thus Leroy-Beaulieu wrote in the preface to the second edition of *On Colonization*, "Our Continental politics, lest they bring us nothing but setbacks, henceforth must be essentially defensive. It is outside of Europe that we can satisfy our legitimate instinct for expansion. . . . [Colonization] is the only great undertaking that destiny allows us."[25]

Such an intertwined relationship between national destiny and national space is the foundation of Leroy-Beaulieu's most famous pronouncement in

On Colonization, that "the people that colonizes most is the first people. If it is not so today, it will be tomorrow."[26] The orientation toward the future implicit in such a statement presents the conquest of foreign lands not simply as an index of greatness—i.e., size matters—but as an essential quality of the development of nations. Put another way, this view of history held that for a mature nation *not* to colonize—following the typical lexical dichotomy between "mature" colonizers and "childish" colonized—was for it to risk history coming to a halt. Upon predicting alarming growth in the Anglo-Saxon, German, Russian, and Chinese populations of the world, Leroy-Beaulieu thus warns that a small France will have no hope of ranking among such giants. "Our country has one means to escape this irreparable downfall—to colonize."[27] He adds:

> Colonization for France is a question of life or death: either France
> will become a great African power, or in one century or two it will
> not be more than a secondary power in Europe. In the world it
> will count for close to what Greece or Romania count in Europe.
> We aspire to greater destinies for our *patrie*: may France resolute-
> ly become a colonizing nation, for when it does, great expecta-
> tions and vast thoughts will reopen before it.[28]

Like Fukuzawa and Turner, Leroy-Beaulieu considers France to be at a crossroads in national history in which it faces a choice between a path of progress and a path leading to the diminution and even dissolution of the nation *per se*.

Leroy-Beaulieu's argument for colonization could be dismissed as a fairly banal nationalism were it not for his striking reliance on the tropes of intercourse and theories of national development already observed in the historical narratives of Fukuzawa and Turner. Beginning with the diagnosis of France's national ill itself, the details of Leroy-Beaulieu's argument derive from the market imaginary of history and its conception of national space far more than from simple nationalistic fervor. In the work of late-century colonial propagandists such as Leroy-Beaulieu, liberal arguments on intercourse as the engine of national history became prescriptive: colonization, they argued, would reverse a national decline that they considered to be the result of blocked circulation in Continental France. National progress would recommence with the liberation of national circulation through trade with colonies.

Thus in Leroy-Beaulieu's work liberal faith in the value of the extension of the division of labor is linked to colonial commerce, through which, Leroy-Beaulieu writes, "exchange is energized and extended, and the division of labor increases. Industry, having before itself larger outlets, can and must produce more, and this production on a larger scale leads to new improvements and new progress."[29] In an unusual turn on the treasured notion of transportation in liberal political economy, Leroy-Beaulieu even went so far as to compare such an invigorating effect of colonies on the metropole to that of provincial canals and roads: if the government was willing to spend time and money developing the latter, it was folly to beggar colonial expansion and administration.[30] The colonies as a whole, his argument went, would compensate for the blockage of intercourse that hexagonal France suffered from the loss of Alsace-Lorraine and its diminished position on the Continent.

Leroy-Beaulieu predicted the same beneficial results for the overseas territories that were to be the means of metropolitan renewal. The colonial propagandists of the early Third Republic considered barbarian or semi-civilized areas (again, following the colonialist lexicon of the day) to suffer, like France, from blocked circulation. In contrast to France, however, natural geographical deficiencies in colonized areas were to blame for the sluggish movement of history. By correcting such deficiencies, colonial administration would allow intercourse, and thus history, to recommence in these areas. In keeping with the liberal valorization of transportation, Leroy-Beaulieu called this process the "acheminement à la civilisation" of subject peoples, that is their "transport to civilization" or more literally their being *put on the road* to it.[31] Subject peoples would be made to circulate whether they liked it or not, because it was only through imperially administered circulation that their history could be made to commence.

In this view of colonization colonies become a space in which the problems of circulation in the national-historical space proper, the space of the metropole, can be redressed. With the addition of colonies the division of labor can continue to deepen, networks of exchange can continue to extend their reach, circulation can continue to quicken: history can continue to unfold. Leroy-Beaulieu thus represents the entire enterprise of colonial conquest and administration, the extraction of resources and the metropolitan accumulation of capital, as a necessary stage in the development of nations *per se*. What results, paradoxically, is a Smithian argument in favor of colonization—paradoxical because Smith, as is well known, opposed colonialism on economic grounds. We can see how such a prescription for regeneration would emerge, however, if we recall that in the historical imaginary that we are examining the movement of history depends on free circulation within the national-historical space. Any blockage of such circulation, whether by incomplete realization of national unity (as in Turner) or by its destruction through the imposition of an unnatural internal border, would threaten to bring the historical process to a halt. It is precisely such a blockage that Leroy-Beaulieu foresaw for a France confined to its European frontiers. One singular advantage of colonial circulation, moreover, was that it would be subject to rational planning. Unlike the movement of history on the Continent, history in the colonies would unfold logically under the careful gaze of administrators. This is to say that national history would be taken out of the hands of politicians and put into those of technocrats (or in Paul Rabinow's phrase, techno-cosmopolitans) who could manage its pathways with proper care.[32] Such a perspective gave rise to grandiose public-works projects for the development of transportation, including proposals for a Trans-Saharan railroad and for an inland sea north of the Sahara.

Deeper links between the arguments first observed in *The Wealth of Nations* and this variety of imperialist ideology further attest that such a legitimation of colonial expansion follows logically from liberal conceptions of the nature of society. Recall that in Smith the division of labor exhibits two essential tendencies: toward increasing specialization, but also toward the integration of ever more territory into its dynamic structure. "Society" therefore is inherently expansive in Smith's logic. Such a view of the division of labor underlies both Fukuzawa's and Turner's representations of national history, in which expansive integration serves as a spatial measure of the temporal movement of history. Leroy-Beaulieu exhibits a similar perspective when he defines colonization as "the expansive force of a people, its power of reproduction, its expansion and multiplication across space."[33] Leroy-Beaulieu's overt use of liberal tropes to champion colonialism as the means to satisfy what he calls above "our legitimate instinct for expansion" thus is far from an opportunistic rationalization. Rather it is only an amplification of a position that always had been present in liberalism's fundamental notions of society. On this most basic level, Leroy-Beaulieu's work is not marked by any paradox of "liberal colonialism" but is fully consistent with the representations of national history that we have observed elsewhere in the world at this time.

Despite such a consistency in logic and representation, however, colonial space has an ambivalent status in *On Colonization* that indicates basic instabilities in the way that this system of rhetoric establishes the space of national history. Such instabilities are clear in the two different ways that Leroy-Beaulieu characterizes the relationship between colonial and metropolitan space: on the one hand colonial space is an *addition* to metropolitan space, as an extension of metropolitan networks of intercourse; on the other it is a *substitute*, a self-contained space that is not subject to the setbacks and irrationalities of history on the Continent. In neither case is the nationality of colonial space clear. Lacking the capacity for social development, this space can not be host to its own nation, but it nonetheless is not truly a part of the national space of France. In a sense, colonial space in such a view of history is dependent on the colonizer for its nationality. As we have seen, however, this space is to be the site of metropolitan renewal, and thus its existence seemingly is necessary for the further progress of history in the metropole itself: without colonial expansion, national history will stop.

The ambivalent status of colonial space in Leroy-Beaulieu's representation of history suggests that as a category, colonial space emerges in response to the failure to appear in reality of the perfectly apposite relationship among national-historical spaces that "national history" supposes to exist. The appearance of such perfect apposition, along with its corollary of the natural unity of the people, is blocked by internal divisions, cross-border identities, and the movement of capital over frontiers. All of these violate the assumptions of national history about the character of physical space; it can account for none of them. Epistemologically, colonial space therefore serves in the market imaginary of history to account for the breakdown of historical interiority, of the assertion that the history of the territory claimed by a nation-state unfolds as the sole result of tendencies within its "nation." To borrow a term from Derrida, the space of the colony is a "supplement" to that of the nation, serving to account for an excess that cannot be contained within historical interiority. To be clear: I am not asserting that the violence of colonialism was the result of fairly obscure problems in historical thought. Rather, I am saying that the particular way that Leroy-Beaulieu inserted colonialism into a liberal narrative of the life of nations transformed it to suit changing metropolitan ideological needs and at the same time postponed the disintegration of the narrative itself by shoring up its epistemological foundations.

Leroy-Beaulieu's argument for colonization as an essential stage in national history thus illustrates general problems in liberal historical imagineries at the same time that it reflects the specific ideological exigency with which he was faced, that of justifying colonial expansion by establishing a necessary relationship between colony and metropole. Once again, comparisons to Fukuzawa and Turner suggest reasons that the liberal narrative of national history took this specific form in early Third-Republic France. As we have seen beginning with Fukuzawa, the liberal historical imaginary served above all to naturalize the establishment and extension of capitalism and its relations of production as the ordained course of national progress. In Japan, among the most pressing tasks in such a project was to locate Japan in the world as a nation among nations, possessing its own history of progress. In the United States, in contrast, the conditions of a settler colony made narratives of unity a comparatively more important goal. Finally in France, with a comparatively stable national identity but radically changing boundaries, the problem rather was to naturalize the relationship of the nation to newly acquired colonies. Colonization became a necessary extension of the movement of national history. To a certain degree the need to reorient narratives of nation-formation to account for expansion was particular to Europe: while Japan and the United States were busily colonizing border areas, they did not seize formal colonies until a few decades later. Nonetheless the specific strategies of Leroy-Beaulieu's legitimation of colonialism followed closely from the rhetoric he shared with Fukuzawa and Turner, and thus from the shared problem of articulating the relationship between the economic and juridical space of the nation-state and the various pasts of the territory it claimed.

The concern to rationally administer circulation that I briefly observed earlier in Leroy-Beaulieu's work points to further commonalities among my French, American, and Japanese examples on the most fundamental historiographical level: that of writing. In light of the link between intercourse and history in *On Colonization*, Leroy-Beaulieu's desire to rationally administer circulation so as to protect it from the vicissitudes of Continental politics finally is a concern to administer national history itself. The undertaking of "civilization and enlightenment" that was the foundation for histories of civilization in Japan and the projects of "Americanization" in the late nineteenth- and early twentieth-century United States share the same perspective, in which the rhetoric of liberalism and indeed the very category of national history serve to make representable and thus administrable the "nation" as a social totality.

If the commonality among my diverse examples can be traced genealogically to early European liberalism and hence to Enlightenment rationalism, the reasons for the spread of this historical imaginary must be sought in systemic conditions that rendered it particularly valuable in national ideology. At the late nineteenth-century turning point in historiography and geopolitics, the consolidation of the world market and the establishment of an international system of states of global reach were the key conditions supporting the travel of the market imaginary of history. This historiographical problematic best can be understood as a system of rhetoric that makes possible specific strategies of representation; in this sense it was a "theory" of history that took the nation as its privileged scale. Nonetheless those who employed it always had *praxis* as their goal: they sought to establish a determinate representation of history that legitimated the nation-state's claim on territory. Such a method of writing history thus ultimately supported the enclosure and administration of the living inhabitants of specific spaces, and a thorough critique of its operations finally must confront its representation of space.

The group of techniques for representing national history that I have examined serves a dual function in historical practice. It nationalizes the past of the territory that is claimed by the nation-state, and it negotiates the relationship of this space of history to other such spaces, according to the particular position of the nation-state in question. The examples that I have chosen by no means exhaust the range of possibilities. They reveal, however, that one problem that "national history" must grapple with is the continual shifting of the limits of the territory claimed by the nation-state. Thus in the United States, the writing of national history had to account for continuous expansion, while in France it had both to confront the loss of Continental provinces and to explain the relationship of colonies to the metropole. Late nineteenth-century Japanese intellectuals faced perhaps an even more difficult task of creating a representation of an integral national territory from prior conceptions of political space and inserting that territory into the space of the world. It is only a slight leap in logic therefore to say that the central problem in the spatial operations of national history finally was not one of changing frontiers but of novelty and indeed foreignness: as a rule the territory over which the nation-state declares sovereignty always is foreign to it, even if that territory is identical to the territory of a previous regime. The reason is that the spatial parameters of sovereignty of the nation-state depart from those of preceding eras by incorporating new ideas of spatial contiguity and of the identity of juridical and economic boundaries, for example. One great problem that national ideology therefore faces is that of explaining the relationship of the territory of the nation-state to that thing called the "nation" that is supposed to be sovereign within it. The writing of national history resolves this problem by establishing a single past for this territory, a national past. In this kind of historical practice the various pasts of the areas claimed by the nation-state are annexed to the history of the nation.

Returning to the question of the position of national-historical space in the world, the rhetoric that these late nineteenth-century historians appropriated from economic liberalism made possible the representation of the world as an array of apposite national-historical spaces. According to this perspective there is no space without its national history, with the corollary assertion that if a space is found to be lacking such a history it may and indeed must be annexed to the space of a proper nation. In such a spatial matrix the relative power of nations, political and economic, is explained by the course of their separate national histories. "National history" thus serves as a simultaneous explanation of the political and economic formations of the nation-state and of the geopolitical relations between different nation-states. The writing of "national history" naturalizes the nation-state as a local political form and as the basic unit of a differentially defined system. This is to say that "national history" does not simply naturalize the nation-state by making it the *telos* of history—a point that is well established—but in a more fundamental sense naturalizes the nation-state by defining the space over which it claims sovereignty as the space within which history occurs. The existence of this space is the ground of history. Moreover, to the extent that "national history" naturalizes the nation-state as a local political form it also naturalizes the organization of the world into a system of nation-states.

"National history" as a system of rhetoric therefore aspires to totality on a grand scale: not simply an all-encompassing and coherent representation of the nation, but rather of the world. The logical problems and inconsistencies of category of this system result from disjunctures between the totality that it seeks to construct and the world as it exists. Indeed, the *writing* of the history of nations (that is, historiography as an attempt to create representations rather than as theory or paradigm) exists between this totality and the world. "National history" was, and indeed still is, a method for rendering social phenomena intelligible, for apprehending the world. There should be little doubt that the intellectuals involved in propagating this paradigm advanced the interests of particular groups such as the colonial lobby of France or the modernist (that is, nationalist) political-economic vanguard in Japan. When these intellectuals naturalized the nation-state they legitimated the forced nationalization of populaces, fed alarm about the presence of strangers in the land, justified the seizure of territory overseas. Nonetheless we should acknowledge that intellectuals like Fukuzawa, Turner, and Leroy-Beaulieu also were observing a world in which territoriality quickly was being reduced to two types, that of the nation-state and of the colony. Their work ultimately naturalized these circumstances, but we should acknowledge that it had the immediate purpose of rendering such circumstances intelligible by making them representable. These were no politically neutral representations—there are no such things—but representation nonetheless was and is necessary.

I do not say this to try to redeem Fukuzawa, Turner, and Leroy-Beaulieu on the basis of circumstances, but rather as a caution to myself and other historians at our own geopolitical turning point. I have argued that the rhetoric that late nineteenth century historians drew from economic liberalism helped to articulate the ideology of world capitalism at the time. The same rhetoric, however, plays an obvious role in *neo*liberalism as it strives to legitimate the transnational capitalism of our own time, a new form of domination that one often hears will make the nation-state obsolete. By making clear the connection between the writing of history as the history of nations and the world capitalism of the late nineteenth century, a spatial critique of national history of the sort that I have attempted should temper the occasionally uncritical enthusiasm of recent years to embark on a study of history proclaimed to be transnational or international. The most zealous proponents typically promote this sort of study by arguing that the nation-state is dead and therefore should be cast out of history. In other words, much of the enthusiasm for writing transnational history has not come from a serious, critical reflection on the history of historiography but appears rather to be driven by observation of contemporary economic transitions, indeed by an unskeptical endorsement of them. In the absence of such historiographical reflection, which must include a more thorough examination than I have been able to provide of the relationship between the practice of national history and the economic circumstances of various eras, I fear that transnational historiography, should it ever become an established pursuit, simply will give substance to the ideology of transnational capitalism as the national historiography of the late nineteenth century advanced the economic ideology of its own time.

References

1. The argument of the present paper is condensed from the first three chapters of my Ph.D. dissertation, "National History and the World of Nations: Writing Japan, France, the United States, 1870–1900," Columbia University, 1999.

2. On the pre-liberal background see Eli Heckscher's *Mercantilism*, trans. Mendel Shapiro and E. F. Söderlund, rev. ed. (London: Allen & Unwin, 1955).

3. Pierre Rosanvallon, *Le libéralisme économique. Histoire de l'idée de marché* (Paris: Seuil, 1989), 74.

4. Adam Smith, *An Inquiry into the Nature and Causes of the Wealth of Nations* (Chicago: University of Chicago Press, 1976), 17. Smith presents this propensity as the cause of the division of labor a few pages later with the declaration that "it is [the] trucking disposition which originally gives occasion to the division of labor." *Wealth of Nations*, 19.

5. *Wealth of Nations*, 21–23.

6. Rosanvallon discusses the status of division of labor as a philosophical concept in Smith in *Le libéralisme économique*, 76.

7. *Wealth of Nations*, 7–8.

8. In English, see Carmen Blacker, *The Japanese Enlightenment: A Study of the Writings of Fukuzawa Yukichi* (Cambridge: Cambridge University Press, 1964), 90–100, which also discusses the importance of historiography to "civilization and enlightenment" thought in Japan. For an overview of the genre see Ienaga Saburō, "Keimō shigaku," *Meiji shiron shū I*, ed. Matsushima Eiichi, Meiji bungaku zenshū 77 (Tokyo: Chikuma Shobō, 1965), 422–27.

9. Fukuzawa Yukichi, *Bunmeiron no gairyaku*, ed. Matsuzawa Hiroaki (Tokyo: Iwanami Shoten, 1995), 57. The translation is my own. A complete translation is available as *An Outline of a Theory of Civilization*, trans. David A. Dilworth and Cameron G. Hurst (Tokyo: Sophia University, 1973).

10. *Bunmeiron no gairyaku*, 114–15.

11. *Bunmeiron no gairyaku*, 273.

12. Mill uses the phrase "a portion of humanity" in the passage from *Considerations on Representative Government* (1861) that Fukuzawa is paraphrasing. Later in the same paragraph he identifies common "race" as one basis for nationality, but not the only possible one. Others include language, history, political form, etc.

13. *Bunmeiron no gairyaku*, 40–41.

14. In "National History and the World of Nations" I theorize the relationship between the two tropes of intercourse in the genre of history of civilization through the concept of inversion that Karatani Kōjin develops in *Marukusu sono kanōsei no chūshin* (Tokyo: Kōdansha, 1974), an analysis of Marx' theory of value. I argue that while irreconcilable, the two tropes jointly invert and obscure causality in the systemic constitution of nation-states. Although the nation-state as a form of territory is the manifestation of systemic conditions in world capitalism in the nineteenth century, the logical inversion in histories of civilization allows the nation-state to appear as if it existed prior to its differential relationships to other nation-states. Systemic conditions thus appear in the genre as the effect of relations among nation-states, rather

than nation-states as the effect of such conditions. In texts such as Fukuzawa's the development of "civilization" within the self-contained space of the nation-state therefore emerges as the key to understanding the place of the nation-state in the world: the synchrony of global geopolitics is replaced by the diachronic interiority of national history.

15. See Samir Amin, *Eurocentrism*, trans. Russell Moore (New York: Monthly Review, 1989), 76–77, 109–11, and Enrique Dussel, *The Invention of the Americas: Eclipse of "the Other" and the Myth of Modernity*, trans. Michael D. Barber (New York: Continuum, 1995), 66–67, 136–37.

16. John Higham offers a concise overview of Progressive history and Turner's place in it in *History: The Development of Historical Studies in the United States* (Englewood Cliffs: Prentice-Hall, 1965), 171–82. Ernst Breisach examines Turner's contribution in the first chapter of *American Progressive History: An Experiment in Modernization* (Chicago: University of Chicago Press, 1993).

17. Drawing on the work of J. G. A. Pocock, Dorothy Ross examines the history of the Jacksonian view of history in "Historical Consciousness in Nineteenth-Century America," *American Historical Review* 89.4 (Oct. 1984), 910–13.

18. On Turner's borrowing from Loria, whom he encountered partly through the work of political economist Richard Ely, see Lee Benson, *Turner and Beard: American Historical Writing Reconsidered* (Glencoe: Free Press, 1960), 1–34.

19. Frederick Jackson Turner, "The Significance of the Frontier in American History," in *Rereading Frederick Jackson Turner: "The Significance of the Frontier in American History" and Other Essays*, ed. John Mack Faragher (New York: Henry Holt, 1994), 40–41.

20. "Significance of the Frontier," 33.

21. Despite his reputation as a progressive, Turner dismissed Populism as a lingering outcropping of lower stages of civilization. "A primitive society can hardly be expected to show the intelligent appreciation of the complexity of business interests in a developed society," he wrote. ("Significance of the Frontier," 55) Turner discussed the persistence of outmoded frontier-era ideals at length in "The Problem of the West" (1896).

22. For a parallel examination of the problem of origins in contemporary Australia see Elizabeth A. Povinelli, "Settler Modernity and the Quest for an Indigenous Tradition," *Public Culture* 11.1 (Winter 1999), 19–48.

23. Chapters three and four of Agnes Murphy's *The Ideology of French Imperialism, 1871–1881* (Washington, D. C.: Catholic University of America Press, 1948) give background on Leroy-Beaulieu and his work as an academic and journalist.

24. See Claude Digeon's remarkable *La Crise allemande de la pensée française, 1870–1914* (Paris: Presses universitaires de France, 1959), 1–4, and Raoul Girardet, "Présentation," *Le nationalisme français, 1871–1914*, (Paris: Seuil, 1983), 17, 30–32.

25. Paul Leroy-Beaulieu, *De la colonisation chez les peuples modernes*, 2nd ed. (Paris: Guillaumin, 1882), viii. The translation is my own.

26. Paul Leroy-Beaulieu, *De la colonisation chez les peuples modernes* (Paris: Guillaumin, 1874), 606.

27. *De la colonisation*, 2nd ed., viii.

28. *De la colonisation*, 2nd ed., viii–ix.

29. *De la colonisation,* 502.

30. *De la colonisation,* 530–31.

31. *De la colonisation,* vii.

32. Paul Rabinow, *French Modern: Norms and Forms of the Social Environment* (Cambridge, Mass.: MIT Press, 1989), 12.

33. *De la colonisation,* 605.

10. China's Search for National History

Q. Edward Wang[1]

This essay aims to trace the origin of national historical writing in twentieth-century China, yet it is clear to the author that this can be a perplexing task, for the term "national history," or *kuo-shih*, in modern Chinese is not a neologism; it is rather an old usage that has existed in Chinese historiography for a number of centuries. Referring to a contemporary account of the history of the reigning dynasty, "National history," or *Kuo-shih*, first appeared in historical texts as early as the third century. It performed a similar function as the *Shih-lu* (veritable records) and *Ch'i-chü-chu* (court diary) and offered a useful basis for a much more comprehensive account to be compiled later by historians of the succeeding dynasty.[2] In China's long historiographical tradition, therefore, the writing of national history had been an integral component of dynastic historiography, its most celebrated historical practice. However, towards the beginning of the twentieth century when China was forced to enter the West-centered "modern" world, the practice of dynastic historiography came under siege—Chinese intellectuals began to use the term "national history" again, only to assign it with a different meaning that heralded a new experience the country was to go through in the years to come.

This new *Kuo-shih*, or national history writing, as I would like to argue, marked a turning point in modern Chinese historiography in the early twentieth century. In order to show its importance, let us take a look at its earliest advocates, or Chinese national historians of their very first generation. As is well known, China's entrance to the modern world was not a pleasant experience; it was fraught with defeats and humiliations. These shattering defeats and shameful losses urged some Chinese to search for means to regain wealth and power (*fu-ch'iang*) in the world outside of their own. The protagonists of my study were such a pioneer group of intellectuals who, while receiving a classical education when young, relentlessly pursued a new knowledge offered by the new world. Most of them sojourned in post-Meiji Japan at the turn of the nineteenth and the twentieth centuries, where they were exposed to Western learning through Japanese translation. As national historians, therefore, their interest in national history was inspired by the works of Japanese and Western predecessors. Leaders of this group were some well-known individuals in modern Chinese history, such as Chang Tai-yen (1868–1936) and Liu Shih-p'ei (1884–1919), whose accomplishments, in the past few decades, have caught the eyes of many students of Chinese history.[3] Yet few of these studies have looked at their historical careers and contributions from the perspective of Chinese historiography.

In 1905 when these individuals launched their careers in both politics and scholarship, they organized the National Learning Protection Society (*Kuo-hsüeh pao-ts'un-hui*) and published two journals: *National Essence Journal* (*Kuo-tsui hsüeh-pao*) and *Comprehensive Review of Politics and Arts* (*Cheng-i tung-pao*). While both journals were equally influential at the time, it was the *National Essence Journal* with which the group was most closely associated and how it was known in history: National Essence Group (*Kuo-tsui pai*).[4] Judging by the name of the group—"national essence," or "*kokusui*" in Japanese, and the timing of its formation, we see an apparent Japanese influence on these intellectuals. Considering their Japanese education, it is not surprising. In the 1880s and the 1890s, Miyake Setsurei and Shiga Shigetaka, two Japanese thinkers, invented and introduced the term "*kokusui*" into the Japanese language for translating the English word "nationality." By advocating the Japanese national essence, or nationality, Miyake and Shiga criticized the ongoing Westernization movement introduced by the Meiji Restoration a couple of decades earlier. In their opinion, the Westernization movement caused a great cultural turmoil in post-Meiji Japan and, as a result, the Japanese had become indifferent, if not oblivious, to their own cultural and national roots.

The decision of these Chinese intellectuals to use the term "national essence" was an example of the cultural and linguistic exchanges frequently seen between China and Japan at the turn of the twentieth-century. Studies have shown that it was quite common for the Chinese, at the time, to borrow neologisms in *kanji* (Chinese characters used in Japanese) created by the Japanese for accommodating Western terms and ideas.[5] The Chinese acceptance of these neologisms suggested not only the cleverness and proficiency of the Japanese in using Chinese characters—*kanji* by that time had been an important part in Japanese for over a millennium—but also a parallel experience between these two countries in coping with the Western intrusion. Both countries encountered the Western challenge in the mid-nineteenth century and, as China chose to fend it off through war, Japan decided, after witnessing China's defeat in the so-called Opium War (1838–42), to circumscribe it through diplomacy. Japan's attempt was hardly successful. But it did help the country to avert an ill-fated war and embark early on the cause of Westernization. Indeed, even before the Meiji Restoration (1868), in which the Japanese summrai (warriors) installed a Western-style government masked in a traditional power transition, Westernization movement had already well under its way in the country.

Thus viewed, although both countries bore similar experiences in encountering the West, there were visible differences between their approaches to coping with the experiences. In contrast to relatively quick actions taken by the Japanese summrai in absorbing knowledge from the West, the Chinese appeared hesitant and unwilling, adhering more to their long cultural tradition. As a result, the Chinese Westernization movement, focusing on importing advanced technology from the West, was not begun until the 1860s after the so-called Second Opium War, while in Japan the interest in Western learning, through the Meiji era, became gradually and steadily intensified and expanded to become a wholesale Westernization through the second half of the nineteenth century. There appeared hence a time gap, close to two decades, in the attitude toward Western learning in nineteenth-century Japan and China. And this gap caused an obvious and important difference in the use of the term National Essence by the intellectuals of the two countries.

When Miyake Setsurei and Shiga Shigetaka addressed the importance of cherishing the "national essence," for instance, they were concerned about Japan's national identity which, in their opinion, had become somehow obscured due to the overwhelming Western influence at the time. When the Chinese scholars came across the Japanese term National Essence and used it to name their journal two decades later in the early twentieth century, their interest derived from the same identity concern that had motivated their Japanese counterparts. However, their pursuit was situated in a different political and ideological milieu. To some Chinese intellectuals at the time, China's military weakness, shown not only in its previous defeats by Western powers but also in its recent shattering loss to Japan, proved that their country's problem lay in its grudging acceptance of advantageous foreign experiences. Liang Ch'i-ch'ao, an active political reformer as well as a prolific essayist, was among the earliest to have noticed the National Essence question raised by Japanese scholars.[6] However, when in 1902 he asked his friend Huang Tsun-hsien, a Chinese diplomat who had lived in and written a history of Japan, about it the latter drew Liang's attention to the difference between Japan and China in their experiences with the outside world. Huang wrote, Japan was:

> a country with a long history of cultural borrowing, and in recent years it had "worshipped" the West. Therefore, it was healthy for Japanese to develop a theory of nationalist essence. In China the problem was the persistence of bad old customs; therefore, "new" studies should be encouraged, and it would be a long time before any movement for national essence would be necessary.[7]

Huang's analysis provides us with one contemporary and critical view of the National Essence movement. In his eyes, this movement represented an untimely conservatism, unneeded by China.

Despite Huang's objection, the idea of National Essence remained attractive to some Chinese students in Japan; Liang Ch'i-ch'ao later renewed his interest in it.[8] After Liang, Huang Chieh (1873–1935), later a founder of the National Learning Protection Society, also noticed this cultural trend in

Japan. At the end of 1902, Huang published the first essay in Chinese, giving a comprehensive and sympathetic review of the Japanese National Essence school.[9] Three years later, in 1905, Huang and his friends Teng Shih (1877–?) and Ma Hsu-lun (1884–1970) founded the Society; they were later joined by Chang Tai-yen and Liu Shih-p'ei, and published the *National Essence Journal*. Their slogan was "to protect the race, to love the country, and to preserve the learning" (pao-chung, ai-kuo, tsun-hsüeh), suggesting a strong nationalist sentiment based on Han Chinese ethnicity and cultural tradition. Their emphasis on protecting the so-called Chinese race was related to the fact that China was then ruled by the Ch'ing Dynasty, founded by the Manchus. It reflected an anti-Manchu attitude, shared not only by the Society members but also by the revolutionaries such as Sun Yat-sen who, in the same year, organized the Revolutionary Alliance (Tung-meng-hui).

I. Imagining Modern in History

Huang Tsun-hsien's concern about the conservative side of the National Essence movement proved to be unjustified. Judging by the essays published in both the *National Essence Journal* and the *Comprehensive Review of Politics and Arts*, the Chinese National Essence group were different from their Japanese counterparts in both approach and agenda. Needless to say, both groups were motivated by nationalist impulses and thereby represented a nativist intellectual reaction to the Westernization movement. As noticed by Cheng Shih-chu, however, the Chinese group not only was charged by a revolutionary motive, absent from the Japanese experience, but pursued the nationalist goal with a more traditional and historical perspective. Compared to Shiga and Miyake, who were modern scholars with scientific and/or professional training, Chinese National Essence promoters were schooled more or less in classical learning; their understanding of the "new" knowledge remained superficial compared to their Japanese contemporaries and their own countrymen of later generations.[10] Perhaps because of that, the Chinese group felt much more comfortable at adopting a historical approach in their presentation of the National Essence, whereas the Japanese scholars were more drawn to the characteristics, both physical and spiritual, of modern Japan to identify the "uniqueness" of the Japanese nationality, refusing "to link it [National Essence] up to either Shinto Buddhism, Confucianism, or any specific religion or philosophy."[11]

What I mean by a "historical approach" refers to the attempt made by the Chinese National Essence group to trace the Chinese National Essence in the country's past. Compared to their Japanese precursors, thus the Chinese group were more interested in cultural elements in the Chinese tradition. To present the national characteristics of China's cultural tradition, historical study constituted an effective medium. In their journals, especially the *National Essence Journal*, we can find a number of essays that were intended to trace the origins and principles of institutions, customs, culture, and scholarship. For example, Liu Kuang-han (1884–?) wrote a series of essays in the journal, discussing the development of China's political system, territory, family system, rulership, law, land ownership, school, social class, and music, which appeared in almost every issue for the entire first year. Tien Pei-hu's long treatise on the evolution of scholarship, too, was serialized in several issues.[12] More importantly, not all historical essays, such as the above two, were necessarily published in the designated "history" column. Essays on a topic in history could appear almost anywhere, sometimes as the lead article, sometimes in the columns "culture" and "scholarship," and sometimes in "politics," "forum," and/or "letters." To a certain extent, we can say that the whole journal was centered on history, making it the most favorite subject for both the journal editors and contributors.

This strong interest shared by the National Essence group is not coincidental, but reflective of their understanding of the National Essence idea. In the broadest sense, these Chinese intellectuals simply equated National Essence with Chinese culture and history. In his "Introductory Remarks" to the journal, Teng Shih, one of the journal editors and its most prolific contributor, stated that, paraphrasing Ssu-ma Chien, the goal of scholarship was to obtain a historical perspective on the changes that had taken place in different time periods. To that end, they must arm themselves with a variety of knowledge, domestic and foreign, and past and present. This historical perspective was most necessary for perceiving and preserving the National Essence. In fact, Teng claimed, since there had not been such a perspective developed in the past, China's National Essence was no longer clear to many Chinese. And this problem—the lack of understanding of their own National Essence among his own compatriots—was exacerbated in more recent times by the confusion caused by the Western intrusion.[13]

Chang Tai-yen took the same historical approach to defining the National Essence. He stated that it was the same as history in its broadest sense, which "included three categories: spoken and written languages; institutions and laws, and people's ideas and actions." He then offered his suggestion for how to preserve and promote the "Essence" (tsui). In order to discover and preserve the Essence, one must distinguish right from wrong and important from unimportant, using both subjective and objective means.[14] The subjective means referred to the way in which one passes his/her moral judgment whereas the objective means, defined by Chang, referred to a historical judgment. Chang believed that while one historical event could be reckoned with in different ways, either politically or morally, its importance was often unequivocal to many. Like Teng, therefore, Chang called upon his colleagues to engage in a careful study of China's past.

Historical study was necessary because, in Huang Chieh's opinion, it helped explain why China failed to develop a scientific knowledge in the same way as the West had, which resulted in its failure in competing with modern powers in the world. This failure was not a mistake in the recent past. Rather, Huang argued, it was caused by Ch'in-shih-huang, China's first emperor in the Ch'in Dynasty, who ordered books and scholars burned and buried in the early third century B.C.[15] To offset the aftermath of this atrocity committed over two thousand years ago, one must first discover the national spirit and essence in China's remote past, namely the pre-Ch'in period. Secondly, one must learn from other cultures, for the "National Essence was not the same as what had been produced by our country [in later times]." To make his point, Huang offered a metaphor. Plants and flowers can grow very well in a strange land. One is often amazed by their ability and vitality in adjusting to the new environment. However, what really deserves one's attention ought to be the land that accepts them. In other words, Huang believed that once the plants take root in the land, they become part of the native, no longer foreign. He explained:

> If what is suitable and appropriate happens to be produced by our country, it is of course the National Essence. However, if what is workable happens to be from foreign countries, it should also be seen as the National Essence.[16]

Huang Chieh's understanding of the National Essence seems to have a great influence on his colleagues. To be sure, given the limitation of their knowledge of the Western world, the National Essence activists could not engage in a study of Western culture; this work did not gain a full momentum until the New Culture Movement of the 1920s.[17] But they did make, from time to time, comparative remarks and observations.

Likewise, Huang's observation of the supposed breakdown of Chinese culture in the Ch'in Dynasty was a point of departure for the group's endeavor. It provided an important theoretical premise for their proposed National Essence study. As discussed above, to these intellectuals, the National Essence was not something that had always existed in China, nor was it a castle in the air. It was rather something in between. It had existed before in the remote past but later became diluted and distorted, and eventually disappeared. Their work therefore was to recover and revive it. To do so, they must try to remove all the historical debris and remains that had buried it for the last two millennia.

Besides the term National Essence which the group borrowed from their Japanese scholars, they also liked the term "National Studies" (Kuo-hsüeh). Since their definition of the National Essence, as seen in Huang Chich's discussion, was not based on national boundaries at their time, they also defined the meaning of National Studies from a historical viewpoint. When they proposed National Studies, they did not mean to study Chinese learning at their time. Instead they were interested in the much earlier and purer form of Chinese culture in the remote past prior to the Ch'in Dynasty. In their minds, the National Studies were equivalent to the "studies of antiquity" (Ku-hsüeh), a term which they invented themselves; for them the two terms were almost interchangeable.

Teng Shih, who first to recommended National Studies, wrote a lead article entitled "On the Origins of National Studies" (Kuo-hsüeh yuen-lun), which appeared in the first issue of the *National Essence Journal*. He tried to identify two schools in the pre-Ch'in period, the "ghosts and gods school" (Kui-shen hsüeh-pai) and the "technique and number school" (Shu-shu hsüeh-pai). These names do not make much sense to most of his contemporaries. What Teng intended to do was to trace and present a scientific element in ancient Chinese culture. He argued that scholarship originated in ancient times from the people's observation of nature. Since they were not able to explain fully all the natural phenomena, they worshipped ghosts and gods and developed religious and cultural rituals, hence the "ghosts and gods school." When ancient people gained more knowledge of their environment, they worked out more systematic and sophisticated theories, such as the "five elements" (wuxing) thesis; based on which they also developed social and political theories. To be sure, Teng pointed out, both schools appeared primitive and superstitious to most modern people, but religious ideas and rituals were the origin of scholarship in many cultures.[18] His viewpoint was echoed by Liu Kuang-han, who wrote "On Religion as an Origin of Ancient Learning."[19] Besides religion, Liu also supported Teng in stating that the rise of ancient scholarship was due to people's experience with nature.[20] In other words, while they acknowledged the religious influence, they also attempted to add a scientific element, one's observation of heaven and earth, as a most fundamental source of ancient culture.

Having explained the meaning of National Studies, Teng and Liu then drew one's attention to China's antiquity. Their real purpose, as I understand it, was to propose a hypothesis that had there not been the cultural breakdown caused by the Ch'in unification, Chinese culture could have moved in a different direction and might have gained a quite different appearance than the one the modern Chinese saw at the time. Of course, it was a bit too late to reverse the course of Chinese cultural development that had moved along for the last two thousand years. But Teng and his colleagues felt it necessary to trace the most remote and therefore most authentic cultural origin in ancient China and also to seek a way to revive it and make it the basis of the National Studies.

To that end, Teng Shih called for the revival of antiquity. Several months after he wrote the "On the Origins of National Studies," Teng published another important essay entitled "On the Revival of Ancient Learning" (Ku-hsüeh fu-hsinglun), in which he presented his thesis in a more definitive way: the development of Chinese culture was interrupted by several events in the Ch'in Dynasty and the following Han Dynasty, such as Ch'in-shih-huang's burning of the books and the Wu Emperor of Han's promotion of Confucianism in the second century B.C., which, consequently, suppressed the development of other schools of thought. The task for modern Chinese was to revive the ancient form of Chinese culture of the pre-Ch'in period. To drive home his argument, Teng drew readers' attention to the path of development in Western culture. In fact, the phrase "Revival of Ancient Learning" (Ku-hsüeh fu-hsing) was Teng's translation of the term Renaissance. Modern Western culture, he observed, was first developed in the Renaissance period when classical culture of ancient Greece and Rome was brought back to life and became the foundation of modern literature, law, and philosophy. "If the fifteenth century witnessed the revival of ancient European culture," Teng proclaimed, "then the twentieth century should be the period for reviving of ancient Asian culture."[21]

Like nationalists of many other countries, the endeavor of the National Essence group obtained a bifurcated characteristic. At one end, of course, there was an overt nationalist sentiment out of their keen concern over China's supposedly belated awakening to the modern world. At the other end, however, this sentiment led them to search for a remote yet ideal past that had, as they claimed, been buried long ago due to various reasons. Their cause, as shown above, involved efforts to imagine and invoke a historical past that were at once "modern" and "ancient." Benedict Anderson states, "If nation-states are widely conceded to be 'new' and 'historical,' the nations to which they give political expression always loom out of an immemorial past, and, still more important, glide into a limitless future."[22] It was ancient because the past was so distant from one's memory. But it was also modern because, as these intellectuals found, it contained possible elements, in its most original form, for building the modern nation.

II. Reconstructing Tradition

If the creation of nation involves imagination of a historical past, this imagination is premised on a new understanding of tradition, which is what connects the imagined past and the imagining present. In his important work, *Nations before Nationalism*, John Armstrong has made it clear that in the case of Europe, where one witnessed the first tide of nationalism, there had been elements such as nomadism that were conducive to the growth of modern nations.[23] Of course, opposite cases are abundant too. When Eric Hobsbawm made his famous phrase, "inventing tradition," I think he tried to emphasize the fact that in most cases, nationalists must make anew the cultural tradition they inherited from the past.[24] Hobsbawm does not mean that the invention can totally discard the past. Invention, as suggested by Anthony Smith, often constitutes a process of reconstruction.[25]

In the case of twentieth-century China, to create a modern nation involves both reconstruction and invention. If Armstrong's thesis can hold, China in its long past has made frequent contacts with the nomadic world. As a result, a sense of ethnic identity ought not be entirely strange and for-eign to the Chinese. In fact, when the National Essence group began to tap the nationalist sentiment, they wasted no time in kindling the ethnic feeling of the Han Chinese against the Manchu rulers of the Ch'ing Dynasty. The same strategy was also used at the time by the revolutionaries led by Sun Yat-sen. Their dislike of the fact that China was ruled by a non-Han ethnic group showed the political side of the group's activity. The other side of the same coin was the group's cultural endeavor. In order to present a pure form of "Han Chinese culture," Teng Shih, Liu Kuang-han and others all fixed their eyes on China's most remote past.

However, no matter how nostalgic they appeared and how much they intended to discover, invent, an ideal past in ancient China, they could not eschew the less pure, less ideal legacy they had inherited at the time. In other words, in order to carry out the task of changing China, they must deal with tradition, or the cultural heritage with which they grew up and were most familiar. Needless to say, they disliked it, just as they disliked the Manchu rule. The *National Essence Journal* published a number of essays that sharply criticized the Chinese cultural tradition from the Ch'in-Han period onward. At the same time, they hastened to point out that a country without "scholarship" (hsüeh) would be even more disheartened and devastated. In Teng Shih's words, "People these days tend to say that national learning presented no usefulness for the country. But they don't know that what caused a country's weakness is its lack of scholarship, not vice versa." For that reason, he and his colleagues proposed to establish the National Essence School (Kuo-tsui hsüeh-t'ang), whose curriculum included such traditional subjects as classics, history, and philosophy as normally seen in the Ch'ing Dynasty, and new disciplines like psychology, religion, sociology, archaeology, politics, and law.[26] If scholarship of a country is extinguished, the group warned, then the country would become really doomed.[27]

The group's ambivalent attitude toward scholarly activity—considering it both the cause and cure for China's modern ills—was also extended to Western culture. In their criticism of the Chinese tradition, Western culture was held to be a yardstick, or a mirror, and was used to measure and reflect the problems in China's past. For example, by some superficial comparison, they quickly pointed out that from the Ch'in Dynasty onward, Chinese scholarship served only aristocrats and monarchs. In Teng Shih's words, knowledge in China belonged only to the monarch, not to the people. All forms of knowledge, namely those about cultural customs, political theories, institutional development, and scholarship, were monarchal rather than democratic. If one wanted to divide them, then sixty percent was for the monarch and the rest was for his ministers; nothing was left for the people.

Teng went on to take the six classics as an example and broke them down to make his point. Except the *Classic of Music*, which was no longer available, he analyzed:

> The *Classic of Changes* recorded the deeds of the so-called Three Emperors and Five Kings in the Hsia, Shang and Chou Dynasties, the *Classic of Poetry* were collections of poems to be presented to the kings, the *Classic of Rites* had nothing to do with commoners, and the *Spring and Autumn Annals* were a pure monarchical text.[28]

In a word, if the six classics were compared to a fishing net, the monarch was its headrope and his ministers were its meshes.

To the National Essence group, Western learning was not only a contrast to the Chinese cultural tradition, but also a serious competitor for the proposed national learning. It had already become a fashion, the group noticed, that many in the country tended to look up to Western culture and look down upon the Chinese. "Today's people," wrote Liu Shih-p'ei, "follow only what is the powerful and stay away from the old. Even if they read old texts, they still want to compare them with Western works."[29] It is worth noticing that Liu made these remarks for the third anniversary of the *National Essence*

Journal. The group seemed to have lost earlier enthusiasm for the exemplary Western experience and became more concerned about its hegemonic influence. Teng Shih, the journal's frequent contributor, also warned his readers about the extinction of the native Chinese scholarly tradition.[30] In his study of modern nationalism in India, Partha Chatterjee has found that while Asian nationalists were inspired by their Western precursors, they also pursued a different approach to the national identity question; they were aware of the cultural "difference" from the modular forms of the Western experience.[31] Chatterjee's analysis seems quite illuminating for the case discussed here.

Accordingly, while criticizing the monarch-centered scholarship in traditional China, the National Essence group made sure that the criticism would not lead to a total rejection of Chinese learning. To Teng Shih and his colleagues, China's past was not singular, but plural; what they intended to do was to make clear distinctions among these pasts and choose one that was suitable and even conducive to the changes they, the modern Chinese, would like to introduce to the country. In defining the meaning of National Learning and defending its usefulness, Teng Shih carefully differentiated it from "monarchical learning" (chün-hsüeh) and advised people not to mix one with the other. In fact, he proclaimed, these two forms of learning formed an antithetical relation; one's rise would cause the decline of the other. What was unfortunate was, according to Teng, from the Han Dynasty onward scholarship in China was by and large centered around the interest of the monarch, which made the task of National Studies ever more difficult as well as compelling.[32]

If the Chinese cultural tradition after the Han Dynasty was essentially a monarch-oriented one, how did the National Essence group view the Confucian legacy? Naturally, the group did not consider the legacy a healthy one, as they strove to discover the more suitable and better "other" in China's pasts. In the meantime, they did not consider Confucianism an "unchanging and invariant" tradition either.[33] Their critique of Confucianism was historicist. On the one hand they regarded it as a most important cultural and political heritage, one with which modern scholars should reckon with care and respect. On the other hand, they wasted no time in blaming the disappearance of the ancient, hence the more authentic, form of national learning on the ascendance of Confucianism in the Han. Teng Shih wrote, "After the Han Dynasty China's scholarship was seen only in Confucianism and Confucianism was seen only in the six classics." Yet before the Han, Teng found, Chinese scholarship had presented itself in different forms. Prior to the Spring and Autumn period, it was characterized by the "ghosts and gods school," as he pointed out elsewhere. "Afterwards it was centered around history up till the Han Dynasty when Confucianism came to acquire the dominant position. Since then, alas, there has been very little change for over two thousand years."[34]

The recognition of Confucianism as an official ideology by the Wu Emperor of Han, therefore, caused other ancient schools of thought to fall into oblivion. In fact, those schools that had once flourished and competed with Confucianism in the pre-Ch'in period eventually were cast out almost entirely from the Chinese tradition. Because of their disappearance, there also went any possibly useful elements from which the country could have perhaps benefited in modern times. "From the Chou to the Ch'in," Teng Shih pointed out, "China experienced the proliferation of scholarship. There were hundreds of schools and many philosophers competing with one another." As a result, many modern subjects that were later developed and only seen in the West had appeared in ancient China, such as logic, law, theology, mathematics, medicine, and military strategy. Their appearance was not only contemporaneous of ancient Greek culture but also, Teng believed, comparable to the latter in quality. But after the Wu Emperor of Han's promotion of Confucianism, in a rather coercive way, many of the knowledge contained in those schools were forever lost. To some extent, he lamented, the promotion of Confucianism in the Han was worse than Ch'in-shih-huang's burning of the books and the destruction of Hsien-yang capital in a revolt against the Ch'in, for it played a more direct part in causing the disappearance of ancient schools of thought in the Chinese tradition.[35]

Nevertheless, the group understood that the Wu Emperor of Han's choice of Confucianism over other philosophical schools was political rather than intellectual. It therefore did no justice to Confucianism if one blamed it for all the perceived problems in Chinese tradition. In fact, according to Teng Shih, one should perhaps thank Confucius for his preservation of ancient learning as he edited the six classics. Of course, when Confucius edited them he had made some changes. As a result, it was difficult for later scholars to recover the original texts. But without his editing work, the Tao of ancient sage-kings would have forever fallen into oblivion, for China experienced a chaotic period from the late Chou to the early Ch'in.[36] Hence the National Essence group held an ambiguous attitude toward Confucianism. On the one hand they exercised a historicist viewpoint and appreciated that Confucious played a role in protecting ancient texts in which, they believed, the National Essence could be discovered. On the other hand, they regretted the fact that what was preserved in Confucianism was just part of ancient learning; they were more interested in learning more about it.

Confucianism therefore became both the object of their criticism as well as the subject of their research. In their study, the National Essence group soon realized that they had to adopt the same way in treating Confucianism as they treated National Essence, namely they needed to take a historical approach and discover the real Confucianism that had been hidden in the disguise of Han scholarship. Liu Kuang-han, for example, wrote an essay entitled "On Real Confucian Learning" (Kung-hsüeh chen-lun) in which he argued that Confucianism (Ju-hsüeh) and Confucian Learning (Kung-hsüeh) were two different ideas; the latter was not only earlier, hence original, but also more comprehensive. First of all, echoing Teng, Liu stated that Confucian Learning rose on the foundation of Chou scholarship; it played a role of a cultural transmitter. Secondly, in its transmission, Confucian Learning absorbed a variety of ideas from many other schools, such as the Mohist school, the Yin and Yang school, Legalism, and even Taoism. However, he lamented, in later times Confucian Learning was replaced by Confucianism, gradually losing its comprehensiveness and becoming both dogmatic and exclusive. Through his dissection, Liu presented the Confucian legacy in two sides. He praised on one hand its educational emphasis and political pragmatism and criticized its disinterest in nature and natural science on the other.[37]

As the National Essence group called for a historical evaluation of the Chinese cultural heritage, they had to deal with China's long historiographical tradition. Indeed, for the group, history was at once a useful method and an important subject. History was important because, following the teaching of Chang Hsüeh-ch'eng, a Ch'ing historian whom the group regarded very highly, all ancient texts, including the classics, were historical accounts.[38] Teng Shih wrote that in searching for the National Essence, one should look not only for the origin of scholarly activity, which, as he already found, was the so-called "ghosts and gods school," but also for its basis that was history. In his words, "The knowledge of Heaven and men was in the hands of the historian (shih) in the early Three Ages." The historian as a court official was responsible for everything, ranging from government, religion, and society to geography and cultural rituals. As a result, all important philosophers such as Lao-tzu, Confucius, and Mo-tzu played the role of historian in their times.[39]

However, although the National Essence group intended to follow these ancient examples to become the historians of Chinese culture, they were not satisfied with the status quo of historical study in their time. To them China's long historiographical tradition offered little help for their work. Rather it demonstrated many shortfalls of the Chinese tradition they mostly disliked, such as its sole interest in dynastic succession, the monarch-minister relation, and its negligence of the common people. The group's attitude toward the status quo of historiography was best shown in an interesting quote in one of Teng Shih's essays. It goes as follows:

> What is unfortunate is not that China does not have history, but that it does not have good historians. It is not because of no historians but because of no attempt [at history]. It is not because of no attempt but because of no good method [in history]. It is not because of no method but because of no passion [for history]. It is not because of no passion but because of no title [for history]. It is not because of no title but because of no previous model [in historiography]. Without all these, history cannot exist. Without history there will be no scholarship and without scholarship there will be no national state.[40]

Despite his rhetorical circumlocution, Teng Shih made it quite clear that in order for the group to discover and display the National Essence in China's past, they must first change the way in which history was written and studied.

III. National History in Chinese Historiography

Indeed, that a Historiographical Revolution (shih-chieh ko-ming) was necessary had already become a consensus among many Chinese intellectuals in the early twentieth century. Although Liang Ch'i-ch'ao coined the term in his *New Historiography* (Hsin shih-hsüeh) in 1902, it was the National Essence group who conscientiously pursued its cause and made some initial yet substantive contributions to its growth. In studying the genesis of modern Chinese historiography many scholars, Chinese and Western alike, have noticed rather naturally Liang Ch'i-ch'ao's role and have given it an extensive coverage.[41] It was not until quite recently that the work of the National Essence group also received some attention.[42] To a great extent, the group shared Liang's many ideas in criticizing traditional historiography, especially his eagerness to make history useful for the nationalist cause.

Liang Ch'i-ch'ao began his *New Historiography* with a strong statement:

> Of the subjects studied in Western countries today, history is the only one which has existed in China for a long time. History is the foundation of scholarship. It is also a mirror of people's nature and the origin of patriotism. The rise of nationalism in Europe and the growth of modern European countries are owing in a great part to the study of history. But how can one explain the fact that, despite this long tradition of historical study in China, the Chinese people are so disunited and China's social condition is so bad?[43]

Huang Chieh, the historian of the National Essence group who wrote the famous *Yellow History* (Huang-shih), the first national history in modern China, made a similar observation:

> Western thinkers believe that history is related to nation and race. In the historical meeting held in Berlin, they declared that the historian's first and foremost task was to advocate nationalism and promote new citizenship. Otherwise the nation would be overrun by a foreign hegemony.[44]

Both Liang and Huang advocated national history, of which they indirectly gained some knowledge from the Japanese translations. In his recent survey of the development of national history in modern China, Yü Ying-shih states that "the new conception of national history as enthusiastically espoused by the new generation of Chinese scholars in the early twentieth century was not an innovation on their part but primarily a borrowing from the West via Japan."[45]

As known to many, Liang Ch'i-ch'ao wrote his *New Historiography* in his exile in Japan where he learned the language and used it to become acquainted with Western theories in politics, economics, history and sociology.[46] Chang Tai-yen, an important member of the National Essence group, had a similar experience. In 1902 Liang and Chang, who had just returned from Japan, corresponded with each other, discussing the possibility of writing a new history of China and departing it from the annals-biographic tradition in Chinese historiography. What distinguished Chang from Liang was that the latter coined the term "new history," whereas Chang chose to call it "general history" (T'ung-shih), a term that had been used before. In Chang's plan for such a "general history," he wanted to go beyond the outlines of dynastic succession and offer a more comprehensive account about the Chinese people. This suggests that his "general history," if ever written, would have been broader in scope and different in perspective than the general histories of Ssu-ma Chien and Ssu-ma Kuang in the past. Chang acknowledged that it was Japanese historians who provided inspirations for his idea about it.[47]

Compared to the practice of national history Liang and the National Essence group perceived in the Western experience, the Chinese tradition of historical writing appeared woefully inadequate and culturally obsolete for their pursuit of a modern China. Despite their different political outlooks on China's future—Liang remained attracted to the idea of a constitutional monarchy whereas the National Essence group were anti-Manchu revolutionaries—they were equally interested in changing historical writing in China. Their complaints against the Chinese historiographical tradition were focused on three areas.[48]

First, they criticized its content. Traditional historians focused their writings on the royal family, especially the reigning emperor. They recorded in detail how the emperor ascended to the throne, chose the color for his dynasty, decided his calendar, paid his sacrifice to Heaven, and gave his edicts to his subjects. When the emperor went onto an inspection tour or waged a military campaign against foreign kingdoms or rebellions, he would receive extensive coverage in history books. In fact, even if the emperor chose to do nothing particular, his words and deeds would still be recorded into the *Chi-chü-chu* and the *Shih-lu*, as demanded by the tradition. As a result, the National Essence group charged, "there was only history of the monarch but no history of the people" in dynastic historiography. History became an account that only interested "one person and one family," but not the entire nation. It left out many aspects the group considered essential to historical writing, such as culture and customs, economics and finance that were related to the lives of ordinary people. Concisely, as Hsu Chih-heng put it, dynastic histories "were nothing but the records of the changing names of the monarchical families. . . . It is not an exaggeration to say that the twenty four dynastic histories were twenty four genealogies of the royal families."[49] His conclusion is almost identical to Liang Ch'i-ch'ao's criticism in *New Historiography*, in which Liang said that "the twenty-four dynastic histories are not real history (chen li-shih), but twenty four genealogies."[50]

Second, they disliked the approach of traditional historians to historical interpretation. In fact, they did not think that traditional historians had ever thought about interpreting historical movement; they had only wanted to record events according to the order of chronology. As they were so fond of recording events, they were not interested in finding out a relation among

historical events. Consequently, Chang Tai-yen noted, there was no clear outline of the evolution of Chinese civilization. Teng Shih went even farther and
declared that China "had no history" for "history must have its spirit. What
is strange was that in China's three thousand year history, there was no history of the spirit."[51] What Teng meant by "the spirit in history" is, as I
understand it, not an idealistic, hence Hegelian, abstraction that directs the
movement of history from above, but the attempt by the historian to develop a perspective on historical interpretation. Teng's remarks should remind
us of Liang Ch'i-ch'ao's attack on traditional historians for their inability to
offer historical insights (pie-ts'ai).[52]

Third, the National Essence group did not believe that traditional historiography was even factual. Since historical writing was always under the
tight control of the ruling dynasty, most historians, except Ssu-ma Chien and
Pan Ku whose relations with the rulers were a bit ambiguous, did not study
history for the public. In order to justify the founding of their dynasty, they
often condemned the previous emperor and even a few of his predecessors.
On the other side, they would refrain from saying anything negative about
the reigning royal family. The main reason, as understood by the National
Essence group, was that historical writings in imperial China served a very
different purpose than the one in their mind. Past historians never understood the necessity of writing a national history centering on the common
people. This was what Liang Ch'i-ch'ao meant that "old historians" (chiu
shih-chia) only knew "individuals" (ko-jen) but not "group/communities"
(chün-ti).[53]

The group's main concern was shown in their criticism of the historical
writing in the Ch'ing Dynasty. This is of course related to their political
stance against the Manchu rule of China. But it is also because they had a
better knowledge about the situation in their own time. They were very
much worried about the fact that due to the intellectual oppression under the
Ch'ing, many historical records were irrevocably lost. As a result, historians
of later times might never be able to know what was really going on in the
Ch'ing. In addition, even if there were records, these records might not show
the real situation due to the government corruption. These criticisms show,
as Charlotte Furth notes, that despite their strong political agenda, the
National Essence group also showed an interest in the so-called "disinterested history," which had two meanings:

> Intellectually, disinterested history implied that there is an objective
> historical truth and that obstacles to knowing it lie simply in the prej-
> udicial use of evidence. Socially it was a protest against two thousand
> years of scholarship in the service of the state—including that of schol-
> ar-officials in the service of the Manchu dynasty—as gentlemen made
> careers through mastering the classics for examinations and made pub-
> lic policy by manipulating the canon to support their plans.[54]

In fact, to the National Essence group, the writing of "disinterested history" was identical to their pursuit of national history; the latter in their

opinion was scientific and public, hence more factual than the dynastic histories whose purpose was only for serving the royal family.

With such a strong belief and commitment, the National Essence group embarked on the writing of national history. In Huang Chieh's *Yellow History*, which appeared as a series of essays in the *National Essence Journal* starting in its very first issue, he traced following Ssu-ma Chien the beginning of the Chinese nation to its legendary Yellow Emperor (Huang-ti), and declared that "all later generations shared the same origin." However, Huang Chieh was not so proud of China's long history, for in subsequent centuries, Han China was overrun by many non-Han groups who occupied China proper. As a result, though there were more than twenty so-called "standard histories" (cheng-shih), many of these were written under the rules of an alien dynasty. In fact, Huang noted, in China's four thousand year history, over thirty percent of the time China was ruled under an alien government, which was "the shame of Chinese national history." "That China is no longer a country," Huang sighed, "is more than the historian can tell." Yet since there were few in the past who actually composed a history of the Han Chinese nation, Huang believed, it was necessary for the people to know about their country's shame in history. "In our four thousand year history, there were only individual biographies, not histories of the society. Although ethnic differences remained, there was not much progress in our society." As a believer in evolution, Huang stated that if a nation failed to go forward, then it would only go backward, for others had progressed. The purpose of his writing was not to share with his countrymen how great their nation had always been, as seen in many writings of national history, but to present the evidence (events and figures) of the once glorious yet now declining Han Chinese nation.[55] Like the humanists in the Renaissance, Huang and his colleagues developed a tripartite interpretation of Chinese history. They admired China's antiquity and attempted its revival, or the Chinese renaissance. In the meantime, they despised its subsequent decline in the later ages and attributed China's current weakness to it. In their outlook for China's future they, again by following the example of the Renaissance, placed their hope on the revival of ancient culture and considered scholarly pursuit the first and sole means to the end of preserving both the Han Chinese nation and culture. Huang stated, "if history goes out, our country and race will go along with it." With such an understanding, he decided to write the *Yellow History* in over two hundred chapters under the categories of "treatise" (shu), "chronological tables" (piao), "biographies" (chi) and so on,[56] and began it with the chapter on the origin of the Chinese race.

While Huang held that the Yellow Emperor was the common ancestor of the Chinese people, he, like his colleagues such as Chang Tai-yen and Liu Shih-p'ei, believed that the Chinese race originated in West Asia. Following the theory of Terrien de Lacouperie (1844–94), a French sinologist brought up in Hong Kong, Huang wrote that the Yellow Emperor was the leader of the Baks, an ancient people who arose from West Asia, or Chaldea, and entered China proper in the third millennium B.C. Having defeated the aborigines, they established their political dominance in the region.[57] It is of course quite strange that a committed nationalist like Huang Chieh would accept Lacouperie's theory and believe the Western origin of the ancient Chinese people. But the theory definitely had its special appeal, as analyzed by both Yü Ying-shih and Martin Bernal.[58] To name just one thing, Lacouperie's thesis was intended to suggest that given the Western origin, Chinese culture contained compatible elements to modern Western culture. This finding lent a strong support to the National Essence group for their search of "modern" traces in China's distant past. It reinforced their main argument that the key to the success of a modern China lay in the revival of its ancient culture, which was vigorous as well as Western. Chang Tai-yen made it most clear why the group bought Lacouperie's theory, as quoted by Bernal, "The Chinese race came from Chaldea. . . . Early Greeks were from Chaldea as were the Romans, Saxons, and Slavs."[59]

At this point, we can perhaps discuss the group's attempt at the construction of the Chinese nation and national history. Much has already been said about their effort to change the Chinese worldview held in the past.[60] As known to many, prior to the nineteenth century when the Chinese were forced to make close contacts with Western powers, they had developed a firm belief in a world that was centered on China. The Chinese perception of the world, or "all under Heaven" (Tien-hsia), was not only unitary, it was also unified under the Son of Heaven who was supposed to carry Heaven's mandate for his rule. Heaven's mandate was defined first by culture, namely the Confucian teaching, and later by space, or the occupation of China proper, which allowed historians to accommodate in their writings the rules of alien government from the tenth century onward.[61] In any case, the search of the National Essence group for national history had a great impact on changing the Sinocentric view of the world. To be sure, in the second half of the nineteenth century, Lin Tse-hsü, Wei Yuan, and others had noted the existence of the Western and other worlds, it was however the National Essence group who, by proposing the writing of national history, replaced the Sinocentric worldview with a pluralist worldview. China was now considered a member of many nations.

Nevertheless, the group's acceptance of the Western origin of the Chinese nation suggests that what they have done is more complex than recognizing the changes in the world. No doubt the group realized that the view of a Sinocentric world could no longer hold. But their emphasis on the Chaldean presence in ancient China, especially Chang Tai-yen's consideration of the Chaldeans as the common origin of the peoples in both China and the West, suggests that they have not completely departed from the unitary approach to perceiving the world in earlier times. With regard to their openness to new theories seen in the West, we should agree with Yü Ying-shih's criticism of Martin Bernal and others that the National Essence group ought not be regarded "as a conservative strain in modern Chinese intellectual history."[62] But their emphasis on world unity (although they later turned their backs on Lacouperie), suggests that they were not immune to the influence of traditional thinking.

In fact, the group's wavering between the modern and the ancient is what characterized their search for China's national history. Homi Bhabha has argued that the nationalist discourse is often ambivalent and Janus-faced.

"It is an exact statement about nationalism," he quotes Tom Nairn, "to say that it is by nature ambivalent." And the "the ambivalent figure of the nation is a problem of its transitional history, its conceptual indeterminacy, its wavering between vocabularies. . . ."[63] As much as the National Essence group liked Lacouperie's thesis on the Western origin of ancient China, they also insisted on the distinctness of Chinese culture through its long evolution. As noted by Yü Ying-shih, Chang Tai-yen and Liu Shih-p'ei, who championed Lacouperie's theory, emphasized more the cultural than the racial aspect in their nationalist discourse.[64] From the cultural perspective, Chinese culture heroes Fu Hsi and Shen Nung "were universal rulers who introduced all civilization."[65] This kind of wavering reminds us of their ambivalent attitude, as shown earlier, toward the contrasting and competitive relationship between Chinese and Western learning. The issue here is that in constructing a national identity for modern China, to borrow Homi Bhabha's analysis once more, the group wanted not only to "recall the past as social cause or aesthetic precedent," but also to renew it, "refiguring it as a contingent 'in-between' space, that innovates and interrupts the performance of the present."[66]

History—the "in-between" space of past and present—is therefore revisited for new reasons that require some alteration of the past. Needless to say, "The most compelling motive for altering the past is to change the present."[67] But as many know, what one can really alter is not the past but history, or a society's collective memory of its past in a given time. The nationalist discourse of the National Essence group not only provided a new perspective on China's past, but also paved a way for a new direction in Chinese historiography and historical thinking. Viewed in the development of the history of Chinese historical writing, the group's approach to history served as a distinct turning point. Its significance has gone beyond national history per se and has touched many areas central to modern Chinese historiography.

First, they came to appreciate the difference between what should be called historical events and what is considered its records, or historical writings and sources, thereby redefined the nature of historical study. According to Ma Hsu-lun, history has two meanings: one refers to what happened in the past and the other refers to what is recorded by historians. The term "history" (shih) therefore can be viewed in two aspects: "name" (ming) and "content" (shih); the former begins at the dawn of human civilization whereas the latter coincides with the very beginning of the universe. In other words, the so-called content of history existed long before one began to have a historical consciousness. But, Ma argues, it is one's desire for knowing the past that made historical study a special subject in scholarly learning, which could be named as "the study of history" (li-shih chih-hsüeh). More importantly, since historical study is a product of human civilization, it is naturally written for the further development of civilization.[68] Through his etymological analysis of the origin of historiography, Ma assigned both a purpose and a new meaning to historical study.

Secondly, given the group's primary interest in the study of history, they began to view history more as an independent, autonomous discipline than as a supplement to the study of the classics. Many of their writings on history were aimed at offering a systematic review of the tradition of Chinese historiography, which turned them into the pioneers of historiographical study in modern China. Lu Shao-ming, for example, studied the Chinese historiographical tradition from many perspectives. He noticed the change of focus in the works of historians at different periods of time. While the initial purpose of historical writing was for political experience and moral teaching, it became more and more interested in faithful recording in a later time, as exemplified by Ssu-ma Chien's *Historical Records* (Shih-chi). Historiographical changes, in his opinion, often corresponded to the change of history, or the manners, morals, and intellectual climate of the time.[69] Lu's interest in the study of historiography also enabled him to discern different historiographical schools by ideas and methods. He found, for instance, that although similar in appearance, the twenty-four dynastic histories were actually quite different in their approaches and emphases; all depended on the preference and training of their composers.[70]

Thirdly, in keeping with their interest in new ideas of historical study, they have greatly expanded the Chinese historians' horizon. In addition to their pioneering study of the history of Chinese historiography, National Essence historians suggested many new fields in historical study. Liu Kuang-han, for instance, published a series essays that appeared in the first five issues of the *National Essence Journal*, proposing a variety of new fields, such as intellectual history, psychohistory, ethic history, social history, religious history, military history, history of science, history of education, history of philosophy, history of mathematics, history of artifacts, history of languages, and history of law. In proposing these new fields, Liu Kuang-han was of course inspired by the examples of both Japanese and Western historians. But what is interesting was that he also believed that these were components of pre-Ch'in Chinese scholarship. This is probably why Yü Ying-shih said that "National Essence historians by and large tried to justify Western values in terms of Chinese tradition."[71] In this justification, new ideas are integrated, congenially and persuasively, into their imagination of a "modern" and ideal past, known to be China's national history.

———————————

References

1. The author is grateful to Roger Des Forges of the University of Buffalo for his critical comments on an earlier version of this essay.

2. Denis Twitchett, *Writings of Official History of the T'ang* (New York: Cambridge University Press, 1992).

3. See Laurence A. Schneider, "National Essence and the New Intelligentsia," Charlotte Furth, "The Sage as Rebel: The Inner World of Chang Ping-lin," and Martin Bernal, "Liu Shih-p'ei and National Essence," in *The Limits of Change: Essays on Conservative Alternatives in Republican China*, ed. Charlotte Furth (Cambridge MA: Harvard University Press, 1976), 57–150; Peter Zarrow, *Anarchism and Chinese Political Culture* (New York: Columbia University Press, 1990); Arif Dirlik, *Anarchism in the Chinese Revolution* (Berkeley: University of California Press, 1993); and Cheng Shih-chü, *Wan-ch'ing kuo-tsui-pai: wen-hua ssu-hsiang yen-ch'iu* (The National Essence group in the late Qing: a study of culture and ideas), 2nd ed. (Peking: Peking shih-fan ta-hsüeh chu-pan-she, 1997).

4. See Cheng Shih-chü's *Wan-ch'ing kuo-tsui pai*.

5. Lydia Liu, *Translingual Practice: Literature, National Culture, and Translated Modernity—China, 1900–1937* (Stanford: Stanford University Press, 1995).

6. Cheng Shih-chü, *Wan-ch'ing kuo-tsui-pai*, p. 4.

7. Martin Bernal, "Liu Shih-p'ei and National Essence," p. 104.

8. Cheng Shih-chü, *Wan-ch'ing kuo-tsui-pai*, pp. 4–5.

9. Huang Chieh, "Kuo-tsui pao-ts'un chu-i" (On protecting National Essence), *Cheng-i tung-pao*, hereafter *CITP* (1902), reprinted in *Jen-yin cheng-i tsung-shu* (Taipei: Wen-hai chu-pan-she, 1976), 27:1, pp.180–81.

10. Cheng Shih-chü, *Wan-ch'ing kuo-tsui-pai*, pp. 51–55.

11. Martin Bernal, "Liu Shih-p'ei and National Essence," p. 102.

12. See *Kuo-tsui hsüeh-pao* (National Essence Journal), hereafter, *KTHP*, No. 2–6 (1905).

13. Teng Shih, "Kuo-tsui hsüeh-pao fa-kan-tz'u" (Introductory remarks to the *National Essence Journal*), *KTHP*, No. 1 (1905): 8.

14. Chang Tai-yen, "Tung-ch'ing liu-hsüeh-sheng huan-ying-hui yen-shuo-tz'u" (A speech at the welcoming party for Chinese students in Tokyo), in *Chang Tai-yen cheng-lun hsuen-chi* (Chang Tai-yen's political speeches and essays), ed. Tang Chih-chün (Peking: Chung-hua shu-chü, 1977), pp. 275–78.

15. Huang Chieh, "Kuo-tsui hsüeh-pao hsü" (Preface to the *National Essence Journal*), KTHP, No. 1 (1905): 11.

16. Huang Chieh, "Kuo-tsui pao-ts'un chu-i" (On protecting National Essence), *CITP* 27:1 (1902): 180–81.

17. Cf. Laurence Schneider, *Ku Chieh-k'ang and China's New History: Nationalism and the Quest for Alternative Traditions* (Berkeley: University of California Press, 1971) and Q. Edward Wang, *Inventing China through History: The May Fourth Approach to Historiography* (Albany NY: SUNY Press, 2000).

18. Teng Shih, "Kuo-hsüeh yuen-lun" (On the origins of national studies), *KTHP*, No. 1 (1905): 21–31.

19. Liu Kuang-han, "Lun ku-hsüeh ch'u-yü tsung-chiao" (On religion as an origin of ancient learning), *KTHP*, No. 8 (1905): 897–905.

20. Liu Kuang-han, "Lun ku-hsüeh yu-yü shi-yen" (On experiment as an origin of ancient learning), *KTHP*, No. 11 (1905): 1277–81.

21. Teng Shih, "Ku-hsüeh fu-hsing-lun" (On the revival of ancient learning), *KTHP*, No. 9 (1905): 1024.

22. B. Anderson, *Imagined Communities: Reflections on the Origins and Spread of Nationalism, rev. ed.* (London: Verso, 1991), pp. 11–12.

23. J. Armstrong, *Nations before Nationalism* (Chapel Hill, NC: University of North Carolina Press, 1982).

24. Eric Hobsbawm, "Introduction: Inventing Tradition," in *The Invention of Tradition, ed.* Hobsbawm and Terence Ranger (Cambridge: Cambridge University Press, 1983), pp. 1–20.

25. Anthony D. Smith, "The Nation: Invented, Imagined, Reconstructed?" in *Reimagining the Nation,* ed. Marjorie Ringrose and Adam J. Lerner (Buckingham: Open University Press, 1993), pp. 9–28.

26. Teng Shih, "Ni-she kuo-tsui hsüeh-t'ang ch'i" (A proposal for the establishment of the National Essence School), *KTHP*, No. 26 (1907): 3161–68.

27. Teng Shih, "Kuo-tsui hsüeh-pao ti-san chou-nien chu-tien hsü" (Preface to the third anniversary of the *National Essence Journal*), *KTHP*, No. 38 (1908): 13–16.

28. Teng Shih, "Chi-ming feng-yü-lou min-shu, tsung-lun" (The people's book in the mansion of cockcrow and winds and rains, a general discussion), *CITP*, No. 5.

29. Liu Shih-p'ei, "Chu-tz'u" (Congratulatory remarks), *KTHP*, No. 38 (1908): 3–6.

30. Teng Shih, "Kuo-tsui hsüeh-pao ti-san ch'ou-nien chu-tien hsu" (Preface to the third anniversary of the *National Essence Journal*), *KTHP*, No. 38 (1908): 13–16.

31. P. Chatterjee, *The Nation and Its Fragments: Colonial and Postcolonial Histories* (Princeton, NJ: Princeton University Press, 1993), p. 5.

32. Teng Shih, "Kuo-tsui chen-lun" (On real national learning), *KTHP*, No. 27 (1907): 3291–97 and "Kuo-hsüeh wu-yung pien" (In defense of the usefulness of national learning), *KTHP*, No. 30 (1907): 3685–88.

33. Eric Hobsbawm, "Introduction: Inventing Tradition," p. 2.

34. Teng Shih, "Kuo-hsüeh t'ung-lun" (A general discussion on national studies), *KTHP*, No. 3 (1905): 261–78.

35. Teng Shih, "Kuo-hsüeh fu-hsing-lun" (On the revival of ancient learning), *KTHP*, No. 9 (1905): 1023–30.

36. Teng Shih, "Kuo-hsüeh tung-lun" pp. 261–78.

37. Liu Kuang-han, "Kung-hsüeh chen-lun" (On real Confucian learning), *KTHP*, No. 17 (1906): 2083–92.

38. See Chang Hsüeh-ch'eng, *Wen-shih tung-i* (General meanings in literature and history) (Peking: Ch'ung-hua shu-chü, 1985). Also Tsang Hsiu-liang, *Chang Hsüeh-ch'eng ho Wen-shih T'ung-i* (Chang Hsüeh-ch'eng and his *General Meanings in Literature and History*) (Peking: Ch'ung-hua shu-chü, 1984); David Nivison, *The Life and Thought of Chang Hsüeh-ch'eng, 1738–1801* (Stanford: Stanford University Press, 1966); and Yü Ying-shih, *Lun Tai Chen yü Chang Hsüeh-ch'eng* (On Tai Chen and Chang Hsüeh-ch'eng) (Taipei: Hua-shih chu-pan-she, 1977).

39. Teng Shih, "Kuo-hsüeh wei-lun" (A discovery of national studies), *KTHP*, No. 2 (1905): 133–44.

40. Ibid.

41. See Wu Tse, ed. *Ch'ung-kuo chin-tai shih-hsüeh-shih* (History of modern Chinese historiography) (Nanking: Chiang-su ku-chi chu-pan-she, 1989), vol. 1; Joseph Levenson, *Liang Ch'i-ch'ao and the Mind of Modern China* (Cambridge MA: Harvard University Press, 1958); Tang Xiaobing, *Global Space and the Nationalist Discourse on Modernity: The Historical Thinking of Liang Qichao* (Stanford: Stanford University Press, 1996); and Chiang Chün, *Ch'ung-kuo shih-hsüeh chin-tai-hua chin-ch'eng* (The process of the modernization of Chinese historiography) (Chi-nan: Ch'i-lu shu-she, 1995).

42. See Chang Wen-chien and Hu Feng-hsiang, *Chung-kuo chin-tai shih-hsüeh ssu-ch'ao ho liu-pai* (Historical trends and schools in modern China) (Shanghai: Hua-t'ung shih-fan ta-hsüeh chu-pan-she, 1993); Cheng Shih-chü, *Wan-ch'ing kuo-tsui-pai*; Yü Ying-shih, "Changing Conceptions of National History in Twentieth-Century China," in *Conceptions of National History*, ed. Erik Lönnroth, Karl Molin, and Ragnar Björk (Berlin: Walter de Gruyter), pp. 155–74; and Lydia Liu, *Translingual Practice*, pp. 239–64.

43. Liang Ch'i-ch'ao, *Liang Ch'i-ch'ao shih-hsüeh lun-chu san-chong* (Liang Ch'i-chao's three works in history) (Hong Kong: San-lien shu-tian, 1980), p. 3.

44. Huang Chieh, "Huang-shih tsung-hsü" (A general preface to the *Yellow History*), *KTHP*, No. 1 (1905): 41–46.

45. Yü Ying-shih, "Changing Conceptions of National History in Twentieth-Century China," p. 161.

46. Chiang Chün, *Ch'ung-kuo shih-hsüeh chin-tai-hua chin-ch'eng*, pp. 32–39.

47. Tang Chih-chün, *Chang Tai-yen nien-pu chang-pian* (A manuscript of the chronicle of Chang Tai-yen), 2 vols. (Peking: 1979), vol. 1, pp. 139–40.

48. Cheng Shih-chü, *Wan-ch'ing kuo-tsui-pai*, pp. 163–70.

49. Hsu Chih-heng, "Tu kuo-tsui hsüeh-pao kan-yen" (A review of the *National Essence Journal*), *KTHP*, No. 6 (1905): 651.

50. Liang Ch'i-ch'ao, *Liang Ch'i-ch'ao shih-hsüeh lun-chu san-chong*, p. 4.

51. Teng Shih, "Shih hsüeh tung lun" (General discussion on history), *CITP* 27:2 (1902): 714.

52. Liang Ch'i-ch'ao, *Liang Ch'i-ch'ao shih-hsüeh lun-chu san-chong*, p. 7.

53. Ibid., p. 5.

54. Charlotte Furth, "The Sage as Rebel: The Inner World of Chang Ping-lin," in *The Limits of Change*, p. 122.

55. Huang Chieh, "Huang-shih tsung-hsü"), pp. 43–45.

56. Ibid., p. 45.

57. Huang Chieh, "Huang-shih chung-tsu-shu" (The race treatise, *Yellow History*), *KTHP*, No. 1 (1905): 50 and Martin Bernal, "Liu Shih-p'ei and National Essence," pp. 96–98.

58. Yü Ying-shih, "Changing Conceptions of National History in Twentieth-Century China," pp. 162–64, and Martin Bernal, "Liu Shih-p'ei and National Essence," pp. 97–99.

59. Martin Bernal, "Liu Shih-p'ei and National Essence," p. 98.

60. Yü Ying-shih, "Changing Conceptions of National History in Twentieth-Century China," pp. 155–74.

61. Cf. Q. Edward Wang, "History, Space, Ethnicity: The Chinese Worldview," *Journal of World History*, 10:2 (Sept. 1999): 285–305.

62. Yü Ying-shih, "Changing Conceptions of National History in Twentieth-Century China," p. 163.

63. Homi Bhabha, ed. *Nation and Narration* (London and New York: Routledge, 1990), Introduction, p. 2.

64. Yü Ying-shih, "Changing Conceptions of National History in Twentieth-Century China," pp. 162–63.

65. Martin Bernal, "Liu Shih-p'ei and National Essence," p. 98.

66. Homi Bhabha, *The Location of Culture* (London and New York: Routledge, 1994), p. 7.

67. David Lowenthal, *The Past is a Foreign Country* (Cambridge: Cambridge University Press, 1985), p. 27.

68. Ma Hsü-lun, "Shih-chieh ta-tung-shuo" (On the unity of history), *CITP* (1903), reprinted in *Kui-mao cheng-i tsung-shu* (Taipei: Wen-hai chu-pan-she 1976), 28:3, pp. 617–22.

69. Lu Shao-ming, "Lun shih-hsüeh chih pien-ch'ien" (On changes in historiography), *KTHP*, No. 10 (1905): 1181–86.

70. Lu Shao-ming, "Shih-chu chih-hsüeh pu-tung lun" (On the differences in historical annotation) and "Shih-ch'ia ts'ung-chih pu-tung lun" (On the differences in historians' ideas), *KTHP*, No. 17 (1906): 2059–68.

71. Yü Ying-shih, "Changing Conceptions of National History in Twentieth-Century China," p. 163.

11. Nationalism and African Historiography

Toyin Falola

The foundation for the turning points in writing about Africa was laid as far back as the fifteenth century. As the fifteenth century was about to close, Europeans began to ensure contacts with Africa. A century later, the primary motivation in the contact had become the trans-Atlantic slave trade. This trade was abolished in the nineteenth century, only to be replaced by the trade in raw materials. In the last quarter of the nineteenth century, commercial relations gave way to direct territorial control as Africa was partitioned by aggressive European powers. New countries emerged, under colonial control for most of the first half of the twentieth century. The struggles for independence were the most intense expression of nationalism by Africans during the twentieth century, a practical and intellectual response to imperialism. All these events affected the emergence of African historiography and historical thinking about Africa in the following interrelated manner:

> 1. The slave trade promoted and consolidated a feeling of racial superiority to Africans. Treated as inhuman, Africans were presented as people without civilization and capacity to think. Older stereotypes were reinforced, in addition to new ones that arose out of racism.
> 2. Racism promoted an arrogant desire to spread civilization to Africa, in a way that further "infantilized" Africans.
> 3. Christian missionary enterprise was invigorated during the nineteenth century, leading to the spread of Christianity, Western education, and the rise of new elite.
> 4. In trying to justify imperialism, a number of scholar-administrators created a "colonial library," which combined racism with arrogance to present Africa in a most demeaning manner.
> 5. As an African educated elite emerged, they began to use their education in a nationalistic manner to confront the

negative presentation of their continent and people. They
revisited the past, to draw from history and traditions to
create an identity and self-assertion, and to blend with contemporary changes to create the idea of progress. Africans
have had to struggle to create their own authentic past, to
present their tradition and culture to a wider world, and to
use the past to fashion an identity and build hope during
the eras both of colonial domination and of postcolonial
failures.
6. The emergence of academic history writing about Africa
was against the background of the "colonial library" and the
need to respond to all the negative attacks on Africa. Thus,
without a doubt, nationalism, both of a cultural and academic nature, instigated the rise of African historiography.
The nationalism focused on a vigorous defense of Africa's
past as well as a commitment to the concept of the nation-
state constructed along European lines, but with borrowing
from indigenous institutions. African thinkers and scholars
turned to the past to define African identity in a colonized
and postcolonial world. They resented the slave trade,
European domination, and imperialism, and they believed
that the glories of the African past would disprove the negative images. Histories, tales, ceremonies, and religion,
sometimes presented in idealistic ways, constitute the
knowledge of counterdiscourse.

The turning points in African history are more or less the elaboration of
the aforementioned points: negative conception about Africans and their
past instigated a nationalistic response by Africanists to reconstruct that past
in an "objective" manner, and to use the past to connect to present agenda
at nation-building.

To start with the chronology of the negative misconceptions that acted
as the foundation, Eurocentric ideas about Africa before the fifteenth century presented Africans as primitive, even sometimes in the exaggerated image
of men with untamed beards, and with heads located in their shoulders.
While an earlier generation of Europeans showed respect for Africans and
underplayed color differences, a later generation close to the fifteenth century regarded Africans as inferior beings. Africans were described as savages by
Europeans of the Christian era, many of whom also believed that they were
cursed people, the so-called sons of Ham condemned by Noah.

When anatomy could no longer be made an issue, the image changed to
that of a grossly distorted past, for the entire duration of the slave trade era.
Africans were presented as beasts, incapable of arts, sciences, and manufac-
tures. They were more of imitators than creators, primitive savages who
played no role in history. The slave trade was justified, even by Christians
who cited affirmative passages in the Bible and discounted the value of conversion. The slave trade era saw the saturation of negative opinions about

Africa. Presented as animals, strange, uncivilized and crude, the slave trade was even seen by some European writers as a blessing to Africans.[1]

During the eighteenth century, philosophers of the so-called Enlightenment era added their voices to the negative presentation of Africa. "I am apt to suspect the negroes," wrote David Hume, the famous philosopher, "to be naturally inferior to the white. There never was a civilized nation of any other complexion than white, nor even any individual eminent either in action or speculation. No ingenious manufacturers amongst them, no arts, no sciences."[2] Georg Hegel, another notable philosopher, added his voice to the stereotype in a major lecture delivered in 1830–31, accusing blacks of a lack of self-control, development, and culture, and concluding that the continent be ignored:

> At this point we leave Africa, not to mention it again. For it is no historical part of the World; it has no movement or development to exhibit. . . . What we properly understand by Africa is the Unhistorical, Undeveloped Spirit, still involved in the conditions of mere nature, which had to be presented here only as on the threshold of the World's history."[3]

In the nineteenth century, the attempt to spread Christianity was presented as an inroad of civilization to Africans who were regarded as children deserving of both strong parents and government. Like their predecessors, many European missionaries believed that Africans were savages. Philosophers, European traders and even scholars joined missionaries in the presentation of Africans as docile, incompetent, and inferior. Arguably the most circulated essay on racism during the nineteenth century was that by Joseph de Gobineau, a Frenchman, who advocated racial purity, an idea subsequently developed by others into a concept of "master race." Ideas of race, as to be expected from this frame of mind, saw little of value in Africans who, together with other blacks, were placed at the lowest end of race classification.

During the colonial period, many older ideas were repackaged. To European administrators and scholars of this period, imperialism brought hope to the primitives, transforming their lives to those of modern people. Having failed to invent any civilization, they could lay claim to no history. Their so-called history, before the coming of Europeans, was nothing but chaos, stagnation, ignorance, and savagery. In the "colonial library," Africans were "natives"—defined as inferior people—or as "tribes," a rather primitive and disorganized group of people. To the colonial administrators, imperialism was presented as a "White Man's Burden," to help the "natives," rather than as an exploitative agency.

After 1945, when academic history writing about Africa began to be accepted, skepticism about the study of Africa was expressed in some circles. How can people without writing have a past? The most notorious remark was made by H. R. Trevor-Roper, the Regius Professor of Modern History at Oxford, who, like Hegel, dismissed Africa as "the unrewarding gyrations of barbarous tribes in picturesque but irrelevant quarters of the globe."[4] Part of the challenge that Africanists faced was to assert the validity of oral traditions as sources of history and to show that the Africa's past was far more than the narration of the activities of Europeans in Africa.

I. The Cultural Response

The response by Africans to challenge the European image of their continent began during the nineteenth century, primarily as what I prefer to label as the "cultural response," a perception of self and of one's past that called into question received ideas. This was both intellectual and practical, and it continued well into the twentieth century, subsequently feeding the intellectual agenda that defined African historiography more broadly. The cultural response was the first turning point in historical thinking about Africa. It set out to restore the dignity of Africans, and point to and celebrate the achievements of past Africans. If Europeans devalued the African past, culturalists would romanticize it.

A new generation of African elite emerged during and after the nineteenth century. Many were Christians, and they accepted or reconciled with the changes of the era and nurtured a vision of progress. Ideas about nationalism took deep roots, expressed in the love for Africa, in demands for reforms under European rule, and subsequently in anticolonial resistance. But elitism and nationalism did not necessarily emerge at about the same time. In the first half of the nineteenth century, many elite actually sought assimilation into European ways of life. Such a notable figure as Africanus Horton[5] even called for the Westernization of Africa, while many others advocated greater European contacts. The elite occupied a number of important positions in church, school, firm, and government, and many looked forward to greater mobility.

The tide changed in the second half of the nineteenth century, when the elite began to experience marginalization, as Europeans believed that Africans were not competent to serve in leadership position or deserve racial equality. Demands for empowerment, antiracial sentiments, and the promotion of the interests of Africans led to fresh thinking and ideas along nationalistic lines. Some elite members were dissatisfied with the European presence, as in the case of Reversible Johnson among the Yoruba or a number of assimilated Africans in Senegal. African missionaries began to criticize their white counterparts. Even the pro-European Bishop, Ajayi Crowther, called for the use of African languages and customs in the promotion of Christianity. Greater rebellion came in the creation of African Independent Churches, a movement that gained currency over a wider area after the 1880s.[6] Great intellectuals of this period included Mojola Agbebi, James Johnson, and Attoh-Ahuma.

It was at a time of profound cultural expression that the partition of Africa began its course. As new countries emerged, so too the grip of Europe on Africa was strengthened. Africans, elite or peasant, were now colonial subjects, treated as second-class citizens. The intellectual attitude was to revisit the past and evaluate the present. The response was eclectic—the elite would take elements from the past, without rejecting all the changes foisted on them by the Western colonial agency, an attitude that shaped the intellectual ideas espoused by Africans.

Among the leading scholars who illustrate the aforementioned issues, Edward Wilmot Blyden (West African, 1832–1912) stands out as the most erudite. Blyden established the foundation of Africa's historical and cultural thought, creating themes that many thinkers and academics would re-examine during the twentieth century. Blyden formulated a theory of racial equality and achievements which completely denied Eurocentric formulations of inferiority. While not denying Europeans of their own successes and achievements, he credited a lot as well to Africans and blacks in general, stressing in particular their contributions to religion, morality and spirituality. Blyden showed that the past achievements of Africans were phenomenal—a theme that was later to dominate the attention of pioneer academic scholars—and that the future was certain to be great—prophecy that is yet to fulfill itself.

Africans are different, asserted Blyden, and they must protect this difference. African-Americans must return to Africa, to join in building a new society. Nothing, asserted Blyden, had damaged the African race, in spite of the slave trade and colonization. "Love of race must be the central fire to heat all his energies and glow along all his activity. He must be animated by the earnest purpose and inspired by the great idea of a genuine race development."[7] So promising and so great was the future of Africa that Blyden concluded that "I would rather be a member of this race than a Greek in the time of Alexander, a Roman in the Augustin period, or an Anglo-Saxon in the nineteenth century."[8]

Associated with the concept of race is that of the "African personality," that is, an identity peculiarly African that Blyden associated with Africa's past, history, love of nature, and connection to God. He rejected any assimilation that would destroy this personality, and called for Africans to reject all attempts that would redefine their identity. In a book published in 1908,[9] he extolled the virtues of African institutions and presented them for adoption to all Africans, including the educated; he dismissed European values as "naked" and assimilated products as "waste products" that will ultimately come into destruction, and he stated that any attempt to imitate Europeans in any form was like "broken cisterns that hold no water."

Blyden's ideas were adopted by many African missionaries and elite converts to Christianity who were able to adopt a new religion without having to reject most of their culture and customs or accept the notion of black inferiority. Pioneer historians such as Samuel Johnson and C. C. Reindorf advocated the unity of their people and the adoption of new ideas without necessarily destroying all of the old.[10] Blyden's ideas were also favorably received by nationalists who demanded reforms under colonial rule or who later struggled for complete European disengagement. Notable among those who drew and expanded on his ideas were Mensah Sarbah, Attoh-Ahuma, James Brew, and Casely Hayford, all of Ghana; and John Payne Jackson of Lagos.[11]

All used the medium of a European language and emerging newspapers and other outlets to enunciate their ideas on African history, future, progress, identity, race equality, nationalism, and self-assertion. In an influential book published in 1911, *Ethiopia Unbound*, Hayford returned to the theme of race emancipation, making a case for the intellect and personality of the African:

> Before this time, however, it had been discovered that the black man was not necessarily the missing link between man and ape. It had even been granted that for intellectual endowments he had nothing to be ashamed of in an open competition with the Aryan or any other type. Here was a being anatomically perfect, adaptive and adaptable to any and every sphere of the struggle for life. Sociologically, he had succeeded in recording upon the pages of contemporary history a conception of family life unknown to Western ideas. Moreover, he was the scion of a spiritual sphere peculiar unto himself; for when Western Nations would have exhausted their energy in the vain struggle for the things which satisfy not, it was felt that it would be to these people to whom the world would turn for inspiration, seeing that in them only would be found those elements which make for pure altruism, the leaven of all human experience.[12]

There was much discussion about the identity of Africa and its peoples. In a colonized world, the elite maintained an ambivalence: they wanted many indigenous institutions to survive, albeit in a modified manner; but at the same time, they wanted progress, defined as the introduction of Western ideas, institutions and infrastructure. Writing about Africa ultimately involves this ambivalence, irrespective of ideological positions. There are those thinkers such as Henry Carr who wanted a rapid spread of Western civilization, or a number of elite in the francophone Africa who advocated assimilation to French culture, but the leading opinion was usually close to that of Edward Blyden: the search for an appropriate blend of tradition with change.

If Blyden set the stage in the nineteenth century, Léopold Senghor (b. 1906) poet and first president of Senegal from 1960 to 1981, was his twentieth-century successor in connecting the past to contemporary identity and history, in a concept that became widely known as negritude. Senghor regarded Africa as the homeland of a united race, with an outstanding heritage capable of transforming the present. The elements of negritude, as defined by Senghor, included Africans' way of life, religion, compassion, humanity, and love of nature. Senghor saw in African family traditions a socialist philosophy.[13] While he studied Marxism, Senghor rejected the Leninist-Stalinist tradition which, according to him, did not create room for spirituality and did not understand African institutions. To Senghor, Africans fall more on intuition than analysis: they are sensitive and emotional, focusing more on the reality of an object than its appearance.[14] In the paraphrase by Robert July, the African is "sound, odour, rhythm, form and colour; he feels rather than sees, senses within his flesh, projects his own being into and thus knows it."[15] In creating a community, with great harmony, dialogue, and cooperation, Senghor concluded that Africans have a great deal to teach others. Like Blyden, he rejected the notion of race inferiority and worked with that of race complementarity. Europeans can give the world science, and Africans can offer spirituality and communalism, thereby creating an amalgam of a new and better human civilization where all people will live in harmony, "free from contradictions and from all forms of slavery," including alienation.[16]

Disciples of negritude are many, including historians, artists, poets, essayists, and novelists. Unlike Senghor, his disciples were far more critical of Europeans, especially of imperialism, and were far more sympathetic to the celebration of African culture and history. Negritude became an expression of cultural nationalism, anticolonialism and antiracism. It affected the education system, as schools indegenized their curricula to pay attention to African cultures and customs. It was also employed as an agency of insertion into world civilization, as Senghor argued that the West should learn about humanity and spirituality from Africans in order to build a "universal civilization." However, there are also critics who regard negritude as an idealization, far from the reality that existed in Africa.

II. The Academic Response

Academic history writing about Africa began during the twentieth century in multiple centers: in the United States, where black intellectuals such as W.E.B. Du Bois and Leo Hansberry deployed African history to elaborate on black identity and the achievements of black people; in Europe, where African studies emerged as a discipline after the Second World War; and in Africa itself, where universities began to emerge after the 1940s. In all the centers, the creation of a respectable discipline called African history was a revolution; the themes and the methods to validate them were turning points in historical thinking.

Except for the United States, where the academic interest grew much earlier, in particular among black intellectuals, developments elsewhere occurred after the Second World War. In Europe, Africa was conceived as part of "overseas history," and respect for it did not come until after the war.[17] Interest in Africa revolved around the histories of European expansion, colonial rule, and the so-called native populations. Specialists had to master the tools of interdisciplinarity, languages, and the methods of using non-conventional sources. The decline of Europe after World War II and the crumbling of its empire in Africa imposed a forced need to rethink the presentation of overseas history. Areas previously regarded as peripheries became new centers of knowledge and ideas. About the same time, social and economic history began to gain currency, with shifts in focus away from the nation-state to social groups, working classes, and rural and urban histories. The writing of history witnessed an emancipation in focus and a recognition that non-European histories were both viable and valid. African history developed rapidly in Europe, gaining respectability within a short span of fifteen years after the Second World War. As the discipline of history itself witnesses changes, either in focus or concepts, Africa becomes either integrated into the mainstream, as in the case of world history, cultural theories, and postmodernism. Studies on imperialism, dependency theory, world system analysis, revolution, social movements, and decolonization have all had to confront Africa, thereby creating conditions to sustain the interest in Africa in the Western academy.[18]

In Africa, conditions for reforms were laid during the war, and the tide of nationalism was difficult to control. Ex-servicemen and students in higher institutions in Western countries preached egalitarian ideas, with a few of them already dreaming of replacing whites in various occupations and leadership roles. The colonial governments initiated a number of concessions, including the creation of the first set of universities in three British colonies. Africans intensified their campaigns for freedom and decolonization, using writing and combative speeches as part of their weapons. The number of educated elite had increased, and thousands of new ones were added in subsequent years. Modern facilities in media, communication, and transportation enhanced not just the ability to reach a large number of people, but the idea that nationalist ideas could energize the masses as well. A more combative and articulate leadership emerged, represented by such figures as Kwame Nkrumah in Ghana, Sekou Touré in Guinea, Léopold Senghor in Senegal, and Nnamdi Azikiwe in Nigeria. Leaders such as Nkrumah and Touré believed that modernization could be attained within a generation, if Africans had power and colonialism was terminated. Nkrumah and Touré's commitment to change often meant that they had to question African tradition and culture in such aspects as gift-giving, crafts, chieftaincy titles, large families, and polygamy. The role of tradition in development became a vibrant academic subject. So, too, did it become the core of literary creativity, as poems, stories, and essays dealt with culture encounter and suggested how Africans could negotiate the acceptance and rejection of African culture. There are authors, such as Camera Laye who wrote *L'Enfant Noir*, who pursued the theme of negritude, or Chinua Achebe, whose novels (among them *Things Fall Apart*), pursued ideas of culture conflicts and the necessity of cultural assertion by Africans.

The changes represented great turning points in radical political thought, while African academic history was also born during this era. The confidence by the nationalists affected not just political emancipation but intellectual freedom as well. Notions of race equality were not being defended, as a previous generation did, but merely assumed. Indigenous African philosophies and cultures were being articulated as relevant to the modern age, as Senghor, Cheikh Anta Diop, and others said. In North Africa, Islam was offered as a way of life to combat the erosion caused by Western imperialism. Robert July observed major cultural shifts in West Africa, from the wearing of English coat to that of African indigenous ones; in the spread of the philosophy of negritude, with the writings of Senghor and Aimé Césaire;

in the ideology of non-alignment of African countries in the Cold War; in pan-Africanist meetings to talk about African unity; and "in the postwar efforts to develop a new African art and literature [and history] which enunciated cultural independence from former colonial masters and gave meaning to the image of the new nations."[19]

Part of the postwar changes was the attention to the Africa's past by pioneer historians. There were two dual interests. The first was to reconstruct the past, to show that Africa had no stagnation, as claimed by the "colonial library"; that there were revolutionary changes and movements; and that continuity with the past was strong. In other words, not only did Africans had history, contrary to the views expressed by certain opinions in Europe, its history was recoverable and glorious. The second was to show that Africans understood the idea of a modern nation-state and could manage it. Historians, like politicians and statesmen, would talk about the past and modernization at the same time. Theses, books, and essays would be devoted to both—the representation of the past as well as the articulation of freedom and development.

Most pioneer Africanists showed a commitment to the use of oral sources. Originally maligned as useless, it soon acquired respect, with its own tools and methods.[20] There is a clear demonstration that almost all African societies had practiced history, with their own notion of time, space, and chronology. Pioneer Africanists were eager to demonstrate the African knowledge of history, if only to show the depth and breadth of African history.

African historians turned to the past primarily to unearth the knowledge of greatness and to use the evidence to build sentiments of pride and nationalism. All the errors and misconceptions about Africa by Europeans became points of attacks for African historians. A discussion on origins becomes the search for heritage so that Africans would have confidence to govern themselves in the modern world.[21] Knowledge about African heroes was pursued with dedication, as evidence was published on great kings and queens. So also is the evidence on leadership, state formation, kingdoms, alliances, and others that shows clearly Africa's management capability long before Europeans set foot on the continent. Historians also struggled to decolonize the curricula, turning Africa into the center of study in schools. Like Blyden and Senghor, historians explored issues of identity. At the forefront of the identity research is Cheikh Anta Diop who pointed to the creation of Egyptian civilization by blacks, the role of women in African history, and other aspects of complex indigenous African institutions.[22]

The combination of everything they did can be described as "nationalist historiography," that is, the use of history in the service of the nation, a way of writing that makes history very valuable in defining the nation and shaping its future. It is the representation of elite interest in the nation, as the elite uses its power to define its leadership in the nation. It is a counterdiscourse for attacking the European representation of Africa and deliberately providing credible evidence on the achievements of Africa and the glories of the past in order to indicate possibilities for the future and combat racist views that Africa is incapable of managing itself. It is a recognition of the fact that the agenda of development should not prevent an interest in the liberal arts, and that a discipline such as history can be integrated into the developmentalist agenda itself. Successful achievers of the past have been used as models for contemporary leaders to emulate. The heroes may inspire the youth to seek greater success in future. The recent history of anticolonial struggles shows the worth of resistance, and how resistance ideologies and committed fighters could provide yet another model for civil society and radical leaders.

Nationalist historiography is about power: the ability of an intelligentsia to assert itself, to use its knowledge to generate knowledge about its own people and continent, to show that others are either wrong or right about what they say of its people and continent, to attack views and people that are perceived as hostile or racist, to defend members that are "politically correct" in their representation of Africa, to justify or explain all aspects in African history and institutions that outsiders condemn, and to create a response to the consequences of European domination of the continent. It can be combative and revisionist, as in all the works of Cheikh Anta Diop who demonstrate the black origins of Egyptian civilization.

I want to illuminate the development of nationalist historiography by focusing on one major example, an African attempt to control the production of knowledge, and to create a discourse that will combat Western domination and represent the knowledge about Africa.

III. Nationalist Historiography: The Ibadan School

In the 1960s, the University of Ibadan, Nigeria, was able to center its History Department as the new frontier in the advocacy of the "African perspective of history" or of the "African factor" in the unfolding of African history. Not that the orientation of the Ibadan historians differed substantially from those of their colleagues elsewhere, but a pioneer status and the publication in London by Longman of the Ibadan History Series brought an important, even if temporary, international recognition. It became labeled as the "Ibadan School of History," originally by outsiders who wanted a descriptive category for the presentation of nationalist historiography.

The school created a counterdiscourse, a rejoinder to what is commonly called the "Eurocentric perception of Africa." This perception pre-dated the twentieth century and also survived in the first half of the twentieth century with the creation of a "colonial library" on Africa. In Eurocentric thinking, not much was good about Africa, a "place of complete and anarchic savagery" before European colonial rule.[23] African history was presented as static—the primeval African man was assumed to have only a limited capacity to transform his society and environment, and there was little or nothing to show for his uncreative talents until the Europeans appeared on the horizon.[24] Racist notions constructed Africans as inferiors, and used the idea of European superiority to justify domination and colonial policies designed to generate changes. In many Western institutions, the study of Africa was not considered to be important, and historians were interested in the continent primarily as part of the understanding of European imperial expansion. No doubt, the trans-Atlantic slave trade was one of the causes of Western negative stereotypes about Africa. Imperialism was yet an additional factor, as many European writers regarded the partition of Africa as a small price for a "barbaric people" to pay for receiving "civilization." An influential opinion in the recycling of negative ideas about Africa was that expressed by the British administrator in Central Africa, Sir Harry Hamilton Johnston, who wrote a widely cited book that justified imperial control.[25] To him, Africans were like retarded children, and would require miscegenation (cross-breeding with another race) before they could progress. Other variants of the colonial philosophy of trusteeship were developed, including that of the "dual mandate" by Lord Lugard,[26] which stated that European rule was for the benefit of both Europe and Africa—Europe would take resources and Africa would receive "civilization."

The concerns that drove nationalist historiography were similar to those that instigated Edward Blyden and his successors to write: race pride and the defense of Africa, all in a nationalistic spirit. Thus, in a sense, the motivation of academic writing was not so much different from those of the non-academic. But the mode and the site were different. The academic mode was based in universities, comprised of a tiny elite with power to speak to students and a larger broadly defined academic audience. The mode itself was an "objective" production of history, within the framework of how the Western academy defined research and university education.

Many have credited Kenneth Onwuka Dike for pioneering the emergence of the Ibadan school, a successful example of nationalist historiography.[27] In 1954, Dike became the first Nigerian to head the History Department at the University of Ibadan. He had to combat the "colonial library," which attacked the ideas of the colonial period as one of profound ignorance about Africa. The University itself was created by the British in 1948, with the Department of History as one of the pioneer academic departments. As to be expected, recruiting teachers was a problem. C. J. Potter, the first Head of Department, had a first degree in History, but with interests in Theology and administration. Potter did not regard himself as a researcher or an author, and his contribution was limited to university administration.[28] There was also the problem of limited resources for teaching, especially the lack of a good library.

The addition of K. O. Dike to Ibadan in 1950 was a breath of fresh air. He received his training in the United Kingdom, where he formed his vision of an African perspective of history. He received his first degree at Durham University, and his Masters at Aberdeen University in Scotland. He completed his Ph.D. in 1950 at King's College, London, with a thesis on "Trade and Politics in the Niger Delta, 1830–1885," later published in 1956 under the same title. While not based on oral traditions as many have assumed, but largely on archival materials, the topic itself could be described as revolutionary for rejecting the logic of imperial history and emphasizing instead the African side of the interactions with Europeans during the nineteenth century. In his preface, Dike informed his readers that he would present an alternative history, by dealing not with the external factor of the British interactions with his people, but only as their presence helped to understand events. "In West African history," Dike concluded, "the concentration of students on external factors has tended to submerge the history of the indigenous peoples and to bestow undue prominence to the activities of the invaders."[29]

Dike's impact at Ibadan was not immediate. Between 1950 and 1952, he was a lone fighter in the call for changes. Other teachers were being recruited at the same time, such as Jean Copeland (later Jean Mellamby), with an interest in European and American history, and Evelyn C. Martin, a specialist in Imperial History. Much power resided in the Heads of Departments, and the pioneer expatriate Heads and the staff they recruited were not oriented towards the development of African history. They had no training in African history, and were not too keen on its development. Still under the guidance of the University of London, Ibadan could only sponsor what London would accept, at a time when many believed that African history was not a proper academic subject. Still under colonial rule, the new university college could not be encouraged to become the seat of opposition to British authorities. Western education was intended to be an appendage of colonialism, with college students showing an appreciation for colonial changes, elitism and British values, with their history teachers emphasizing the relevance of imperial history. The goal was for the students to understand not the history of Africa, but of Europe, Canada, and the Commonwealth. There was only one course devoted to Africa, titled "History of European Activities in Africa from the Middle of the 14th Century to the Present Day." Even then, this was more about the history of European expansion to Africa, a reinforcement of the myth that there was little or no history before European contacts. The leading textbooks for use by the general readers and students also privileged the role of Europe, or of European heroes, in the development of Africa.[30] With the control by British faculty, the orientation was to imitate the University of London, with courses on political ideas, and outline courses on European and English history.

From the point of view of the expatriate teachers, the overriding aim of the university was to supply a pool of manpower, and they did not see how courses on Africa would lead to the production of better administrators and school teachers. The History Department was also expected to play a complementary role in the training of others in the Humanities and Social Sciences. When the syllabi of such other courses as Literature and Classics are examined in relation to that of History, the design to emphasize the importance of Europe is rather clear.[31] A few Nigerian contemporaries believed that the grip of the University of London prevented the radicalization of the curricula since they were unable to inject as much of a dose of Africa as they would have wanted.

Dike's impact began in 1952 when he relocated to the West African Institute for Social and Economic Research (WAISER), a research agency attached to the University of Ibadan. With a greater access to resources and freedom to operate, he began to make some of the changes that would outlive him. He began the process that led to the creation of the National Archives of Nigeria. He conducted a survey of available records in government and missionary hands, and wrote a report that formed the basis of the request for the creation of the archives.[32]

In 1954, he returned to the History Department as the Head, now with the power to direct changes. Dike's fortunes improved, as he moved from one office to the other, eventually becoming the first indigenous Vice-chancellor of the university. He used this power to reshape the practice of the profession, and to connect history as a discipline to the task of nation-building and nationalism. In the mid-1950s, the British had fully accepted the need for Nigerianization—the transfer of power to Nigerians and the recruitment of competent Nigerians to new positions and those being vacated by the expatriates. New lecturers were recruited to the Department, mainly those with interest in African history, and with an orientation that also promoted nationalist historiography. Notable additions included H. F. C. Smith (later Abdulahi Smith), J. C. Anene, R. E. Bradbury, J. D. Omer-Cooper, A. Ryder, C. W. Newbury and V.W. Treadwell. All later made their marks on different aspects of African history. In 1953, Saburi Biobaku, with a Ph.D. thesis on the Yoruba group of Egba obtained from the United Kingdom, joined the University College of Ibadan as the first indigenous Registrar, and he could be counted upon as an ally in the development of African studies.[33] J. C. Anene did his Ph.D. on the early years of British rule and stages in the conquest of Nigeria; A. B. Aderibigbe wrote on the British in Lagos during the nineteenth century; J. D. Omer-Cooper on the Mfecane in South Africa; J.F.A. Ajayi on Christian missions; H.F.C. Smith worked on northern Nigeria; and Allan Ryder and R. E. Bradbury devoted their time to the study of Benin kingdom.

The new books of the 1950s by Dike and Biobaku (and the others that followed in the 1960s) are not to be judged solely on their academic merits but their symbolic significance. Africans could now do original research and write books and essays about their own people; they used the language of the academy, and the works were intended to be consumed by their colleagues all over the world. With varying degree of success, they stressed the relevance of oral sources. In their prefaces and thrusts, they offered an "African perspective" of the past: Africans no longer appeared as docile and passive agents of their own history, as many Europeans had presented them, but the real agents, the heroes and the architects of their fortunes. At last, they were able to show that African history, as a discipline, was not only possible, but viable.

A new generation of students benefited from the changes. Nationalist historiography changed the teaching curricula by way of orientation, courses, and their contents. Colonial education was accused of failure to adapt teaching to African needs, and for stressing European history, making European expansion in Africa the core of historical knowledge, and turning European explorers and administrators into the heroes of African history. With Dike and others came a new way of presenting materials. If the Europeans had presented such men as Taubman Goldie as "the maker of

Nigeria," Dike would present him only as the "maker" of the Royal Niger Company, the company that he formed, and not of Nigeria. If Europeans had presented Jaja of Opobo as a Nigerian chief who stood in the way of free trade, Dike and others would present him as a resistance hero, a patriot who did not want the British to cheat him in trade and deny him of power. A new orthodoxy in teaching was about to replace an older orthodoxy.

Changes had to be made to the course offerings and to the content of a number of courses. There were limitations in the early years, even when Dike and his colleagues wanted rapid changes. The books to teach the courses they had in mind did not exist, a situation which encouraged the use of theses, published and unpublished, as textbooks. Until the university freed itself from control of London in 1962, the degree requirements did not require the students to take more than one course in African history. For an honors student, this was one out of ten courses. To surmount both obstacles, the scholars had to publish, organize seminars, and create an autonomous university. Within a decade, they were very successful.

The doctoral theses formed the basis of the first major publications. Many of these were printed with minimal revision, but they were widely received as part of the new writings on Africa. The scholars also paid attention to local sources, notably oral traditions and the writings of amateur scholars. Before the emergence of the university, writings in Arabic, local languages, and English had become established.[34] They used the available ones in their writings, as in the cases of Bradbury making use of Jacob Egharevba's works or of Smith falling on Arabic sources. They also encouraged the production of new ones.

Although his own research and writings were to suffer,[35] Dike had to join the other pioneers to establish the infrastructure of intellectual production and elitism. An academic society was organized in 1955, the Historical Society of Nigeria, one of the oldest in the continent, again with Dike as its first president.[36] In addition to its annual conferences, regular seminars were held to exchange ideas with graduate students, especially in the 1960s and beyond. The society attempted to involve school teachers and members of the public in its activities, but it was not very successful at building viable alliances with academics. In 1956, the Historical Society of Nigeria established its journal, the *Journal of the Historical Society of Nigeria*, edited by Omer-Cooper. The journal acquired an instant reputation for disseminating works of original scholarship and new ideas. In the mid-1960s, a journal, the *Tarikh*, to present general materials to students and teachers was also added. In 1980, the Society attained its peak with the publication of *Groundwork of Nigerian History*,[37] a tentative synthesis of the history of Nigeria.

In a nationalistic spirit, Dike and the pioneer scholars attempted to embark upon a rescue mission to recover the African past through the establishment of what was called the Historical Research Schemes. The schemes were conceived as a collaborative effort to involve many disciplines and scholars, and Nigeria was broken into regions to be covered by each scheme and with possible funding from the Nigerian federal and regional governments and international organizations. All available sources would be gathered, and the scholars were expected to write definitive accounts of the past of the region, fill existing gaps in knowledge, and contribute to the development of historical and national consciousness. An administrative groundwork was established, many scholars were co-opted, and the regional governments were approached for funding. Within the university, a separate center was established for research and documentation, the Institute of African Studies, which became the hub of cultural activities, especially the promotion of local artists and writers.

In the Western Region, the Yoruba Historical Research Scheme received support in 1955, with a five year grant for "cultural research." Under the leadership of S. O. Biobaku, it was expected to bring together archaeologists, anthropologists, historians, and others to explore the origins of the Yoruba. A small team embarked upon the collection of Yoruba oral sources. Another small group began pioneer archaeological excavations in Ile-Ife, the ancient city of the Yoruba. Both the oral sources and archaeology demonstrated the antiquity of Yoruba kingdoms, their great civilizations and artistic talents. A number of the members of the Yoruba Historical Scheme were later to distinguish themselves.

The Department of History was directly in charge of the three remaining historical schemes—those on Benin, Arochukwu, and Northern Nigeria—with financial support from the Federal Government of Nigeria and grants from the Colonial Development and Welfare Fund and the Carnegie Trust of America.[38] As with the Yoruba Scheme, the aim was to pool the resources of historians, anthropologists, and archaeologists to write a comprehensive account of the past. The efforts on Benin yielded results published by Allen Ryder and Bradbury, both historians, and the archaeological work on Benin walls and art. In the case of the north, G. E. Connah carried out archeological works in the Kanem-Borno area. An historian, Murray Last, used Arabic sources to write an account of the Sokoto Caliphate. The enormity of the data in the north and further financial support from the regional government led to the establishment of the Arewa House, a center for historical documentation, and the Sokoto History Bureau.

Dike initiated the Arochukwu project, with the aim of investigating the power and impact of the Aro, a trading network that profited from the manipulation of a religious oracle in Eastern Nigeria. Owing to Dike's administrative appointments and the civil war from 1967 to 1970, the project suffered considerable delay, and its major result was published in the 1980s. Archaeologists also worked here as well, and Thurstan Shaw distinguished himself with his work on the Igbo Ukwu, which shows the antiquity of the Igbo and their extensive trade connections with their neighbors.

Although the majority of the scholars in all these interdisciplinary projects saw themselves primarily as academics, there was a sense in which the leaders of the projects were connecting with the earlier views of cultural nationalists in obtaining government support. Grant applications and public defense of the projects show a tendency to affirm the concept of negritude, to show how historical research would enhance the identity of the nation or group, and to show that scholars were part of the elite interested in the pro-

ome northern states to collect documents and present local histories.

The Department of History also played a leading role in the academic revolution at the secondary school level. Not only did it produce the school teachers, it influenced the school curricula and produced books for them. The West African Examination Council started new syllabi in African history. Workshops were conducted for school teachers in West Africa, with the financial support of the Carnegie Foundation. The papers presented at these workshops became the first set of two textbooks in African history in the region: *A Thousand Years of West African History*[39] and *Africa in the Nineteenth and Twentieth Centuries*.[40] Later on, other historians wrote four textbooks in a series, *The Growth of African Civilization*,[41] to cover the entire continent. The textbooks reflect the orientation of nationalist historiography—the stress on the achievements of Africans, and their ability to understand their environments and initiate important changes. Rather than present Africans as members of "isolated tribes" as the "colonial library" did, the texts discussed a number of issues in a regional framework, using trade, war, and culture to link many African groups. In the 1970s, advanced texts and comprehensive works of synthesis also appeared, most notably the two-volume book on West Africa.[42] UNESCO also published eight volumes of comprehensive history which, no doubt, represent the ultimate achievement of nationalist historiography. The control of graduate education passed rather quickly to Dike and the first generation of scholars. This was again another revolution, as the first generation was able to reproduce itself very quickly. The undergraduates of the 1950s became the graduate students and academics of the 1960s and beyond. In the early years of the university, the award of a General Degree (rather than honors in single subjects) took priority, since the primary aim was to produce manpower for the civil service.[43] Beginning from 1952, an honors program enabled a student to focus on one discipline, while taking others as subsidiaries. This enabled brilliant students with at least a Second Class (Upper Division) to develop the ambition to pursue graduate studies, with the encouragement of the university and the regional and federal governments. Among those who benefited from this in the 1950s were C. C. Ifemesia, who specialized in Eastern Nigeria, and T. N. Tamuno, the historian of colonial administration and the future Vice-chancellor of the University of Ibadan.

There was, however, pressure and politics to train graduate students locally. Dike and others believed that they themselves could provide the best training in the new orientation they were developing. In other words, to avoid the contamination of African students by Eurocentric opinions and imperialist historians, it was better for them to stay at home. Locally generated research would also boost the image of the school. There was also the added pressure for manpower, as new universities were created in the early 1960s.[44] They would require academics to function, and Ibadan could produce them cheaper and faster. At Ibadan itself, by the time Dike's term ended in 1967, twenty of the alumni of the school had held teaching appointments in the Department.[45]

The graduate students of Ibadan continued with the theme of the "African factor," or the agency of Africans in the process of change. They were expected to collect oral materials and written sources and fill major gaps in the literature, especially of Nigeria. Murray Last and Adiele Afigbo were the pioneers who obtained their Ph.D.s in 1964. Murray Last completed his thesis on the Sokoto Caliphate, the largest state in West Africa during the nineteenth century.[46] The caliphate was used to inspire modern-day nation builders as evidence of how Africans in the past used Islam to create change and a stable polity. A. E. Afigbo, another pioneer student, did his study on the "The Warrant Chief System in Eastern Nigeria 1900–1929,"[47] showing the need to understand indigenous institutions before policy change. A year later, Obaro Ikime graduated with a Ph.D. on intergroup relations in southern Nigeria, and began his entire career in his alma mater.[48] A configuration of themes emerged on Christianity, British rule, trade and politics, and Islam, all designed to reflect the genius of Africans.

A successful graduate program enabled Ibadan to create a diaspora of scholars from the 1960s and beyond. The four new universities created in the early 1960s had to be staffed, and they drew from existing faculty from Ibadan or recruited their graduate students. H.F.C. Smith relocated to Zaria, and A. B. Aderibigbe moved to Lagos. The Nigerian crisis that led to the civil war in 1967 saw the migration to the East of J. C. Anene, the historian of boundaries,[49] A. Afigbo, C. C. Ifemesia, and K.O. Dike himself, with the University of Nigeria, Nsukka as the new base for most of them. Two expatriates left in the 1960s—Omer-Cooper to the University of Zambia as the first chair of department, and Bertin Webster to Makarere University in Uganda, also as Chair. There were more movements within Nigeria itself. While a number of courses offered at Ibadan were duplicated elsewhere, attempts were also made to create major changes, especially at Ahmadu Bello University, Zaria. As many researchers focus on societies close to their universities, the dispersal boosted the development of local historiographies and ethnic histories.

In influencing the world of scholarship beyond its shores, the Ibadan History Series became the agency. The idea occurred in the 1950s,[50] and the books began to appear in the 1960s. The purpose of the Ibadan Series and similar essays and books relating to it are, first, to show that Africans had history, to identify and praise many examples of great civilizations (e.g., the empires of Ghana, Mali, Songhai, and Zimbabwe) and that Africa's greatness pre-dated the European contact. The Eurocentric opinion that Africa was "without writing and so without history," received one of the most vigorous attacks as African historians demonstrated that there was indeed evidence, both in written forms (as in the case of Arabic writings) but even more in oral traditions. While academic history may be said to share similar objectives and methods, a few even suggested that the writing about Africa can be different, if scholars can draw from the way the people themselves interpret history, especially in their comprehensive philosophy of life which does not partition knowledge as academics do.[51] The argument of nationalist historiography is that colonial rule and European contact distorted the African past as well as its history.[52] This is a great challenge to the "colonial library" on Africa.

To nationalist historiography, precolonial history was glorious and successful. The argument and the data demonstrate that most areas were already well developed before the European contacts. The slave trade is blamed for initiating a long period of disaster in Africa.[53] The services of archaeologists came handy, as they showed successful results of established civilizations at Nok, Ile-Ife, Benin, and Igbo-Ukwu, all in Nigeria. The past offers models to develop the present, concluded a number of scholars.

Second, nationalist historiography challenged the notion in the "colonial library" that the primary determinant of African history was the European presence in Africa. This view was challenged in two ways. The first was to present the history of Africa without the European impact—in pre-fifteenth century histories of places, and in the explanation of the causes and nature of great changes in Africa (such as the Islamic revolution of the nineteenth century). The other approach was to say that the European presence was an interlude in African history, a short phase in a long history. Even under colonial rule, Africans were said to have responded to the changes through a creative process of adaptation than of imitation.

Third, nationalist historiography adds the African dimension to an historical or cultural episode, without necessarily presenting it as a counterdiscourse. Thus, there are studies which may show that Africans think differently on certain issues such as colonialism,[54] or that things are different in their own environments and societies,[55] or that it is only Africans who can actually dominate certain aspects of knowledge, as in the case of indigenous literatures and languages.

Fourth, they wanted to demonstrate the African capability for nation-building and leadership. Not a few European writers had expressed the opinion that Africans would mismanage their freedom and that their indigenous political systems were inferior. The historians had to rescue the African kings, queens, merchant princes and princesses, and warriors if only to show that there were great men and women in Africa with leadership abilities. There is a tone in most of the work to affirm that precolonial institutions were well suited to the needs of the people before colonialism began to destroy them and that precolonial states were stable "with all the paraphernalia of a 'modern' state."[56] Omer-Cooper made a direct claim that leaders such as Shaka the

Zulu offer examples for modern leaders on how to transform their people: ". . . the task of instilling a sense of political unity into people of different languages and cultures in a limited time, the task which faces every political leader in the newly independent countries, is not so difficult as pessimists tend to maintain."[57]

Only a few of the studies can be used here as illustrations. As a collective, the books and essays offer a respectable outline of Nigerian history from antiquity to the present. The first local thesis by Murray Last relates the Islamic revolution of the nineteenth century to the preceding history, with details on the conditions that necessitated a revolution. He saw the new Islamic leaders in positive ways. In what appears as a follow-up study, R. A. Adeleye examines how the British conquered the caliphate and imposed colonial rule, cleverly adapting the caliphate structure to the system of Indirect Rule.[58]

In the south, among the Yoruba where the University of Ibadan was located, studies on the nineteenth-century wars and colonial rule were the most prominent. Ajayi and Robert Smith collaborated to write a small book on the Ijaye war (1860–65) and the general features of the military and warfare. S. A. Akintoye wrote an excellent account on the last and longest war, the Kiriji, from 1878 to 1893,[59] and Kola Folayan on the groups to the south and west.[60] The aims of the books were similar: to show that the wars were not primitive or barbaric as the European writers and missionaries had portrayed them, but were motivated by genuine political reasons; that the wars were not instigated by the slave trade, but by efforts at state formation; and that the wars had revolutionary impact on demography and politics. In the studies on Islam and the jihad, Yoruba wars and South Africa on the Zulu, the message was clear: Africans could initiate their own changes, and leaders did emerge at appropriate periods in history to produce the necessary changes. Dan Fodio and Shaka Zulu represent great leadership. If the former used Islam, the latter fell on African customs and a warrior culture to create far-reaching innovations in the military system and society.

The study of Indirect Rule dominated the studies on the south, with Afigbo writing on the Igbo, J. A. Atanda on the Yoruba, P. Igbafe on the Bini, and A. Asiwaju on the groups in the southern Republic of Benin.[61] The studies are very much alike in their structure and arguments: they celebrate local leadership, especially of the kings such as the Alaafin and Oba of Benin.

A few studies look at Nigeria or other countries.[62] Thus C. N. Anene and T. N. Tamuno examine the evolution of British rule up until the first World War.[63] Jide Osuntokun examines the war years,[64] and Fred Omu concentrates on the media, especially in the context of nationalism.[65] Ajayi and E. A. Ayandele examine the spread and impact of Christianity, while T. G. Gbadamosi looks at the spread of Islam among the Yoruba.[66] What is slighted is the historical study of traditional religions.

As the universities became fully established, research emanating from them also more and more reflected regionalism and their locations. In Zaria studies are on the Hausa-Fulani states and other groups. E. J. Alagoa, based in Port-Harcourt, wrote about the Niger Delta and the Ijo where the university is located. The elaboration of precolonial state structures and state formation gave prominence to the history of the precolonial period, and was usually positive in its description of power and institutions of society. Great kings such as Idris Alooma of Kanem-Borno, Mansa Musa of Mali, and Jaja of Opobo became the celebrated heroes of Africa. The histories of big states and kingdoms were presented as monumental success stories, even if there was evidence of political absolutism or of many cases of warfare, as in the case of the building and consolidation of the empires of Oyo and Dahomey. A merchant-prince, Jaja of Opobo was forgiven for his other lapses, which included rivalries with his neighbors and support for the British army against the Asante. Little was said of the dysfunctional elements in those systems and of the lapses in leadership, even if the methods were authoritarian.

H. F. C. Smith (now Abdulahi Smith), originally part of the Ibadan team before locating to Zaria in the north, to join the History Department of Ahmadu Bello University (ABU), provided an alternative vision that led to the emergence of what has been called the "Islamic legitimist,"[67] and a vibrant Marxist tradition. Among the principal achievements of the emphasis on Marxism are the reinterpretation of the causes of the nineteenth-century Islamic revolutions, and a class analysis of contemporary Nigeria. On the former, the study of the Sokoto caliphate received a central attention, with some scholars calling for Nigeria to draw models and ideals from it to improve the society, instead of looking to the West.[68] Although presented in Zaria as "new and different" from the scholars of Ibadan, both the Islamic and Marxist visions were definitely nationalistic in agenda: the Islamists, like negritudists, turned within African societies for ideas; the Marxists turned to a materialist interpretation to seek an end to the Western domination of Africa.

IV. Nationalist Historiography: A Critique

As the membership of the Ibadan school grew, and as the conditions in Africa changed for the worse, it became clear that a narrow definition of nationalist historiography could not be sustained. Some even began to express self-doubt as to whether it was the right way to write history. Criticisms and responses to them have been varied, while an alternative model is yet to take root in many African Departments of History.

The first, and perhaps the most sustained, modification was to develop additional themes in addition to the original fields for the doctorate degrees. In broadening research interests and agendas, the emphasis was to create a shift to the more contemporary period, so that historians could be useful to the nation or they could demonstrate the worth of their knowledge in the management of the nation. This is a variant of nationalist historiography, with a stress on the relevance of history to contemporary realities.

Second, there were those who called for a shift away from political history. Political history was and still is the dominant theme. E. A. Ayandele criticized the emphasis on political history which enabled kings and elite to dominate historical reconstruction at the expense of others.[69] Thus, members of the school began to pay attention to social, labor, and economic history. In the 1980s, new works were encouraged on modern Nigeria and international relations. In spite of the shifts, concerns were still dominated by sources and the importance of Africans.

Third, many were concerned about the issue of relevance, the extent to which a work of history should help to explain or solve a contemporary problem. Why should historians be preoccupied with the past if their present societies have too many problems? Why should they not use the past to explain the problems of the present? These and related questions were posed in the 1970s as a critique of the school. Indeed, the most important remark made by the members of the school against itself is that its works should be more relevant to the needs of contemporary Africa. This awareness owed in part to the failure of politics, the rise of military regimes, and the civil war from 1967 to 1970 which showed the fragility of the new independent state and the limitation of nationalist historiography in promoting the idea of the nation-state. Thus, Ajayi had to admit that "of all the branches of African Studies, African history is the most useless of all disciplines. Its failure to relate research to the practical problems of Africa is phenomenal."[70] Yet another issue is the extent to which the African people identify themselves with the various essays and books being presented on their behalf, one that raises the need to evaluate the type of history being written, the language of communication, and even accessibility to the African audience.

The views of A. Afigbo and Obaro Ikime, another distinguished member trained at Ibadan, are representative. To start with Ikime, his most important remarks were made in 1979.[71] He called for a linkage between historical studies and current issues, how some problems have their origins in either colonial or precolonial eras. As the historians searched for areas where they could be most useful, a few chose to focus on the historical explanation of ethnicity, on developing new courses on intergroup relations, and writing national histories so that their people could be united in a modern nation-state. Ikime defined relevance as the use of history in the service of the nation-state, a variant of nationalist historiography. In his own case, history was to be used to integrate the country, a sort of Nigerian perspective that would treat the people as united and promote those things that unite them, even at the expense of local histories.[72] Afigbo's comments are more polemical and ideological.[73] He sees a lack of paradigms and theories in most of the writings, and like Ikime, he wants historians to use their writings to unite the nation.[74]

A fourth issue is that most of the books display an ambivalent attitude towards change. On the one hand, external contacts, notably Islam and colonial imposition, are presented as agencies of change, and the outcome can be described as revolutionary. Yet on the other hand, they see great damage arising from them. Islam corrupted indigenous traditions, concluded R. A. Adeleye, while at the same time noting its pervasive role and entrenchment in culture and society. British rule was important, but then it is criticized for not doing enough, as all the studies on indirect rule stated. The colonial era was a major phase, but historians do not want it to be a dividing line in African history. Dike complained that the African factor has been ignored but opened his most important book with the claim that "[t]he history of modern West Africa is largely the history of five centuries of trade with European nations." While rejecting Europe on the one hand, many of the writers wanted Africa to aspire to the models of Europe. The main message was that Africa can be like Europe if given time; or that Africans had shown the capability of inventing and running systems that were either superior to or at par with those of Europe.

Fifth, the crisis of the African academy also impacted upon the growth and regeneration of nationalist historiography. Economic decline devastated the production of new knowledge, as there is no money to fund new research or rehabilitate existing infrastructure.

There are a number of devastating criticisms of the Ibadan School, partly arising from the studies published by it and also a critique of nationalist historiography in general. A common criticism from the Left and radical scholars is that the school is basically conservative, looking at society from the perspective of elite privileges and failing to use scholarship to create the conditions for change. It is also accused of empiricism, that is, merely collecting data about the past without a challenging ideological framework to study them, or at the minimum, providing a paradigm to make the data more meaningful. The works lack theoretical perspectives, many are fond of concluding, a view supported by such members of the school such as E. A. Ayandele.[75]

To start with, the claim of being a "school" is dismissed as too misleading a label for a group of scholars with an incoherent philosophy, ideology, or mission. It can still be described as a school, primarily in the elaboration of an African perspective of history and the use of multiple sources. It is not autonomous as a school, by which I mean that it did not publish something entirely unique unto itself. Neither did it have a "philosopher-king" whose ideas shape the orientation of all the texts, in spite of the towering stature of Dike and Ade Ajayi.[76] Even one Marxist work is represented in the Series, the study on the Nigerian mine workers by Bill Freund.[77]

Still on the charge of conservatism, its discussion of colonialism, in spite of the preponderance of the literature on this, is regarded as too generous to Europeans and too weak in capturing the great changes caused by imperialism. Even a member of the school, Omer-Cooper, agreed with this comment, and called for "new interpretations and analyses" to transcend what he regards as views that are "conservative and out of date."[78]

Not different from the criticism of conservatism is that of elitism. What comes across, concluded E. A. Ayandele, is an aristocratic view of history. By focusing on the nobles and the rich, historians are accused of representing the ruling class of the past. Where are the poor of history, the powerless, the exploited? The kind of the history of "everyday life,"[79] social and cultural history broadly defined, is missing from nationalist historiography.

The aforementioned critique constitutes a challenge to nationalist historiography as a new generation writes about Africa. If nationalist historiography started on the premise of anticolonial nationalism and the need to defend Africa, it has to be transcended by the need to confront independent Africa and the obstacles to its development. Present obstacles to development and political stability will constitute the turning points for writing about Africa for the greater part of the next millennium.

References

1. See for instance, William Bosman, *A New and Accurate Description of the Coast of Guinea* (London, 1705; reprint 1967); James Houston, *Some New and Accurate Observations of the Coast of Guinea* (London, 1725); and John Barbort, *A Description of the Coasts of North and South Guinea* (London, 1732).

2. Quoted in Joseph E. Harris, *Africans and Their History* (New York: Mentor, 1972), p. 19.

3. G.W.F. Hegel, *The Philosophy of History* (New York: Wiley Book Co., 1944), p. 99.

4. H. Trevor-Roper, *The Rise of Christian Europe* (New York: Harcourt, Brace, 1968), p. 9.

5. Horton (1835–83) was one of the pioneer professionals—a surgeon, businessman, and political thinker. He grew up in Sierra Leone, trained in England as an army medical doctor, and served for 20 years in British West Africa. After his retirement, he established a bank and a mining company, while retaining his interest in writing and politics.

6. See for instance, James B. Webster, *The African Churches among the Yoruba, 1888–1922* (Oxford: Clarendon Press, 1964).

7. Edward Wilmot Blyden, "Africa for Africans," quoted in Henry S. Wilson, ed., *Origins of West African Nationalism* (New York: St. Martins, 1969), p. 233.

8. Blyden, "The Prospects of the African," quoted in Wilson, ed., *Origins*, p. 240.

9. Blyden, *African Life and Customs* (London: C. M. Phillips, 1908).

10. Johnson, *The History of the Yorubas* (Lagos: C.M.S., 1921); Reindorf, *History of the Gold Coast and Asante* (Basel: Basel Mission, 1895).

11. Robert W. July, *The Origins of Modern African Thought: Its Development in West Africa during the Nineteenth and Twentieth Centuries* (New York: Praeger, 1967), p. 464.

12. Hayford, "Introduction," quoted in full in Wilson, ed., *Origins*, p. 334.

13. Léopold Senghor, *On African Socialism* (New York: Praeger, 1964).

14. Senghor, "African-Negro Aesthetics," *Diogenes* 16 (Winter, 1956): 23–24.

15. July, *The Origins of Modern African Thought*, p. 474.

16. Senghor, *On African Socialism*, p. 140.

17. For the development of the discipline in the West, see for instance, Jan Vansina, *Living with Africa* (Madison: University of Wisconsin Press, 1994); Roland Oliver, *In The Realms of Gold: Pioneering in African History* (Madison: University of Wisconsin Press, 1997); and A.H.M. Kirk-Greene, ed., *The Emergence of African History at British Universities* (Oxford: Worldview Publications, 1995).

18. See, for instance, Henk Wesseling, "Overseas History," in Peter Burke, ed., *New Perspectives on Historical Writing* (University Park: Pennsylvania State University Press, 1992), pp. 67–92.

19. July, *The Origins of Modern African Thought*, p. 468.

20. See for instance Jan Vansina, *Oral Tradition: A Study in Historical Methodology* (London: Routledge and Kegan Paul, 1965).

21. K. O. Dike, "African History and Self-Government," *West Africa*, no. 1882 (March 21, 1953): 251.

22. For examples of his writings, see *Civilization or Barbarism: An Authentic Anthropology*, translated from the French by Yaa-Lengi Meema Ngemi; edited by Harold J. Salemson and Marjolin de Jager (1981; translated edition, Chicago: Lawrence Hill, 1991); and *Precolonial Black Africa*, translated from the French by Harold Salemson (Chicago: Lawrence Hill, 1987).

23. M. Simmons J. Perham, *African Discovery* (London: Faber and Faber, 1962), p. 16.

24. Basil Davidson, *The African Past* (London: Longman, 1964), p. 36.

25. H. H. Johnston, *A History of the Colonization of Africa by Alien Races* (Cambridge: Cambridge University Press, 1899).

26. F. D. Lugard, *The Dual Mandate in British Tropical Africa* (London: Frank Cass, 1965).

27. Born at Awka in Eastern Nigeria in 1917, he went to school in Nigeria and Sierra Leone before proceeding to the United Kingdom for higher studies.

28. See for instance Michael Omolewa, "The Education Factor in the Emergence of the Modern Profession of Historians in Nigeria, 1926–1956," *Journal of the Historical Society of Nigeria* 10, 3 (December 1980).

29. K. O. Dike, *Trade and Politics in the Niger Delta, 1830–1885* (Oxford: Clarendon, 1956), pp. iv–v.

30. See for instance, John Flint, *Tubman Goldie and the Making of Modern Nigeria* (London: Oxford University Press, 1960).

31. For useful literature on the courses and the college in the early years, see K. Mellanby, *The Birth of Nigeria's University* (Ibadan: Ibadan University Press; T. N. Tamuno and J. F. Ade Ajayi, eds., *The University of Ibadan, 1948–73* (Ibadan: Ibadan University Press, 1973).

32. K. O. Dike, *Report on the Preservation and Administration of Historical Records in Nigeria (Mimeo, 1956)*.

33. Biobaku had a varied career as an administrator and professor. In 1956, he was appointed by the Western Region in Nigeria as the head of the Yoruba Historical Research Scheme to collect data and write on the Yoruba. Biobaku's thesis was also published as one of the pioneer academic books on the Yoruba: *The Egba and their Neighbours, 1842–1872* (Oxford: Clarendon, 1957).

34. See Toyin Falola, *Yoruba Gurus: Indigenous Production of Knowledge in Africa* (Trenton: Africa World Press, 2000).

35. Apart from his revised thesis, he published two small studies in the 1950s: *A Hundred Years of British Rule in Nigeria* (Ibadan: Ibadan University Press, 1957) and *The Origins of the Niger Mission* (Ibadan: Ibadan University Press, 1958).

36. C. C. Ifemesia, "Funeral Orations," *Bulletin of the Historical Society of Nigeria*, Special edition (1984): 5.

37. Obaro Ikime, *Groundwork of Nigerian History* (Ibadan: Heinemann, 1980).

38. See for instance J. D. Omer-Cooper, "The Contribution of the University of Ibadan to the Spread of the Study and Teaching of African History," *Journal of the Historical Society of Nigeria* 10, 3 (December 1980).

39. Edited by J. F. Ade Ajayi and Ian Espie (Ibadan: Ibadan University Press, 1965).

40. Edited by J. C. Anene and Godfrey Brown (Ibadan: Ibadan University Press and London: Nelson, 1966).

41. Published by Longman, the four titles are: *A History of West Africa 1000–1800, The Revolutionary Years: West Africa since 1800: The Making of Modern Africa 1800–1960*, and *East Africa to the Late Nineteenth Century*.

42. J. F. Ade Ajayi and M. Crowder, eds., *History of West Africa* (London: Longman, 1985).

43. J. F. Ade Ajayi, "Post-Graduate Studies and Staff Development," *The University of Ibadan 1948–73* (Ibadan: Ibadan University Press, 1973), p. 153.

44. These were the University of Nigeria, Nsukka, established in 1960, the University of Ife, the University of Lagos, and the Ahmadu Bello University, all established in 1962.

45. T. N. Tamuno, *Department of History, 1948–73: Commemorative Brochure* (Ibadan: Department of History, 1974) pp. 13–14.

46. D. M. Last, "Sokoto in the Nineteenth Century with Special Reference to the Vizerate," Ph.D. thesis, University of Ibadan, 1964.

47. Ph.D. thesis, University of Ibadan, 1964.

48. O. Ikime, "Itshekiri-Urhobo Relations and the Establishment of British Rule, 1884–1936," Ph.D. thesis, University of Ibadan, 1965.

49. His major work is the *International Boundaries of Nigeria, 1885–1960* (London: Longman, 1970).

50. See J. D. Omer-Cooper, "My time in Ibadan," in T. N. Tamuno, ed., *Ibadan Voices* (Ibadan: Ibadan University Press, 1981), pp. 127–35.

51. See for instance, C. C. Ifemesia, "Current Demands of African Historiography," Conference paper presented at the Silver Jubilee of the Historical Society of Nigeria, Ibadan, September, 1980.

52. See for instance, Toyin Falola, ed., *Tradition and Change in Africa: The Essays of J. F. Ade Ajayi* (Trenton: Africa World Press, 1999).

53. See for instance, Walter Rodney, *How Europe Underdeveloped Africa* (Dar-es-Salaam: Tanzania Publishing House, 1972).

54. See for instance, Adu Boahen, *African Perspectives on Colonialism* (Baltimore: Johns Hopkins University Press, 1987).

55. See for instance, Jomo Kenyatta, *Facing Mount Kenya* (London: Secker and Warburg, 1938).

56. M. Phares Mutibwa, *The Malagasy and the Europeans* (London: Longman, 1974), p. xiii.

57. J. D. Omer-Cooper, Preface to *The Zulu Aftermath* (London: Longman, 1966). .

58. *Power and Diplomacy in Northern Nigeria: The Sokoto Caliphate and Its Enemies, 1804–1906* (London: Longman, 1971).

59. S. A. Akintoye, "The Ekiti Parapo and Kiriji War," Ph.D. thesis, University of Ibadan, 1966.

60. Kola Folayan, "Egbado and Yoruba-Aja Power Politics, 1832–1894," M.A. thesis, University of Ibadan, 1967.

61. Afigbo, *The Warrant Chiefs: Indirect Rule in Southeastern Nigeria, 1891–1929* (London: Longman, 1972); Atanda, *The New Oyo Empire: Indirect Rule and Change in Western Nigeria, 1894–1934* (London: Longman, 1973); Igbafe, *Benin under*

British Administration: The Impact of Colonial Rule on an African Kingdom, 1897–1938 (London: Longman, 1979); and Asiwaju, *Western Yorubaland under European Rule, 1889–1945: A Comparative Analysis of French and British Colonialism* (London: Longman, 1976).

62. Among the studies on other places beside Nigeria are: B. O. Oloruntimehin, "The Segu Tukulor Empire, 1848–1893," Ph.D. thesis, University of Ibadan, 1966.

63. Anene, *Southern Nigeria in Transition, 1885–1906* (Cambridge: Cambridge University Press, 1966); T. N. Tamuno, *The Evolution of the Nigerian State: The Southern Phase, 1898–1914* (London: Longman, 1972).

64. Osuntokun, *Nigeria in the First World War* (London: Longman, 1978).

65. J.I.A. Omu, "The Nigerian Newspaper Press, 1859–1957: A Study in Origin, Growth and Influence," Ph.D. thesis, University of Ibadan, 1966.

66. Ajayi, *Christian Missions in Nigeria, 1841–1891: The Making of a New Elite* (London: Longman, 1965); Ayandele, *The Missionary Impact on Modern Nigeria, 1842–1914: A Political and Social Analysis*; and Gbadamosi, *The Growth of Islam among the Yoruba, 1841–1908* (London: Longman, 1978).

67. Paul Lovejoy, "Nigeria: The Ibadan School and Its Critics" in Bogumil Jewsiewicki and David Newbury, eds., *African Historiographies: What History for Which Africa?* (Beverly Hills: Sage, 1986), p. 202.

68. A. Smith, "The Contemporary Significance of the Academic Ideals of the Sokoto 'Jihad'" in Y. B. Usman, ed., *Studies in the History of the Sokoto Caliphate* (Lagos: Third Press International, 1979).

69. E. A. Ayandele, "How Truly Nigerian is our Nigerian History?" *African Notes* 5, 2 (1969): 19–35.

70. J. F. Ade Ajayi, "Canada Provides Food for Thought," *West Africa* (May 26, 1980): 296.

71. Obaro Ikime, "Nigerian History Yesterday, Today and Tomorrow," Inaugural Lecture, History, University of Ibadan, Nigeria, 1979.

72. See for instance Obaro Ikime, *The Fall of Nigeria: The British Conquest* (London: Heinemann, 1977).

73. *The Poverty of African Historiography* (Idanre: Afrografika Publishers, 1977).

74. A. E. Afigbo, "Nigerian History and Unity," Conference Paper, Annual Congress of the Historical Society of Nigeria, University of Ilorin, 1983.

75. E. A. Ayandele, "How Truly Nigerian Is Our Nigerian History?" Conference Paper, 14th Annual Congress of the Historical Society of Nigeria, 1969.

76. Toyin Falola, ed., *African Historiography*.

77. *Capital and Labour in the Nigerian Tin Mines* (London: Longman, 1981).

78. "The Contribution," p. 30.

79. For its definition and relevance, see for instance Alf Ludtke, ed., *The History of Everyday Life: Reconstructing Historical Experiences and Ways of Life*, trans. William Templer (Princeton, NJ: Princeton University Press, 1995).

12. The Subaltern School and the Ascendancy of Indian History

Vinay Lal

I. Footnotes to a History

It is a rare moment indeed when a school of thought, whether in history or in any other discipline, from a formerly colonized nation that is still resoundingly a part of the Third World (whatever its pretensions to nuclear or great power status), receives in the Western academy the critical attention that has been bestowed upon the Subaltern School of historians, whose work revolves largely around the colonial period of Indian history. Historians might recall that even the *American Historical Review*, which is seldom a journal at the cutting edge of theory, or otherwise prone to the bacchanalia of postmodern excesses, devoted the greater part of the pages of one of its recent issues to Subaltern Studies and its rather wide impact across not only historical studies in the Anglo-American academy, but beyond as well.[1] A Latin American Subaltern Studies Group, citing the inspirational work of the Indian historians, has declared its intent to install the subaltern at the center of Latin American studies, though it is revealing that their programmatic statement appears in a cultural studies journal.[2] There is, in the warm reception given to Subaltern Studies in some circles in the Anglo-American world, more than just a whiff of avuncular affection: trained almost entirely in British universities, the core group of subaltern historians stand forth, or so it is sometimes fondly imagined, as living testimony to the continuing power of the 'mother' country to influence its peripheries.[3]

However, if I may mix metaphors, the return of the prodigal son is not an unmixed blessing. A few years after the publication of the first volume of *Subaltern Studies*, the first rumblings of discontent about the ascendancy of subaltern history, which have since greatly increased, began to appear. Social historians, for instance, argued that in substance there was little to distinguish subaltern history, stripped of its veneer of post-structuralism and Gramscian thought, from "the history from below" associated with E. P. Thompson, Eric Hobsbawm, and many others belonging to the venerable tradition of British Marxist history. Others are inclined to attribute the success of the subalternists to the fact that Indians could with relative ease take advantage of the English language's inescapable hegemony in the global marketplace of scholarship, though incipient in this criticism are numerous unsavory suggestions about the manner in which colonialism's deep structures continue to inform the political economy and political sociology of scholarship in the formerly colonized world. When, a mere few years into the emergence of the journal *Subaltern Studies*, Edward Said and Gayatri Chakravorty Spivak lent their formidable voices to the enterprise, its short-term future was certainly assured. Thus, argue the critics, subaltern history was propelled into fame not as a mode of doing history, but as another form of postcolonial criticism. This impression is reinforced by the rather bizarre recommendation with which the new *Subaltern Studies Reader* (1997), whose contributors are described as being "instrumental in establishing" postcolonial studies, is brought to the reader's attention.[4]

I will address some of these criticisms later, but suffice to note that just as India is represented as having sought to gate-crash its way into the estate of the nuclear powers, only to be rebuffed by the zealous guardians at its doorway, so subaltern scholarship is sometimes seen as an intruder into domains whose inhabitants are scarcely accustomed to seeing themselves in need of interpretive and analytical lessons from the East. It is one thing to turn to India for its wisdom, and indeed what would India be (for the West) without its mystics, sages, yogis, gurus, and half-naked fakirs, but no one is prepared to countenance the view that in the realm of history and reason, these being construed as one and the same, Western social scientists and historians could turn with profit to the work of Indian historians. Let us remind ourselves that, writing in 1817, James Mill, whose *History of British India* would become the indispensable historical manual for the young employees of the East India Company and its successor regime throughout the nineteenth century, could aver with perfect confidence that the Hindus, being "perfectly destitute of historical records", displayed every signs of being an irrational people: "all rude nations neglect history, and are gratified with the productions of the mythologists and poets".[5] If one should dismiss this cavalier assessment with the trite observation that Mill was merely a creature of his times, a captive of an European age unabashedly fond of its imperialist credentials, it behooves us to listen to the words, not so far removed from our times, of that 'friend' and historian of India, Edward Thompson, the father of E. P. Thompson:

> Indians are not historians, and they rarely show any critical ability. Even their most useful books, books full of research and information, exasperate with their repetitions and diffuseness, and lose effect by their uncritical enthusiasms. . . . So they are not likely to displace our account of our connection with India.[6]

Nearly twenty years after the emergence of subaltern history, no one doubts that the old colonial histories have been displaced, and even that though Delhi and Calcutta may not entirely rule the roost, the interpretation of Indian history is now largely an affair of the Indians themselves. The likes of Edward Thompson have been confined to oblivion, and the British accounts of their connections with India lie largely in tatters, worthy only of the dustbin of history. But it is also equally the case that no one can say with complete confidence what subaltern history stands for, with what voices the subaltern historians speak, and to what purposes. Ten volumes of *Subaltern Studies* have appeared so far, and the fifty-some historians associated with the enterprise, a few of them since its very inception, have between them produced hundreds of articles and several dozen monographs. A certain coherence seemed to mark the work of the collective in the first decade of its existence, when Ranajit Guha, then based at the Australian National University, presided over its deliberations and saw the first six volumes of *Subaltern Studies* into print. However, the imperatives to diversify the membership of the collective, and bring subaltern history into a more palpable relationship with literary narratives, the discourses of political economy, the intellectual practices of the other social sciences, and the contemporary realities of India, must have been present even then, and were only to become accelerated in the 1990s. Volume IV, which appeared in 1986, featured a critical intervention by Gayatri Spivak, and so marked subaltern history's first engagement with feminism, and indeed the first explicit attempt to locate it in relation to deconstructionism. It also established the pattern whereby one or more contributions in most of the subsequent volumes of *Subaltern Studies* were to offer a critical perspective on the enterprise as a whole, and in Volume V this was attempted by placing *Subaltern Studies* under the scrutiny of historical materialism and Marxist economics,[7] just as the following volume featured an anthropological perspective on the enterprise, accompanied by a debate on the representations of women in Indian feminist histories.[8]

Still, it is a striking feature of the first six volumes of *Subaltern Studies* that, with the exception of a solitary piece by Tanika Sarkar,[9] the work of no women practitioners of Indian history was on display. This may not be entirely surprising, since the impulse towards feminist critiques in India had emanated from largely literary circles, where the disposition to engage in what was considered 'theory' was also more clearly visible. Though the debate on feminism's relation to subaltern history had commenced in *Subaltern Studies*, feminist readings of history were nowhere to be seen, except somewhat tangentially in Gayatri Spivak's translation of, and commentary on, a short story by Mahasweta Devi,[10] one of India's leading women writers and an activist who has worked extensively alongside women and tribals in Bengal. Spivak had forged a unique but nonetheless ambivalent and curiously disjunctive intellectual relationship with Mahasweta, but the history of this collaborative work forms a chapter in the sociology of Indian intellectual life, rather than a chapter in subaltern historiography.

There were doubtless other sources of discomfort for certain members of the collective. In his opening salvo on elite historiography, Ranajit Guha had condemned it for neglecting and obscuring the "politics of the people",[11] but it was not until 1996, when Volume IX of *Subaltern Studies* was published, that the politics of the Dalits, historically the most disempowered segment of India's population, and now at least 150 million in number, received its first explicit articulation.[12] Despite the grandiose celebrations of subalternity, and the promise to furnish complex and compelling narratives of how far the "people *on their own*, that is, *independently of the elite*", had contributed to the nationalist movement and the making of Indian society, Subaltern Studies seemed far too interested in the activities of the middle classes. This disenchantment with Subaltern Studies's alleged abandonment of its originary ambitions, namely to understand how far the activity of the people constituted an "autonomous domain", and what were the modes of their resistance to both imperialist and elite nationalist politics, can be witnessed in the caustic assessment by Ramachandra Guha, who had himself once been a member of the collective, of Volume VIII of *Subaltern Studies* (1994). Guha gave his considered opinion that the essays comprising the volume, though unquestionably constituting "intellectual history, reframed as 'discourse analysis'", were "emphatically not Subaltern Studies". Guha described it as a shift towards "*bhadralok* studies", fully aware that no greater insult was possible. The word "bhadralok", made common in the 1960s by American scholars working on India, who have specialized in taking the politics out of knowledge (a characteristically American trait),[13] refers to the 'gentle folk', or the gentry, but its far more pejorative connotations call to mind a class of people who, being the progeny of Macaulay, were imitative of their colonial masters, and even professed to be more English than the English themselves. Solidly middle-class, and unfailingly enslaved to the narratives of science, reason, and progress, the *bhadralok* disassociated themselves equally from Gandhian politics, which smelled too much of disloyalty, and the politics of the masses.

To say that Subaltern Studies had transformed itself into *bhadralok* studies, in a curious return of the repressed, was to aver that the subaltern historians, for the most part, had moved from studies of popular consciousness to unraveling the mentalities of nationalist leaders and the world of middle-class Bengali domesticity, "from documenting subaltern dissent to dissecting elite discourse, from writing with (socialist) passion to following the postmodernist fashion".[14] Similarly Sumit Sarkar, himself one of India's most distinguished historians and a founding member of the Subaltern Collective, in tracing the postmodernist turn in Subaltern Studies to what he alleges is the wholesale and unreflective deployment of the Saidian framework among a section of the subaltern historians, has not only disavowed any further association with his former colleagues, but is unremitting in his critique of Subaltern Studies for those very sins of essentialism, teleology, and fetishization which were associated with elite historiography.[15] Sarkar's apostasy has not gone unnoticed: thus Ranajit Guha's introduction to his *Subaltern Studies Reader* (1997) was to excise all trace of Sarkar and his important role in the collective.[16]

Thus, as the Subaltern Studies collective prepares to enter into the third decade of its existence, the enterprise of Subaltern history means many different things to different people. Over the course of time, people drift into different sets of habits, take up new ideas, and form new associations. However, Subaltern Studies's sharpest critics are some former members of the collective, and it is a trifle too gentle to speak of the fragmentation of the collective as though one were describing the tendency of rivers to form tributaries. The high priest of the collective, Ranajit Guha, is no longer formally associated with his own creation, and the group of younger historians he gathered around him rendered him an intellectual tribute by designating Volume VIII of *Subaltern Studies* as a collection of essays in his honour. If some members of the collective had wandered into postmodernism, or were more seriously engaged with Western philosophy or feminist theory, Volume IX of *Subaltern Studies* was to show that the collective had the capacity to reinvent itself in yet more diverse ways, by embracing voices more generally associated with postcolonial theory and cultural studies, as well as with the study of contemporary Indian society. Indeed, in the American academy especially, Subaltern Studies is seen as the form in which "cultural studies" has taken root in India, while others recognize it as constituting the particular Indian inflection of postcolonial theory. In all this, Subaltern Studies is beginning to look like the banyan tree, whose magisterial presence pervades the Indian landscape, and under its enormous canvas social and cultural historians, postmodernists, postcolonialists, feminists, post-structuralists, and—if I may put it this way—post-Marxist historians have alike found some sustenance. A banyan tree, I might add, is not the same thing as a tropical jungle, whatever the temptation to let those luxuriant metaphors which the study of India invites inform our understanding of the particular relationship of Indian intellectual endeavors to Indian history and society. One does not tackle a banyan tree as a whole; and, in like fashion, I can only lop away at some of its branches, and merely hint at some of the trajectories that a critique of Subaltern Studies, around which a formidable mass of critical literature has developed, should take.

II. Backdrop to a History

In the words of one of the newer members of the Subaltern collective, "subalternist analysis has become a recognizable mode of critical scholarship in history, literature, and anthropology".[17] Yet very few people outside the field of Indian history understand its particular place in Indian historiography, and fewer still are able to assess the precise departures signified by subaltern history. Subaltern Studies has certainly thrived on the impression, which it did everything to encourage, that all previous histories of India represented the collusion of imperialist and nationalist forces, just as they were singularly lacking in any theoretical impulse. It is noteworthy that, despite the avowedly Marxist orientation of some of the subaltern historians, and certainly their repudiation of neo-Hindu histories, their work offers no engagement with an entire generation or two of Indian Marxist historians (and sometimes sociologists) who preceded them, such as Rajne Palme Dutt, D. D. Kosambi, and A. R. Desai, or even with their older and still active contemporaries such as Romila Thapar and Irfan Habib. One might well think, on reading the subaltern historians, that nothing in the tradition of Indian historiography speaks to their interests, and that insofar as one might wish to evoke any worthwhile lineages, the past is a *tabula rasa*. Here subaltern history echoes, ironically, the early nineteenth-century British histories of India, which were predicated on the assumption that, the Indians being supremely indifferent to their past, the British were faced with the onerous task of starting entirely afresh, dependent only on their own resources.

Though the history of Indian historiography, and the precise relations of subaltern histories to Marxist histories, can scarcely be delineated in this paper,[18] the advent of subaltern history might be better appreciated against the backdrop of other trajectories of twentieth-century Indian history, howsoever briefly these are delineated. The first generation of Indian historians such as R. C. Dutt (1848–1909) and R. G. Bhandarkar (1837–1925) had expended its labors largely on the study of ancient India, which was envisioned as the high point of Indian civilization. The tomes of the Bengali historian Jadunath Sarkar (1870–1958) on the Mughals and Aurangzeb were based on a representation of political Islam as tyrannical and iniquitous, an impression equally conveyed by his celebratory biography of the Maratha leader Shivaji, who was elevated as the founding father of Indian nationalism. With the attainment of independence in 1947, the creation of an Indian history, for and by Indians, became something of a national imperative, and it was never doubted that the "freedom struggle", waged under the leadership of Mohandas Gandhi and the Congress party, would constitute one of the more glorious chapters of Indian history. An official *History of the Freedom Movement in India*, authored by Tara Chand, made its appearance in four volumes (1961–72),[19] but the enterprise of state-sponsored histories extended much further, as most Indian states released their own histories of the "freedom struggle".[20] In the gargantuan eleven-volume *History and Culture of the Indian People* (1951–69), under the general editorship of R. C. Majumdar, whose own contributions to the volumes were formidable, the nationalist devotion to the Hindu past saw its most sustained expression, and history was to be yoked to a particular vision of nation-building.

From the point of view of locating subaltern history, however, it is other trajectories, associated with Marxist or materialist historians such as Saumyendranath Tagore, D. D. Kosambi, Romila Thapar, R. C. Sharma, Irfan Habib, and Bipan Chandra, or with Calcutta-based historians and scholars—Barun De and Asok Sen, among others—of the Bengal Renaissance, that demand our attention. The latter group, in revisiting the hagiographic accounts of the Bengal Renaissance, had come to the realization that Rammohan Roy, Iswar Chandra Vidyasagar, Keshub Sen, and other nineteenth-century social reformers were constrained by the colonial context and unable to enter into anything but an uncritical engagement with Western modernity.[21] This insight, though shorn of any theoretical apparatus, would clearly inform the work of subaltern historians. Among the Marxist historians, a number of other considerations, stemming from the immense political and social dislocations of the 1970s, predominated. Under

Jawaharlal Nehru, the country had seemed committed to secularism, but this consensus began to show signs of strain under his daughter, Indira Gandhi. The war with Pakistan in 1971, leading to the creation of Bangladesh, brought to the fore questions of ethnicity, language, and nation-formation, just as the massacre of Bengali intellectuals by the retreating Pakistani army brought an awareness of the precariousness of intellectual life in South Asia. Yet four years later Indira Gandhi was to impose an internal emergency, and political calculations impelled her, as well as other various other politicians, to court religious bodies and organizations. Henceforth the 'religious vote bank' would be an invariable factor in Indian politics.

At the same time, 'communalism', or the supposition that identity in India was constituted preeminently through membership in religious communities, broadly defined as 'Hindu', 'Muslim', 'Sikh', and so on, was assuming a heightened importance in historical narratives. The effect, from the Marxist standpoint, was to introduce manifold distortions in the understanding of Indian history: not only were Hindu-Muslim relations being cast as drenched in blood, but conflicts among the ruling elite were being construed as conflicts at the broader social level. Marxist historians who dared to challenge conventional orthodoxies found themselves ostracized or ridiculed: such was the experience, for instance, of R. S. Sharma, who in his school textbook, *Ancient India*, had put forth the view that the ancient Aryans were beef-eaters, a view that the Hindu right construed as calculated to demean their faith. But the Marxist historians by no means were an undifferentiated lot: while Bipan Chandra veered towards the view that the nationalist movement could not be dismissed as a bourgeois endeavor, other historians were hostile to the received view and pointed to the Congress party's unwillingness to stand for radical economic and land reform, or its inability to draw workers, peasants, minorities, women, and other disenfranchised into the nationalist movement or into the mainstream of public life in the period after independence.[22]

In the delineation of the circumstances under which the Subaltern Studies collective was formed, it becomes important to dwell at length on what was then the dominant strand in Indian historiography, namely the so-called Cambridge School. Earlier generations of imperialist historians had sought to make a decisive link between education and politics: in their view, it is the largely English-educated Indian middleclass, nourished on the writings of Mill, Locke, and Milton, and brought to an awareness of the place that institutions, organized along rational and scientific lines, could play in the life of a society, which had first raised the demand for some form of political representation. Cognizant of the principles of liberty, democracy, the separation of powers, constitutional agitation, and freedom of speech enshrined in Western political practices, these Indians were construed as the main, and only rightful, actors in the drama of nationalism that began to unfold in overtly political ways in the late nineteenth century. They recognized, or so it was argued, that political action must be within the framework of the law, and nothing should violate the 'rule of law'. The British themselves might well be despotic, as the wise and the just must often be, but among a people such as the Indians who before the blessings of Western civilization were brought to their doorstep had never experienced anything but despotism, the adherence to the 'rule of law' served as the indispensable condition of their acceptance in the political domain. All other political activity must perforce be 'criminal'. The British could well be proud of these middle-class or *bhadralok* Indians, as they provided unimpeachable evidence of the bountiful effects of the civilizing mission, the judiciousness of British policies, and the universal truth of the great narratives of science and reason. The only Indian politics was the politics of the English-educated *bhadralok*, and as it is they who stoked the fires of nationalism, Indians were bound to recognize that even their nationalism was the very gift of a magnanimous people endowed with enlightened traditions.

Trite and comical as this narrative might now sound, it appears in a refurbished and seemingly more subtle form in the writings of the 'Cambridge School' of historians. Many commentators have been fixated on Anil Seal's *The Emergence of Indian Nationalism* (1968), where it is argued that education was "one of the chief determinants" of the politics of Indian nationalism, the genesis of which "is clearly linked with those Indians who had been schooled by Western methods",[23] as the originary point of the Cambridge School's explorations in Indian history, but in point of fact the framework for this school of thought is derived from a broader swathe of work on the partition of Africa and the economic history of the British empire. Rejecting the view of both Marxist theoreticians and late Victorian historians that the essence of imperialism consisted in the scramble for colonies, in the extension of Western political control over territories in the non-Western world, John Gallagher and Ronald Robinson argued in an article published in 1953 that the emphasis on formal empire had blinded scholars to the continuity between formal and informal empires, as well as to the history of continued expansion of British trade and investment. Gallagher and Robinson posited a *reluctant* imperialism; their Empire, moreover, had nothing to do with power. The "distinctive feature" of British imperialism, they boldly argued, resided in the "willingness to limit the use of paramount power to establishing security for trade"; and power was deployed only when native collaborators could not be found to preserve British interests.[24]

The thesis for the "Non-European Foundations of European Imperialism" emerges more clearly in Robinson's article by the same name, significantly subtitled "Sketch for a Theory of Collaboration".[25] The use of the word 'theory' implies something lofty, but Robinson had no more prosaic observation than that "imperialism was as much a function of its victims' collaboration or non-collaboration—of their indigenous politics, as it was of European expansion". If imperialism had perforce to be rescued (though why that should be necessary—at a time when Britain had already been divested of India, Burma, and Ceylon, and was facing insurgencies elsewhere in its empire, at a time, that is, when the writing was on the wall and Britain could choose to leave with grace—is another question), it only remained to demonstrate that the natives, or the class of natives that alone mattered, were enthusiastic in their embrace of colonial rule: as Robinson puts it, "the choice of indigenous collaborators, more than anything else, determined the organisation of colonial rule". Imperial takeovers in Africa and Asia were actuated less by the expansion of European capitalism than "by the breakdown of collaborative mechanisms in extra-European politics which hitherto had provided them with adequate opportunity and protection". Moreover, if imperialism is only another name for collaboration, then it is even possible to say that the natives were imperialists in their own right. Robinson can, thus, quite brazenly even speak, apropos the Tswana tribe of Bechuanaland, of the natives "exploit[ing] the European". European imperialism is moved to the margins, rendered into an epiphenomenon: "Imperialism in the form of colonial rule was a major function not of European society, but a major function of indigenous politics". Imperialism was consequently not the cause but the consequence of the partition of Africa; to adopt the formulation of Eric Stokes, more well-known for his work on India, "the powers were scrambling in Africa and not for Africa".[26]

Seal's work on Indian nationalism, to which I have alluded, points to the ways in which this purportedly "new" view of imperialism found its way into the study of late British India. The subtitle of his work, "Competition and Collaboration in the Late Nineteenth Century", gives the game away. In accounting for the origins of Indian nationalism, Seal constructs an entire narrative around the lives and activities of a handful of English-educated men in the Presidencies, who competed for those jobs and opportunities that the British had provided through educational and administrative reform. A new class of people had also emerged as a consequence of the disruption of the village economy and the increasing penetration into the town and countryside of trading companies which employed educated Indians in increasing numbers as middlemen, brokers, and agents. However, the growth of this middle class soon outpaced the availability of jobs, leading to increasing disaffection among the educated youth. In the altering conditions of British rule, characterized by new opportunities for advancement, social change, and institutional reform, the existing rivalries that divided one caste from another, the Muslim from the Hindu, community from community, became even more accentuated. Now the educated, whether Brahmins or Muslims, tradition-bound or modernizers, Bengali or Tamil, forged their own horizontal alliances—a natural enough response, but one that Indians, among whom the idea of the 'individual' has no salience in the colonial sociology of knowledge, were bound to adopt in a predictable surrender to primordial community instinct. Seal stops short of describing all these beneficiaries of English education as a "new social class", for in his view the changes introduced in the economy were not so substantial as to "give India social classes based on economic categories". Seal could not argue otherwise, for to impute a form of social stratification based on social classes would be to obscure the differences between a colonized people and the more advanced society of the 'mother' country.[27]

In a later paper on "Imperialism and Nationalism in India", Seal professes to have abandoned the theory so elaborately constructed in his earlier work, on the grounds that the "graduates and professional men in the presidencies [Bombay, Calcutta, and Madras]" were "not quite as important as they once appeared".[28] But in fact the "horizontal alliances" that had once seemed so paramount to Seal now turn into "vertical alliances" of "bigwigs and followers", "factions" with patrons and clients. Accordingly the nodal point of the analysis is shifted from the presidencies to the localities, where "the race for influence, status and resources", which alone "decided political choices", is better observed. In the localities "the unabashed scramblers for advantage at the bottom" become more visible; and it is not incidental that this scrambling is all done by Indians, not Englishmen. Driven by self-aggrandizement, by the lust for economic gain and political power, "Hindus worked with Muslims, [and] Brahmins were hand in glove with non-Brahmins";[29] and the religious taboos and social constraints of centuries were cast aside. Money will make untouchables even of Brahmins; so much for the incorruptible purity of the sacerdotal caste. In the words of one of Seal's colleagues at Cambridge, "the most obvious characteristic of every Indian politician was that each acted for many interests at all levels of Indian society and in so doing cut across horizontal ties of class, caste, region and religion".[30] Indians jockeyed with each other for position and power in this wild scenario of collaboration and competition.

In the view of Indian history propounded by the 'Cambridge School', there is no room for ideology.[31] Indian nationalists, animated only by self-interest, relentlessly pursued rationally calculated ends, and their pious declarations must not be allowed to obscure the nature of "Indian nationalism" as "animal politics".[32] Annie Beasant, an Irishwoman who came to occupy an important place in Indian politics, is described as joining the Congress "undoubtedly . . . to bring her increased public attention", and militancy in the Kistna-Godavri deltas during the Civil Disobedience movement is attributed to the inability of some people to "find a satisfactory niche in local government".[33] When Indians fail to become clerks, they opt for rebellion: such are the doings of a highly impulsive people. Writing about politics in the South, David Washbrook, one of the more sophisticated of the Cambridge historians, avers that "the provincial political struggle was not about the nature of interests which were to be represented to the British; it was about who was to earn the money and achieve the prestige which came from carrying out the representation".[34] Political activity at the provincial level, in other words, is thus seen to revolve around the institutions of government. Here, again, Seal had set the tone for the argument: as he wrote, "It is our hypothesis that the structure of imperial government can provide a clue to the way Indian politics developed".[35] Where before the "genesis" of Indian politics was said to lie in the actions of the English-educated elite in the presidencies, now the motor of political behavior was described as the government, which itself showed Indians the way to political activity. The argument is rendered more explicit in Gordon Johnson's monograph on Bombay, where Indian politicians are generally described as being consumed by local politics, and compelled to take interest in national politics only when prompted by the government at the national level: in Johnson's words, "nationalist activity boons and slumps in phase with the national activity of the government".[36] Indians had to be pushed towards nationalism; they could not think beyond their village or town, nor was their gaze set on anything nobler than short-term tactics, local grievances, and petty gains. Imperialist stimulus, nationalist response: the scientist in the laboratory, the rat in the cage; here is the story of Indian nationalism, that sordid tale of every man desperately seeking to find his place under this sun.

III. The Moment of Arrival:
The Birth of the Subaltern in Negation

It is against the immediate backdrop of the 'Cambridge School' that subaltern history emerged, though this is scarcely to say that there was anything in a history of "vertical" or "horizontal" alliances to warrant the claim that it represented a novel reading of Indian nationalism or political history. But in the writings of the historians belonging to the 'Cambridge School' was to be found a template which pointed, in the most tangible way, to what Ranajit Guha has described as the "bad faith of historiography", to everything that a historiography which is responsible to its subjects, politically emancipatory, sensitive in its treatment of the evidence, and theoretically astute must avoid.[37] (I may here note, and shall advert to the matter in greater detail later, that subaltern history knows itself principally as negation, as the opposite of what it does not desire.) Since the emphasis in earlier imperialist writings on the activities of a small segment of the English-educated elite now appeared as a gross caricature of Indian political activity, the 'Cambridge School' historians, let us recall, were to shift the locus of their attention to the government, whose actions were eagerly watched by the nationalists. Seal attempted to seal this argument with a cryptic formulation: "The British built this framework; the Indians fitted into it".[38] *Agency* never belongs with the Indians; they are condemned to be reactive. Moreover, whether the chief "determinant" of Indian political activity is construed as the activities of the educated elite, or the actions of the government, the 'Cambridge School' history of India is a history of native *collaboration*. As is quite transparent, the effect of this argument is to make *resistance* invisible, to write it out of the political history of nationalism altogether; collaboration also renders Indians into willing partakers of their own submission. This is the house-cleaning and refurbishing of the 'Cambridge School' variety: since Indians must be conceived as agents in their own right, they were to be endowed with a greater share in the institutional mechanisms that kept them suppressed and bid them to look to the *state* as the principal locus of political agency.

No one reading Ranajit Guha's programmatic note in the first volume of Subaltern Studies would have missed the implicit references to the 'Cambridge School', or to the older liberal-imperialist histories from which its arguments are derived. But Guha was to be equally unsparing of nationalist histories, which in some respect, since they invited and even demanded allegiance from loyal-minded Indians, were more insidious in their effect.

"The historiography of Indian nationalism has for a long time been dominated by elitism", Guha wrote in the opening sentence, and added in elaboration that elitism contained both "colonialist" and "bourgeois-nationalist
elitism", the former defining Indian nationalism "primarily as a function of
stimulus and response".[39] "The general orientation" of nationalist historiography, on the other hand, "is to represent Indian nationalism as primarily an
idealist venture in which the indigenous elite led the people from subjugation to freedom". In either case, Guha argued, elitist historiography failed to
"acknowledge, far less interpret, the contribution made by the people *on their
own*, that is, *independently of the elite* to the making and development of this
nation". Nationalist historiography understood the "mass" articulation of
nationalism mainly "negatively", that is as a problem of "law and order", and
positively, if at all, "as a response to the charisma of certain elite leaders or in
the currently more fashionable terms of vertical mobilization by the manipulation of factions". Colluding with the imperatives of imperialist histories,
nationalist historiography had no space for "the politics of the people".
Consequently, the task of a non-elitist, or subaltern, historiography is to
interpret the politics of the people as "an autonomous domain" that "neither
originated from elite politics nor did its existence depend on the latter".

In the inelegant, albeit passionate, formulations of Guha's agenda-set-
ting document lie the seeds of *Subaltern Studies*'s peculiarities and failures;
and the novel readings of familiar phenomena encountered in some of the
papers in the ten volumes, and in other related scholarly works, occur inspite
of the extraordinarily clumsy attempt to theorize the grounds for a new historiography.[40] The peculiarities can be said to begin with Guha's deployment
of the words "elite" and "subaltern", and the particular manner in which they
stand in relation to each other. In a note appended to his programmatic statement, Guha states that the term "elite" signifies "dominant groups, foreign
as well as indigenous". Though even his use of the term elite, where a crude
distinction is drawn between "foreign" and "Indian"—as though "Indian"
were a given category, not one that is constantly put into question in India
itself—hearkens back to the equally crude notion of *false consciousness*, as
when he describes dominant indigenous groups at the "regional and local
levels" as those which "acted in the interest" of the dominant groups at the
national level "and not in conformity to interests corresponding truly to their
own social being", it is his deployment of the word "subaltern" which beg-
gars belief.

In the introduction to the opening volume of the series, Guha describes
the word "subaltern" as meaning a person "of inferior rank", for which his
authority is the *Concise Oxford Dictionary*. "It will be used in these pages",
Guha writes, "as a name for the general attribute of subordination in South
Asian Society whether this is expressed in terms of class, caste, age, gender
and office or in any other way"; and as he adds, the inspiration for this usage
came to him from a reading of Gramsci's "Notes on Italian History". But as
Guha is undoubtedly aware, the word subaltern, which can hardly be
described as having general currency in the English language, properly
belongs to the realm of the military, to designate a non-commissioned offi-

cer of very inferior rank, or even an orderly. Indeed, the *Oxford English Dictionary* concedes, in its 1989 edition , that the word subaltern, to designate a person or body of person of "inferior status, quality, or importance", is "rare", and the last quotation from any text that is furnished as an instance of the word's usage is from 1893. This, too, is the colonized Bengali's mentality: an archaic, or nearly archaic, word from the English language is resuscitated, the writings of an esoteric Italian Marxist theoretician are evoked, and all this in the cause of delineating the *autonomous* realm of a people in a colonized country who are stated as having acted under their own impulse. Beckett could have done no better, if the intention was to furnish a preliminary sketch of the theatre of the absurd. Guha has sense, but clearly lacks sensibility.

Doubtless, one could argue that the word "subaltern" in "Subaltern Studies" stands for something resembling the subordinate "classes" that are not quite "classes", for much the same reasons that E. P. Thompson once hinted at an eighteenth-century English history as a history of "class struggle without class".[41] If even apropos England, where the industrial revolution was born, there was some risk of speaking of classes as reified and bounded identities, how much more difficult is it to speak of classes in colonial India, where social relations were in a state of very considerable flux and class formation, in conditions resembling 'feudalism', existed in the most rudimentary form?[42] Since "subaltern" sufficiently points to relations of subordination and domination without the entrapment of the more familiar but rigid categories of class derived from orthodox Marxism, categories that moreover are most meaningful when the language of "citizen-politics" prevails (as it mostly does not in India), is not much gained by the deployment of subalternity as an analytical notion and as a locus for the location of consciousness?[43] But does not this argument return us to the formulations of Anil Seal and his Cambridge brethren, to the contention indeed that India did not quite have social classes based on economic categories? Must India be condemned, in subaltern history as much as in the Cambridge School monographs, to remain an inchoate mess—something that, in a typical demonstration of Indian recalcitrance, remains resistant to the categories of social science discourse? Moreover, if the notion of the "subaltern" is lifted from Gramsci to explicate the social relations prevalent in Indian history, it is well to recall that Gramsci's discussion of subalternity is framed alongside his deployment of the idea of "hegemony". Suffice to note, as I shall advert to the matter later, that Guha has throughout been insistent on characterizing the British Raj as an exemplification of "dominance without hegemony", yet he does not reflect on whether the deployment of the notion of subalternity is not contingent upon the deployment of the idea of hegemony.

As a further explication of Guha's usage of the word "subaltern" shows, the entire edifice of subaltern studies is fraught with the most hazardous philosophical and political conundrums. Whether by his very usage of "subaltern" Guha sought to impart a militancy to rebel consciousness, or to suggest that the realm of everyday life is inherently suffused with the spirit of insurgency, the suppression of which is a task to which dominant forces set themselves, is a question brought to the fore by his *Elementary Aspects of Insurgency in Colonial India* (1983),[44] the book with which Subaltern Studies is sometimes seen to have been inaugurated. Ranging widely and oftentimes indiscriminately across materials on rebellions, jacqueries, and insurgencies in India, Guha gave the distinct impression, howsoever subtly conveyed, that the consciousness of the subaltern is the consciousness of militancy. Peasants somehow appear not as persons who spend the greater part of their lives toiling on the fields, but as figures of resistance: that is to say, if I may invert Victor Turner, peasants are not only immersed in communitas, but also spend a good part of their life serving the structure.[45]

Other, more obvious, objections have been raised to Guha's notion of the "subaltern". There are hierarchies among both elites and subalterns, and at what point one shades into another is not clear. As colonial rule was indubitably to establish, local elites were merely subalterns to the British, and even in the ranks of the indigenous elites, subalternity was a matter of negotiation. Guha is evidently sensitive to these questions, for instance in his recognition that local indigenous elites were sometimes subservient to indigenous elites at the national level, but nonetheless the contrast between elites and subalterns is too sharply drawn. Consequently, as one critic has argued, those groups which "occupy an uneasy marginal role between the elite and the subaltern, crossing and re-crossing the conceptual boundary according to the precise historical circumstances under discussion", receive "short shrift" in subaltern history.[46] In *Elementary Aspects*, moreover, Guha appears to be unable to distinguish between tribals and peasants, and often his discussion of peasant insurgency, such as in the chapter on "modalities" of insurgency, draws mainly upon materials pertaining to tribal insurrections. This is no small problem, because this confusion obscures the fundamentally different manner in which colonialism affected tribal communities and peasant societies. Colonialism knew of no other way to profit from tribal economies than by destroying them altogether, to pave the way for plantations or for extraction of forest and mineral wealth; in peasant communities, on the other hand, the colonial expropriation of surplus took the form of rent or taxes.[47] This meant, as well, that disaffection in tribal areas was more widespread, and given the relatively egalitarian basis of most tribal societies, the resistance to colonial rule was more thorough, integrated, and uniform.

If all this seems problematic enough, Guha yet moves from one distinctly odd formulation to another. In the supplementary note to his programmatic statement, he ventures to say of the "people" and the "subaltern classes", used synonymously in his statement, that "they represent the demographic difference between the total Indian population and all those whom we have described as the elite".[48] If we recall his ambition to understand subaltern politics as an "autonomous domain", it is extraordinary that his definition of the subaltern is made contingent upon the definition of the elite, and the elite is given ontological priority. That the elite constitute a miniscule portion of the Indian population only exacerbates the problem. Guha could well have said that the elite represent the demographic difference between the entire Indian population and all those who are described as subaltern, but the priority given to "elite" clearly suggests that he considers it a less ambiguous category. It betrays as well his own tendency to slip into those habits of elite thinking which he otherwise deplores: when all is said and done, Guha's habits of thinking are firmly Brahminical, and consequently he appears not to recognize that at least some "subalterns" may have welcomed British "elites" as carriers of norms that promised them legal, social, and political equality.

Having set apart, then, the elites and the subalterns, Guha admits that the subaltern classes could not originate initiatives "powerful enough to develop the nationalist movement into a full-fledged struggle for national liberation". The working-class did not have consciousness as a "class-for-itself", and was unable to forge alliances with the peasantry; and so the numerous peasant uprisings eventually fizzled out, having "waited in vain for a leadership to raise them above localism and generalize them into a nation-wide anti-imperialist campaign". If the subaltern classes "waited in vain", to stress Guha's own words, one can only conclude that Guha does not consider their autonomy to be a fully desirable feature of their politics, which is hardly consistent with the very project of Subaltern Studies. If they "waited in vain", the subalterns were betrayed by the bourgeoisie, who failed to exercise the requisite leadership; and so we come to Guha's explication of the principal task of subaltern historiography:

> It is the study of this *historic failure of the nation to come to its own*, a failure due to the inadequacy of the bourgeoisie as well as of the working class to lead it into a decisive victory over colonialism and a bourgeois-democratic revolution of either the classic nineteenth-century type under the hegemony of the bourgeoisie or a modern type under the hegemony of workers and peasants, that is, a 'new democracy'—*it is the study of this failure which constitutes the central problematic of the historiography of colonial India.*[49]

Subaltern history, if we are to follow Guha's argument, commences with a recognition of "failure", and its provenance is the study of "failure", that is, the realm of what did not transpire. Somehow that "failure" seems all but natural, since the native seldom arrives at the destination: either he is still averse to clock-time, or has overstepped his destination, or failed to keep his appointment; and when, after much expenditure of energy, the destination is in sight, and the threshold is eventually reached, the native finds that everyone else is departed. When India arrives at the doorstep of modernity, it is to find that the West is already living in the era of postmodernity; when the great industrial targets set by the five-year plans are eventually met, the part of the world that the Indian nation-state seeks to emulate is already post-industrial, living in the mad throes of the information superhighway; when the great dams, those "temples" of the modern age as Nehru saw them, are finished to the cheering of the leaders of the nation-state, the news arrives that megaprojects of the state are demeaning to the human spirit, productive only of waste, pollution, and ruined lives. The history of India is always "incomplete", and here is Sumit Sarkar, one of the founding members of the Subaltern Collective, to remind us of the modernity which we in India still await: "The sixty years or so that lie between the foundation of the Indian National Congress in 1885 and the achievement of independence in August 1947 witnessed perhaps the greatest transition in our country's long history. A transition, however, which in many ways remains grievously incomplete, and it is with this central ambiguity that it seems most convenient to begin our survey".[50] India is not lacking in people, poverty, or pandits, but the "history" of India is conceptualized as a "lack", a "want" for something better—call it the bourgeoisie that could have, to quote again Guha, led the nation to a "decisive victory" over colonialism, or call it a revolution of the "classic nineteenth-century type". If only India had been like France, we might have been a fulfilled nation.

IV. The Journey: The Practice of Subaltern History

From a reading of Guha's programmatic note, as well as of other subaltern histories which bemoan the incompleteness of modernity in India, one would be entitled to draw the conclusion that subaltern history itself exists in a position of subalternity to Europe. This is an argument that can be developed at several levels. The ten volumes of *Subaltern Studies*, as well as the other works of the scholars associated with the project, suggest that India still furnishes the raw data, while the theory emanates from Europe. India is the terrain on which the investigations are carried out, and the analytical tools are derived from the West: this is hardly a departure from the older models of indological scholarship. The subaltern historians are comfortable with Marx, Hegel, Heidegger, Jakobson, Habermas, Foucault, Barthes, and Derrida, as well as with French, American, and British traditions of social history, but the interpretive strategies of the Indian epics or puranas, the political thinking of a Kautilya, the hermeneutics of devotional poetry, the philosophical exegesis of Nagarjuna, and the narrative frameworks of the *Panchatantra* or the *Kathsaritsagara*, are of little use to them; and even the little literature of the countless number of little traditions, such as proverbs, ballads, and folk-tales, *seldom* enters into their consciousness.

Still, perhaps this is not so substantive a criticism of subaltern history as one might imagine. The origins of the modern social sciences lie in Western intellectual practices, and it is not unreasonable that the interpretive models should also be derived from these practices, though that does not obviate the path of inquiry that some scholars have taken, which is to ask whether one can speak of an 'Indian sociology', 'Indian anthropology', and so on. There is also the argument that India is at least as much heir, for example, to Marxist thought as any other place, and in some respects India has made more of Marx than have the Western democracies. Consequently, the objection that is frequently encountered, namely that Guha and his colleagues show an inconsistency in denouncing Western historiography at the same time that they draw upon the work of Gramsci, would strike the subaltern historians as having little merit. The precise uses to which Gramsci is put is certainly, as I have suggested, an open question. But what is quite certain is that in intellectual matters, there is still no reciprocity, and one wonders what reception, if any, subaltern history would have received in the West had it not so obviously been the carrier of theoretical trajectories that were simultaneously finding a resonance in the Western academy. That this is not an idle question is clearly demonstrated by the fact that the work of many fine Indian historians—Majid Siddiqui, Neeladhri Bhattacharya, and Sabyasachi Bhattacharya, to name three—whose work is less indebted to streams of post-structuralist thinking or postcolonial theory remains almost entirely unknown outside the Indian academy and certainly the field of Indian history.

The more critical point is that Europe is still, in two fundamental respects, the site of all histories. The present of India is the past of Europe, and India's future is only Europe's present. In fact, if the recipe furnished by the developmentalists and the modernists were followed, one suspects that India's future will merely yield a poor version of Europe's present. If history already happened somewhere else, India has no history to speak of, a proposition to which Hegel would give his joyous assent. Secondly, subaltern historians, except occasionally,[51] have fundamentally stopped short of asking how is it that history came to be so decisive a terrain for establishing the autonomy and agency of a subject people or understanding the modality of resistance, and what the consequences are for locating agency, subjecthood, and resistance in the discourse of history, tethered as it is to the narratives of modernity, the nation-state, and bourgeois rationality. It is history, more than any other discourse, which has enshrined the narrative of the nation-state as the reference point for all agency, and which has made it difficult to derive other arrangements for the organization of human affairs. This is not a point I wish to belabor here, as I have addressed it at very considerable length in a number of other papers,[52] but it bears reiteration that history as a universalizing discourse, which is less tolerant of dissent than even the master narratives of science, is not merely a novel phenomenon, but has immeasurably narrowed the possibilities for conceptualizing alternative modernities, political identities, and different forms of community. History is not the only mode of accessing the past; it may not even be the most desirable one, at least for certain communities, but I shall return to this point later.

Poor theorizing does not always yield poor histories, and so it is with very considerable surprise, given the rather ill-conceived programmatic agenda as set out by Ranajit Guha, that one finds the practice of subaltern history to have far outpaced its theoretical ambitions or philosophical posturing, and to have often yielded some remarkable insights into the study of colonial India. In *Elementary Aspects of Peasant Insurgency*, Guha provided a reading of peasant insurgency through the texts of counter-insurgency, a strategy with particular salience for the study of subaltern agency in colonial India, given that the rebels and insurrectionists rarely if ever left behind any texts. This point is similar to Dipesh Chakrabarty's observation, apropos his study of the jute workers of Calcutta, that unlike E. P. Thompson's study of the working class in England, which could make use of the diaries, journals, and pamphlets left behind by his subjects, he was constrained in having to use only the documents of the ruling class, which would then have to be "read both for what they say and for their 'silences'".[53] It is the reading of these silences, of the insurgent consciousness, that leads Guha, in his essay "The Prose of Counter-Insurgency", to develop, with the aid of semiotic analysis, a typology of the discourses of counter-insurgency, which he describes as constituting three layers, primary, secondary, and tertiary. The primary discourse, which is constituted by the immediate accounts of insurgency produced by colonial officials or what were fondly called the men-on-the-spot, furnishes the first instance of what Guha calls the "counter-insurgent code"; at a further remove in time and place, this account is processed and transformed into official reports, memoirs, and administrative gazetteers, but even this secondary discourse is unable "to extricate itself from the code of counter-insurgency". The secondary discourse shares in primary discourse's commitment to the "code of pacification", which entails turning the language of insurgency upside down: thus peasants become insurgents, "Islamic puritans" become "fanatics", the resistance to oppression is written as "daring and wanton atrocities on the inhabitants", the self-rule desired by the peasants is turned into treason, and "the struggle for a better order" is reduced to the "disturbance of public tranquility". The "rebel has no place", writes Guha, "in this history as the subject of rebellion", and whatever the sympathies for the peasants, the "official turned historian" opts to come down on the side of what he thinks of as law and order. At the final or tertiary level of historiography, the "code of pacification" encountered in the primary and secondary levels is redistributed, regurgitated, and replicated, since this discourse is read without the acknowledgment of the occluded other, that is the insurgent. Indeed, tertiary discourse is in some respects more nefarious, emboldened and fattened with the authority of the historian and the purported impartiality produced by the passage of time: and so the "discourse of history, hardly distinguished from policy, ends up by absorbing the concerns and objectives of the latter". If, for instance, the primary and secondary discourse of colonial officials pinned the responsibility for a peasant rebellion on the local elites for their exploitative behavior towards the peasants, in the tertiary discourse of nationalist historiography this blame is shifted onto British rule, which is said to have aggravated the sufferings of the peasants. In either case, the peasant is not seen as a rightful subject, as an agent possessing a will of his own, as the maker of his own destiny.[54]

Not only "canonical" texts, but the revered figures of the nationalist movement, none more so than Mohandas Karamchand Gandhi, become the proper subjects of inquiry for subaltern historians. How Mohandas became transformed into the Mahatma is a long story, but what his deification might have meant to the subaltern masses, and how they read the message of the Mahatma, is the theme of Shahid Amin's brilliantly original study of "Gandhi as Mahatma".[55] In the received version of Gandhi's life that predominates in nationalist historiography, Gandhi captured the Indian National Congress a few years after his return from South Africa, moved the masses with his principled attachment to truth and commitment to non-violence, and led the country to independence after waging several movements of civil disobedience and non-cooperation with the British. All this may very well be true, but nationalist historiography has had no place for Gandhi except as the example par excellence of the 'great man', and contrariwise no place for the masses, who are seen as the flock that humbly followed the great master, though on occasion they may have been led astray by trouble-mongers, the advocates of violence, or those other elements in society which refused to act in the national interest. We know of the impression that Gandhi left on Nehru, Patel, Maulana Azad, and others who were to rise to the helm of political affairs in the nationalist movement, but how did Gandhi's charisma register with the masses? The burden of Amin's essay is to establish that there was no single authorized version of the Mahatma, and the masses made of the Mahatma what they could; indeed, they stepped outside the role which nationalist historiography habitually assigns to them. This historiography also seeks to marginalize competing or varying accounts of the Mahatma. For all their religious beliefs and alleged superstitions, the subaltern masses appear to have been more worldly-wise than the elite as they attempted to grapple with the mystique of the Mahatma.

Amin's narrative of the subaltern engagement with the Mahatma commences with an account of Gandhi's visit, at the height of the non-cooperation movement in 1921, to the district of Gorakhpur in the then eastern United Provinces. Here Gandhi addressed numerous "monster" meetings at which immense crowds gathered to have a *darshan* of their Mahatma. Ordinarily, in Hindu religious practices, the worshipper seeks a *darshan*, or sight of the deity; this sighting is said to confer blessings upon the worshipper.[56] Gandhi's hagiographers were to summon this as an instance of the reverence in which the Mahatma was held, but they seem to have been less alert to the fact that, as Amin suggests, the worshipper does not, as did many of Gandhi's followers, demand *darshan*. The crowds nearly heckled him, and after a long day of traveling and speech-making, the Mahatma might have nothing more to look forward to than a long stream of visitors who desired to have his *darshan*, and who forced themselves upon him. At one point in his travels the crowds had become so obstinate that Mahadev Desai, Gandhi's secretary, stepped forth when the crowd started shouting Gandhi's name, and presented himself as the 'Mahatma'; whereupon the people bowed to him, and then left the train.[57] Their fervor was quite possibly increased by the rumours that circulated about the Mahatma's capacity to cause "miracles", and certainly the local press was fulsome in its description of the 'magic' that the Mahatma had wrought on the villagers. "The very simple people in the east and south of the United Provinces", adjudged the editorialist of the *Pioneer* newspaper shortly after Gandhi's visit to Gorakhpur, "afford a fertile soil in which a belief in the powers of the 'Mahatmaji', who is after all little more than a name of power to them, may grow". The editorialist saw in the various accounts of the miracles purported to have been performed by Gandhi "the mythopoeic imagination of the childlike peasant at work", and expressed concern that though the events in question all admitted of an "obvious explanation", one saw rather signs "of an unhealthy nervous excitement such as often passed through the peasant classes of Europe in the Middle Ages, and to which the Indian villager is particularly prone".[58]

It was, however, far more so than the "mythopoeic imagination of the childlike peasant at work" in the circulation of the rumours. Gandhi's teachings—among others, the stress on Muslim-Hindu unity; the injunction to give up bad habits, such as gambling, drinking, and whoring; the renunciation of violence; and the daily practice of spinning or weaving—were doubtless distilled in these rumors, but an entire moral and political economy was also transacted in their exchange. One set of rumors and stories referred to the power of the Mahatma; another enumerated the consequences of opposing him, or particular aspects of his creed; and yet another referred to the boons conferred on those who paid heed to Gandhi's teachings. In one story, a domestic servant declared that he was only prepared to accept the Mahatma's authenticity if the thatched roof of his house was raised; the roof lifted ten cubits above the wall, and was restored to its position only when he cried and folded his hands in submission. A man who abused Gandhi found his eyelids stuck; another man who slandered him begin to stink; more dramatically, a lawyer of some standing in the local area discovered shit all over his house, and no one doubted that this was because he opposed the non-cooperation movement which Gandhi had initiated. Gandhi was said to punish the arrogance of those who considered themselves exempt from his teachings, or, much worse, boldly defied his creed of non-violence, vegetarianism, and abstention from intoxicants. One pandit who was told to give up eating fish is reported to have said in anger, "I shall eat fish, let's see what the Mahatmaji can do". When he sat down to eat, it is said, the fish was found to be crawling with worms.[59]

In the name of the Mahatma, an entire nation could be swung into action. That much is clear, and the "elite" histories have belabored that point; but as Amin's study shows, at the local level another set of meanings was imparted to the Mahatma's name. Gandhi's name could be used to enforce order in the village, establish new hierarchies, expunge violators of caste norms, drive the butcher out of the village, settle old scores, compel the wearing of khadi, or restore communitas. In Gorakhpur, faulting debtors were threatened that Gandhi's wrath would come down on them if they failed to meet their obligations; likewise, the Cow Protection League, eager to halt the killing of cattle, impressed upon recalcitrant Muslims the consequences of ignoring the Mahatma's message. Utilizing the name of the Mahatma, money-lenders and Hindu zealots sought to refurbish their image; contrariwise, peasants heavily in debt and burdened by enormous tax burdens, invoked the name of the Mahatma, who had warned moneylenders that they should not bleed their poor brethren, and suggested that unimaginable blessings would fall upon those moneylenders who saw fit to offer them financial relief. The Mahatma's name, Amin argues, could lend itself to all kinds of purposes, and as he argues towards the conclusion of his study, even the violence that was committed at Chauri Chaura in February 1922, when a score of policemen were killed by a crowd provoked to extreme anger, was done in Gandhi's name.[60] The very understanding of Gandhi's teachings to which the masses held often conflicted with the tenets of Gandhi's creed. No nationalist historiography has had room for those masses who, turning the Mahatma into a floating signifier, thought that they could justifiably, for the higher end of Swaraj or self-rule, commit violence in the name of the very prophet of non-violence.

In Amin's use of local literatures, vernacular newspapers, rumors, and village proverbs, in the service of a reading which establishes the extraordinarily polysemic nature of the name of the 'Mahatma', we have a demonstrably good instantiation of subaltern studies at work.[61] But if his concern is with the silences effected by nationalist historiography, in Gyanendra Pandey's work we are furnished with a powerful reading of the overt posturing and palpable presences of colonial historiography—a historiography that, in this case, offers a seamless account of Hindu-Muslim conflict, as if it were the eternal condition of Indian existence.[62] In reviewing British writings on Banaras in the nineteenth century, Pandey found, with respect to a Hindu-Muslim conflict that took place in October 1809, widely different colonial accounts of the events that are said to have transpired at that time. The colonial government records of that time described the "outbreak" as having occurred at the "Lat Bhairava" [site of an image] between 20–24 October 1809, and placed the number of casualties at 28 or 29 people killed, and another 70 wounded; the cause of the conflict is described as a dispute over attempts by Hindus to render a Hanuman shrine built of mud into a more permanent structure of stone, and the subsequent Hindu outrage over the alleged pollution of the "Lat Bhairava". Writing some twenty years later, James Prinsep was inclined to attribute the cause of the conflict to "the "frenzy excited by Muharram lamentations"; and writing still another 20 years later, in 1848, the colonial official W. Buyers considered the conflict as having emanated from the clash between Muslims celebrating Muharram and Hindu revelers playing Holi. But all agreed at least that the initial outbreak had taken place at the "Lat Bhairava". How, then, asks Pandey, did the *District Gazetteer* of 1907 transpose the site of the initial rioting to the Aurangzeb mosque, and even more significantly, how did the 28–29 people who were killed become transformed into "several hundreds killed"? Is this the much celebrated colonial respect for "facts", the supreme indifference to which was described by colonial officials as a marker of the Indians' poor rational faculties?[63]

It is the particular features of the colonial construction of 'communalism', that is the narrative of a Hindu-Muslim conflict that is said to be timeless, beyond resolution, and the eternal condition of Indian society, which Pandey illuminates in his study of British discourses. Many of his interpretive strategies are familiar to students of colonial discourse, for instance his analysis of the "type-casting" commonly found in Orientalist writings, such that the Muslims become "fanatics" or given to "frenzy", or the Brahmins are viewed as "crafty". He notes the tendency in colonial texts to describe the reaction of the Hindus as a "conspiracy" instigated by the "wily" Brahmins, and the depiction of the rioting as a "convulsion" that shook Banaras: "convulsion" seeking to indicate the spontaneous, primordial, pre-political, near-ly cataclysmic nature of the "outbreak". Hindu and Muslim practices—the lamentations of the Muslims at Muharram, the excitability of the Hindus over their images, the fanatic attachment to places of worship—become the predictable sites of representations of an exotic, bizarre, and primitive Other. But Pandey takes us much further along in his understanding of how the "communal riot narrative", purporting to describe the event, itself creates the object of its discourse. The 1907 *Gazetteer*, which had described the dead as numbering in the "several hundreds", when previous sources placed them at less than 30, introduced the 1809 riots with the observation that "the city experienced one of those convulsions which had so frequently occurred in the past owing to the religious antagonism of the Hindu and Musalman sections of the population". A *history* of *Muslim-Hindu conflict* did not have to be established; it could be presumed: as another colonial writer put it much later in his book *Dawn in India*, "the animosities of centuries are always smouldering beneath the surface".[64] If Banaras had Hindus and Muslims, they had perforce to be in conflict; and perforce they had to be in conflict over religion, that being the preeminent marker of Indian identity. More remarkably still, the observations of the 1907 Gazetteer appear, virtually verbatim, in the report of the Indian Statutory Commission of 1928, drawn up to consider the constitutional condition of India and the arrangements to be devised for granting Indians a greater degree of self-rule. Only now, the "grave Banaras riots" of 1809 are furnished not as an instance of Hindu-Muslim antagonism in Banaras, but as an indicator of the state of Muslim-Hindu relations all over India: it was one of those "convulsions which had frequently occurred in the past owing to the religious antagonism of the Hindu and Moslem sections of the population".[65]

The "communal riot narrative" ranges widely over time and space, a scant respecter of history or geography; events can be transposed, the locale of disturbances can be shifted, one riot can stand in place for another,[66] an analog to what I have elsewhere described as the *principle of infinite substi-tutibility*, whereby any one native was construed as capable of standing in place for any other.[67] No history ever transpired in India: so, writing apropos Hindu-Muslim conflict in Mubarakpur, the district gazetteer described the Muslims as made up mainly of "fanatical and clannish Julahas [weavers], and the fire of religious animosity between them and the Hindus of the town and neighbourhood is always smouldering. Serious conflicts have occurred between the two from time to time, notably in 1813, 1842 and 1904. The features of all these disturbances are similar, so that a description of what took place on the first occasion will suffice to indicate their character".[68] Even the future can be read from this history: the colonial official as futurist, prophet, forecaster. Like animals, Indians have no past or future: they live only in the present, for the present, but this is not the present of the enlight-ened who have gained *satori*. In this colonialist form of knowledge, "'vio-lence' always belonged to a pre-colonial condition",[69] and the Hindu-Muslim conflict becomes the very justification for the intervention by a transcendent power, namely the British. If this strife did not exist, it would have to be invented—and invented, too, so that the colonial state, the mender of fences, can become the locus of all history. Earlier, but not the twentieth-century, accounts of the 1809 Banaras riots had invariably also noted that the conflict was accompanied by a fast commenced at the riverside by Brahmins and other upper-caste Hindus, but this form of political action, which was deemed to be only an instance of native eccentricity and mendacity, had to be excised out of history. The following year, the Hindus and the Muslims joined together in Banaras in a great movement to resist the imposition of house tax: a rather unhappy circumstance for the British, who by the early twentieth century, as resistance to their rule became more marked, had further political compulsions for sketching the Hindu-Muslim past as a bloody affair. But because these histories of independent political action, resistance, and political pluralism could not be reconciled with the history of the colonial state, which refuses to grant the people any legitimate agency or will of their own, they had to be rendered invisible. Another history, which it was the task of the state to create and nourish, all the better that it should become the handmaiden to policy, would stand in for the Indian past. In the twentieth century, Pandey observes, a name had to be found for this history: that name was 'communalism'. We are still living with that history.

V. Accessing the Past, and the Subalternity of History

Of the dozens of papers that have been published in the ten volumes of *Subaltern Studies* and associated works, the papers of Guha, Amin, and Pandey, which I have discussed at some length, appear to be subtle demonstrations of the power and promise of subaltern studies. I have, at the same time, already pointed the way to a partial critique of subaltern history, but its limitations need to be addressed at greater length, particularly in view of the consideration that subaltern history has a very substantial following outside India, just as historians in India have themselves become something of public figures, however inconsequential their part in the formulation of policy. The ascendancy of historians is all the more remarkable in a country where historical knowledge had, until recently, an altogether subaltern status in relation to other forms of knowledge and other modes of accessing the past, and it is not particularly clear that even today history enjoys wide legitimacy among the common people. Not long ago, when the Babri Masjid, a sixteenth-century mosque in Ayodhya claimed by Hindu militants as the original site of a Hindu temple allegedly built to mark the very spot on which Lord Rama was born, was declared by the government to be a "disputed structure" before being brought down by a crowd numbering in the thousands, historians became prominent in the public controversy surrounding the mosque.[70] Ironically, questions of faith were largely dispensed with, as both the proponents of the temple theory, that is those Hindus alleging that the mosque was built after a temple on the same site was razed to the ground in a brazen display of Muslim prowess, and the defenders of the mosque, which included not only Muslims but the avowedly secular elements of the

Hindu intelligentsia, decided to wage the battle on the field of history. The proponents of the temple theory, whom the secularists preferred to address as Hindu fascists, militants, or fundamentalists, gave it as their considered view that it was an *"undisputed historical fact* [italics added] that at Ramjanmabhumi [the birthplace, allegedly, of Lord Rama] there was an ancient mandir [temple]", but the *"authentic history books"* [italics added] they cited in their support turn out to be, on closer examination, accounts by European writers and travelers whose testimony on many other points is impugned by these same people.[71] The rejoinder was equally framed in the language of historical authority, far more formidable than anything that the militants could command. Jointly authoring a pamphlet entitled "The Political Abuse of History", twenty-five historians at the prestigious Jawaharlal Nehru University demolished, or so they thought, the view that a Hindu temple might have stood at the spot where the Babri Masjid had been built, and rejected, with evidence they considered decisive, the claim that this temple, had it stood there in the first place, could possibly have been built to mark the birthplace of Rama.[72]

Doubtless the secular historians had by far the "better" evidence in support of their views, but this seems to have left hardly any impression upon the militants and their scholarly supporters, or even among the general public. The only shared area of agreement among the 'secularists' and the 'fundamentalists' is seen to be their readiness to deploy historical evidence,[73] though the secular historians added the necessary caveat that irrespective of the historical evidence, the destruction of the mosque could not conceivably be justified. From the standpoint of secular historians, moreover, the eventual destruction of the mosque signaled the (evil) triumph of myth over history, blind faith over principled reason, religious fundamentalism over secularism. Not many of these historians, however, asked whether the language of secularism spoke to the condition of those Hindus who, without supporting Hindu militancy, nevertheless felt themselves to be devout Hindus. What did the secular historians have to say about belief, except to acknowledge, most likely with a tinge of embarrassment, its presence in the life of most Indians? Few paused to ask why the "hard" evidence of historical "facts" had little attraction for most Indians, and not only the upwardly mobile Hindus who were held to be responsible for creating a climate of opinion hospitable to the resurgence of Hindu militancy. Fewer still reflected on the adequacy or even soundness of their proposed solution to the dispute, which was to turn the mosque over to the Archaeological Survey of India, which would in effect transform it from a place of religious worship claimed by both Hindus and Muslims into a dead monument existing in 'museum time', of interest to no one except archaeologists, antiquarians, scholars, and Western tourists. None of the historians or secularists showed themselves capable of a creative response to one of the most pressing crises to face India in the post-independent period, and it devolved upon the philosopher and cultural critic, Ramachandra Gandhi, to transcend the parameters of historical discourse within which the discussion over the Babri Masjid had been trapped, and furnish a radical and emancipatory reading of the events that transpired in Ayodhya. As Gandhi showed, historians had been grossly negligent in failing to take serious notice of a building, Sita-ki-Rasoi ("Sita's Kitchen"), adjoining the mosque; and from this proximity Gandhi spins a tale, and moral fable, which allows us to consider the conflict at Ayodhya as part of the violent ecological disruption of the world.[74]

It is particularly noteworthy, from the perspective of this paper, that the subaltern historians, who are concentrated at Delhi University (rather than Jawaharlal Nehru University) and the Centre for Studies in Social Sciences, Calcutta, had almost no part to play in the debate. An eloquent plea or two appeared from the pen of Gyanendra Pandey, but the subaltern historians appeared stunned and paralyzed: subaltern history seemed unable to speak to the present. Though subaltern historians are able to theorize communalism, they are still unable to speak with ease about religion or the supernatural. In common with social scientists, quite unlike the physicists or biologists who have shown themselves perfectly capable of distinguishing their own religious beliefs from the epistemological assumptions of the sciences which they practice in their professional lives, the subaltern historians are still captive to positivism and its disdain for anything which cannot be encompassed within the circle of reason. Thus, willy-nilly, subaltern histories, on closer inspection, appear to echo those familiar juxtapositions of 'faith' and 'reason', 'Enlightenment' and 'superstition'; and at every instance of religious belief, the subaltern historian falters, slips, and excuses himself. How else can one explain Guha's constant slippage into the language of that very elite historiography which he so unequivocally condemns? He writes of the peasants that their "understanding of the relations, institutions and processes of power were identified with or at least over determined by religion", but adds in the same breath that they were possessed of a "false consciousness" on account of their "backward . . . material and spiritual conditions".[75] Though the subaltern historian is inclined to concede autonomy and agency to the subaltern, how does the historian negotiate the problem that arises when the subaltern, disavowing any agency, declares—as happened often—that he or she was instigated to act by the command of God, or the local deity? The voices of the subalterns do not always, or even seldom, speak to us, and yet it is the ambition of subaltern history that it desires to make these voices, by transforming them into the language of modernity, scholarship, or narratives organized along other principles of 'rational' ordering, touch us.

That the subaltern historians did not so much as lift their voices while the debate over the Babri Masjid raged across north India may be indicative of a wide and disturbing disjunction between the espousal of radical politics and history in the academy, and a nearly complete surrender in the public domain. I am by no means suggesting that historians that should become policy makers, but rather adverting to the failure of historical discourses to transplant themselves into the public consciousness, and the abject failure of those who describe themselves as opponents of 'elite' histories to speak in the voices of public intellectuals. This brings me to a more commonly expressed general criticism, which I would argue should be treated with considerable caution, that subaltern history has thrived on the fetishism of exile encoun-

262   TURNING POINTS IN HISTORIOGRAPHY

tered in the American academy.[76] Of the core members of the collective, the greater majority of them are placed in some of the leading universities in the United States and Britain, and of those who are settled in India, they have sinecures and arrangements for leave that are the envy of Indian academics. They sometimes represent themselves, usually informally, as unwilling exiles, as receiving a more sympathetic hearing in the Western academy than in Indian universities, as speaking in a language that places them at odds with their Indian colleagues. There are other ambivalent narratives woven into this tale as well, since educated Indians, who are sworn to the motto that 'there is no honor in one's own country', like to believe that recognition in the West is a pre-condition of success in India.

The criticism that seems to deserve a more sympathetic hearing, and which is a corollary to the suggestion that the subaltern historians have rendered themselves into exiles, pertains to the manner in which subaltern historiography has itself been rendered into exilic history. The argument, encountered in the eloquently written essays of Gyan Prakash, who has become something of a spokesperson for the subaltern historians in the West, that subaltern historiography can content itself with deconstructing master narratives, with—in his words—not unmasking "dominant discourses" but rather exploring their "fault lines in order to provide different accounts, to describe histories revealed in the cracks of the colonial archaeology of knowledge", justifiably lends itself to the multiple charges that subaltern history, in something of a mockery of its name, is committed, if only negatively, to the printed text, to elite discourses, and to a revived form of colonial textualism. According to Prakash, "subalterns and subalternity do not disappear into discourse but appear in its interstices, subordinated by structures over which they exert pressure", and there is the insistent reminder that "critical work seeks its basis not without but within the fissures of dominant structures".[77] If the fissures and gaps in dominant, almost invariably printed, discourses are enough to furnish us clues and even histories of subalternity, why go outside the realm of elite texts at all? Indeed, Prakash admits as much, and calls for a "complex and deep engagement with elite and canonical texts",[78] which is what the "elitist historiography" that Guha and the collective so roundly condemned has been doing since the inception of historical work.

And what of the voices of the subalterns? What of the lived experiences, so celebrated in the abstract, of peasants, workers, the slum dwellers, the Dalits, rural and urban women, and countless others? If one can repair from time to time to "elite and canonical texts", and repeatedly deploy those interpretive strategies that teach us how to read between the lines, which show us the precise moments at which these texts unwittingly betray themselves, then why bother with the archive at all? What makes the subaltern historian so radically different from James Mill, who authored an eight-volume history of British India without having ever visited the country about whose destiny he pontificated, or from Max Muller, the revered father of late-nineteenth-century indology, who absolutely forbid his students from visiting India, lest the contemporary India of colonial rule should irretrievably suffer in comparison with the Aryan India of the sages and philosophers which he had instilled into their imagination? If subaltern history is to become another species of postcolonial criticism, as Prakash's very title of his essay so bids us to understand, why call it "subaltern history" at all? Moreover, though this point is deserving of far greater elaboration, nowhere does Prakash show any comprehension that postcolonial criticism arose in the societies of the West where the forces of homogenization had historically operated with such power as to create a desperate need for plural structures, while India is a society where the ground reality, so to speak, has always been plural, whatever the attempts of militant Hindus in recent years to transform India in the image of the West. To speak, then, of "subaltern history" as "postcolonial criticism" is to lose sight of the fact that the task of criticism and intellectual inquiry is substantively of a different order in India and the West.

Subaltern India, one suspects, will prove itself rather more recalcitrant to subaltern history than Prakash and some of his cohorts in the collective imagine. Until very recently, subaltern history showed itself as entirely impervious to contemporary urban India, as if the slum-dwellers, urban proletariat, small-town tricksters, the countless number of street vendors, and even the millions of lower middle-class Indians suffocating in dingy office buildings do not constitute the class of clearly subordinate people that Guha designated as the "subalterns". The Subaltern Collective is doubtless moving towards a more expansive conception of its mandate, even while Gyan Prakash has been announcing that "elite and canonical texts" furnish subaltern historians with their most effective material, and in Volume IX one finds the first explicit attempts to engage with subalternity in the contemporary urban context.[79] But as yet there is little to warrant the optimism that Subaltern history will be able to extricate itself from the legacy of anthropology, with its conception of "Village India", or from the stress on rural India with which post-independent anthropology and sociology have been preoccupied.[80] One wonders whether subaltern history does not also, in the fashion of indology and Orientalism, secretly hold to the view that the India of villages and peasants, that realm of rebellion and insurrectionary activity, is somehow the authentic India, the India where the "autonomous" realm of the people is more clearly discerned.

Though Indian subalterns have been making their history in myriad ways in post-independent India, and have moved from one form of subalternity to another, and often to other destinations, it is transparent that subaltern historians have themselves been left behind. Even their understanding of village India, to advert to one instance, seems curiously predictable, though this limitation may well have to do with the poverty of historical thinking than with their own shortcomings. India characteristically transforms its urban areas into villages, and ruralizes its urban landscapes: in India the village is everywhere, and there is the village outside the village. There may well be the villager in most urban Indians, though increasingly urban Indians are getting disconnected from the village. Many of the subaltern historians—Shahid Amin, Partha Chatterjee, Sumit Sarkar, and Ranajit Guha—have tackled Gandhi, but it seems that they are yet to understand the village within Gandhi. This may seem like an unlikely proposition, considering that Gandhi spent a very considerable part of his life in urban settings, whether London, Durban, or Ahmedabad. Notwithstanding his very long spells in Britain and South Africa, Gandhi never left the village; he inhabited its structures, its modes of thought, and its imagination. That is no discredit to him at all, and Amin's reading of the polysemic nature of the Mahatma myths, which as I have suggested is accomplished with extraordinary verve and imagination, could have been richer still had he had understood not only how the peasants worked on Gandhi, but how the village served as a symbiotic link between the Mahatma and the masses.

The subaltern historians, to put the matter bluntly, have been riding along with the academy, but they must now walk with the subalterns. There is great merit in walking, and the subaltern historians may take a lesson or two from Gandhi, who walked at least ten kilometres every day, and often a great deal more. It is with the walk to the sea that a revolution was launched, but Gandhi would have said that walking puts us in touch with our body in different ways, as well as in touch with India. Walking introduces a different conception of time, working with (not only within) the boundaries set by clock-time: it formulates, to evoke Raymond Williams's phrase, "structures of feeling" that cannot be encapsulated by the body put in mechanical motion. The subaltern historians have mastered the analytical models derived from European philosophy and the social sciences; they are placed in conversation with some of the other academic trajectories of thought that have become inspirational for our times; their work offers a trenchant critique of colonial, neo-colonial, and nationalist historiographies; and, though this consideration will be of more interest to Indians, and perhaps to those in the Southern hemisphere of the world, they have succeeded in placing Indian history on the world map. Yet the subalterns on whose behalf they speak are not very responsive to the historical mode of inquiry, or even to the historical mode of living in the body. Their language has more in common with the epics, puranas, bhajans, folk-tales, proverbs, songs, and poems than it does with the language of history. The subaltern historian, reliant on modern knowledge systems, theorizes the subaltern and works on the village; the subaltern, who inhabits the village within and without, has not entirely abandoned the indigenous knowledge systems. There is something fundamentally out of joint with subaltern studies, and a recognition of that disjointedness may yet lead to a more enriched conception of this historical enterprise.

_____

References

1. See Gyan Prakash, "Subaltern Studies as Postcolonial Criticism"; Florenica E. Mallon, "The Promise and Dilemma of Subaltern Studies: Perspectives from Latin American History"; and Frederick Cooper, "Conflict and Connection: Rethinking Colonial African History", all in "AHR Forum", *American Historical Review* 99, no. 5 (December 1994): 1475–90, 1491–1515, and 1516–45.

2. Latin American *Subaltern Studies* Group, "Founding Statement", *boundary 2* 20, no. 3 (1993): 110–21. See also John Beverley, *Subalternity and Representation: Arguments in Cultural Theory* (Durham, N.C.: Duke University Press, 1999), which focusses on Latin America.

3. Some readers may recognize that I am rendering far more ambivalent the characterization, made popular by Edward Said among others, of subaltern history as 'the empire striking back', or 'writing back to the centre'. See his foreword to Ranajit Guha and Gayatri Chakravorty Spivak, eds., *Selected Subaltern Studies* (New York: Oxford University Press, 1988);Edward Said, "Third World Intellectuals and Metropolitan Culture", *Raritan* 9, no. 3 (Winter 1990): 27–50; and, Edward Said, *Culture and Imperialism* (New York: Viking, 1993).

4. Ranajit Guha, ed., *A Subaltern Studies Reader, 1986–1995* (Minneapolis: University of Minnesota Press, 1997), back cover.

5. James Mill, *History of British India*, ed. with notes by Horace Hayman Wilson, 10 volumes (5th ed., London: James Madden, 1840–48), 2:46–48; 1:114–15.

6. Edward Thompson, *The Other Side of the Medal* (London: Hogarth Press, 1925), pp. 27–28.

7. See Asok Sen, "*Subaltern Studies*: Capital, Class and Community", and Ajit K. Chaudhury, "In Search of a Subaltern Lenin", both in *Subaltern Studies V: Writings on South Asian History and Society*, ed. Ranajit Guha (Delhi: Oxford University Press, 1987): 203–35 and 236–51, respectively. All volumes of *Subaltern Studies*, hereafter cited as *SS*, have been published by Oxford University Press, Delhi; the first six volumes (1982, 1983, 1984, 1986, 1987, and 1989), were edited by Ranajit Guha. Volume VII (1992) is edited by Partha Chatterjee and Gyanendra Pandey; Volume VIII (1994) by David Arnold and David Hardiman; and Volume IX (1996) by Shahid Amin and Dipesh Chakrabarty.

8. Veena Das, "Subaltern as Perspective", *SS* VI: 310–14; and for the debate on feminist readings of Indian women, see Julie Stephens, "Feminist Fictions: A Critique of the Category 'Non-Western Woman' in Feminist Writings on India", and Susie Tharu, "Response to Julie Stephens", both in *SS* VI: 92–125 and 126–131, respectively. Vol. IV also offered, in Dipesh Chakrabarty's "Invitation to a Dialogue" (pp. 364–76), a defence of Subaltern Studies against its critics.

9. Tanika Sarkar, "Jitu Santal's Movement in Malda 1924–1932: A Study in Tribal Protest", *SS* IV: 136–44.

10. Mahasweta Devi, "Breast-Giver", Appendix A to *SS* V: 252–76, and Gayatri Chakravorty Spivak, "A Literary Representation of the Subaltern: Mahasweta Devi's 'Stanadayini'", ibid., pp. 91–134.

11. Ranajit Guha, "On Some Aspects of the Historiography of Colonial India", *SS* I: 4.

12. Kancha Ilaih, "Productive Labour, Consciousness and History: The Dalitbahujan Alternative", *SS* IX: 165–200.

13. I refer here to the work, among others, of John Broomfield and Leonard Gordon.

14. Ramachandra Guha, "Subaltern and Bhadralok Studies", *Economic and Political Weekly* 30 (19 August 1995), p. 2057.

15. Sumit Sarkar, "Orientalism Revisited: Saidian Frameworks in the Writing of Modern Indian History", *Oxford Literary Review* 16, nos. 1–2 (1994): 205–24, especially pp. 205–7.

16. See Guha, ed., *A Subaltern Studies Reader*, pp. ix–xxii, and my review of the volume in *Emergences* 9, no. 2 (November 1999): 397–99.

17. Prakash, "Subaltern Studies as Postcolonial Criticism", p. 1476.

18. I have taken up the history of Indian historiography in a series of loosely connected published papers: "The Discourse of History and the Crisis at Ayodhya: Reflections on the Production of Knowledge, Freedom, and the Future of India", *Emergences* 5–6 (1993–94): 4–44; "History and the Possibilities of Emancipation: Some Lessons from India", *Journal of the Indian Council for Philosophical Research*, Special Issue: Historiography of Civilizations (June 1996): 95–137; and "Claims of the Past, Shape of the Future: The Politics of History in Independent India", in *India Briefing*, ed. Philip Oldenburg and Marshall Bouton (New York: M. E. Sharpe, 1999).

19. Tara Chand, *History of the Freedom Movement in India*, 4 vols. (New Delhi: Government of India, Ministry of Information and Broadcasting, Publications Division, 1961–72).

20. See, for example, S.A.A. Rizvi, ed., *Freedom Struggle in Uttar Pradesh*, 6 vols. (Lucknow: Government of Uttar Pradesh, Information Department, Publications Bureau, 1957–61), and K. K. Datta, ed., *History of the Freedom Movement in Bihar*, 3 vols. (Patna: Government of Bihar, 1957–58).

21. V. C. Joshi, ed., *Rammohun Roy and the Process of Modernization in India* (Delhi: Vikas, 1975) and Ashok Sen, *Iswarchandra Vidyasagar and His Elusive Milestones* (Calcutta: Riddhi-India, 1977).

22. A more detailed account of history in post-independent India can be found in my article, "History and Politics", in Marshall Bouton and Philip Oldenburg, eds., *India Briefing* (New York: M. E. Sharpe , 1999).

23. Anil Seal, *The Emergence of Indian Nationalism: Competition and Collaboration in the Late Nineteenth Century* (Cambridge: Cambridge University Press, 1968), p. 16.

24. John Gallagher and Ronald Robinson, "The Imperialism of Free Trade", *Economic History Review* (2nd Series) 6, no. 1 (1953), reprinted in *Imperialism: The Robinson and Gallagher Controversy*, ed. William Roger Louis (New York: New Viewpoints, 1976), p. 60; cf. also Gallagher and Robinson, "The Partition of Africa", in *The Decline, Revival and Fall of the British Empire*, ed. Anil Seal (Cambridge: Cambridge University Press, 1982), p. 71.

25. Ronald Robinson, "Non-European Foundations of European Imperialism: Sketch for a Theory of Collaboration", in Louis, ed., *Imperialism*, esp. pp. 130, 133–34, 141, 144, 146–47, from where the quotations in this paragraph are drawn.

26. Eric Stokes, "Imperialism and the Scramble for Africa: The New View", reprinted in Louis, ed., *Imperialism*, p. 183. Cf. Ronald Robinson, John Gallagher, and Alice Denny, *Africa and the Victorians: The Climax of Imperialism* (London: St. Martin's Press, 1961; paperback ed., New York: Anchor Books, 1968).

27. Seal, *The Emergence of Indian Nationalism*, p. 34.

28. Seal, "Imperialism and Nationalism in India", in John Gallagher, Gordon Johnson, and Anil Seal, *Locality, Province and the Nation: Essays on Indian Politics 1870 to 1940* (Cambridge: Cambridge University Press, 1973), p. 2.

29. Ibid., p. 3.

30. Gordon Johnson, *Provincial Politics and Indian Nationalism: Bombay and the Indian National Congress 1880 to 1915* (Cambridge: Cambridge University Press, 1973), p. 10.

31. In a different context, it is worth recalling Louis Dumont's lamentation that studies of Indian society and specifically the caste system had been wholly insensitive to questions of ideology, and that empirical studies could not substitute for the understanding of the caste system as an ideology. This is not to say that his work is free of other problems, or that it is not totalizing in its own fashion, but these problems have been addressed in the critical literature surrounding his book. See *Homo Hierarchicus: The Caste System and Its Implications*, trans. Mark Sainsbury (Chicago: University of Chicago Press, 1970); and for a 'subaltern' reading of Dumont, see Partha Chatterjee, "Caste and Subaltern Consciousness", *SS* VI: 169–209.

32. See the scathing review of 'Cambridge School' history by Tapan Raychaudhuri, "Indian Nationalism as Animal Politics", *Historical Journal* 22 (1979): 747–63.

33. Ibid., p. 750.

34. D. A. Washbrook, *The Emergence of Provincial Politics: The Madras Presidency, 1870–1920* (Cambridge: Cambridge University Press, 1976), p. 255.

35. Seal, "Imperialism and Nationalism in India", p. 6.

36. Gordon Johnson, *Provincial Politics and Indian Nationalism*, p. 193.

37. Guha, "Dominance without Hegemony and Its Historiography", *SS* VI: 210–309, esp. p. 290.

38. Seal, "Imperialism and Nationalism in India", p. 8. The modern variant of this argument has been expressed all too often by V. S. Naipaul, who opines that the Third World knows how to use the telephone, but is incapable of having invented it.

39. Guha, "On Some Aspects of the Historiography of Colonial India", *SS* I: 1–7, esp. p. 1.

40. This is less heretical than it might sound to an informed outsider, who, cognizant of the acute differences that have sometimes arisen among the original and present members of the collective, would have noticed the near deference that they accord to Guha's writings. Though members of the collective will doubtless signal their profound unease with 'essentialisms', they have handled their differences with Guha, whose role in bringing them together and nurturing a new generation of teachers and scholars of Indian history is readily acknowledged, in characteristically *Indian* fashion. His formulations have not been explicitly contested, or critiqued; but the most viable of the exercises in 'subaltern' history have, it seems to me, bypassed Guha's naked sociological equations.

41. E. P. Thompson, "Eighteenth-Century English Society: Class Struggle Without Class?", *Social History* 3, no. 2 (May 1978).

42. I use the word 'feudal' advisedly, as there is considerable debate, to which I do not propose to speak, as to whether one can reasonably transfer an understanding of feudalism derived from the history of Western societies to the study of Indian history.

43. This is the argument of Dipesh Chakrabarty, "Invitation to a Dialogue", *SS* IV: 375–76.

44. Ranajit Guha, *Elementary Aspects of Insurgency in Colonial India* (Delhi: Oxford University Press, 1983). A glowing assessment of this work, and of Guha's entire corpus, is to be found in T. V. Sathyamurthy, "Indian Peasant Historiography: A Critical Perspective on Ranajit Guha's Work", *The Journal of Peasant Studies* 18, no 3 (October 1990): 92–141.

45. See Victor Turner, *Dramas, Fields and Metaphors: Symbolic Action in Human Society* (Ithaca, N.Y.: Cornell University Press, 1974).

46. C. A. Bayly, review article on Volumes 1–IV of *Subaltern Studies*, "Rallying Around the Subaltern", *Journal of Peasant Studies* 16, no. 1 (1988): 116.

47. That large body of administrative and scholarly literature which deals with patterns of land settlement and revenue management in colonial India speaks entirely of peasant, rather than tribal, communities.

48. Guha, "On Some Aspects of the Historiography of Colonial India", p. 8; see also p. 4.

49. Ibid., pp. 6–7; emphasis in original.

50. Sumit Sarkar, *Modern India, 1885–1947* (Delhi: Macmillan, 1985), p. 1.

51. See, in particular, the following series of papers by Chakrabarty: "History as Critique and Critique(s) of History", *Economic and Political Weekly* 26, no. 37 (14 September 1991): 2162–66; "Postcoloniality and the Artifice of History: Who Speaks for 'Indian' Pasts?", *Representations, no.* 37 (Winter 1992): 1–26; and "Minority Histories, Subaltern Pasts", *Postcolonial Studies* 1, no. 1 (1998): 15–29.

52. I would refer the reader to "The Discourse of History and the Crisis at Ayodhya: Reflections on the Production of Knowledge, Freedom, and the Future of India", *Emergences* 5–6 (1993–94): 4–44; "History and the Possibilities of Emancipation: Some Lessons from India", *Journal of the Indian Council for Philosophical Research*, Special Issue: Historiography of Civilizations (June 1996): 95–137; "Discipline and Authority: Some Notes on Future Histories and Epistemologies of India", *Futures* 29, no. 10 (December 1997): 985–1000; and "Gandhi, the Civilizational Crucible, and the Future of Dissent", *Futures* 31 (March 1999): 205-219.

53. Dipesh Chakrabarty, "Conditions for Knowledge of Working-Class Conditions: Employers, Government and the Jute Workers of Calcutta, 1890–1940", *SS* II: 259–310; see p. 259.

54. Ranajit Guha, "The Prose of Counter-Insurgency", *SS* II: 1–41; quotations are from pages 15, 26–27.

55. Shahid Amin, "Gandhi as Mahatma: Gorakhpur District, Eastern UP, 1921-2", *SS* III: 1–61.

56. The idea of 'darshan' is not as distinctly 'Hindu' as is represented in the literature, for instance in Diana Eck's book by the same name. What is lacking from Amin's account is the notion of *darshan* as it came to be seen with reference to the Mughal Emperors. Akbar's trusted aide and biographer, Abu Fazl, was to write in the *Ain-i-Akbari* that Akbar would come out on to the balcony of his palace and confer *darshan* on the crowds, and so provide his subjects with an assurance that he was well and capable of discharging his duties. In an era when palace rivalries could lead to the dethronement of kings, and the Emperor himself commanded the armies on the field

at risk to his life, it was perforce necessary to demonstrate with a vivid display of sovereignty that the ship of the state was afloat.

57. Amin, "Gandhi as Mahatma", pp. 1–3, 18–20.

58. Ibid., p. 5, citing the *Pioneer* (Allahabad), 23 April 1921, p. 1.

59. Ibid., pp. 22–45.

60. Ibid., pp. 51–55.

61. One of the other pieces which offers a similarly complex, detailed, and nuanced reading of local sources is Sumit Sarkar's "The Kalki-Avatar of Bikrampur: A Village Scandal in Early Twentieth Century Bengal", *SS* VI: 1–53.

62. Gyanendra Pandey, "The Colonial Construction of 'Communalism': British Writings on Banaras in the Nineteenth Century", *SS* VI: 132–68.

63. Ibid., pp. 135–40.

64. Ibid., p. 151, citing Francis Younghusband, *Dawn in India* (London, 1930), p. 144.

65. Ibid., p. 136.

66. Ibid., pp. 166–67.

67. Vinay Lal, "Committees of Inquiry and Discourses of 'Law and Order' in Twentieth-Century British India", Unpublished Ph.D. Dissertation, Department of South Asian Languages and Civilizations, The University of Chicago, 2 vols. (1992), Vol. 2, Ch. 8.

68. D. L. Drake-Brockman, *Azamgarh: A Gazetteer, being Vol. XXXIII of the District Gazetteers of the United Provinces of Agra and Oudh* (Allahabad, 1911), pp. 260–61, cited in Pandey, "The Colonial Construction of 'Communalism'", p. 165.

69. Pandey, "The Colonial Construction of 'Communalism'", p. 151.

70. Sushil Srivastava, *The Disputed Mosque: A Historical Inquiry* (New Delhi: Vistaar Publications, 1991), provides a balanced historical account, and finds it probable that a Buddhist stupa stood at the original site of the mosque (pp. 113–24).

71. Citations are from Sarvepalli Gopal, ed., *Anatomy of a Confrontation: The Babri Masjid-Ram Janmabhumi Issue* (Delhi: Penguin Books, 1991), p. 138 notes 6–7.

72. Sarvepalli Gopal et al, "The Political Abuse of History", as reprinted in *Social Scientist*, nos. 200–201 (Jan.-Feb. 1990): 76–81. Almost the only historian at Jawaharlal Nehru University who did not append his signature to the document was Majid H. Siddiqi, himself a Muslim. Siddiqi offered the argument, which is deserving of attention, that historians "must exhibit intellectual self-confidence in their discipline and determine their own agenda in terms of their own questions and not allow the existence of communalism in this society . . . to force its agenda upon them". See his "Ramjanmabhoomi-Babri Masjid Dispute: The Question of History", *Economic and Political Weekly* 25, no. 2 (13 January 1990): 97–98.

73. I have discussed this question in detail in "The Discourse of History and the Crisis at Ayodhya", and in Sections V–VI of "Claims of the Past, Shape of the Future".

74. Ramachandra Gandhi, *Sita's Kitchen: A Testimony of Faith and Inquiry* (New Delhi: Penguin Books, 1992).

75. Guha, *Elementary Aspects*, pp. 265–68.

76. I would associate this argument with the likes of Aijaz Ahmad, whose voice is mistakenly seen to carry greater moral authority as he is himself a US-returned Indian academic.

77. Prakash, "Subaltern Studies as Postcolonial Criticism", pp. 1482, 1486–87.

78. C. A. Bayly, "Rallying Around the Subaltern", quite rightly anticipates Prakash in his observation that in contrast to those American historians who had used "indigenous sources (including popular ballads)", the "subalterns' forte has generally lain in rereading, and mounting an internal critique, of the police reports, administrative memoranda, newspapers and accounts by colonial officials and the literate", in other words 'elite texts', "which earlier historians had used for different purposes" (p. 111).

79. See Vivek Dhareshwar and R. Srivatsan, "'Rowdy-sheeters': An Essay on Subalternity and Politics"; and, to a much lesser extent, Susie Tharu and Tejaswini Niranjana, "Problems for a Contemporary Theory of Gender", both in SS IX: 201–31 and 232–60, respectively. It is a telling comment that of these four authors, only Vivek Dhareshwar, who earned his Ph.D. from the History of Consciousness Program at the University of California, Santa Cruz, has any training in history.

80. This problem is encountered in other domains of Indian life and intellectual work. I am reminded of the poignant observations of one of India's most famous environmentalists, Anil Agarwal, founder and director of the Centre for Science and Environment. In one of the recent issues of the magazine that he founded, *Down To Earth* (31 January 1999), Agarwal relates how, when he was asked in 1986 by the then Prime Minister Rajiv Gandhi to address his council of ministers on the "environmental challenges" facing the country, he spoke forth with confidence that "rural environmental problems are more important than urban environmental problems". He admits that he did not anticipate the extraordinary speed with which industrial pollution would become a nightmare for virtually the entire country, and so provided the country with "poor environmental leadership" (p. 6). The historical, sociological, and anthropological literature on modern India seems largely oblivious of the fact that there is an urban India, where nearly twenty-five percent of the country's one billion people live, and an ethnography of urban India has barely emerged. The observations of small-town India of one young writer, Pankaj Mishra, make for better subaltern history than the laborious postcolonial ruminations of Indian academics. See his *Butter Chicken in Ludhiana* (Delhi: Penguin, 1995).

13. A Critique of the Postmodern Turn in Western Historiography

Keith Windschuttle

This conference is about turning points, and postmodernism certainly represents a turning point for historiography. However, rather than postmodernism leading somewhere fruitful, this essay will argue that it is a movement that turns the writing of history into a blind alley and leads it up to a dead end.

Perhaps the most dramatic indicator of the state of the discipline of history in English-speaking countries today is that young people are abandoning it in droves. This was a tendency that, admittedly, was underway in the United States and elsewhere long before the 1990s, but as this decade has progressed, the reversal has become a rout. In America, the proportion of high school students studying history had declined from two-thirds in the 1960s to less than twenty per cent by the 1990s. At university level, the annual number of graduates in history from American colleges peaked in 1970 at 45,000 but had declined to less than 20,000 two decades later. The number of Ph.D.s awarded in history in the United States also fell by more than fifty per cent at the same time. This all occurred, moreover, during a period of great increase in overall college enrollments and degrees awarded. This absolute and relative decline in the number of history students has fed through to employment opportunities in the discipline and produced a similar result. By 1995, the American Historical Association recorded that the proportion of history doctoral graduates employed by universities had fallen to the lowest level on record. Commenting on these statistics, one of the most distinguished American historians of the twentieth century, C. Vann Woodward, observed in 1998 that, although there were several factors at work, including a shift in undergraduate preferences towards more vocational courses, postmodernist theorists deserved a significant share of the blame:

> I am of course aware that radicals in cultural studies and their postmodern precursors are by no means the only causes for the decline that history and some of the other humanities have suf-

fered in the academy in the last few years. . . . But [it] is my conviction that unless we of the academy, here and abroad, muster the
courage and find effective means to counter these forces, we face
a shabby end to the discipline we have served and to any system
of education we can respect.[1]

In Australia, there has also been a deterioration in student demand to the
point where a large proportion of academic historians have been forced into
what is euphemistically called 'early retirement', that is, they have been
retrenched. The total number of Australian historians employed by universities declined from 451 in 1989 to less than 300 in 1998, with the number in
some of the once most prestigious departments being reduced by half.[2] As in
the United States, there are obviously several influences at work here as well.
The fact remains, however, that until the end of the 1960s the writing and
teaching of traditional history corresponded to the period of greatest health
of the discipline, while the subsequent emergence of postmodern theory and
identity group politics corresponds to its worst decline of the century.

This dramatic shrinking of the historical enterprise, however, has not
had some of the effects that one might have expected. Since the publication
seven years ago of my own book *The Killing of History*,[3] there has been little
reappraisal by the proponents of postmodernism about what has gone
wrong and whether they deserve any responsibility for it. Instead, there has
been an even greater proliferation of publications pushing their now-famil-
iar critique of the discipline: that historians can only express the ideology of
their times, that they are deluded if they think they can be objective enough
to see beyond their own class, sex, ethnic, or cultural background, and that
traditional historiography reflects the views and interests of white, middle-
class, European males. Some of these new works have been devoted primarily to the theory or philosophy of history, such as Alun Munslow's
Deconstructing History,[4] Robert Berkhofer's *Beyond the Great Story: History as
Text and Discourse*,[5] Mark Poster's *Cultural History and Postmodernity*,[6] and
Frank Ankersmit and Hans Kellner's *A New Philosophy of History*.[7] Others are
surveys of historiography from the perspective of postmodernism or post-
structuralism. These include Keith Jenkins's *On 'What is History?' From Carr
and Elton to Rorty and White*,[8] Beverley Southgate's *History: What and Why?
Ancient, Modern and Postmodern Perspectives*,[9] David Harlan's *The
Degradation of American History*,[10] Joyce Appleby's *Knowledge and
Postmodernism in Historical Perspective*,[11] and Donald Kelley's *Faces of History:
From Herodotus to Herder*.[12]

The influence of this theory and the politics that accompany it can now
be seen in the design of the history curriculum at both high school and university levels. Among those who designed the new national history standards
for American high schools were educationalists opposed to the traditional
notion that history should be disinterested and above ideology. According to
Gary Nash, Charlotte Crabtree, and Ross Dunn, this concept is both out of
date and politically contaminated. 'Modern historiography has taught us that
historians can never fully detach their scholarly work from their own educa-

tion, attitudes, ideological dispositions and culture.' Disinterested scholarship, they assure us, 'is not simply an uneducated view. It is also an ideological position of traditionalists and the political Right that particular facts, traditions, and heroic personalities, all untainted by "interpretation", represent the "true" and "objective" history that citizens ought to know."[13] Fortified by the claim that it is impossible to be non-political, they advocate a reversal of the traditional account of American history with its emphasis on the War for Independence, the making of the Constitution, westward expansion, and the Civil War. Instead, they recommend a high school syllabus that focuses on how women, blacks, and ethnic minorities 'have suffered discrimination, exploitation, and hostility but have overcome passivity and resignation to challenge their exploiters, fight for legal rights, resist, and cross racial boundaries'.[14] Were it not for the unprecedented intervention of the Republican-dominated U.S. Senate in November 1994 voting to prevent two government educational bodies from certifying these national history standards, a program of this kind would now be taught to the majority of American high school students.

The university syllabus the critics recommend for the methodology of history has a similar theoretical bent. It is described in the 1997 anthology edited by Keith Jenkins, *The Postmodern History Reader*. Although this book contains a token number of anti-postmodernist articles by Lawrence Stone, Gertrude Himmelfarb, Geoffrey Elton, and a handful of old-style Marxists, the bulk of the selection comes from the familiar pantheon of French theorists—Jean François Lyotard, Jean Baudrillard, Roland Barthes, and Michel Foucault—as well as the latest English-language theorists mentioned above—Berkhofer, Ankersmit, and Kellner—plus a sprinkling of poststructuralist feminists.

Like the advocates of the new high school curriculum, the editor of this collection is quite frank in supporting a political agenda as much an academic one. Jenkins candidly admits that the collection is neither balanced nor disinterested and that 'the weight of the readings come down in favour of postmodernism'.[15] He justifies his position by the claim that all approaches to history are themselves already politicised, even those that think themselves above ideology, and that politicisation is impossible to escape. This is equally true for traditional empirical historiography, Jenkins claims, which has a hidden prejudice that needs to be outed. Traditional academic history is, in his own words, nothing but 'bourgeois ideology'. He arrives at this conclusion by the following reasoning: Traditional historians say they are opposed to teleological versions of history, which hold that history has a purpose that leads either to a Communist utopia (Marxist version), or to ever-improving progress (Whig version). The proper role of history, the traditionalists say, is not to create some kind of trajectory into the future but to study the past for its own sake. But if they take this line, Jenkins argues, this means they must be satisfied with the status quo. Because they don't want to change the present, he says, they must be committed to it.

> The fact that the bourgeoisie doesn't want a different future (the
> fact that it has now arrived at its preferred historical destination—

liberal, bourgeois, market capitalism) means that it doesn't any longer need a past-based future-orientated fabrication. Thus at this point, the point where the links between the past, present and future are broken because the present is everything, the past can be neutralized and studied not for our various sakes but for 'its own'. For this is exactly what is currently required, a history which is finished now that it has led right up to us.[16]

Now, this is plainly a specious argument. The wish to understand the past in its own terms is compatible not only with satisfaction with the status quo but with several other positions as well, including a critical attitude towards, and even despair about, the present condition of society. The ranks of traditional historians constitute a broad church that includes apolitical cynics as well as conservative, romantic, social democratic, Christian, and even some old-fashioned empirical Marxist historians who each, in their different ways, regard the prevailing social system as far from satisfactory. Yet all believe that the proper role of the historian is to try to shake off his own prejudices and interests and to study the past for its own sake. To argue that positions of this kind represent bourgeois ideology is to enforce the crudest kind of ideological reductionism, more akin to vulgar Marxism than postmodernism's purported appreciation of 'difference'. Rather than any revelation about traditional historiography, all that Jenkins's argument illustrates is, first, the level of politicisation that prevails within the postmodernist mindset, and, second, how quickly this political approach descends into ad hominem abuse. In this kind of debate, instead of addressing the evidence and reason deployed by your opponent, the tactic is simply to identify his political position and then rest your case as though enough has been said. This is not only an unsatisfactory way to assess historians but is the antithesis of any kind of respectable intellectual activity.

Most pointedly, it represents the desire to continue the Marxist critique of western society by other means. Instead of the transformation of society being made in the name of old blue collar proletariat, the approved constituency is now composed of anyone who can claim to be oppressed by Western culture—feminists, blacks, gays, indigenes, ethnics, the disabled, the insane, prisoners, drug addicts, or members of any other minority group. The politics of all this are crude enough on their own but to base an education program on a critique of this kind is to destroy the probity of any field through which it is taught. Yet in the past decade this has increasingly been the fate of history. What was once the central discipline through which Western culture defined itself is now being used by radical educationalists to deny the integrity of the West altogether.

Even when they are focussing specifically on methodological issues, the critics of history openly acknowledge that this is their aim. Robert Berkhofer claims that traditional history is an authoritarian practice that reflects the 'ethnocentrism' and 'cultural hubris' of contemporary Western society. This is true, he argues, no matter which of the prevailing political divisions within Western culture—conservative, liberal, or radical—its authors support. All are couched within the same humanistic tradition and are driven by the same desire for power. 'Normal history orders the past for the sake of authority and therefore power over its audience. . . . By assuming a third person voice and an omniscient viewpoint, authors, be they left or right or in between politically, assert their power over their readers in the name of REALITY.'[17] By undermining history's claims to represent the past, Berkhofer hopes to demystify the discipline and to replace it with the methodology of 'poetics', which will introduce different methods and endorse different voices.

This is a prospect that also excites Keith Jenkins who, in endorsing Berkhofer's approach, argues that it opens the way for those who are currently excluded to write their own histories, while at the same time silencing the voice of traditional authority.

> Such demystification can thus 'free up' historians to tell many equally legitimate stories from various viewpoints, with umpteen voices, emplotments and types of synthesis. It is in this sense that we can interpret the past 'anyway we like'. And it is this conclusion which signals to many (normal) historians the end of their kind of history.[18]

On this issue, I agree that the last implication drawn by Jenkins does follow, except that, unlike him, I find it appalling. It is also, ironically, self-defeating for the political aims of the postmodernists themselves. They are happy to legitimise a multiplicity of voices as long as they all belong to leftist groups of which they approve. However, by abandoning truth and endorsing the interpretation of the past 'anyway we like', they unwittingly provide equal legitimacy to political positions they might find less congenial, such as those of neo-Nazis, neo-Stalinists, white and black supremacists, holocaust deniers, ethnic cleansers or any other variety of political depravity. If we accepted Jenkins's view, we would deny ourselves both the right and the ability to contest their versions of history, no matter how offensive, absurd or inaccurate they might be.

Although the view that history has been fatally compromised is now more entrenched than ever, there are also growing signs of a fight back in defence of traditional values. In 1998, in response to the postmodern influence on the American Historical Association and its journal, the *American Historical Review*, a group of U.S. historians formed The Historical Society. They described their objective as being to 'concentrate on the constructive work of reshaping our profession'. By mid-1999 they had attracted 1200 members. The society's membership is drawn from across old political boundaries—'from the Marxist Left to the traditionalist Right', according to the open letter that announced its founding. It deplores what it calls the endless controversies of the 'cultural wars', and intends to avoid 'the perpetuation of the irrationalities of recent years'.

There have also been a number of new books analysing the challenge to history and providing persuasive counter arguments. They include Richard Evans's *In Defence of History*[19] and Behan McCullagh's *The Truth of History*.[20]

Of the two, Evans, who is professor-elect of modern history at the University of Cambridge, has had the most publicity, being widely reviewed in both the popular and intellectual press.

Evans presents a number of effective arguments against attempts by postmodernist critics to undermine the credentials of history, especially their denial of the historian's use of facts and pursuit of the truth. He shows how the critics cannot even state their objections without depending on the very notions they deny. For instance, the postmodernists Ellen Somekawa and Elizabeth Smith argue that 'within whatever rules historians articulate, all interpretations are equally valid'. Hence, they say historians should reject the traditionalists' belief in the truth of what they are writing, and instead affirm the moral or political position they are taking. But if all interpretations are equally valid, then these authors should admit that their own perspective is just as valid as that of its opposite, traditional realism. But they only arrive at their postmodernist position by arguing that realism is false. 'Once post-modernism's principles are applied to itself', Evans observes, 'many of its arguments begin to collapse under the weight of their own contradictions'.[21] Evans also dissects the claims of the feminist historian Diane Purkiss who, in her book, *The Witch in History*, rejects the use of empirical methods to investigate her subject and instead decides to 'tell or retell the rich variety of stories told about witches'. Evans points out, however, that in telling these stories she acknowledges that she has 'assembled evidence' about witches and has thus adopted the very procedures she derides in others. And although she dismisses the notion of truth in empirical history as 'male', this does not stop her from criticising the claims of some other feminist historians as inherently 'improbable'. Evans points out that she is thus 'arrogating to herself a right of scepticism which she denies to men—a sexist double standard if ever there was one, and an impossible one too, for if truth were really a male concept, then Purkiss could never even begin to claim that anything she said herself was true'.[22]

The publishers of Evans's book claim it is a 'worthy successor' to E. H. Carr's *What is History?* which has stood since the 1960s as one of the standard accounts of the practice of the discipline. There are at least two reasons, however, why Evans will have difficulty in filling these shoes for a similar length of time. First, he addresses his arguments almost exclusively to the phenomenon of postmodernism, which, even as he wrote, was a label some of its original proponents were beginning to evade. In late 1997, one of the principal progenitors of the postmodernist mindset, the American philosopher Richard Rorty, was recommending that, since nobody has 'the foggiest idea' what the term postmodernism means, 'it would be nice to get rid of it.'[23] If there is one thing that is consistent about the current generation of radical academics it is their penchant for intellectual fashion. Their views about what is intellectually chic shift as rapidly and as regularly as that of the garment industry. In a little more than two decades the same people have been adherents of structuralism, semiotics, post-structuralism, postmodernism, postcolonialism, radical feminism, queer theory, critical theory, and cultural studies. The main reason academics have adopted this shifting pattern of allegiance has been to immunise themselves against empirical criticism. On several occasions in the recent past when they have seen a strong body of opinion emerge to publicly deride the currently favoured position, they have quickly declared the latter out of date (their own sharpest rebuke) and have abandoned it.[24] (Indeed, in the very week I write this, the post brings a review copy of the galleys of a book by the poststructuralist literary critic, Gayatri Spivak, in which she announces she is abandoning 'postcolonialism', a movement that until now counted her as one of its celebrities.[25]) Unfortunately for Evans, he is likely to find his targets will soon be dismissing him on the grounds that nobody subscribes to postmodernism any more. In fact, the majority already prefer the less provocative term cultural studies which, although it endorses the same combination of anti-realist philosophy and anti-Western politics, has a terminological blandness that offers a thicker veneer of academic respectability.

The second problem for Evans is that, in wanting to be diplomatic and to promote a spirit of academic ecumenism, he concedes too much to the movement he is criticising. In its more constructive modes, Evans writes, postmodernism has 'encouraged historians to look more closely at documents, to take their surface patina more seriously, and to think about texts and narratives in new ways'.[26] The principal piece of evidence he offers for this assessment is Robert Darnton's 1983 book, *The Great Cat Massacre*. Its author based his entire work on a three-page pamphlet written some thirty years after the incident it purports to describe. The 'cat massacre' was supposedly conducted by a group of apprentices in the 1730s and Darnton used it as a symbolic prefiguration of the great massacres of the French Revolution during the 1790s. Apart from the one pamphlet published in 1762, however, Darnton has found no other evidence the massacre took place. Although Evans acknowledges that some critics have charged that Darnton's thesis does not stand up to even the most cursory scrutiny, he still goes on to praise the sophistication of the book's interpretation of its single text.[27] However, Evans's early chapters provide a clear enough account of the development of historical scholarship to show that the close scrutiny of documents long predates postmodernism and has been part of the province of history for the past 170 years. The German historian, Leopold von Ranke, who introduced rigorous new criteria for veracity in the 1830s, derived his techniques from the textual practices of philology, in which he had initially trained. Moreover, unlike postmodernist studies, the traditional historical approach brings a scepticism to its analysis of texts that allows it to distinguish between the relevant and the irrelevant, the verifiable and the unverifiable, and the authentic and the fraudulent. There is nothing in Evans's book to persuade historians they have anything to learn from postmodernism about the scrutiny of documents.

Two other claims for postmodernism made by Evans are, first, that it has shifted the emphasis in historical writing away from social-scientific to literary models, thus making history more accessible to the general public, and, second, that it has restored individual human beings to history, whereas social science approaches had largely written them out. The first claim is plausible in view of the postmodernist credentials of Simon Schama, who has been one of the best-selling authors of the past decade. However, it is hardly accurate as far as some of the works cited by Evans himself are concerned, such as that of Diane Purkiss, which would be appetizing to the palate of only the most hardened radical feminist. Nor does it apply to several of the works discussed in *The Killing of History*, such as the anti-narrative theoretical poses struck by Greg Dening and Paul Carter. Similarly, Evans's second claim has a surface plausibility but overlooks entirely the legacy of the anti-humanist genre of Michel Foucault with its assertion that the autonomy of the human subject is an illusion and that the individual is merely an instrument of language and culture. Foucault and his followers have rendered the individual human agent non-existent in ways that few of the social sciences ever thought possible or desirable.

There is one outcome of postmodernism, however, about which Evans is certainly correct. Its emergence has, as he says, forced historians to interrogate their own methods and procedures as never before. His own book is itself good evidence of this. Despite the reservations I have recorded above, *In Defence of History* is indeed a fine defence, a valuable contribution which would have been unlikely to be produced were it not for the provocation of postmodernist theory. However, one question raised by this fight back is whether historians themselves are the people best qualified to engage an adversary of this kind. In *The Truth of History*, Behan McCullagh points out that because this debate is ultimately over such fundamental concepts as truth and objectivity, and because the postmodernist critique takes place more at the level of philosophy than historical method, a defence mounted primarily through the rationality of the procedures used by historians is less than adequate. McCullagh is a realist philosopher who wants to defend the practice of history from its philosophical opponents. He maintains that, in this debate so far, the historians have focussed on the justification of historical descriptions, interpretations, and explanations while the philosophical critique has been aimed at the assumptions historians make and the standards of rationality they employ. Hence, he claims, each side has not done justice to the other's arguments.[28]

Now, this characterisation is not completely accurate as far as the historians are concerned. Evans, for instance, certainly tackles the postmodernists over their own standards of rationality, and my own book attempts the same in terms of the logic of their position and the philosophy of science that has influenced them. Nonetheless, it is true that there are a number of philosophical issues in this debate that the historians have not addressed. McCullagh not only takes up these additional issues but he pursues the arguments involved to a depth that is more characteristic of a philosophical than an historical controversy. Although I am not persuaded by all his arguments, his book is a *tour de force*. It deserves to be seen as the best defence of history yet made by any philosopher and a major contribution to the field.

McCullagh takes the debate into the philosophy of language, which is the original source of a number of postmodernist critiques of historical knowledge. For instance, the French theorists Roland Barthes and Jacques

Derrida, and their more recent English-language followers like Robert Berkhofer and Keith Jenkins, argue that language has no important or regular relation to the world. Words and texts get their meaning not from their relation to the world itself but from their relation to other words and texts. Hence descriptions couched in language about what has happened in the world cannot reveal reality. History thus refers not to the reality of the past but, like language, only to itself. As Jenkins puts it: 'The signified (the past) is thus nought but the signifier (history)'.[29] However, McCullagh draws on the work of other philosophers of language, Michael Devitt and Kim Sterelny,[30] to refute this. He shows that when people make assertions through language they are not merely producing a set of words related to other words. Instead, they are referring to something in the world that is capable of producing certain kinds of experience. To learn what the word 'brown' means, McCullagh points out, one must be shown brown objects and not just learn that brown objects are not yellow, blue, red, and so on. The word 'brown' is associated with the experience of a certain colour.[31] Hence, the meaning of words and the use of language are compatible with both referentiality and realism.

McCullagh also examines Derrida's claim about the textual dependence of historical descriptions, which is another that both Berkhofer and Jenkins have repeated. This case is as follows: Although historical descriptions purport to be about the world, their authors refer not to the real world but to other texts, such as reports about what occurred and documents about how people experienced events. So these descriptions are not related directly to the real world, but are themselves products of other texts. As Greg Dening puts it: 'I retext the already texted past'.[32] McCullagh notes that it is of course true that historians draw inferences about what happened in the past from largely documentary evidence, that is, from written texts rather than from their own direct observations. However, he points out that this only implies their accounts of the past cannot be true if that textual evidence is not connected with, or does not establish, what happened. 'It is not the fact that their descriptions are inferred from other texts which makes their truth suspect,' he observes. 'It is suspect only if the evidence does not strongly entail their truth in the first place. When the evidence strongly supports the truth of an historical description, one is rationally entitled to believe it is very probably true'.[33]

Another thesis advanced by Derrida, and developed into a critique of history by Jean François Lyotard, is that descriptions of the world always omit details. Historical descriptions use common nouns and verbs that pick out only general features of what they refer to. It is thus naïve to assume that our descriptions of the world can portray reality accurately. No description using language can capture the whole. In particular, Lyotard says, readers of works of history need to be reminded that they are looking at artifices, that the text and the event are separate, different things. Lyotard argues that since it is impossible to represent past events in all their particularity, history is thus impossible.[34] But as McCullagh points out, the fact that an historical description refers only to some aspects of an event or situation, and makes no reference to others, does not mean that it must be false. It simply means it is not exhaustive. The fact that a description does not capture every detail about the past, that descriptions are always incomplete and can never 'mirror reality', does not mean they cannot represent it with some degree of precision. 'The more general the description, the less precise it is,' McCullagh acknowledges. 'Nevertheless, very general descriptions can be completely accurate, in that they are entirely warranted by the known facts, even though they are far from precise.'[35]

Now, at this point in his discussion, McCullagh says that the postmodernists deserve some credit for their having advanced this last case. 'We must honour the postmodernists for having exposed the limitations of descriptions so vividly. There is no denying that descriptions do use common nouns and verbs, and there is a range of sets of the truth conditions for any statement about the past. They do not capture every detail. . . .'[36] This seems to me, however, a strange compliment to offer. No historian has ever seriously claimed that his work 'mirrors reality' in the sense of reproducing the past in all its particularity. No description of the world, as McCullagh himself acknowledges, could ever pretend to tell everything, and there is no historian who ever imagined he could perform such a feat. Moreover, no reader of history has ever been so innocent that he needed a Lyotard to remind him that the historical text and the historical event are different things. The postmodernists' argument is an assault on a straw man, the demolition of a position their opponents have never held. It is also extraordinarily patronising towards readers, who are assumed to have the mentality of pre-school children watching television. Historians certainly claim to have uncovered truths about the past but they have never maintained that these constitute the entire truth about everything. It should be perfectly obvious to anyone not mesmerised by theory that descriptions on the printed page of a history book could never pretend to be a reproduction of the whole of the lived past. The Rankean entreaty to discover 'what actually happened' is a recommendation to pursue truth about the past, not to pursue *all* the truths or to reconstruct everything that happened in it.

As I noted above, McCullagh is a realist who defends traditional historiography. Rather than supporting a correspondence theory of truth, which is the usual accompaniment of the realist position, McCullagh offers what he calls a 'correlation theory' of truth, which is similar but, he argues, more sophisticated. The correspondence theory holds that a description of the world is true if there is something in the world that resembles one of the conventional truth conditions of the description. The theory is normally accompanied by the belief that we can check the truth of a description by directly observing whether part of the world resembles or corresponds to the truth conditions of the description or not. McCullagh's correlation theory modifies this to take into account the perceptions of different cultures. He believes that the knowledge of different peoples is conditioned by their culture, even though the things in the world are not determined by culture. He states his correlation theory as follows: 'A perception of the world is accurate if there was some state of the world such that it would normally cause a person of a certain culture to have perceptions of that kind.' Thus, he says, realism about the world is compatible with cultural relativism about knowledge.[37]

Without recapitulating the objections I raised to cultural relativism in *The Killing of History*, let me point out that one of the problems in this debate is that philosophers and historians come to it from opposite directions. Philosophers usually approach from the abstract end of the spectrum by asking questions to do with how we justify our beliefs or whether we can know anything for certain. Historians often start from the position that we actually do have knowledge and a high degree of certainty about many aspects of the past. They then seek to justify why this is so, or to respond to objections from those who claim that historical knowledge is not well grounded.

From this latter perspective, there is a crucial distinction that needs to be made. This is between propositions about history and works of history. This is the distinction between particular pieces of knowledge about what happened in the past, or the facts of history, and the explanations made by historians, that is, explanations made in extended pieces of writing such as articles and books. Some of the philosophical critics of history, even those like Keith Jenkins who claim 'epistemology shows we can never really know the past', acknowledge the existence of historical facts but dismiss them as inconsequential. Facts such as the dates of events, Jenkins says, are '"true" but trite'.[38]

It is not difficult to show that there are a great many facts or propositions about history that are not subject to any doubt or uncertainty at all. That such facts exist is itself quite enough to dispel any attempt from philosophy to impose a blanket scepticism on the whole of the field. Historians know countless numbers of facts about the past that no sane person would question. The names of the elected officials of most democratic nations over the past two centuries, for instance, are obviously in this category. Or take the following proposition: The Viet Minh defeated the French at Dien Bien Phu in 1954. Every term in this proposition—the names of the two protagonists, the concept of military defeat, the name of the place, the date the event occurred—is a construct of language and culture. Yet the proposition is true. What's more, it is true in a culturally objective sense. There is nothing relativistic about it. It is a proposition that is equally true in either French culture or Vietnamese culture, as well as the culture of any other peoples of the world. Moreover, far from being trite, this is a very important proposition. Because the event it describes actually occurred, it affected the subsequent history of the whole of South East Asia. The political allegiances and the lives of the inhabitants of the countries of the region would not be as they are today if this proposition were untrue.

Any reader with the slightest familiarity with the world he inhabits can immediately think of dozens of historical facts with the same status, that are just as objectively true and just as substantial in their consequences. Moreover, facts with this degree of certainty are by no means confined to events within living memory but go back to the medieval and ancient worlds, and even well beyond antiquity. That the Turks conquered Constantinople in 1453, that the ancient Greeks wrote poetry and philosophy, and that human beings have inhabited Australia for at least 10,000 years, are all facts that one would have to be either highly ignorant, or decidedly perverse, to want to question. Of course many of the details surrounding or supporting these facts may not themselves be finally known. We may not know all the tactics or armaments General Giap used when he surrounded the French forces at Dien Bien Phu, but incompleteness in our accounts of his victory does not affect the fact that we know it occurred.

On the other hand, whole works of history are often culturally biased. An extended historical explanation may use as evidence historical propositions that in themselves are objectively true, but may nonetheless provide a cultural or political slant on this material that distorts the reality under discussion. Lack of objectivity often derives from the process of selection when the historian chooses some facts as evidence for his case but omits others. But just because the process of selection is often based on the historian's cultural predilections, this does not mean that it must necessarily or always be so. The simple act of selection does not endorse Simon Schama's assertion that 'claims for historical knowledge must always be fatally circumscribed by the character and prejudices of its narrator'.[39] The selection process of the historian is a contingent matter that may itself be criticised by other historians. Indeed, the charge of cultural, political, or moral bias is one of the most common criticisms that historians make of each other's work. In some cases, criticism of this kind might mean that the historical community jettisons an entire explanation. In others, however, it may allow some aspects of a work to be rejected while permitting the remainder to go on to become part of the overall store of historical knowledge. But if all historians were as cocooned within their own cultural mindset as postmodernist philosophers claim, they would lack the very ability to detect cultural bias in their colleagues. They would be unable to make the kind of extra-cultural critique of each other's work that is so common. Bias and lack of objectivity among historians are issues that have to be decided in individual cases, not by an appeal to epistemological necessity.

We should also recognise that the concept of objectivity is crucial to historical debate, to the resolving of historical controversies and, indeed, to the ability of historians to discuss matters sensibly with one another. Historians from widely different cultural backgrounds can often agree that some historical explanations do not work, either because the known evidence does not support them, or because the evidence actually contradicts them. This kind of exchange is possible only because many of the propositions that constitute historical evidence are themselves independent of any one historian's culture. A person of any cultural background who investigated the history of the Byzantine empire would find the same outcome for the siege of Constantinople in 1453. If the notion of objectivity were to be eliminated from the historian's methodological tool box, the use of evidence to resolve issues in historical debate would become impossible. Scholars would simply talk past one another, confined to their own cultural and political shells, insulated in their own beliefs but unable to contest the views of others or, indeed, to learn anything from members of other cultures.

The experience of participating in a number of debates and seminars on this topic over the past five years has taught me that this quarrel often appears to many of those not directly involved as an esoteric matter confined to the margins of methodological disputation. Yet it deserves to taken more seriously than this for it has much wider implications. If we deny the possibility of discovering objective knowledge about human affairs, if we succumb to cultural relativism, linguistic idealism, and the kind of overt politicisation advocated by postmodernist critics, we give away history altogether. Ever since Thucydides wrote the *History of the Peloponnesian War*, historians have been distinguished by their efforts to distance themselves from their own political system and their own culture and to write from a position beyond both. The attempt to be objective and self-critical, rather than subjective and self-defensive—fraught with all the difficulties that we know this involves—defines the historian's profession. In the current contest with the postmodernists over methodology, what is ultimately at stake is the preservation of this intellectual heritage.

References

1. C. Vann Woodward, 'The core curriculum as intellectual motivation', *Partisan Review*, 3, 1998, pp. 406–7.

2. *The Australian*, 30 June 1998, p. 3, citing figures produced by the president of the Australian Historical Association, Stuart Macintyre.

3. Keith Windschuttle, *The Killing of History: How a Discipline Is Being Murdered by Literary Critics and Social Theorists* (Sydney: Macleay Press, 1994; New York: Free Press, 1997; paperback edition San Francisco: Encounter Books, 2000).

4. Alun Munslow, *Deconstructing History* (London: Routledge, 1997).

5. Robert Berkhofer, *Beyond the Great Story: History as Text and Discourse* (Cambridge MA: Belknap Press of Harvard University Press, 1995).

6. Mark Poster, *Cultural History and Postmodernity: Disciplinary Readings and Challenges* (New York: Columbia University Press, 1997).

7. Frank Ankersmit and Hans Kellner (eds.) *A New Philosophy of History* (London: Reaktion, 1995).

8. Keith Jenkins, *On 'What is History?' from Carr and Elton to Rorty and White* (London: Routledge, 1995).

9. Beverley Southgate, *History: What and Why? Ancient, Modern and Postmodern Perspectives* (London: Routledge, 1996).

10. David Harlan, *The Degradation of American History* (Chicago: University of Chicago Press, 1997).

11. Joyce Appleby et al. (eds.) *Knowledge and Postmodernism in Historical Perspective* (London: Routledge, 1997).

12. Donald R. Kelley, *Faces of History: From Herodotus to Herder* (New Haven: Yale University Press, 1998).

13. Gary B. Nash, Charlotte Crabtree and Ross E. Dunn, *History on Trial: Culture Wars and the Teaching of the Past* (New York: Alfred A. Knopff, 1997), p. 10.

14. *Ibid.*, p. 101. For a review and critique of this program see Keith Windschuttle, 'The problem of democratic history', *The New Criterion*, 16, 10, June 1998.

15. Keith Jenkins (ed.) *The Postmodern History Reader* (London: Routledge, 1997), p. 2

16. Jenkins (ed.) *The Postmodern History Reader*, pp. 15–16.

17. Robert Berkhofer, 'The Challenge of Poetics to (Normal) Historical Practice', in Jenkins (ed.) *The Postmodern History Reader*, pp. 152–53, 155n (his upper case).

18. Jenkins (ed.) *The Postmodern History Reader*, p. 20.

19. Richard J. Evans, *In Defence of History* (London: Granta Books, 1997).

20. C. Behan McCullagh, *The Truth of History* (London: Routledge, 1998).

21. Evans, *In Defence of History*, pp. 219–21.

22. *Ibid.*, pp. 98–99.

23. Mark Leyner, 'Geraldo, Eat Your Avant-Pop Heart Out', *New York Times*, 21 December 1997.

24. In fact, as long ago as 1991, the Australian literary theorist John Frow displayed a very French predilection for keeping one step ahead of the pack by publishing a monograph entitled *What Was Postmodernism?* (Sydney: Local Consumption Publications, 1991).

25. Gayatri Chakravorty Spivak, *A Critique of Postcolonial Reason: Toward a History of the Vanishing Present* (Cambridge MA: Harvard University Press, 1999).

26. Evans, *In Defence of History*, p. 248.

27. *Ibid.*, p. 248.

28. McCullagh, *The Truth of History*, pp. 3–4.

29. Jenkins (ed.) *The Postmodern History Reader*, p. 20.

30. Michael Devitt and Kim Sterelny, *Language and Reality: An Introduction to the Philosophy of Language* (Oxford: Blackwell, 1987).

31. McCullagh, *The Truth of History*, p. 38.

32. Greg Dening, *Mr Bligh's Bad Language: Passion, Power and Theatre on the Bounty* (Cambridge: Cambridge University Press, 1992), p. 5.

33. McCullagh, *The Truth of History*, p. 40.

34. *Ibid.*, pp. 40–41.

35. *Ibid.*, p. 42.

36. *Ibid.*, p. 42.

37. *Ibid.*, pp. 26–28.

38. Keith Jenkins, *Re-Thinking History* (London: Routledge, 1991), pp. 19, 32.

39. Simon Schama, *Dead Certainties (Unwarranted Speculations)* (London: Granta Books/Penguin, 1991), p. 322.

14. Postmodernism and Chinese History
Arif Dirlik

The discussion below considers questions raised by postmodernism with specific reference to issues in the historiography of China. If I spend more time working through questions of postmodernism than on the historiography of China, it is because the former demands considerable clarification before there can be any evaluation of what it may imply for the study of Chinese history, where its effects have become visible only in the last few years. The few self-proclaimed efforts at writing postmodern histories of China have provoked an almost unthinking hostility among some historians, based mostly on a misunderstanding, if not a caricaturing of what postmodern historiography might entail.[1] To be fair, this hostility is provoked in part by the advocates of these new approaches who, taken by their own novelty, make exaggerated claims for postmodernist innovation which may be sustained only by *their* caricaturing of the historiography they would depart from. But it is driven also by a conservative attachment to what is considered to be proper historical method, and an even more conservative urge to police disciplinary boundaries. We need to confront both the abuses of postmodern historiography, and the abusive hostility it provokes; for the issues involved are too important to be lost in the mazes of what often seems to be little more than trivial professional politics. What is at issue, most fundamentally, is the relationship of history as discipline and epistemology to its broader cultural environment, whether in China or the United States, which are the locations of concern in this discussion.

I. Historicizing Postmodernism

"Postmodernism is an exasperating term," Hans Bertens writes, because, "in the avalanche of articles and books that have made use of the term since the late 1950s, postmodernism has been applied at different levels of conceptual abstraction to a wide range of objects and phenomena in what we used to call reality."[2] Not only does the meaning assigned to the term differ from one artistic realm to another, Bertens suggests, but these meanings often point in conflicting directions, especially in the relationship of the postmodern to the modern. If the postmodern has generated its own intellectual and artistic styles, moreover, its domain has been enlarged also by the incorporation within the idea of the postmodern of intellectual developments that preceded, and owed little to, postmodernism as it emerged in the 1980s, which both defenders and critics have nevertheless come to attribute to postmodernism, adding further to the difficulty of distinguishing the postmodern from the modern.

The varied and contradictory guises in which postmodernism appears rules out any easy definition of the term, suggesting instead that it is best grasped in the concrete historicities of discourses on the postmodern. How the postmodern appears in its relationship to history is discussed at some length below. Suffice it to say here that given the apparently antagonistic relationship between history and postmodernism, it is ironic that developments within historiography should have contributed both to the generation of postmodernism, and the broadening of its scope. On the other hand, while postmodernism in its more extravagant guises appears to be inimical to history, it also has legitimized ways of thinking about the past that may rescue history from the teleologies of modernity, and enrich our understanding of the past and its relationship to the present. The contradictory relationship between history and postmodernism is entangled in the cultural legacy of the 1960s, with its own blend of hope and disillusionment, that would produce both new departures in history and a radical questioning of the cultural and political meaning assigned to history under the regime of modernity.[3]

The relationship of the postmodern to the modern is highly ambiguous because, arguably, it is the modern that in its commitment to ceaseless change generates the postmodern in its self-realization, which by the very logic of modernity must be continually deferred. The postmodern, in other words, exists within the modern at every moment as its dialectical negation. But is it possible that there is a point at which the postmodern breaks with the modern and sets itself against the latter with its own claims to history? This is suggested by Marxist periodizations of postmodernity, such as those of Frederic Jameson and David Harvey, who, while they recognize the common material foundation of modernity and postmodernity in a capitalist mode of production, nevertheless acknowledge a profound transformation within capitalism that calls forth a new "cultural logic," as Jameson has put it.[4] Where history is concerned, the intellectual break appears most intrusively in the repudiation of the teleology of modernity, so that postmodernism is no longer simply an expression of the dialectics of modernity, but is set against its dialectical claims, which are then extended throughout the past to repudiate all "metanarratives."[5] The postmodern, then, provides a new vantage point from which to "re-read" modernity, not just to expose its "underside," which had never been too far below the surface, but more importantly to impugn responsibility for modernity's misdeeds to the culture of modernity based on claims to reason, science, and history.[6] The "cultural turn" of the last two decades is traceable to a new awareness of culture not just as a function of material structures, but as an autonomous force itself in the making of modernity. The awareness was to be reinforced by the "cultural turn" in the operations of capital, as information and communication technologies became crucial to its functioning.

What makes postmodernism problematic as a principle of historical periodization is that its is a "cultural logic" that denies logic (or *logos*) and points to nothing beyond itself. While it is liberating in its repudiation of structures and metanarratives that have constrained human activity, and erased alternatives to modernity, the liberation it promises has neither spatial nor temporal depth. Postmodernism itself, as implied by the prefix "post-," is always residual, defining itself by what it rejects, without an immanent logic of its own; indeed, denial of the possibility of any such logic lies at the very heart of postmodern claims to break with the modern. While the products of modernity are everywhere in postmodernity, they appear there in their fragmentation, without the structural or the historical coherence with which modernity had endowed them. The postmodern may be no more than a way of naming the disintegration of the modern-liberating in its open-endedness, but also highly problematic in its seemingly boundless tolerance for difference, including tolerance for oppression. Bertens writes of postmodernism that it serves "to accommodate a number of critico-political utopias and dystopias, varying from visions of liberation and emancipation (of both the Enlightenment and the anti-Enlightenment varieties) to equally sincere visions of the apocalypse."[7]

Ernst Cassirer wrote of "the philosophy of the Enlightenment" that it proclaimed "the pure principle of immanence both for nature and for knowledge," which were thereby made available to rational understanding.[8] The rinciple of immanence has also informed historical thinking since the Enlightenment, and would find its most uncompromising expression in Marxism. The practice of history, especially by professional historians, has derived its "cultural logic," and public legitimacy, from the assumption that reason, working through the evidence of the past—any past—could get at the truth of its inner workings, which enabled the subsuming of all differences, including cultural ones, to a history that claimed universal understanding.

The universalist claims of history as a way of knowing the past need to be distinguished, however, from a unilinear account of the past demanded by the Enlightenment ideology of progress, that for the next two centuries would place Europe at the pinnacle of human development. The principle of immanence may have been crucial to the universalist claims of reason, but it also forced a recognition of difference as a principle of nature and society. History as we have known it is a product of the insistence on difference against Enlightenment universalism.

Post-Enlightenment history has been characterized by the pursuit of two contradictory goals, both of which are traceable to contradictions in Enlightenment thinking, which sought at once to recognize difference and to formulate universal propositions out of difference. The universalist logic of the Enlightenment that presupposed a common history along which people could be graded differently, also produced different histories that could not be so graded because they were driven by circumstances which, by the very logic of Enlightenment "immanentism," had their own claims to rationality, this time a historical rationality. The Enlightenment, in the idea of immanence, contained the seeds of its disintegration, once difference could be recognized, and given its due place in historical development.

It is fashionable these days to hold the Enlightenment responsible for the hegemonic, or oppressive, consequences of modernity. This makes for a reluctance to view the Enlightenment in its contradictory affirmations of universality and difference, which was suppressed in post-Enlightenment historiography but not, therefore, extinguished. Postmodernism, in this perspective, may be viewed as the resurfacing of the contradictions that were present at the very origins of modernity, that were suppressed in the ensuing two centuries—not by the cultural logic of the Enlightenment, but the appropriation of that cultural logic in the legitimation of Eurocentrism, driven by the logic of capitalism which has held center stage in historical interpretation both by its ideologues and its opponents, primarily Marxists. The Enlightenment's legacy no doubt has served purposes of cultural oppression and erasure; what needs to be remembered is the liberating impulse that also informed it, which is as much a part of post-Enlightenment history as the oppressiveness that is presently attributed to it. Postmodernism in thought expresses above all disillusionment with the forms that this liberating impulse took under the regime of modernity, which may explain why its portrayal of the Enlightenment is one of unrelieved cultural oppression.

If contradictions in Enlightenment premises concerning the past came to the fore with German Enlightenment thinkers who, in their very invention of national differences, were to invent history as we know it, in our times the same contradictions have produced the postmodern fragmentation of history with the explosion on the scene of seemingly endless claims on the past— which may be incomprehensible without reference to the universalist promise of the Enlightenment, globalized through the agencies of capitalism, imperialism, and colonialism. If dissatisfaction with Enlightenment universalism created history at one time and demands its abolition at another, the change may well have to do with the proliferation of constituencies, from nations to cultures, and genders to ethnicities, that have been empowered by the very modernity that is now called into question. History, for all its hegemonic complicity with modernity, has played a part in this empowerment, and may well be a victim of its success.[9] The failure of the aspirations of 1968, no less than the radical visions that inspired it, would come together in producing what now is postmodernism and, in its Third World variations, postcolonialism. "1968" is not just a year but a symbol of a temporality that had different durations and boundaries in different places.[10] What is important is that it marked an urge to make a break with past ways of thinking history, which in many ways it did. Many of the histories that have become familiar by now, from women's history to ethnic histories, from microhistories to the histories of "people without history," and, most important methodologically, from cultural history to the history of the invention of culture—which would make culture into the prime location for the production of histories through the medium of language—were products of a radical urge that brought to the surface of historical consciousness much that had been suppressed earlier. This would complicate immensely what had been considered up until then the proper domain of history. Viewed presently as attributes of postmodernism, these histories represented but the fulfillment of the promises of modernity that, when they acquired a hearing, would call into question the most fundamental premises of post-Enlightenment historiography. A most significant consequence was the new attention to the part played by discourses and representations, including those of history, in suppressing alternative voices.[11] The new histories are the consequences of modernity, not of postmodernity, but they have served in their own right to generate postmodernism in history by questioning the ways in which they were suppressed in the historiography of modernity.

The radical break with the past also ushered in the end of radicalism, as the failure of the radical visions of 1968 left history without a compass, and the new histories, rather than re-visioning history, were to end up in questioning the very premises that had informed modern radicalism, which had been motivated by the same universalist assumptions as the hegemonic structures it opposed. If historians assuming the existing *status quo* to be the end of history placed it at the end of history, radical historians did them one better by pointing to a future that would not only be different but better. The dissipation of historical temporality into so many social and cultural spaces has rendered moot any question of future betterment—or, more accurately, has made for a suspicion of any promise of future betterment, as the utopianism that drove earlier radicalisms now appears as one of the oppressive consequences of modernity.[12] Radicals of various stripes for two centuries located oppression in social structures, and sought to overcome it through social transformation in accordance with some vision or other of the future. As the sources of power and oppression have been relocated in discourses and representations, issues of social transformation have faded into the background, and hopes for liberation invested in the deconstruction of discourses and representations which, in their seeming inexhaustibility, drive the task of deconstruction to a spiraling devolution into seemingly endless fragmentation, ruling out the possibility of a common language out of which to formulate new radical visions. The implications of such fragmentation for history are obvious. History, assigned the task of adjudicating social and cultural difference for two centuries, now appears as a socially and culturally limited epistemology that is only one among a whole range of possible ways of knowing the past. It has been cut down to size and, in the process, lost its direction—no less for the radicals who drew upon the past to point to directions for the future than for the powers that used the past to legitimize the political arrangements of the present. Postmodernism and postcolonialism are heirs at once to the radical visions of 1968, and to their disintegration in the face of failure.

One aspect of the historiographical developments to issue from the 1960s is of particular importance in the context of this discussion: the emergence of the Third World. Discussions on postmodernism are often carried out without reference to its context outside of Europe and North America—which is very strange, as there is widespread agreement that postmodernism, as it has been shaped by post-structuralism, was very much a product of the 1960s, crystallized around the events of 1968. And what were the 1960s, but the emergence to the forefront of Euro-American consciousness of the "Third World," the postcolonial societies that now demanded a hearing in history? The results have been even more far-reaching than within European dialogues on the Enlightenment, as they now involved societies that could not be accommodated within a European, or Euro-American, cultural space; that demanded their own spaces in order to dislodge Euro-America from the center of history. Postmodernism as we know it is also a response to the conflicting cultural legacies of 1968. In an obvious sense, it represents a retreat from the Eurocentrism that had informed modern historiography by its very emphasis on culture as a determinant of epistemology. But it is also a reaffirmation of Eurocentrism, that retreats from the Marxist structuralism of the 1960s—as in the case of Althusser's Marxism—that sought to incorporate into Marxism the experiences with revolution of the world outside of Europe. The world outside of Euro-America is largely absent from the epistemology of post-structuralism. The incorporation into Euro-American consciousness of the demands of Third World societies for autonomous histories nevertheless has played a crucial part in the postmodernization of history. The internalization by Third World intellectuals of postmodernist assumptions about history has in turn produced what appears in our day as postcolonial criticism, which breaks with an earlier vision of national liberation in the same way that postmodernism breaks with the radical visions that inspired it in the first place. They have, each in its own way, worked to dissolve modernity as it has been understood in the First World or the Third.

Any discussion of postmodernity of necessity makes certain assumptions about the modern, which needs to be addressed in its historical specificity. There may be a common modernity based on material conditions, but the experience of modernity is not therefore the same, especially where it relates to history. European modernity in its overwhelming power could construct a history that confirmed teleologically European supremacy worldwide; the recipients of that modernity in the Third World, beginning in Eastern Europe, experienced modernity as a loss of history, of any connection to the past. When historians outside of Europe began to reconstruct a past in accordance with the requirements of modernity, the histories they constructed appeared as accounts of failure. The question that guided these histories was always in the negative: why could we not achieve that which Europe has achieved? Ironically, the answer to this question, more often than not, has been a "surplus of history," translated into the the vocabulary of tradition: tradition held us back. To overcome tradition it was necessary to turn to the very source that had "invented" the tradition to begin with: the critical historiographies of Euro-America. The modernity that imprisoned also showed the way out of the prison.

The urge to overcome tradition was supported by methods of inquiry imported from Europe. Chinese historians speak of a revolution in historiography that took place in the early part of the century.[13i] And sure enough, there was a revolution in both historical interpretation and the methods it employed. An empiricist historiography, backed up by archeology and linguistics, exposed the "golden age" of a "sacred," classics-based, historiography to have been an ideological construct of later times. The new historiography exposed as "myth" the sacred history that had been imbedded in the interpretation of temporality with the aid of what had been written in classics that were timeless in their pronouncements. The culture-based explanations of that historiography found material explanation as Marxism took over the field of history, providing economic and social explanations for backwardness. A historiography that naturalized development could in the end find justification in the argument that the "natural" development of Chinese society had been stalled by intrusion from the outside, in the form of imperialism, either local (tribal invasions) or of European origin, that had prevented Chinese society from fulfilling its "natural" destiny.

Teleology may make for bad questions, but it does not stand in the way of fruitful answers. Marxist historians in China, in naturalizing a monistic conception of history, uncovered much about China's past that had been suppressed in Confucian and liberal historiographies, obsessed as they were with the political dimensions of history. It is arguable that by the 1930s, Marxist historiography was triumphant in China not only because it had revealed much about Chinese society that had gone unnoticed in previous historiographies, but also because it provided answers to problems that were not just historiographical but also broadly cultural. Its empiricist competitors, from Hu Shi to Chen Yinke, however impressive in the breadth of their research, had no grand narratives in which to ground their findings, other than a resort to the scientificity of research, which were most notable for avoiding the "larger" questions of the role history played in defining national identity and explaining its fate in the contemporary world.

The premises of modernization discourse (in both its liberal and Marxist guises), that had been internalized in Third World historiography, was challenged in the immediate aftermath of 1968 both within EuroAmerican thinking, and in the self-assertion of Third World developments. It is interesting that China, which was an inspiration for 1968 in many places through the Cultural Revolution, would also play an important part in the disillusionment with 1968. "Third-worldism" was crucial to 1968, and China with its ongoing "cultural revolution" (along with Vietnam, engaged in a struggle for survival) provided the main inspiration for Third-worldism. It was 1968 in the United States that brought China to the center of attention, and it was the generation of 1968 that brought into U.S. China scholarship the inspiration of Marxist historiography in China which had been dismissed hitherto as "ideological" scholarship. That generation now finds itself beleaguered, as its questions are no longer relevant to a present generation, which does not even remember what there was to be opposed and can make no sense, for the same reason, of the opposition. Most interestingly, it is unable to recognize the ways in which it may have contributed to the dissolution of history that it mourns.

In China, on the other hand, historians celebrate their release from political subjection, and perceive for the first time in half a century possibilities of creating a history that lives up to the demands of historical truth. But there is a crisis there as well, as an ever-widening gap between the present and the past calls into question the relevance of history to understanding the present or guiding the present into the future. History continues to serve as a depository of myths and cultural artifacts, ancient and modern, that may be drawn upon to legitimize conflicting visions of China, but that only further underlines the arbitrariness of history. Modernity, which in its Euro-American guises has assumed the power of a tradition, appears in a Chinese historical context both as a negation of past legacies, and, contradictorily, as a disposable phase that leaves intact the claims of those very same legacies. What is postmodern about Chinese historiography is not its supersession of modernity, which remains as an unfulfilled desire, but the coexistence of many temporalities which historians are no longer able to order and contain in the evolutionary schemes of modernity; these temporalities, on the contrary, raise questions about the cultural role of the historian.

II. Postmodernism and History

Film analyst Vivian Sobchak writes with reference to the film, *Forrest Gump*, that it stands as both symptom of and gloss upon a contemporary—and millennial—moment in which history (with either upper- or lower-case *h*, in the singular or plural) and historical consciousness have been often described on the one hand as 'at an end,' and on the other hand have been the object of unprecedented public attention and contestation.[14] Where the status of history is concerned, it is not too difficult to think of other paradoxes commonly encountered in contemporary discussions: history as the medium at once of discourses of domination and liberation; skepticism over the knowability of the past versus evidence across the disciplines of a preoccupation with historicity; an interpretive voluntarism against a sense of the persistent burden of the past—even a sense that the most important forces shaping human history may be beyond the control of human beings; and, most ironically, an enrichment in our understanding of the past even as we seem to be losing control over the methods, organization, and goals of historical knowledge. Others could be named, but these will suffice for the moment to illustrate the theses I will take up in this discussion, namely: that there is (once again) a crisis in history that is a product of factors that involve both complex considerations of history as discipline and epistemology, and the cultural meaning of history; that it is not clear whether the crisis signals a hopeless disintegration of history or a paradigm shift in historical practice; and, finally, that, whatever the outcome, the transformation of history as we have known and practiced it for the last hundred years or so does not imply either history's end, or an end of the concern with the past. Postmodern history, if that is what it is, is most likely to be also post-historical in the sense of containing history as a significant moment, which may serve as a reminder of the power of history even in its negation. On the other hand, it implies also a significantly diminished cultural role for history than it enjoyed under the regime of modernity.

The current crisis is not a crisis in the disciplinary practice of history as such—at least, not yet. To be sure, over the last three decades, historians have faced challenges which continue to force rethinking both of history's relationship to the past and narrower questions of method.[15] Some of these challenges have been mounted from within the historical discipline; such is the case with the linguistic or narrative turn in theories of history which was to end up questioning the possibility of historical truth, and the appearance of new social and cultural histories which were to lead at once to the thickening (in the Geertzian sense) of historical description and skepticism toward the possibility of holistic comprehension of the past. These tendencies to postmodernity in history were reinforced by the appearance and diffusion of post-structuralism, which resulted in a questioning of all the working concepts of the historian from space and time to subject, context, and event, which underlined in the process the complicity of history in social and political power—to the point where it seems nearly impossible to determine even what is a significant historical problem, let alone how to deal with it. The proliferating claims on the past of new social constituencies, already an important moment in the creation of the new social history, has gained momentum since the 1980s, as the assertion of diasporic identities has further scrambled notions of what is a proper unit of historical analysis. The claims to different pasts at both the national and the global levels have issued, most fundamentally, in a repudiation of history as a cultural artifact of the modern West, that must be rejected if other cultural traditions are to acquire contemporary voices of their own. Finally, if historians could ever pretend to monopoly over interpretations of the past, that pretense seems less credible than ever before as new visual and electronic media make their own claims on representations of the past.

Historians have been able to absorb some of these challenges, and simply ignored others. As Nancy Partner writes, "for all the sophistication of the theory-saturated part of the profession, scholars in all the relevant disciplines that contribute to or depend on historical information carry on in all essential ways as though nothing had changed since Ranke, or Gibbon for that matter; as though invisible guardian angels of epistemology would always spread protecting wings over facts, past reality, true accounts, and authentic versions; as though the highly defensible, if not quite the definitive, version would always be available when we really needed it."[16] How long this disciplinary resilience may last is an open question; for if there is no apparent crisis in the practice of history, there is little question about a crisis in the cultural meaning of history. Georg Iggers, himself a defender of the rationality of history, observes perceptively that the revolt against the conception of historical truth and with it the belief in the applicability of rational criteria, say scientific or scholarly, to the investigation of the past cannot be viewed as a current in historical thought in a narrow sense but as part of a broad reorientation of modern consciousness under the changing conditions of modern existence.[17] We might note, however, that while the current reorientation of historical thought may have roots in the past of European modernity, or draw upon precedents from that past, it is the product more specifically of the social and intellectual ferment of the 1960s, draws upon a much broader range of cultural sources than European modernity, and is informed and shaped by novel technological transformations that produce not only new kinds of information and representations, but also new meanings of being human. The historiographical reorientation of the last few decades, no less than the new social and cultural histories, was informed by a conviction that "scholars should begin to take seriously the cries of the 1960s for involvement and relevance of history that militant social reformers were legitimately demanding of the academic community. Only a radical questioning of the cultural utility of history . . . can contribute to the salvation of the human *species* which it is our duty as thinkers to serve."[18] The turn to the Third World in the 1960s also initiated the assault on Eurocentric universalist conceptions and practices of history, although that turn itself would undergo a reorientation with the appearance of ideologies of globalization and multiculturalism in the 1980s. The transformation of Euro-America's place in the world, and with it of the historiography it informed, prompts Frank Ankersmit to observe that autumn has come to Western historiography.[19] On the other hand, while modernist assumptions may still guide historical practice in the discipline, scholars find no shortage of postmodernist representations in the new visual media.[20]

Tracing debates over history in the 1960s and 1970s, Richard Vann concludes that by the mid-seventies, "something like a paradigm shift had occurred; for the next twenty years historians' language, not explanation or causality [in other words, the relationship of historical to scientific knowledge], would be *the* topic around which most reflections on history would center."[21] The outstanding marker of this paradigm shift was Hayden White's *Metahistory*, "the most revolutionary book in the philosophy of history over the past twenty-five years,"[22] which was to bring to the center of attention an already proliferating concern with narrative. The linguistic turn would derive additional momentum from the rapid diffusion of post-structuralism in the 1970s and 1980s. The result was a reorientation in theory from a positivistic concern with history as a recuperation of the past to a concern with the ways in which the historian constructs the past.

The implications were to be far-reaching, if uncertain in their practical consequences for historians. There may well have been a paradigm shift in the philosophy of history, as Vann suggests, but if we understand paradigm shift in the Kuhnian sense as a new way of ordering knowledge or understanding, the new paradigm represented by the linguistic turn suggests most prominently a dis-ordering, or even the impossibility, of historical knowledge. This is the way White's revolution in historiography appears to another distinguished historiographer, Georg Iggers. What Iggers has to say about

White is worth quoting because it touches on several important aspects of the new revolution in history:

> The new emphasis on history as a form of literature is related to the reduction of history to language. Hayden White is . . . quite right in insisting that every historical text is also a literary text and that as such it is governed by literary criteria. But White goes beyond this to conclude that a historical text is in essence nothing more than a literary text, a poetical creation as deeply involved in the imagination as the novel. The history the historian writes is determined ultimately not by any reference to his subject of study but by literary decisions, by the limited choices permitted by such literary determinants as emplotment and choice of tropes. . . .[23]

Whether or not this is an accurate reading of what White does is open to question. Sidney Monas observes somewhat differently that White's point rather was that differences among the historians and philosophers of history he dealt with "were not to be explained in terms of who was right and who was wrong, who plugged in to objective reality and who did not, but rather in terms of differences of temperament and the relationship of temperament to genre, mode, and emplotment. None of them used evidence improperly."[24]

The question, in other words, is not whether or not historians may dispense with evidence, or engage in arbitrary manipulation of the past, but rather what beyond evidence makes for a work of history, especially a great work of history with seminal consequences for our understanding of the past. Ironically, White's work does not diminish but expands the role of the historian who now appears as the creator of history, the subject of the text, rather than a transmitter of past reality, a task best accomplished by absenting the author from the text.

Recognition of these points is important because they point to the even more ineluctable question raised by the narrative turn: not the relationship between narrative and evidence, but the relationship between narrative (and by implication, evidence) and objective truth. The most significant consequence of the narrative turn is the affirmation of the possibility of multiple narratives on the same event(s) or past(s) that may have equally valid claims on the truth of the past, accompanied by a rejection of the professional historian's assumption that different claims to historical truth may be adjudicated on the basis of evidence alone. We may agree readily with Iggers' statement that a historical text must be understood with reference to the context to which it refers, and that this context contains an element of objectivity not fully identical with the subjectivity of the historian and an element of rationality which presumes elements of intersubjectivity in the methods of historical inquiry.[25] But that still leaves open the question of the historicity of history itself, and the possibility that historical context (no less than the historical event) may be as much a product as a condition of history.

While most historians may write as if they are at the end of history, it is a presumption of modern scientific professional history in particular that while the past as such may lie behind us, history—the effort to understand and write the past—is at all times a project that extends into the future. Like the truths of modernity, the truths of history are deferred truths, which means, on the one hand, that the future is likely to have a better access to truth than the present, and, on the other hand, that there is a built-in obsolescence to historical work at any one time. In the words of J. B. Bury, "This work [the work of history], the hewing of wood and the drawing of water, has to be done in faith—in the faith that a complete assemblage of the smallest facts of human history will tell in the end. The labor is performed for posterity—for remote posterity."[26] This faith in cumulative truth ignores that posterity's notions of time and space may well be quite different than those of the present in the same manner that the present differs from the past, or that the hewing of wood may result in the splintering of the truth of history, not its unification into one comprehensive whole. These are exactly the implications of recognizing equal or at least, comparable, validity to conflicting narratives on the past, which also would suggest that the future does not promise any guarantee of getting closer to truth.

The implications reach beyond the goals of history into its practice. The historian ceases to be *just* a rational excavator of the truth of the past, and is rendered instead into the imaginative creator of the past whose temperament, in Monas' term, becomes at least as important in the creation as claims to reason and method; unlike, say, ideology, the temperament of the historian does not lend itself easily to analysis on the plane of rationality, but requires the confrontation of his/her subjectivity.[27] The new importance assigned to emplotment, structure of the text, etc., on the other hand, shifts attention from the context to which the work of history refers to the text as at least partially an autonomous entity to be read in its own right, or in relationship to other texts. The analysis of text, no less than the analysis of the author, implies a shift in the direction of literary analysis away from strictly historical readings, which in the process renders history into a sub-species of literature.

What may be most important is that such questions are not narrowly epistemological questions, but epistemological questions with broad cultural implications. Unlike earlier discussions on historiography, which revolved around the status of historical versus scientific ways of knowing, and were conducted as if in a cultural vacuum, the turn to narrative almost imperceptibly shifted attention to questions between culture and history. Hayden White from the beginning portrayed his undertaking as a cultural project; the critique of historical practice involved questions not only of historical culture, or the social and political implications of history, but also the relationship of history to its broad cultural context. In the 1973 article referred to above, he contrasted metahistorical to historical as socially innovative historical vision, and offered a historical/cultural explanation why metahistorians found an easier home on the continent than in Anglo-American contexts:

> In Continental Europe, speculative philosophy of history is not
> only very much alive, the kinds of problems it poses and the ques-

tions it raises stand at the center of a debate over the purpose of historical inquiry and the cultural utility of historical conscious- ness. In part, this is due no doubt to the philosophical traditions prevailing on the Continent. Throughout the nineteenth century, European thought remained more metaphysical in its orientation than its British or American counterparts; European thinkers remained much less convinced of the power of science to substi- tute for metaphysics; but more importantly, perhaps, the Continental experience of the two world wars and of fascism served to give ethical thought and ontological inquiry a different orientation.[28]

White has also raised the question of culture as a delimitation on the options available to the historian. He wrote, more than a decade later, that "the plausibility of any given narrative account of real events resides," first, "on the perceived adequacy of a given plot structure to the representation of the meaning of the set of events serving as the historian's referent," and sec- ond, that "the number of strategies available to the historian for endowing events with meaning will be coterminous with the number of generic story types available in the historian's own culture."[29]

The premise that history was conditioned by a cultural context which historians themselves served to shape placed the new turn in historiography squarely within post-1968 intellectual developments that would come to be associated with postmodernism and post-structuralism. The turn to narrative in historiographical discussions in the United States coincided with the ques- tioning of history by Roland Barthes, and the assault on grand or master nar- ratives by post-structuralist thinkers such as Jean-François Lyotard, who would ultimately define postmodernism as the repudiation of master in favor of local narratives and stories, and draw attention to the gaps and fissures in narratives as a better way of getting at the truth of the past than what the documentary evidence provided. While the common attention to narratives and representations easily leads to the confounding of the two developments, it may be best to think of them as independent developments within a com- mon historical situation that intersected in the constitution of a new cultur- al context. Having said this, it is probably fair to observe that the new views of history propounded by White, Louis Mink, and others were to benefit enormously from the diffusion of post-structuralist ideas with which they overlapped, and the increasing popularity of postmodernist representations of the past—just as they may have facilitated the latter.[30]

Ironically, historians who refused to question the validity of claims to truth in history, but turned to historical analysis of the problems thrown up by the social and political circumstances of the 1960s and 1970s, would in the end contribute themselves to the disintegration of history—and play their part in foregrounding the importance of culture and narrative in his- torical work. The new awareness of the cultural context of historical practice was quite evident in a volume published in the late seventies, edited by the same Georg Iggers whom I have cited above as a critic of White, and Harold

Parker, a historian of France at Duke University.[31] Iggers has continued since then to pursue this question, which has acquired increasing attention from historians. The pursuit in itself does not point to postmodernist or cultural-ist intentions, because casting the net broadly over historiographies world-wide does not necessarily imply a resignation to inevitable diversity, but may be motivated by a search for a renewed universalism that seeks to overcome the parochialism of an earlier Eurocentric universalism.[32] It is important, nev-ertheless, that even historians who defend an earlier historicism, or remain committed to notions of historical truth regardless of cultural context, should do their share in raising culture as a problem both in and for history.

Even more important have been the consequences of the varieties of new histories that emerged from the seventies, that further undermined the notion of a coherent, integrated history, but also broke down the notion of culture by radically historicizing it (in a spatial as well as a temporal sense). Inspired by the works of historians such as E. P. Thompson and Eric Hobsbawm, who already had introduced culture into Marxist analyses of social movements in the 1960s, new social historians dealing with labor movements, as well as groups that had hitherto been left out of history—from women to ethnic groups to indigenous peoples—produced histories showing the importance of culture, and history, to the self-definition of these various groups. The location of culture, to borrow Homi Bhabha's felicitous phrase, was moved from the national to the group level; more importantly, these groups were revealed to have a historical consciousness of their own that was bound up with their particular experiences—which challenged not only the sense of history of the dominant groups in society, but also that of historians who played important parts in the formulation and consolidation of dominant history. The question, of course, was how to integrate these proliferating narratives into a coherent whole, relate social to political and cultural history, and reconcile proliferating senses of history. The very deep-ening of historical knowledge, and its extension beyond received boundaries, had by the late 1970s already led to complaints about balkanization of national histories.[33] The problem of coherence was visible also in communi-ty studies, as well as the new microhistory inspired by anthropology, in par-ticular Clifford Geertz's idea of thick description.[34] It is worth repeating here that, in all these cases, the problem was not merely a technical or a theoreti-cal problem of organizing disparate historical narratives, but the confronta-tion of different historical epistemologies. History from the bottom revealed stories and histories that had been suppressed in earlier historiography, but now came forth to make their own claims upon the past, and to challenge the claims of historians—in effect confirming the abstract speculations of his-torians such as White, or postmodernists such as Lyotard.[35] Post-structural-ist assumptions—including the rejection of the distinction between reality and fiction—were explicitly adopted by the new cultural historians, which has led historians and philosophers such as Mark Poster and Frank Ankersmit to declare the arrival of postmodernity in history.[36] This time around, how-ever, postmodernity is not a response to historians' failure, but a product of their very success in getting at the truths of history, which prove to be too complex to be contained in systematic narratives or theoretical systems—or even a single epistemology. The proliferation of claims on the past means not only the proliferation of narratives within the historical profession, but also that the narratives of professional historians are reduced to only one set of narratives among others.[37] The question is no longer whether or not histories can be true in an objective sense, but whether or not truths may be containable in something called history.

This question has been brought to the fore dramatically with a new awareness of global transformations that has emerged since the 1980s. What we may describe as the replacement of the paradigm of modernization by a paradigm of globalization has many dimensions that range from the recognition of new groups, the empowerment of others and questions about the nation-state as an appropriate political, economic, and cultural unit to the disappearance of socialist alternatives to capitalism accompanied by, ironically, an erosion of a Eurocentric teleology of modernity (to be distinguished from the erosion of Euro-American political and economic power). These are the phenomena that inspired Francis Fukuyama's end of history thesis.[38] Fukuyama's ideological reasons for bringing history to an end are misguided, but there may be another reason, quite contrary to that of Fukuyama, for considering a possible end to history. I will describe it simply here as a sense of the reversibility of time that has accompanied the widespread rejection of the teleology of modernity, and the many reversals in history that have accompanied it—most importantly in the case of the great revolutions of the last two centuries. Varieties of claims on history consigned to the past, rendered invisible or simply ignored under regimes of modernity, have reappeared to haunt the contemporary world, propelled to the surface of consciousness by the reconfiguration of social and political relationships globally.

If postmodernism in history means anything, at the very least it points to a proliferation of pasts making claims on the present. Such proliferation is liberating to the extent that it enriches the repertory of pasts to draw upon in order to act in the present and imagine the future. But it can also be devastating in its consequences if it leads not to open-ended dialogue but to resurgent culturalisms, which, against the evidence of history, insist on drawing boundaries around imagined cultural identities—not just to keep out what is constructed as foreign but, more seriously, to suppress the diversity within. The latter seems to be the more likely possibility in a world where identity is not the product of free-wheeling negotiations, but is subject still to the prerogatives of power of various kinds. Rather than usher in renewed hopes for alternative futures, the denial of the teleologies that have informed history instead has rendered the future opaque: as a chaotic present makes a mockery of any effort to contain the pasts it has unleashed, the future itself is caught up in the terrifying anxieties of the present, stripped of its power to inspire or to guide.

Two examples will have to suffice for the purposes here. First is the proliferation of memory literature since the 1980s. Historians long have taken memory as the raw material for history, as a means to getting at the truth of the past. If the new historiography of the seventies discussed above endowed memories with greater status, in its most recent appearance memory has emerged as a competitor with history, in opposition to the latter.[39] Memory may serve different purposes under different circumstances for different groups. The memory literature of recent years is connected most intimately with traumatic events such as the Holocaust or the Cultural Revolution in China. An event such as the Holocaust, Hayden White writes, may "escape the grasp of *any* language even to *describe* it and of *any* medium—verbal, visual, oral, or gestural—to *represent* it, much less of any historical account adequately to *explain* it."[40] Memories of the experiences of traumatic events may in such cases well accomplish what history is unable to capture or explain. Memories may also serve to capture glimpses of the past for groups who have been erased from history. On the other hand, they add moral force to history in the case of groups (such as the Japanese-Americans interned during World War II), seeking for recognition of their grievances. Memory serves to bolster the self-images of newly empowered groups seeking to overcome their images as victims in history.

Loss of confidence in history may be the reason that is most pertinent to the discussion here. Pierre Nora writes that "the loss of a single explanatory principle, while casting us into a fragmented universe, has promoted every object—even the most humble, the most improbable, the most inaccessible—to the dignity of historical mystery. Since no one knows what the past will be made of next, anxiety turns everything into a trace, a possible indication, a hint of history that contaminates the innocence of all things."[41] The decline of the hegemony of the past ("regime of discontinuity," as Nora puts it)[42] has allowed for a proliferation of memory that talks back, not just recent memory, where it is most visible, but even distant forgotten memories that have returned to challenge history. The result is a multiplication of "private memories demanding their individual histories."[43] If historians often have forgotten or suppressed memories not suitable for their purposes, memory often appears as if it is immune to the history or histories that constitute it. Ironically, the confrontation of memory and history seems also to promise abolishing the difference between the two. We may view the proliferation of memory as an indication of the impossibility of history. We may also view it as the proliferation of histories—many histories that do not cohere, and have no hope of doing so, which may be the price paid for "the democratization of social memory."[44]

If memories claim their own truths against history, they may seek also to reverse the latter to create a new history. In many ways this is in the process of happening with the populations of the now fallen Communist regimes, seeking to recuperate suppressed histories. But it is happening also with others, victimized by history, who seek to create new images of themselves once that history has been accounted for, and recedes into distant memory. A Jewish rabbi, heading the struggle for compensation for lost Jewish property, aims "to reconstruct an image of Jewish life before the war, one that will drive out visions of emaciated concentration camp prisoners in their striped uniforms . . . to paint a picture of the Jew before the war properly, not as a victim but as a society."[45] On the other side of the world, peoples in the

Pacific seek to forget their victimization by erasing memories of their colonization.[46] Indeed, replacing memories of colonization, victimization, and
even the distinction between oppressor and oppressed is central to the project of so-called postcolonial criticism.

We have moved here way beyond the recuperation of "people without
history" into history, or the complication of the past, to the reversal of
received historical narratives, where the most important question guiding the
rewriting of the past are identity needs of the present.

The second example of reversal is the cultural reversal of what was taken
to be earlier a relationship between the First and the Third Worlds, as well as
of peoples with or without states—especially of indigenous peoples, again a
major preoccupation of postcolonial criticism. This reversal also implicates
the reversal of historical judgment on what used to be called the Second
World, the world of socialist revolutionary regimes, which have disappeared
from history, leaving behind not images of hope and liberation but of death
and destruction. Their disappearance has also left the other two worlds face
to face with one another, trying to renegotiate cultural relations in a new situation of globality. History is central to such renegotiations. Historians of
the advanced capitalist world seek to accommodate the new situation by a
multiculturalist re-writing of history, that seeks to write back into history
those that had been left out of it, or condemned to backwardness, in the
process also moving Euro-American modernity from the center to the
peripheries of history—albeit also trying to salvage what is left of universalism, as in the case of the renewed preoccupation with world history. Such
efforts to recuperate a declining cultural hegemony are not necessarily
acceptable to the Others of Euro-American modernity. The Others reassert
their own claims by reaffirming their own pasts; traditions relegated to the
past by modernizationist history, and rejected in the 1960s and 1970s by critical intellectuals as Eurocentric concoctions are now upheld by the Others in
claims to alternative modernities, or alternatives to modernity. Indigenous
peoples, whose silencing and oppression in the name of civilization have
been global, similarly reassert their pasts against the claims on history of the
civilized by denying history altogether. Indeed, the most radical challenge to
history lies not in demands for alternative histories, but demands for alternatives to history that have been voiced by widely different Third World and
indigenous intellectuals such as Ashis Nandy in India and Vine Deloria Jr. in
the United States. To quote Nandy,

> The historical mode may be the dominant mode of constructing
> the past in most parts of the globe but it certainly is not the most
> popular mode of doing so. The dominance is derived from the
> links the idea of history has established with the modern nation-
> state, the secular worldview, the Baconian concept of scientific
> rationality, nineteenth century theories of progress, and, in recent
> decades, development.[47]

The end to such dominance, Nandy concludes, requires rejection both
of science and history. These lines were published not in some off-beat jour-

nal, but the same *History and Theory* that served as a medium for the paradigm shift of less than three decades ago. From its universalistic methodological claims of three decades ago, history has come now to be portrayed as a culturally bound epistemology, which must be transcended for the salvation of the human *species*, which it is our duty as intellectuals to serve.

These reversals have good reason, and a great deal of merit, in forcing us to rethink history as a cultural product. But they also point in directions quite different than those that informed the histories of the 1960s and 1970s. Charles Maier writes of the proliferation of memory that "the surfeit of memory is a sign not of historical confidence but of a retreat from transformative politics. It testifies to the loss of a future orientation, of progress toward civic enfranchisement and growing equality. It reflects a new focus on narrow ethnicity as a replacement for encompassing communities based on constitutions, legislation, and widening attributes of citizenship."[48] Ethnicization is even more dramatically apparent in global cultural conflicts over the meaning and status of history. While the attack on history serves a sharply critical purpose in the hands of cosmopolitan intellectuals such as Nandy and Deloria, whose critiques are self-consciously post-historical, it is equally open to appropriation for the most parochial and reactionary essentialisms and exceptionalisms.

IV. Postmodernism and the Historiography of China

The historiography of China can hardly claim immunity from developments in history over the last three decades, or from changes in its cultural environment, especially as events in China—most importantly the disgracing of the revolution—have contributed to the formation of that environment. It is true that historians have shown less sensitivity to these developments than their counterparts in literature and anthropology. It is also true that there has been a blurring of boundaries between these disciplines, with inevitable consequences for the practice of history.

There is no reason here to go in depth into recent transformations in the historiography of China which I have discussed at length elsewhere.[49] Suffice it to say here that the events of 1968 were quite crucial in the United States in redirecting the historiography of China; but even more crucial in historical hindsight may have been the changes that took place in the 1970s with the repudiation of revolution in the People's Republic of China, and the emergence to visibility of other Chinese societies. Not the least important aspect of these changes may have been the influx into U.S.-China scholarship of scholars of Chinese origin, and the intensification of the confrontation between different historical perspectives that has complicated immensely what we understand by Chinese history. It is not a paradigm change that is at issue in these transformations but a breakdown of existing paradigms, which may be the clearest sign of postmodernity in the historiography of China.

The transformations in the U.S. historiography of China may be illustrated most economically by the contrasts between two periodicals founded two decades apart, the one a direct product of the 1960s, the other of changes that took place in the 1980s: *Modern China* and *Positions*. *Modern China*, which started publication in 1975, was the brainchild of historians radicalized by the anti-imperialist mood of the 1960s, and represented a rebellion against liberal historiography with its modernizationist—and predominantly anti-Communist—assumptions. Liberal historiography had also been visibly culturalist, pointing to culture as the primary factor in advancing or obstructing progress toward modernity. Rebellion against it not surprisingly took the form of affirming the historical legitimacy of the Communist revolution in China, accompanied by much greater receptivity to the findings of Chinese Marxist historians, whose work had been dismissed earlier as "ideological claptrap." The charge of ideology was now directed against liberal historiography, which was seen by a new generation as having been complicitous with United States imperialism in providing it with ideological legitimacy. Suspicious of the legacy of culturalism, historians associated with *Modern China* for the most part focused on questions of social and economic development to show that a different developmental trajectory had prevailed in Chinese history, one that called into question the pretensions to universalism of Euro-American modernity. They devoted themselves to the uncovering of historical materials to get at problems of development in China at the ground level, against an earlier top-down history that had been preoccupied mostly with political, diplomatic and intellectual history. The concern for re-writing Chinese history from the bottom up, a general concern of the so-called "new social history" emerging during this period, also included bringing into history those who had been excluded from it earlier: peasants, workers and, possibly most important in its long-term consequences, women. While historians of this generation called upon the insights of sociology and anthropology in their work, they by no means intended to question the validity of historical method, but saw in the mobilization of the insights of those disciplines a way to enhance the validity of historical interpretation; indeed, in their dissatisfaction with questions of ideology and culture, they displayed a tendency to positivism, firmly convinced that the discovery of new materials would enable them to get ever closer at the truth of history—which in many ways it did.

Positions started publication in 1993, nearly two decades later. Its orientation was self-consciously postmodern, but postmodern as it was inflected in its Third World offshoot, postcolonial criticism. While it has not repudiated questions of political economy, the latter unquestionably have receded into the background, overshadowed by a preoccupation with discourse and representation that marks the journal as a product of the cultural turn of the 1980s. *Modern China* forced into historical discussion questions of political economy, regionalism, and class; *Positions* articulates the concerns of a new generation with the question of identity—in particular gender, ethnic, and national identities as they have been shaped and reshaped in the course of colonial encounters, as well as the emergence of modern states. To the extent that questions of political economy appear in the discussions, the tendency there, too, is to forego questions of economic and social "reality," in favor of attention to discursive constructions of those realities. If this marks the return of "culturalism" to the historiography of China, culture is now understood in a different sense than before: implicated as a formative moment of attitude, behavior, and knowledge, but also constantly negotiated and transformed in the course of social and political encounters. Especially noteworthy is the confrontation of culture with ways of knowing the world, which calls into question the role of culture in shaping contemporary knowledge and disciplines. Not surprisingly, in these inquiries history itself comes under intense questioning as a product of social encounters whose truth—claims are often sustained at the cost of erasing other claims to historical truth. Anthropology, now a consciously self-critical anthropology aware of its colonial past, appears conspicuously in the journal's pages, but the most important disciplinary innovation may be the breaking down of the boundaries between history, literature, and new developments in communications studies.

While there may be much that is deserving of criticism in *Positions*' excessive culturalism, the triviality and narcissism of the preoccupation with identity (a general problem of contemporary postmodernism and postcolonialism) which often contributes less to a better understanding of the world than to the reproduction of academic fashions, and the sloppy and superficial scholarship that is frequently the consequence, we may ignore the questions raised by the journal only at the risk of an academic obscurantism that refuses to recognize the temporal and cultural conditions of intellectual practice. It is also important to ask whether those questions, even though they may be threatening to the discipline of history as it exists, bring us closer to historical "reality" even as they raise doubts about the reality of history, and our ability to gain access to it.

This is a general question of postmodernism, as I suggested above. Perhaps we give too much credit to postmodernism for creating the messiness of history, when all it does is recognize an incoherence that is intrinsic to the past, and, on those grounds, questions both our ability to gain access to the past through documentary artifacts, and our efforts to bring coherence to the past through intellectual constructs that are themselves limited by the circumstances of their construction. All we can do is "invent" the past; which is not to be confused with creation *ex nihilo*. *Positions* has played an important part in bringing these questions into the historiography of China in the United States.

Nevertheless, the appearance of *Positions* needs to be viewed within the context of developments since the early seventies, which raises the question of whether the kind of historiographical stance it represents is a product of modernity or postmodernity; a distinction the ambiguity of which I have noted above. It is a postmodernist conceit (conceded readily by critics) that postmodernism reveals the past in all its incoherence, and exposes the vacuity of claims to the truth of history. Postmodernists justify this conceit, however, by claiming for postmodernism intellectual tendencies that owed little to postmodernism *per se*, but were products of problems generated by modernity, that in turn played an important part in the production of postmodernism; in effect suppressing postmodernism's own history. Such claims may enhance the novelty of postmodernism, but they also sweep aside what postmodernism itself has erased in its emergence, that point to *its* limitations. What may be most novel about postmodernism is a renaming of what was there already, in the process endowing the latter with a new meaning.

There has been a good amount of work over the last three decades that has contributed to questioning received ways of conceiving and writing history without rejecting the validity of history *per se*, or claiming postmodernist novelty. *Modern China* and its contemporary, *The Bulletin of Concerned Asian Scholars*, were the first to question the relationship between historical scholarship and power in suggesting complicity between China scholarship and imperialism. Both these journals, moreover, sponsored scholarship that sought to give voice to those who had been excluded from history earlier, most importantly women, but also ethnic groups, minorities, and indigenous peoples suppressed in official histories, that have complicated our understanding of Chinese history—to the point where it has become apparent for some time now that it would be an almost hopeless task to try and contain all these histories within any kind of a coherent narrative. On the other hand, there are also significant examples of transgression against the boundaries of the idea of history, as well as historical method that nevertheless have been acceptable as innovations within, rather than against, history. Most notable may be the works of Jonathan Spence who, in works such as *The Death of Woman Wang* (1978) and *The Question of Hu* (1988), has sought to overcome the paucity of historical documentation by imaginative reconstructions of the past that abolish any clear distinction between history and fiction. Others, such as Paul Cohen, have raised questions concerning national differences in historical scholarship, as well as differences in the experience of history between those who lived the past and those who write it; Cohen's *Discovering History in China: American Historical Writing on the Recent Chinese Past* (1984) argues the former, while his more recent *History in Three Keys: The Boxers as Event, Experience, and Myth* (1997) is a Rashomon'esque inquiry into historical interpretation. Similar to the latter in some ways is Roxann Prazniak's *Of Camel Kings and Other Things: Rural Rebels against Modernity in Late Imperial China* (1999), which places the historian's ways of knowing the past against the stories told by those who lived, and made, the past. The question of history as lived experience versus history as abstract reconstruction is at issue more poignantly in the problems presented to historical work by the memorial literature to issue from the traumatic events of recent Chinese history. In a different vein, questions of the construction of national and ethnic identity through history have been raised not only by anthropologists, but by historians such as Pamela Crossley in her *Orphan Warriors: Three Manchu Generations and the End of the Qing World* (1990). None of these historians, to my knowledge, was motivated by the goal of writing postmodern histories. My own work has been described as postmodern, which it may be for all I know, but it was by no means a product of any self-conscious postmodernist intention.

It is not my intention, in drawing attention to the works above, to suggest that there is nothing new about a historiography that claims postmodern inspiration, but merely to recall the blurred boundary between the two that seems to be ignored both by its proponents and its opponents. If we may find much that is implicitly postmodern in historical developments that do not claim postmodernity, there is also much that is modern in the post-modern. It is possible, however, to point to a distinction that gradually assumed conscious form in the course of the 1980s. While most of the historians (and others) who have gathered around a publication such as *Positions* are themselves products of the intellectual ferment of post-1968 developments, the postmodernity (or postcoloniality) that they claim is mediated by the diffusion of post-structuralist ideas in the 1980s, which distinguishes their postmodernism from the suggestions of postmodernity to be found in the works of historians that I noted above. A self-conscious postmodernism in the historiography of modern China has come of age in the 1990s, and while it has aroused considerable opposition among the erstwhile radicals of the immediate post-1968 period, it obviously has acquired a certain respectability as well, as evidenced by the awarding of a professional prize to James Hevia's *Cherishing Men from Afar*, recognized as a postmodern work.

Once the postmodern is named as such, it is possible to point to these historiographical tendencies to emerge out of the very conventions of modern history as so many different expressions of postmodernity in history. It is equally possible, from an alternative perspective, to question the novelty claimed for postmodernity, and to view its innovations as further unfolding of the contradictions created by the very advances in historical knowledge, and as a response to a changing historical situation that presents the historian with previously unforeseen problems. The claim to innovation is sometimes quite vacuous, and consists merely of renaming historical problems that have been around for some time; as in Prasenjit Duara's *Rescuing History from the Nation*, which merely tags a new label, "postcolonial," to long-standing questions concerning the nation, and creates straw targets to enhance its claims to novelty.[50] It is more convincing in a work such as James Hevia's *Cherishing Men from Afar*, which in fact does overcome old culturalist prejudices to produce new readings of old materials, and in the process brings us closer to the historical situation that it seeks to understand. It is another matter whether or not his achievement has anything to do with "a different sort of history . . . that would focus its attention on networks of relationships among heterogeneous agents, rather than discrete units organized around uncomplicated notions of cause and effect," or a "hybridized" history that exposes as a "modernist fiction" the "presumed gap between past and present, between 'us' and 'them.'"[51] Nice thought, but one that confuses a desire to avoid objectifying the past with an abolition of temporality which is as likely to hybridize the historian as it is to invade the past with the consciousness of the present. That, too, is an old problem.[52]

But the old problem is compounded here by a postmodernist textualization of history that, in its very urge to overcome the power of the present over the past, or of one society over another, ends up sweeping aside structures of power that shape both the course of history, and historians' readings of the past. The new history Hevia calls for is ultimately premised on overcoming history; for what could "closing the gap between past and present" suggest but the dehistoricization of the past? This is a major problem of a postmodernist historiography which renders the temporal and spatial differences that constitute history, or histories, into a matter of the historian's readings, representation, and interpretations. It is also visible in Duara's approach to the nation and nationalism, which ignores the different meanings that those concepts have conveyed under different circumstances, with different political consequences. And it is evident in much discussion of the problem of identity, which treats identity as if it could be grasped as a product of situational negotiations, without the burdens imposed by structures of social, political, and cultural power. Common to them all is a suggestion of arbitrariness in historical interpretation. Postmodernism without reference to structures of power may succeed in bringing us closer to historical situations, but it does so by taking the history out of those situations.

Postmodernism has found less favor with Chinese historians of China. For one thing, postmodernism is a relative newcomer on the Chinese intellectual scene, having arrived there only in mid-1980s, without a significant impact before the 1990s.[53] More importantly, historians in China have been too busy enjoying the newfound, if still relative, freedom from political control they have achieved since the late 1970s to be tempted by postmodernist questionings of history. While official historiography still continues to reaffirm Marxism-Leninism as the ultimate guide to historical research, historians have rediscovered the non-Marxist historians of pre-1949 years, with their commitment to empirical research to uncover the truths of history. The breadth of historical research has enjoyed parallel growth, as previously unthinkable topics and interpretations have found their way into historiography.[54] Chinese historians presently would seem to be more interested in establishing a professional history with claims to a method of its own than in questioning the methods and cultural meaning of history. It is tempting to suggest that historicism of a nineteenth-century bent is alive and well among Chinese historians when it has gone out of fashion here in the United States.

Over the last decade postmodernism (along with other "posts") has made considerable headway in Chinese intellectual circles, giving rise to a new term, hou-hsüeh, translated variously as "postology" or "postism." But there are only a few signs of interest in postmodernism in historiography. Two articles published in recent years have introduced to Chinese readers some of the implications of postmodernism for received ideas and practices of history.[55] These articles are theoretical in orientation and, to the extent that they mention any works in Chinese history that might be construed as postmodern, the works mentioned are some of the works to which I have referred above.[56] A survey of the premier (if semi-official) history journal, *Lishi yanjiu* (Historical Research), during the same period, indicates only two articles dealing with postmodernism/post-structuralism in the sixty issues published during that period; the one a survey of Michel Foucault's historical ideas, the other a review essay on James Hevia's *Cherishing Men from Afar* that discusses the relevance of postmodernism to the study of China.[57] The Foucault essay discusses Foucault's efforts to transcend the dichotomy between rationality and irrationality.[58] The review of Hevia's book, while quite sympathetic, nevertheless concludes that postmodernism, in order to make a lasting contribution to historiography, needs to be able to move on from deconstruction to a more constructive approach to history.

The apparent paucity of interest in postmodernism in a journal such as *Lishi yanjiu*, however, may be misleading. It is possible that a more thorough inquiry, especially in provincial history journals, may reveal greater interest in questions raised by postmodernism, as political controls have usually been less effective in provincial institutions than at the center. Historians in China these days may enjoy greater freedom in the practice of history than in earlier days, but this does not mean the absence of political controls, only that there may be greater possibilities for negotiation between historians and political authorities. But political controls need not be imposed from outside the historical profession. Orthodoxy in China, as elsewhere, is sustained most effectively by internal controls, guaranteed by the domination of the profession by historians loyal to orthodoxy; and there is good evidence that the older generation of historians who continue to dominate the historical profession have little need of outside help when it comes to deciding what may or may not be acceptable historical practice. Postmodernism, it seems, is not in the professional, or the national, interest—which is of deep concern to historians.

What is radically different from the past is that Chinese historians are no longer constrained by national boundaries. It is no longer possible these days to speak of Chinese historiography as if it were limited to historians in China. If we employ this broader definition, postmodernism is in fact already a feature of the Chinese historiography of China, not only through historians working abroad whose views nevertheless are readily accessible to historians within China, but also among historians working in China who can get their works published abroad. As I noted above, many of the Chinese historians who received their education in the United States in the 1980s have been quite interested out of their own existential situation in questions of postmodern and postcolonial identity, and are to be found among contributors to periodicals such as *Positions*. The questions they have raised about Chinese identity (among other things) have made an impact also on historians in China, who themselves have gained access to such publications through intermediaries or through direct solicitation of their contributions.

The Chinese historiography of China is arguably also more open to the intrusion of historical work produced by non-historians *because* of the relative porosity of disciplinary boundaries. As Chinese historians readily incorporate literary devices in their work, literary scholars have produced historical works that are judged not according to their disciplinary loyalties but on their merits in shedding new light on historiographical questions.[59] There is, of course, little that is new or "postmodern" about such practices, as they long have been common features of intellectual life in China, that have survived modern pressures to professional specialization. Differences in cultural practices call for extra caution in judgments of modernity and postmodernity. Andrew Plaks wrote two decades ago that "the question of how to define the narrative category in Chinese literature eventually boils down to whether or not there did exist within the traditional civilization a sense of the inherent commensurability of its two major forms: historiography and fiction," to which his answer was that there was in fact no clear separation between the two.[60] Such practices have been maintained in modern historiography, including Marxist historiography, which often eschews the clear distinction not only of history from literature, but also of history from memory. Not because Chinese historians are lax with sources, which they are not, but because they have a different view of the relationship between sources and history. While such practices draw the opprobrium of the more professionally minded Chinese historians, their intellectual impact in China should not be underestimated.

No less important is the cultural environment within China which, if it does not directly affect historians' work, nevertheless raises questions about the cultural meaning of history. According to some Chinese intellectuals, there can be no room for postmodernism in a China that has yet to go through modernity. This mechanical evolutionism, which is also focused on the nation as a unit of reckoning, as if nations ever experienced development in even homogeneity, ignores the implications of China's incorporation into a global system (or, conversely, the incorporation in Chinese society of global practices). China today may be a country of multiple spatialities and temporalities, which is what makes the concept of postmodernity all the more relevant to understanding it. Where history is concerned, the study of China not only has to address questions of a multiplicity of Chinas, even though that is hardly acceptable to the more patriotic Chinese, but to an unprecedented scrambling of temporalities in popular life that range from the most contemporary global cultural practices to continued affirmations of Communist revolutionary history to revivals of Republican history, from the repudiation of the entirety of the modern Chinese Revolution, informed by nationalist urgings, to the re-confirmation of ancient myths that a modern historiography once seemed to have laid to rest. These conflicting temporalities, moreover, find daily expression in media that, as elsewhere, have far broader cultural reach than anything historians may aspire to, unless they learn to serve its demands. More to the point, historians are themselves divided over these issues, and their historical work contributes to the fragmentation of a past which resists coherent formulations despite brave, and chauvinistic, proclamations of an imagined historical unity. There is, of course, always the possibility, under official direction, of producing a negotiated past, much as the Communist Party has managed to produce a "negotiated past" that at least temporarily could harmonize different readings of its past.[61] But such solutions can be only temporary. Closer to the mark may have been those creative writers of the late 1980s, the producers of what was to come to be known as "the new historical novel" (Xin Lishi xiaoshuo), who saw in history something to be played with, temporalities to be separated or conjoined as they fit in with the author's proclivities, much as postmodernist historians would abolish "the gap between the present and the past" as they see fit to do so.[62]

The affirmations of history in China barely disguise the sense of crisis in historical knowledge that may be of the historians' making as they seek to cope with the consequences of past historical practice; but the crisis also has to do with changes in the cultural environment of history, which call into question the relevance of history as we have known it. In a conference held in Taiwan a decade ago, entitled, significantly, "Whither History?" (Shixue wang nali zou?), the distinguished historian Du Weiyun observed that there was a crisis in history created by a growing gap between economic progress and the spiritual adjustment to it.[63] Historians in China today also acknowledge such a crisis, this time rephrased as a crisis created by "market socialism" and commodification.[64] The crisis of history is apparent in either case, and similarly to the United States, is manifested in a decline of interest in history as produced by professional historians. On the other hand, there would appear to be a simultaneous surge of interest in history in literary production and the mass media which arouse enthusiastic public reception. Part of this may be due to the ability of literature, film, and television to tackle the difficult events of the recent past which historians are unable or unwilling to confront. I would suggest, however, that it also has to do with the appeals of imaginative reconstructions of the past in a cultural situation where the complex realities of the present demand equally complicated recreations of the past that correspond to its perceptions and needs; above all, to bring history to the interior of everyday experience. The Korean literary critic, Uchang Kim, writes with reference to the cultural situation in Korea that "history and politics make humans creatures of externals: physical limits, social constraints, and moral duties. Culture, including literature, is an unceasing attempt to transform or reconstruct these externals so that they appear as if they were part of human interiority."[65] Imaginary constructions of the past may defy historians' ideas of historical reality, but they are not any the less real for that reason because they answer to the cultural needs thrown up by the lived realities of everyday life—and history as we have known it, is only one of those realities. The gap between the practice of history by historians and the cultural demands on history is not new; what may be novel about the contemporary situation in China, as elsewhere, is the legitimacy claimed by alternatives to history. And this may well be the ultimate significance of postmodernity in history.

V. A Concluding Statement

Postmodernism may or may not be acceptable to historians. But it seems to me that there is a condition of postmodernity that constantly throws out new questions, and demands different kinds of answers than those to which historians have been accustomed by professional training or compliance. Whether in China or the United States, historians are faced not just with the questions of historical method, but with the cultural meaning of history. It is unlikely that history will disappear with these new developments, which are more likely to enhance the role historians have always played as record-

keepers, which was their original task, and which becomes even more important in rapidly changing times that look to history for the confirmation of
identity. But this is a considerable demotion from the role historians have
assumed since the nineteenth century as guides not just to the past but to the
future as well, which led revolutionaries no less than conservatives to history as the fountainhead of temporal wisdom. Postmodernism, with all its merits and demerits, needs to be taken seriously as a recognition of this new cultural situation. In a world where the teleology of Eurocentric modernity is
as much out of fashion as the utopias of yesterday, different temporalities
coexist in shifting spatial configurations, rendering history itself into part of
a collage that includes many different versions of the past. The collage itself
is post-historical; without history, and the modernity that informed it and
propelled it globally, there would be no collage but simply a scattering of
times and places. But where does it leave us?

However welcome may be the abolition of the earlier hierarchies of history, there is a price to be paid for the liberation from the hegemony of history: loss of a vision of the future that may help make sense of the present,
and the past as well. Worse still, this loss of vision also leaves us at the mercy
of forces of our own creation. Heilbroner, describing the present mood as
apprehension, writes that if there was ever a time in which the shape of
things to come was seen as dominated by impersonal forces, it is ours.[66] Is
there any point to history when the only choices for the future may be either
endless play, or domination by such impersonal forces?

The historiographical revolution or paradigm shift of the 1960s and
1970s, whether by historians or metahistorians, was motivated by an urge to
democratize history, and in this has succeeded all too well—with the ironic
consequence that it has contributed to the marginalization both of history
and the historian, with consequences that are not necessarily favorable for
democracy. The democratization of history may be visible most readily in the
current productions of history for popular cultural consumption, which are
also revealing of the predicament both of history and democracy. When a few
years back historians objected to Disney's plans to build an American history theme park in Virginia, Disney representatives responded that since history was all constructed, Disney had as much prerogative to construct the
past as the historians who sought to monopolize it! The historian may object
that there is a big difference between historians' construction of the past and
a theme park construction that places Monticello next to McDonald's, com-
modifying an important marker of democracy no less than the past; but such
objections carry less weight when the boundaries of interpretation have been
blurred, and historians become complicitous in the authentication of popular representations of the past.

The latter may be more readily observable in visual media such as film
and television, which reach millions around the globe daily, and are likely to
become increasingly attractive even to professional historians who seek to get
their message to broader constituencies than the few fellow-academics who
are the consumers of written works. History on film may confirm, at least
for the present, Ankersmit's claim that representation (analogous to art)

expresses what the historian does better than interpretation or narrative (analogous to literature).[67] Film, Rosenstone argues, brings us a different, multimedia, version of the past in blending reality and fiction, or actuality and simulation, through poetic overlays of sounds, images, words, and ideas.[68] History in the conventional sense, words and ideas, may be part of the film, but is now part of a larger language of representation, that brings the truth of the past to life in other ways. Historians who are called upon—as consultants or actual participants—to authenticate film or television historical narratives similarly find themselves as part of a production of the past of which they are no longer subjects. In an article he wrote in 1967, the distinguished historian J. H. Hexter pointed to the footnote as a distinctive feature of historical writing.[69] In history on film, historians play the part of footnotes, inserted into the narrative to comment and elaborate on its complexities. The footnoting of historians could be taken to mean that historians are still indispensable to the authentication of the postmodern text.[70] But it also implies a diminished role for the historian in the production of history. From a postmodernist perspective, there is nothing about film or television history that necessarily subverts historical understanding, or truth, but neither can we avoid the questions raised by the production of history in accordance with considerations in which marketability inevitably takes precedence over the pursuit of knowledge, and the public is most important in its role as consumer. Not the least important of these questions is the complicity of such history production in the promotion of technological fetishism.

There may be nothing postmodern about these representations of the past—unless we are prepared to take the postmodern back into the heart of modernity in the nineteenth century. The theme parks of the present have their predecessors in the World's Fairs of the nineteenth century, which also claimed to represent history in its totality; albeit in the service of the technological civilization of which the contemporary West represented the pinnacle.[71] The representation of the past on film is as old as the history of that medium; and historical fiction of which it may be a visual counterpart is even older. And of course there is even less that is novel in the appropriation of the past for a variety of motives, from political to commercial, and democratic to anti-democratic. What may be novel is the disappearance of a counterpart to all of the above in transformative visions of the future, and the attenuation of the conviction that knowing the past might have some value in their realization. As Lutz Niethammer puts it,

> The inflation of the various 'post' concepts might suggest that we are no longer able or willing to define the content of where we are and where we want to go; that we seek only to know where we come from. What used to appear self-evident or desirable has lost its innocence, and now words more or less fail us. 'Posthistory' is the most far-reaching of these concepts, for it denies a future not only to one characteristic element of a phase of history (modernity, revolution, industry, etc.) but to the idea of history itself.[72]

Postmodernism proves to be highly liberating in some ways, self-destructive in others. Postmodernism without history is not only available for appropriation in diverse causes, but may serve to undermine the democratic goals that informed its origins. Partner writes that "the danger inherent in capricious, opportunistic violations of the protocol of historicity is really not that millions of people will absolutely come to believe this or that, but that millions of people will come to be cynical, disabused, and wary, to believe nothing and thus feel no connection with the polity at all."[73]

There is probably not much that historians can do about a problem of this magnitude, which is a broadly cultural and political problem. There may be little that is odd about manufacturing history in a world that is poised on the verge of manufacturing human beings. If historical time is generated by the tension between experience and expectation, as Reinhart Koselleck suggests, it may become increasingly meaningless as expectation comes to mean little more than what is to be consumed next, accompanies visions of the future into oblivion, or disappears into everyday experience of an eternal present; Poster argues that this is in fact what is happening with the electronic media which collapse notions of space and time, and bring the future into the present.[74]

Not the least important aspect of the problem is the relationship between history and culture. Most discussions of the relationship between postmodernism and history take place within a Euro-American intellectual space, ignoring the different meanings that both postmodernism and history may assume in different cultural contexts. It has become quite evident in recent years that it is no longer sufficient to historicize culture, that we need also to address the question of the spatial and temporal boundaries of history as a way of knowing the past. Niethammer's complaint that posthistory challenges the idea of history itself ignores the possibility that history may be perceived differently from other cultural perspectives, such as those of Ashis Nandy and Vine Deloria, Jr. cited above. It would be foolish to assume, needless to say, that a historical understanding of the past is just an attribute of Western culture, as history has accompanied modernity in transforming the consciousness of the past globally, and is by now the dominant, if not the only, way of reading and writing the past. Nevertheless, other ways continue to exist, and recognizing these other ways may be one of the most important contributions of postmodernist questionings of history.

On the other hand, it is important also to note that postmodernism itself carries different meanings in different social, political, and cultural contexts.[75] Postmodernism is as much a matter of contention in a Chinese as in Euro-American contexts, but even its defenders endow it with different meanings there than, say, in the United States; postmodernism places itself in those contexts in opposition not just to modernity, but also to a hegemonic postmodernity guided by Euro-American takes on the world. Opponents of postmodernism in China charge it with a politically and intellectually debilitating mimicry of Euro-American fashions. On the other hand, to its proponents, postmodernism provides a way out of the dilemmas created by entrapment between the past and the West (between a nationalistic historiography, on the one hand, and a modernizationist liberalism that takes for granted the teleologies of modernity, on the other). It offers possibilities, therefore, of reading the past differently so as to envisage alternatives to the present (of both China and the West), which is quite liberationist in its underlying impulse. From this perspective, it is modern historiography, modified by nativist urges, that appears in its commitment to upholding the existing *status quo* while endowing it with some Chinese characteristic or another. What is most remarkable in this historiography is the denial of the challenges of the present, that call into question not only ways of doing history in a postrevolutionary society, but even the spatialities that historians presuppose—the idea of China itself. The re-readings of Chinese history that are informed by postrevolutionary China, while they may yield different conclusions than in the past, are motivated nevertheless by an urge to provide linear accounts of one kind or another to explain how the present came to be; that erase in the process alternative readings that might enable more critical appreciations of the present—in much the same way that a revolutionary historiography, with *its* claims to truth, earlier erased different ways of reading the past. Historicism in this sense serves above all to imprison the present in the past—not just China's past but the past of modernity. In order to achieve this goal, however, it first has to deny all other pasts that might have pointed to different eventualities; to imprison the past, in other words, in the imagined teleology of the present. To release the past from the hold on it of this historicism requires a willingness not only to recognize a multiplicity of pasts, but also different ways of comprehending them, of which history may be only one way. The question here is not merely one of whether or not we may dispense with facts and the evidence of the past, but rather whether different versions of the past may be constructed from different or even the same bodies of evidence: not the relationship of history to the evidence of the past, in other words, but the claims of history to Truth, which is an entirely different matter.

While there is no reason why historical practice should abandon its search for truth as historians have understood it over the years, there are very good reasons why they should not continue to pretend that the cultural challenges of the three decades following 1968 mean little for history, or disavow the very real challenges of the present. Even as staunch a defender of history as Richard Evans is driven to conclude that "postmodernism in its more constructive modes has encouraged historians to look more closely at documents, to take their surface patina more seriously, and to think about texts and narratives in new ways. It has helped open up many new subjects and areas for research, while putting back on the agenda many topics which had previously seemed to be exhausted. It has forced historians to interrogate their methods and procedures as never before, and in the process has made them more self critical, which is all to the good."[76]

The challenge is to face up to the evidence that constructivism in history is here to stay, and construct out of the rich materials of the past possibilities for alternative visions of the future; that are informed not only by age old visions of human dignity and liberation, but also account for problems thrown up by changing times. Such visions in the end will be convincing if only they are grounded in past and present realities, to the uncovering of which history may still have much to offer—so long as it is informed by a critical recognition of its own epistemological and cultural limitations.

———————————

References

1. I am referring here to the gratuitous attack by Joseph Esherick on the study by James Hevia of the McCartney Embassy to China, *Cherishing Men from Afar* (Durham, NC: Duke University Press, 1995). See Joseph W. Esherick, "Cherishing Sources from Afar," *Modern China* 24, 2 (April 1998): 135–61. While I have my own doubts about the claims Hevia makes for his "innovations," he raises questions concerning the use of culture in historical interpretation that are not to be buried under philological nit-picking, which is the strategy Esherick employs in the worst traditions of Sinological trivialism. Esherick's attack on Hevia may be understandable (not excusable), because he seems to think that "postmodernism" is something that may be relevant to literature, but not to history, which is revealing of an obliviousness to the cultural environment of history that is all too common among certain historians, who see in postmodernism not an intellectual challenge to be confronted but a disciplinary threat that must be vanquished—even at the cost of intellectual obscurantism. For Esherick's remarks on postmodernism, see Dong Zhenghua and Han Yuhai, Wan Qing yilaide Zhongguo lishi he xiandaihuade jincheng (Chinese History and the Progress of Modernity since the Late Qing) [interview with Joseph W. Esherick], *Zhanlue yu guanli* (Strategy and Management), No. 2 (1996): 45–50, p. 49. Given Esherick's stance on these issues, one wonders if he is quite aware of what he says when he refers to the Communist Party as a Asocial construct. See Esherick, "Ten Theses on The Chinese Revolution," *Modern China* 21, 1 (January 1995): 45–76, p. 61.

2. Hans Bertens, *The Idea of the Postmodern: A History* (London: Routledge, 1995), p. 3.

3. This is not to suggest that "postmodernism" was a product of the 1960s, although it was to undergo significant transformation in its association with post-structuralism, which was. For the history of the term, see Bertens, *The Idea of the Postmodern*, and Perry Anderson, *The Origins of Postmodernity* (London: Verso, 1998).

4. Frederic Jameson, *Postmodernism, or the Cultural Logic of Late Capitalism* (Durham, NC: Duke University Press, 1991), and David Harvey, *The Condition of Postmodernity* (Cambridge, MA: Basil Blackwell, 1989). Manuel Castells sees the transformation in capitalism in the rise of a "network society." See his *The Rise of the Network Society* (Cambridge, MA: Basil Blackwell, 1996). I prefer the association with "global Capitalism," as the points to the global dimensions of the transformation. See Arif Dirlik, *After the Revolution: Waking to Global Capitalism* (Hanover, NH: Wesleyan University Press, 1994).

5. Jean-François Lyotard, *The Postmodern Condition: A Report on Knowledge*, trans. from the French by Brian Massumi (Minneapolis, MN: University of Minnesota Press, 1984).

6. Francis Barker, Peter Hulme, and Margaret Iverson, *Postmodernism and the Re-reading of Modernity* (Manchester, UK: Manchester University Press, 1992).

7. Bertens, *The Idea of the Postmodern*, pp. 12–13.

8. Ernst Cassirer, *The Philosophy of the Enlightenment*, trans. Fritz C. A. Koelln and James P. Pettegrove (Boston: Beacon Press, 1951), p. 45.

9. In a recent survey of twentieth century historiography, Georg Iggers observes that while history has been challenged throughout the twentieth century, and dislodged from the preeminent place it held in nineteenth-century thinking, these challenges nevertheless did not question the knowability of the past, which is the issue raised by the postmodernist challenge. See Georg G. Iggers, *Historiography in the Twentieth Century: From Scientific Objectivity to the Postmodern Challenge* (Hanover, NH: Wesleyan University Press, 1997).

10. For a more elaborate discussion, see Arif Dirlik, "The Third World in 1968," in Carole Fink, Philip Gassert, and Detlef Junker, eds., *1968: The World Transformed* (Cambridge: Cambridge University Press, 1998), pp. 295–317.

11. Jane Flax, "Is Enlightenment Emancipatory? A Feminist Reading of 'What is Enlightenment?'" in Barker, Hulme, and Iverson, *Postmodernism and the Re-reading of Modernity*, pp. 232–49.

12. Russell Jacoby, *The End of Utopia: Politics and Culture in an Age of Apathy* (New York: Basic Books, 1999).

13. Dai Yi, "Shiji zhijiao zhongguo lishixue de huigu yu zhanwang" (Retrospects and Prospects of Chinese Historiography at the [Impending] Turn of the Century), *Lishi yanjiu* (Historical Research), No. 6 (1998): 5–16.

14. Vivian Sobchack, "An Introduction: History Happens," in Vivian Sobchack, ed., *The Persistence of History: Cinema, Television and the Modern Event* (New York and London: Routledge, 1996), pp. 1–14, p. 3.

15. These challenges, their implications for history, and the methodological questions they raise, have been discussed in a number of excellent collections. For prominent examples, see Robert A. Canary and Henry Kozicki, eds., *The Writing of History: Literary Form and Historical Understanding* (Madison, WI: University of Wisconsin Press, 1978); Henry Kozicki, ed., *Developments in Modern Historiography* (New York: St. Martin's Press, 1993); Peter Burke, ed., *New Perspectives on Historical Writing* (Cambridge, UK: Polity Press, 1993); Frank Ankersmit and Hans Kellner, eds., *A New Philosophy of History* (London: Reaktion Books, 1995). Peter Novick, in *That Noble Dream: The Objectivity Question and the American Historical Profession* (Cambridge, UK: Cambridge University Press, 1988), provides interesting discussions of the impact of the new developments on historians on the U.S. Dominick LaCapra and Steven Kaplan, eds., in *Modern European History: Reappraisals and New Perspectives* (Ithaca, NY: Cornell University Press, 1982), and Mark Poster, in *Cultural History and Postmodernity: Disciplinary Readings and Challenges* (New York: Columbia University Press, 1997), offer important discussions of the relationship between post-structuralism and history. The most extensive defenses of history against postmodernisms is to be found in Joyce Appleby, Lynn Hunt, and Margaret Jacob, *Telling the Truth about History* (New York: Norton, 1993), and Richard J. Evans, *In Defence of History* (London: Granta Books, 1997).

16. Nancy F. Partner, "Historicity in an Age of Reality-Fictions," in Ankersmit and Kellner, *A New Philosophy of History*, pp. 21–39, p. 22. Henry Kozicki writes, somewhat more smugly, that "despite current theoretical distractions the historical discipline is soundly based on traditional practices properly understood," Preface to Kozicki, *Developments in Modern Historiography*, pp. xi–xii, p. xiii.

17. Georg G. Iggers, "Rationality and History," in Kozicki, *Developments in Modern Historiography*, pp. 19–39, pp. 21–22.

18. Hayden White, "The Politics of Contemporary Philsophy of History," *Clio* 3, 1 (1973): 35–53, p. 53.

19. F. R. Ankersmit, "Historiography and Postmodernism," *History and Theory* 28, no. 2 (1989): 137–53, p. 149.

20. Partner, "Historicity in an Age of Reality-Fictions." See also Robert A. Rosenstone, "The Future of the Past: Film and the Beginnings of Postmodern History," in Sobchack (ed), *The Persistence of History*, pp. 201–18.

21. Richard T. Vann, *"Turning Linguistic: History and Theory* and History and Theory, 1960–1975," in Ankersmit and Kellner, *A New Philosophy of History*, pp. 40–69, p. 69.

22. F. R. Ankersmit, "Historiography and Posmodernism," *History and Theory* 28, no.2 (1989): 137–53, p. 143. The reference is to Hayden White, *Metahistory: The Historical Imagination in Nineteenth-Century Europe* (Baltimore, MD: Johns Hopkins University Press, 1973).

23. Iggers, "Rationality and History," p.28.

24. Sidney Monas, "Introduction: Contemporary Historiography: Some Kicks in the Old Coffin," in Kozicki, *Developments in Modern Historiography*, pp. 1–16, p. 6

25. Iggers, "Rationality and History," p. 19

26. J. B. Bury, "The Science of History, quoted in Allan Megill, 'Grand Narrative' and the Discipline of History," in Ankersmit and Kellner, *A New Philosophy of History*, pp. 151–73, p. 159.

27. Linda Orr, "Intimate Images: Subjectivity and History—Stael, Michelet and Tocqueville," in Ankersmit and Kellner, A New Philosophy of History, pp. 89–107, p. 90. Contrast this, for example, with Jean Chesneaux, *Pasts and Futures, Or What Is History For?* (London: Thames and Hudson, 1978), where the argument proceeds on the basis of rationally comprehensible class and social interests in the shaping of history.

28. Hayden White, "The Politics of Contemporary Philosophy of History," p. 49. White also observed with enthusiasm that on the continent, nothing is taken for granted, everything has been brought under question, even the utility of historical consciousness itself (p. 52).

29. Hayden White, "Historical Pluralism," *Critical Inquiry* 12 (Spring 1986): 480–93, p. 488.

30. Richard Vann in his account of the changes suggests independent developments. Vann, *"Turning Linguistic,"* p. 59. White obviously did not oppose metanarratives, per se, and unlike Lyotard, who was driven by anti-Marxism, found critical inspiration in the Marxist tradition in Europe. White suggests in a recent essay, however, that it may be necessary to draw a distinction between modernist (which was the context for metahistory) and postmodernist ways of historical narration: After modernism, when it comes to the task of story-telling, whether in historical or literary writing, the traditional techniques of narration become unusable—except as parody. He also writes, with regard to certain types of events, especially as they are presented on the electronic media, that it may be impossible to tell any single authoritative story about what really happened—which meant that one could tell any number of possible stories about it. The distinction probably should not be carried too far, as it appears to me that White does not care to distinguish postmodernism too strictly from modernism, viewing it more or less as a development of the latter. See H.

White, "The Modernist Event," in Sobchak, *The Persistence of History*, pp. 17–38, p. 24.

31. Georg G. Iggers and Harold A. Parker (eds), *International Handbook of Historical Studies: Contemporary Research and Theory* (Westport, CT: Greenwood Press, 1979).

32. I base this observation at least in part on my own experience with conferences in which I have been a participant along with Georg Iggers, and a more explicitly unreconstructed (I say this with affection) universalist, Jörn Rüsen. For an example, see Rüsen, "Some Theoretical Approaches to Intercultural Comparative Historiography," *History and Theory* 35, No. 4 (December 1996): 5–22.

33. Samuel P. Hays, "Theoretical Implications of Recent Work in the History of American Society and Politics," *History and Theory* 26, No.1 (1987): 15–31, p. 15. The same tendency has been visible within the history of the same group. For a discussion of problems in integrating women's history, see Joan Scott, "Women's History," in Burke, *New Perspectives*, 42–66. Novick, *That Noble Dream*, chap. 14, "Every Group Its Own Historian," provides a detailed account of these developments.

34. Giovanni Levi, "Microhistory," in Burke, *New Perspectives*, pp. 93–113

35. The reference here is to the works of historians such as E. Le Roy Ladurie, C. Ginzburg, R. Darnton, and Natalie Davis. How stories may help us get closer to the truths of the past, and also subvert the truths of history, is the subject of Natalie Davis's *Fiction in the Archives: Pardon Tales and Their Tellers in Sixteenth-Century France* (Stanford, CA: Stanford University Press, 1987). For a recent example from my own field of Chinese history, see Roxann Prazniak, *Of Camel Kings and Other Things: Rural Rebels against Modernity in Late Imperial China* (Boulder, CO: Rowman and Littlefield, 1999).

36. Mark Poster, *Cultural History and Postmodernity*, especially the introduction, and Ankersmit, "Historiography and Postmodernism," and "Historical Representation," in F. R. Ankersmit, *History and Tropology: The Rise and Fall of Metaphor* (Berkeley, CA: University of California Press, 1994), pp. 97–124. It is an open question whether describing works such as the above as postmodern gives an accurate impression of their origins, or merely appropriates them for the postmodern. The authors do not necessarily view their works as postmodern, clearly distinguishable from the modern, as do analysts such as Ankersmit and Poster. Richard Evans, in his extensive defense of history, points out rightly that many of the postmodern issues raised with regard to historical work long have been questions for historians. On the other hand, it may be suggested that whatever the inspirations at their source, such works do contribute to a discourse of the postmodern.

37. I am bracketing in the context of this discussion the obvious fact that history has never been the monopoly of professional historians. Historical fiction and histories produced by journalists are obvious examples. They have been joined in recent years by claims on a better telling of history by disciplines as far apart as economic, historical sociology, and literature. What may be important at the present is the explicit recognition of such claims, as well as the recognition of the claims on history by previously ignored and marginalized groups.

38. Francis Fukuyama, *The End of History and the Last Man* (London: Hamish Hamilton, 1992).

39. Jacques Le Goff, *History and Memory*, trans. from the French by Steven Rendall and Elizabeth Claman (New York: Columbia University Press, 1992), p. xi.

40. White, "The Modernist Event," p. 30. Emphases in the original.

41. Pierre Nora, "Between Memory and History: Les Lieux de Mémoire," *Representations* 26 (Spring 1989): 7–25, p. 17.

42. Ibid., p. 17.

43. Ibid., p. 15.

44. Le Goff, *History and Memory*, p. 99.

45. Richard Wolffe, "Putting a Price on Barbarity," *Financial Times* (March 6/7, 1999), weekend supplement, p. 1.

46. Klaus Neumann, "'In Order to Win Their Friendship': Renegotiating First Contact," *The Contemporary Pacific* 6, no. 1 (Spring 1994): 111–45.

47. Ashis Nandy, "History's Forgotten Doubles," *History and Theory* 34, No. 2 (1995): 44–66, p. 44. Deloria's rejection of history and science is even more total. See Vine Deloriaq, Jr., *Red Earth, White Lies: Native Americans and the Myth of Scientific Fact* (New York: Scribner, 1995). Such repudiations of history are post-historical, in the sense that they are mediated by the history that they reject. This does not trivialize them, but rather enhances their plausibility. If some Australian aborigines believe that the gods sent anthropologists to preserve the traditions of old, Turkish historians in the twenties and thirties used the scholarship of European Turkologists to create a national history. It would be wrong, also, to describe the repudiation of history by a Nandy or Deloria as backward-looking, as they self-consciously take the present as their point of departure. I have elaborated these points, most recently, in my "History without a Center? Reflections on Eurocentrism," in Eckhardt Fuchs and Benedikt Stuchtey, eds., *Historiographical Traditions and Cultural Identities in the Nineteenth and Twentieth Centuries* (forthcoming); "Reading Ashis Nandy: The Return of the Past, or Modernity with a Vengeance," in Vinay Lal, ed., *Dissenting Knowledges, Open Futures: The Multiple Selves and Strange Destinations of Ashis Nandy* (Delhi: Oxford University Press, forthcoming); and, "The Past as Legacy and Project: Postcolonial Criticism in the Perspective of Indigenous Historicism," *American Indian Culture and Research Journal* 20, 2 (1996): 1–31.

48. Charles Maier, "A Surfeit of Memory? Reflections on History, Melancholy and Denial," *History and Memory* 5, 2 (Fall/Winter 1993): 136–51, p. 136.

49. Arif Dirlik, "Reversals, Ironies, Hegemonies: Notes on the Contemporary Historiography of Modern China," *Modern China* 22, 3 (July 1996): 243–84.

50. Prasenjit Duara, *Rescuing History from the Nation: Questioning Narratives of Modern China* (Chicago: University of Chicago Press, 1995).

51. Hevia, *Cherishing Men from Afar*, pp. 247–48.

52. It is difficult, for instance, to see how Hevia's new history represents an advance over a similar study, this time of Portuguese and Dutch embassies to the court of the Emperor K'ang Hsi, by John E. Wills, Jr, *Embassies and Illusions: Dutch and Portuguese Envoys to K'ang-Hsi, 1666–1687* (Cambridge, MA: Harvard University Press, 1984).

53. For discussions of the general state of postmodernism in China, see Arif Dirlik and Zhang Xudong, eds., *Postmodernism and China* (Durham, NC: Duke University Press, 2000). This volume is an expanded edition of a special issue of *Boundary 2* 24, 3 (Fall 1997).

54. Dai Yi, "Shijizhi jiao Zhongguo lishixuede huigu yu zhanwang," *op. cit.*, and Lin Ganquan, "Xinde qidian: shijizhi jiaode Zhonnguo lishixue" (A New Start: Chinese Historiography at the Impending Turn of the Century), *Lishi yanjiu* No.4 (1997): 5–17.

55. Wang Qingjia (Edward Wang), "Ruhe kandai houxiandai zhuyi dui shixue de tiaozhan?" (How to View the Postmodernist Challenge to History?), *Xinshixue* (New History), 10:2 (June 1999): 107–44; and Zhang Yonghua , "Houxiandai guannian yu lishi xue" (Postmodernity and Historiography), *Xinhua wenzhai* (Xinhua Synopses), 241:1 (1999): 85–89, originally published in *Shixue lilun yanjiu* (Research in Historical Theory), No. 3 (1998). It is significant that Edward Wang is a historian of Chinese origin working in the United States, and that the article by Chang was published in journal of the world history section of the Chinese Academy of Social Sciences.

56. Wang, "Ruhe kandai houxiandai zhuyi," pp.139–40.

57. Gao Yi, "Fuke shixue chuyi" (Humble Opinions on Foucault's Historiography), *Lishi yanjiu*, No. 6 (1994): 142–55, and Luo Zhitian, "Hou xiandai zhuyi yu Zhongguo yanjiu: <Huairou yuanren>de shixue qishi" (Postmodernism and the Study of China: The Historiographical Revelations of "Cherishing Men from Afar"), *Lishi yanjiu*, No. 1 (1999): 104–20.

58. The suggestion here is that Foucault's ideas respond to, and are a manifestation of, a European problematic that set the rational against the irrational in the first place. Similarly, Zhang Yonghua, in his discussion of postmodernism, suggests that postmodernism is caught up in a European problematic that derives from an opposition established between subjectivity and objectivity, and concludes that "Chinese wisdom" may have something to contribute to overcoming the problem. Zhang, "Houxiandai guannian," p.89.

59. See, for examples, Xiaobing Tang, *Global Space and the Nationalist Discourse of Modernity: The Thinking of Liang Qichao* (Stanford, CA: Stanford University Press, 1996), and Wang Hui "Modernity and 'Asia' in the Study of Chinese History," in Eckhardt Fuchs and Benedikt Stuchtey, eds., *Historiographical Traditions and Cultural Identities in the Nineteenth and Twentieth Centuries* (Washington, DC: German Historical Institute, forthcoming).

60. Andrew Plaks, "Towards a Critical Theory of Chinese Narrative," in Andrew H. Plaks, ed., *Chinese Narrative: Critical and Theoretical Essays* (Princeton, NJ: Princeton University Press, 1977): 309–52, pp. 311–12.

61. Deng Xiaoping, "Remarks on Successive Drafts of the 'Resolution on Certain Questions in the History of Our Party since the Founding of the People's Republic of China (March 1980–June 1981),'" in *Selected Works of Deng Xiaoping, 1975–1982* (Beijing: Foreign Languages Press, 1984): 276–96.

62. The reference here is to writers such as Su Tong, Qiao Liang, Li Xiao, Wu Bin, Yu Hua, etc., who gained prominence in the late eighties. For discussions, see Wang Biao, "Yu lishi duihua: xin lishi xiaoshuo lun" (Dialogues with History: Discussion of the New Historical Novel, *Wenyi pinglun* (Literature and Art Review) No. 4 (1992): 26–32; Song Xiaoping, "Ba war jiupingde youxi: 'xin lishi xiaoshuo'zhi wojian" (Playing with Old Bottles: My Views on the New Historical Novel), *Huazhong shifan daxue xuebao* (Journal of the Central China Normal University), No. 4 (1995): 94–95, and Sun Xianke, "'Xin lishi xiaoshuo'de yishi

xingtai tezheng" (Ideological Characteristics of 'the New Historical Novel'), *Dandai wentan* (Contemporary Literature Forum) No. 6 (1995): 8–10.

63. Du Weiyun, "Shixue wang nali zou?" *Jindai Zhongguo* (April 30, 1989): 1–14, p. 6.

64. Dai Yi, pp. 13-14, 15-16; Lin, p. 16.

65. Uchang Kim, "The Agony of Cultural Construction: Politics and Culture in Modern Korea," in Hagen Koo, ed., *State and Society in Contemporary Korea* (Ithaca, NY: Cornell University Press, 1993): 163–95, p. 192.

66. Robert Heilbroner, *Visions of the Future: The Distant Past, Yesterday, Today and Tomorrow* (New York: Oxford University Press, 1995), pp. 13, 69.

67. Ankersmit, "Historical Representation."

68. Rosenstone, "The Future of the Past," p. 213.

69. Richard T. Vann, "Turning Linguistic," p. 53.

70. I am paraphrasing here the concluding lines to Grafton's marvelous book on the footnote: Footnotes guarantee nothing, in themselves. The enemies of truth—and truth has enemies—can use them to deny the same facts that honest historians use them to assert. The enemies of ideas—and they have enemies as well—can use them to amass citations and quotations of no interest to any reader, or to attack anything that resembles a new thesis. Yet footnotes form an indispensable if messy part of that indispensable, messy mixture of art and science: modern history. Anthony Grafton, *The Footnote: A Curious History* (London: Faber and Faber, 1997), p. 235.

71. Paul Greenhalgh, *Ephemeral Vistas: The Expositions Universelles, Great Exhibitions and World's Fairs, 1851–1939* (Manchester, UK: Manchester University Press, 1988), and Robert W. Rydell, *All The World's a Fair* (Chicago and London: University of Chicago Press, 1984). It is interesting that historians, but especially anthropologists, were enthusiastic participants in world's fairs as consultants, directors, etc., as they believed them to be golden opportunities for publicizing their work and disciplines.

72. Lutz Niethammer, in collaboration with Dirk Van Laak, *Posthistoire: Has History Come to an End?*, trans. Patrick Camiller (London: Verso, 1992), p. 10. Note that posthistorical as the end of history is quite different from my use of the term above. Niethammer also traces the origins of the concept to right-wing German intellectuals of the thirties. It was adopted subsequently after 1968 by left-wing intellectuals.

73. Partner, "Historicity in an Age of Reality-Fictions," p. 39.

74. Poster, *Cultural History and Postmodernity*, pp. 67–70. Koselleck, quoted in ibid., p. 68. Poster views postmodernism as a resolution of problems presented by new sensibilities of time and space that are inextricable from the new technologies that provide their material context.

75. For discussions of this problem, see the essays in Arif Dirlik and Zhang Xudong, eds., *Postmodernism and China* (Durham, NC: Duke University Press, 2000)

76. Evans, *In Defence of History*, p. 248.

15. Postscript

Richard T. Vann

This chapter could be called "Conclusion" if I as a commentator had been able to reach firm conclusions, much less *a* conclusion. Instead I am left with a substantial array of questions—not because the chapters have failed to be informative, but because the very richness and variety of the contributions have exhibited the puzzling condition in which the still infant study of the comparative history of historiography finds itself. We have been presented with cross-cultural studies, and, appropriately, several authors who come from various non-Western cultures. In consequence, as one might expect, there isn't—and perhaps cannot be (?)—any real consensus on what they are all talking about, not to mention what they say about it.

The notion of "turning point" itself provides the best example of this conceptual diversity. Although, as Wang and Iggers say, the phrase may have entered ordinary historical work as late as the nineteenth century, it was borrowed from the structure of fictional narratives, especially plays. Aristotle in the *Poetics* was already discussing it as *peripeteia* (the Greek word for "sudden change") in terms that, although designed to treat tragedy, are, I would argue, also applicable to all kinds of narratives, including historical ones. The *peripeteia* is the observable point in the drama when things suddenly change from one state of things to another. This usually means a change in fortune for the hero from prosperity to ruin—this after all generally happens in tragedies—but it can also work the other way.

At the *peripeteia* the plot takes its decisive "turn" towards an ending which could not be entirely foreseen, yet in retrospect seems predetermined. Thus, Hamlet has his chance, and does not take it, to kill King Claudius at his prayers. To have done so would have satisfied the demands of justice and brought a conventional revenge play to a satisfying conclusion; Hamlet's declared desire for a more horrid vengeance sets in train the actions which will leave all the principal characters except Horatio dead by the end of the play. It is particularly important to note that such turning points in the plot, though sudden, must be seen to arise from the "probable or necessary sequence of events." The hero can't be undone merely by bad luck.[1]

Due caution of course must be observed in applying this term to histories. In a classical tragedy after the *peripeteia* the action proceeds inevitably to its denouement that, as Aristotle famously claimed, leaves the spectators "purged by pity and terror." These are not sentiments regular enjoyed by readers as they turn the last page of a history. In histories there is usually no hero to focus the cathartic effect, nor any determinate end of the story; but as in any narrative there must be a central subject—for us in this context, historiography itself—and the end is the only one we have, the present. A "turning point" in historiography would thus seem to me to be not necessarily a huge event (not the mass killings at the end of the play, but Hamlet's sparing the king). It could be some sort of "swerve" in which historians made decisions that altered the course of their subsequent thoughts and actions, and perhaps those of some of their readers.

Although real-life actions rarely end, like plays, with the slaughter of most of the characters (or, in a comedy, their coupling), there must be some way in which a turning point is distinguished from a mere development, and it must lead to a state of affairs markedly better or worse—or at least different—than the one which obtained before these decisions and actions were taken.

For "turns" or "swerves" of this kind we have a word derived from the Greek: *tropos*, which means "turn." It gives us the notorious "trope," which has invaded discussions of historical writing in the last quarter century. While I do not quite understand what Humphreys means by denying that "turning point" is a formal concept (can there be an informal concept, or a material one?), I agree that if it is not exactly a metaphor, it behaves like one. In other words, it must be judged on its aptness, and not as a potentially verifiable truth claim. It follows that there are no decision rules governing its applicability; the historian is free to employ it as freely, or loosely, as her taste and aesthetic sense suggest.

Thus it should occasion no surprise, or at least no shock, to see Humphreys beginning his story of Islamic history with a "turning point." In a similar gesture Falola speaks of the "foundations" of the turning point he is to discuss (a twentieth-century one) as far back as the fifteenth century. Hill speaks of the "history of civilization" histories as "a decisive shift in Japanese historical writing," even though they became outmoded within twenty years. In most of the other chapters little or no emphasis is placed on locating a turning point in historiography; Huang, for example, discusses a turning point in Chinese history, but claims that a moralizing construal of history in Chinese historiography has been more or less constant since the earliest times.

Perhaps because ancient history is remote enough for its turns to seem more obvious, the chapters which most directly address the issue of turning points are those by Breisach, Lee, and Hartog. Breisach approaches the question using the well-worn topos of cyclical and linear conceptions of history. He is however justifiably skeptical of any simple dichotomy between "cyclical" Greek or Roman histories and "linear" Christian ones.[2] Romans began their chronology *ab urbe condita*, from the founding of Rome, and Rome was supposed, until the visits of the Vandals and Goths, to continue forever.

Christians started from the creation of the world, or the birth or resurrection of Christ. But just as no histories could claim that there has or ever will be an exact reoccurrence of historical events—not even Nietzsche could hold this view, except as a thought experiment—neither could we understand history at all if there were no repetitive patterns of events. Although St. Augustine poured scorn on the heathens "wandering in circles,"[3] his disciple Orosius was solidly in the Christian and Jewish tradition in detecting a pattern (not unlike the Greek belief in *hubris* and *nemesis*) of persistent human sinning, calls to repentance, and when these are not heeded, condign punishment.

Breisach is on firmer ground when he turns from lines and circles to discuss the relationship of the sacred and profane which puzzled Christian historians as soon as they realized that the end of the world was not as nigh as they have been led to believe. In an argument which seems counter-intuitive, because the "turning point" is succeeded by the quite different conceptions of St. Augustine and Orosius, Breisach nevertheless shows that Eusebius, doubtless owing to his close relationship with the emperor Constantine, had hit upon the right formula for blending ecclesiastical and secular history and giving the latter some meaning beyond the apocalyptic *telos* that was all that interested St. Augustine.

Without disparaging myth, it might be said that Eusebius succeeded in inserting the Christian myth into the course of human history. The problem of the relationship of myth and historiography, and how to distinguish between the two, arises a number of times in these papers. The most sophisticated treatment of it is Hartog's subtle argument about what seems to us a supreme mythical epic, Homer's *Odyssey*. For the ancient Greeks, Homer was an historian; even Thucydides, while criticizing Homer for exaggerating the importance of the Trojan War, does not seem to have thought that the *Iliad* was not an historical text.

Without going nearly this far, Hartog claims that the germ of a turning point towards historiography can be seen embedded in the much-discussed episode in Book Eight where the blind rhapsode Demodocus sings of the siege of Troy and reduces Odysseus to tears. Developing a suggestion first made by Hannah Arendt, Hartog shows that the mastery of its details that Demodocus shows should only have been possible to one who learned them from the Muse; but Odysseus raises the alternate possibility that Demodocus was present at the siege (which he knows cannot be true) or heard what happened from someone else. This, as Hartog puts it, "doubles" the bard as historian (especially since interrogation of eyewitnesses was the chief methodological strategy of subsequent Greek historians). Furthermore, Odysseus was the witness; but hearing the story in the third person, with himself as a major actor, positions him as though he were dead. He thus experiences "the shock of the temporal difference that separates oneself from oneself," which is "the first encounter with historicity."

Hartog is not claiming that this episode amounts to what we could call historiography; it merely opens a space which historiography eventually filled. I am not enough of a classicist to evaluate this argument, but it struck me that even if there were no other consideration of turning points in this volume, Hartog has ingeniously shown how illuminating this trope can be.

The flexibility with which these authors deploy the concept of a turning point is matched by their exploitation of the ambiguities in the word "historiography." Beyond the dictionary definition of historiography (the writing of history or written history), many historians use it to denote what past historians have said about a given subject—histories of small slices of historiography, in other words. This is what they mean when they say "I will research the historiography of this." The word would be really useful if the well-known ambiguity of the word "history" could be removed by reserving it entirely for *res gestae* (things done in the past) so that all accounts of them purporting to be true could be called examples of "historiography."[4] "Historiography" can—I would say must—be the object of both historical and philosophical reflection, and some people also call this "historiography." I would like instead to revive "historiology" for the study of histories or historiography; but as I lack power to compel a rectification of names in the Chinese fashion, the most I can do is try to establish in which sense words are being used and point out where ambiguities may be tripping us up.

This is particularly important, and difficult, when an adjective—especially a national name—modifies "historiography." Leaving aside the question of the temporal and geographical parameters of "France," is "French historiography" all historical writing about France, or only that produced by historians who are French? The contributors to this volume all seem to favor the more restricted sense. "Chinese historiography" for them appears to be only what Chinese historians have written, no matter how much it might have been influenced by Japanese or German models. It is not clear whether Falola would admit historical works about Africa by English, French, or American historians to the canon of "African historiography." I rather think not, since he cites the view that the historiography of Africa should be inflected by popular conceptions of history entertained by Africans, and even that "it is only Africans who can actually dominate certain aspects of knowledge." (He does not give any arguments or data to make us accept such views, and I do not know whether he himself holds them.)

I can imagine arguments and data that might compel me to accept such a view, but I can't conceive any that would justify *excluding* histories of a country by non-citizens of that country from a consideration of its national historiography. American historiography without Tocqueville or English without Halévy would be considerably impoverished. Of course the gift to see ourselves as others see us may be a poisoned one, and Falola properly denounces the racist stereotypes that pervaded European writing about Africa. However it is noteworthy that he treats the beginnings of "academic history writing about Africa" in the twentieth century as entirely the work of black intellectuals such as W. E. B. DuBois and Leo Hansberry, who "deployed African history to elaborate on black identity and the achievements of black people." Have European writers, though neither elaborating on black identity nor saying much about Africans' achievements, contributed nothing at all to historical understanding of any part of the continent?

Falola raises, in a different context, the question of the relationship between historiography and myth. Historiography must surely at least purport to be factually accurate, and in that sense true. Without entering very far into vexed epistemological issues, we can say that to count as historiography, a work must not refer to people who never lived and events that never occurred, and it must produce evidence to support its truth claims. Myths set in the past that do make such references and exhibit no evidence may be in some sense true, even profoundly true; but such truths are not *historiographical* truths.

Falola seems to me to show a certain ambivalence about whether to admit elements of myth into historiography. What he calls "the cultural response" to racist European historiography about Africa "fed" the intellectual agenda of African historiography, which he succinctly summarizes as "If Europeans devalued the African past, culturalists would romanticize it." Once academic history departments were set up in the new African universities that followed independence from the imperial powers, the "tiny elite" of historians used a mode of "'objective' production of history, within the framework of how the Western academy defined research and university education" but they were to use their elite position to create a history usable "in the service of the nation." The use of quotation marks around "objective" in the previous quotation is significant, since these historians defined their task as "providing credible evidence on the achievements of Africa and the glories of the past." The best examples are such works as those by Cheikh Anta Diop that "demonstrate the black origins of Egyptian civilization."[5] What is at issue here is whether historians should produce all the evidence they can find that bears on a claim, rather than simply searching for that which might credibly support a position congruent with nationalist ideology.

No fair-minded person could doubt the propriety of assessing the works of African historians "not solely on their academic merits but their symbolic significance." Myths, however, have pure symbolic significance, and Falola does not discuss what weight is to be given to academic merits, how they are to be evaluated—and who is to judge them.

"Contribution history" of the sort that many African historians have written is by no means limited to them; it is familiar in the historiography of women, immigrants, and other groups that have been subjected to the scorn or, more often, the neglect of mainstream historiography. Nor is the use of histories to inflate national morale confined to Africa. Many European and American historians did much the same thing in the nineteenth century; African historians may have been unique only in doing it later, and in the candor with which they acknowledge their patriotic mission. Lal is quite correct in pointing out that "history, more than any other discourse . . . has enshrined the narrative of the nation-state as the reference point for all agency, and . . . has made it difficult to derive other arrangements for the organization of human affairs."

The theme of the relationship between nationalism and historiography comes up repeatedly in this volume, especially in discussions of historical writing in and about parts of the world subjected to European imperialism.

Fuchs challenges the usual view that "scientific history" was invented in Germany and subsequently exported all over the world by pointing to the actual isolation of the German historical tradition and the stubborn persistence of national schools of historical thought throughout the nineteenth century. Elman's contribution, especially valuable as the only essay based on reader response (actually examiner response) to changes in historiography, emphasizes how those who set the famous Chinese civil service examinations came to a higher regard for historiography because they believed policy decision should be informed by the storehouse of examples in historical writings. What would we give for a comparable seventeenth-century Western set of examination questions and answers, and the cribs for how to take them! If only there had been history courses, examinations, books with examples of the best answers. . . .

This nexus of historiography and nationalism is the key problem for cross-cultural perspectives on historiography. These perspectives are necessarily comparative; but only Hill has given much thought to one of the great logical problems in comparison: the constitution of the entities to be compared. As he points out, a naïve "comparison" of national histories setting them in the context of national cultures presupposes that there *were* national cultures antecedent to the comparison being made. His comparison therefore juxtaposes nineteenth-century French, United States, and Japanese history systemically. Implicitly this is done in places by those articles (by Falola and Fuchs, in particular), which set off African historiography against that of the imperial powers or compared various European historians of the nineteenth century with one another and with those from the United States. Informative as these articles are, I think their impact would have been greater if Hill's strictures about the prior constitution of the entities to be compared had been more explicitly confronted.

Hill also draws attention to the neglected topic of the way nineteenth-century historiography did not problematize the spatial extension of the "nation," and thus naturalized the imperial acquisitions of France and the final dispossession of Native Americans in the western United States. (The latter process was kept invisible by Turner because he accepted the U.S. Census definition of "empty" land. These lands were inhabited by Native Americans, and some had actually been cultivated by them, but since they were not U.S. citizens, the Census Bureau did not count them.) "National" historiography can be deployed against an imperial power, as in China, Japan, and India; or, as Hill demonstrates, to justify imperialism. It can also be used to glorify a national state and discredit or ignore the separatist ambitions or traditions of regions or provinces. French historiography is again an example of this, as is that of the United States in the decades following the Civil War.[6]

If there was ever a turning point from regional to national historiography, it was turned long ago in Europe and the United States. Neither Michelet's "Tableau de la France" or Ranke's view that states are the "thoughts of God" could have been produced in the eighteenth century, but their authors had attained classic status by the end of the nineteenth. The more recent, and politically urgent, task for a national history in Africa and Asia has been to resist the historiographical pressure exerted by the European powers.

This is not easy to do, and almost impossible to do thoroughly, because there is a dialectical tendency for opponents to borrow from one another and thus come to resemble one another. Lal brilliantly uncovers this tendency in the well-known Subaltern School in Indian historiography. Although they would seem at first glance to fit perfectly under the well-known rubric of "history from below," Lal depicts them as comfortably fitting within an older European indological tradition of understanding empirical data from India through European theory. He suggests that to really make the subaltern speak, relying on the firm of Marx, Hegel, Heidegger, Jakobson, Habermas, Foucault, Barthes, and Derrida is not enough. In fact dependence on their theoretical armamentarium makes plausible Lal's claim that "subaltern history itself exists in a position of subalternity to Europe."

Subaltern history doesn't, but presumably should, use, among other resources, "the interpretive strategies of the Indian epics or puranas, the political thinking of a Kautilya, the hermeneutics of devotional poetry, the philosophical exegesis of Nagarjuna, and the narrative frameworks of the *Panchatantra* or the *Kathsaritsagara*." This implied recommendation resonates with Falola's evocation of the possibility that popular African notions of history inflect African historiography, and warns us to be cautious in invoking European standards in judging African or Indian historians. Yet Lal also points to the ease with which Western histories can gain authority when they provide handy ammunition in localized political struggles. Religious Hindus who have recently taken power in India, and who are normally disinclined to praise Western culture, nevertheless cheerfully quote as "authentic history books" supplying "undisputed historical fact" books written by Western writers in support of their claim that there was an ancient temple on the alleged birthplace of Lord Rama. Turns away from hegemonic Western historiography are easier to talk about than accomplish.

Given the very long historiographical tradition of China, it might be expected that the influence of foreign historiographical techniques and concepts would not be great; but in fact Chinese historians were no more immune to the attractions of Western historiography than to Western theories such as Marxism. Both Wang and Elman explore the ambivalent Chinese attitude towards Western historians. Wang identifies it even where it might not be expected, in the National Essence School. "In their criticism of the Chinese tradition," he writes, "Western culture was held to be a yardstick, or a mirror, and was used to measure and reflect the problems in China's past." Finding traditional Chinese historiography of little use, they created in the early twentieth century a "new conception of national history" which was not an innovation but "a borrowing from the West via Japan."

Elman suggests however that there were elements in traditional Chinese learning that the National Essence School might have appropriated. Chang Hsueh-ch'eng and other scholars writing in the late eighteenth century had already applied new empirical methods of source criticism, historicized the

332   TURNING POINTS IN HISTORIOGRAPHY

Classics, and sought out a wider range of source materials for history. In this, however, he sees more similarities to Enlightenment historiography than to nineteenth-century German historicism. A real turning point (and curiously, in the Western direction) seems to have been reached only when "under the influence of German historicism" the Classics lost their classical status and were "desacralized."

One noteworthy feature of this collection is that it is the substantive side of "historiography" which is usually emphasized. I expected turning points in historiography to lie more in methodological developments, rather than changes in historical interpretation, but this is not how the majority of the contributors have read their brief. Elman, as noted above, does remark that eighteenth-century Chinese historians had developed some methods like those of their Enlightenment contemporaries in Europe, and these eventually did lead to the historicization and thus desacralization of the Classics. In Thomas Lee's essay, we find that this sort of similar development in historiography had occurred even earlier, in the Sung Dynasty of the tenth and eleventh centuries; he compared Sung historical writing with European erudite and antiquarian historiography in the seventeenth and eighteenth centuries. Wang shows how the National Essence School developed the history of historiography and expanded the scope of historical writing into many areas new to Chinese historiography. These would certainly have required new historiographical methods, inevitably relying at least in part on borrowing from the West (directly, or through Japan).

Breisach makes the important point that our understanding of historicity implies a nexus among the present, past, and expectations for the future. It is thus appropriate that the collection concludes with discussions of what has often been trumpeted as a decisive turning point in all of contemporary culture: that from modernism to postmodernism.

The two papers by Dirlik and Windschuttle present us with the following problems: how extensively have historians (in Europe, Australia, America, and China) adopted, or been affected by, "postmodernism"; and why has this come about?

There is, alas, one more terminological swamp we must enter. What is "postmodernism"? Windschuttle uses the word quite freely, although quoting with apparent approval Richard Rorty's comment that nobody has the foggiest notion what postmodernism is. Windschuttle associates it with structuralism, post-structuralism, queer theory, radical feminism, cultural studies, and other things of which, one gathers, he does not approve. They all boil down for him to "anti-realist philosophy and anti-Western politics"; postmodernism is simply a mask which can be dropped when no longer convenient. Dirlik is considerably more nuanced, but also acknowledges the difficulty in distinguishing modernism from postmodernism.

It is surprising how useful these articles are, given that both authors acknowledge they are not entirely sure what they are talking about. Dirlik, in particular, offers a comprehensive account of how postmodernism was implicated in the modernist project itself. (Paradoxically, although Windschuttle is a staunch advocate of traditional historical procedures, it is Dirlik who deploys them.) Neither paper, however, confines itself to a purely historicist approach. Both, much to their credit, advance critiques analogous to what literary critics might apply to purely imaginative fictions. We clearly do want the evaluative terms (and Windschuttle provides us with an abundance of them) to analyze and characterize postmodernist historical thinking and writing, not merely to understand how it came to be.

Unlike Dirlik, Windschuttle appears to believe that postmodernism in historical thought and writing is the result of an exogenous catastrophe. The historians—or much more often, the historiologists—that he castigates have apparently been infected by the French flu. They have accepted the view of Roland Barthes that historical writing acts in bad faith by concealing the degree to which it is a construction or—shock, horror!—an invention by the historian. Even worse, some have been tempted by the ideas of Jacques Derrida (in all likelihood incompletely, if at all, understood) summarized in the notorious statements that there is nothing outside texts, and the meanings of all texts are ultimately undecidable. The consequences of the infection are claimed to be a considerable and deplorable desertion of history as an academic discipline, consequent depletion of the ranks of professional historians, and, implicitly, a deleterious undermining of the authority previously accorded to historians as presenters of facts about the past that should inform policy decisions in the present.

If anyone who knew anything about historical writing had ever said that there was *no difference at all*, or no difference of any importance, between histories and novels, or that the physical world which surrounds and impinges upon us either doesn't exist or is itself a text, Windschuttle would be right to refute such statements. However nobody, to my knowledge, holds such views.[7] Everybody agrees that historians can make true statements about the past. It is when they are arrayed in a narrative that problems arise. As an historical realist, Windschuttle must believe that there is at least in principle only one true account of a given set of historical events. Whether historians can achieve that one true account, and know that they have achieved it, is a more complex and difficult question that Windschuttle does not treat in this paper.

Dirlik's much more extensive treatment of the origins of postmodernism in historical thought emphasizes the fragmentation of the field of history brought about by the political tumult of the 1960s and 1970s—above all by the "events" of 1968. There can be no doubt about the political impetus lying behind the expansion of historical studies that began in France in the 1930s and spread to the Anglo-Saxon world after World War II. The demand for "history from below" was articulated by self-proclaimed radical historians in the United States, and was congruent with the program previously announced by the English journal *Past and Present*, which began publication in 1952 with an editorial board in which members of the Communist Party of Great Britain were substantially represented. It reflected the concerns for "relevance" voiced by minority students, newly admitted in numbers to elite American colleges and universities, and even more by women.

From the first Greek histories until the 1930s, it is safe to say, the subjects of historians were almost always high matters of state: wars, revolutions, diplomacy, the constitution, the macroeconomy, the organization of governing bodies. Most of the technical expertise that historians traditionally acquired, such as the detection of forgeries, was developed to study these matters, and it is no accident that the mantra of historical realism, telling it *wie es eigentlich gewesen*, was first uttered by Ranke, who made his reputation by discovering and exploiting the *relazioni* of the Venetian ambassadors. The introduction of new subject areas and subject positions called forth a different set of skills, such as psychoanalysis or a statistical repertoire. As Dirlik points out, the inevitable result was a diffusion or fracturing of history as an academic enterprise.[8] Inevitably, the credibility of master or "grand' narratives"—of progress, modernization, or the inevitable triumph of the proletariat—came into question. Women's historians, for example, realized that the conventional periodizations built into grand narratives, whether of progress or stages of socioeconomic development, made little sense. Did women, Joan Kelly famously asked, have a Renaissance?

These consequences by no means pleased all those who had set them in train. On the left, Marxist and *marxisant* historians were loath to compromise the claims that the historical process could be understood scientifically; they thus rejected relativism with as much vehemence as Windschuttle exhibits, while clinging to a teleological interpretation of history which, one suspects, he does not share.

While the political events of the 1960s (I would not put quite so much emphasis on the single year 1968) undoubtedly played a role in bringing about what Dirlik characterizes as postmodernism in historical scholarship, developments in historiology were tending towards the same consequences. I remain convinced that there is an "internalist" as well as an "externalist" explanation for its development. Constructivist views of historiography can be traced back at least as far as R. G. Collingwood's *The Idea of History* (1948). Collingwood definitively located historical thought in the critical mind of the historian—as opposed to the "scissors-and-paste" compiler who simply records the evidence he or she has found—but he also argued that once the historian had fully grasped the "inside" of historical events (the thoughts which led the agent to act as he or she did) there was nothing more to do. He compared this understanding to working out in the historian's mind the same reasoning process that Euclid had applied to geometrical demonstrations. There would thus be no possibility of more than one truthful account. But this argument always smacked of excessive rationalism,[9] and Collingwood paid no attention to the process by which historical knowledge was expressed in texts.

It seems to me important to make a distinction between "constructivism" in the philosophy of history and full-blown cases of postmodernism. Failure to make this distinction makes it seem that Windschuttle is firing a blunderbuss when a rifle should have been his weapon of choice. Collingwood is certainly a constructivist—and so is Hayden White—but neither is a postmodernist.

Once historical writing as well as historical thinking came under scrutiny, it became apparent that narratives were integral to it; and once people began to think about narrative, the view that it was a genus of which novels and histories were two of the species became inescapable. Once again, this realization did not entail the consequence that grand narratives were no longer tenable. Louis Mink raised a question that seems not have occurred to anyone else: do historical narratives need to be fitted together, and if so, how can this be done? If there is no way to join them, the audience for histories would be confronted with a congeries of accounts which would not necessarily be incompatible (as long as they contained only true statements) but which did not add up to anything—exactly the postmodernist view of history, and indeed of the world. But any way to join them would seem to situate them in some larger narrative, and there would be no logical way to circumscribe the scope such larger narratives. We would thus seem to require what the Romantics called "universal history" as the framework of our individual narratives; and Mink argued that historians still have a tacit belief in such an "untold story," while discontinuing any effort to make it articulate.

This will serve as well as anything to state the postmodern dilemma. Is there any way to escape being gored by its horns? Windschuttle points to one way out, by backing out. He recommends re-erecting the dilapidated walls that have protected history from invasions by other disciplines and defending historical realism and objectivity against its various postmodern critics. This course of action, he implies, would arrest and perhaps reverse the flight of undergraduates from history majors and possibly even restore history to its Victorian pre-eminence. This is a prescription which will have considerable appeal, especially to practicing historians; but like all prescriptions, its appropriateness depends on the accuracy of his diagnosis. I know nothing which contradicts his report of the conditions in Australia, and though I am better acquainted with the American scene, I have found it very difficult to come up with any convincing data that indicate that enrollments in history have suffered because of the rise of postmodernism. No national data exist which would tell us whether fewer undergraduates proportionally are enrolling in history courses; there are data about the number of history majors in American colleges and universities, which has, as Windschuttle says, declined. On the other hand, production of Ph.D.s in history reached a peak in 1998. For everyone who says that history is in crisis, at least one other historian exudes confidence in the state of the discipline, as do the outgoing and incoming presidents of the American Historical Association.[10] I suspect that the enrollment situation in my own university is not untypical: enrollments in history courses modestly increasing, but the number of majors declining. But where are the potential history majors going? More students at Wesleyan now major in economics than in any other subject. It is hard to associate this with postmodernism.

Windschuttle's diagnosis of the baleful influence of postmodernism can cut in several ways. He may think historians themselves have lost confidence in their enterprise, which infects the confidence with which they can offer it to students. Or they may have embraced a full-blooded postmodern approach to history, which is unsatisfying to students because it is too infested with ambiguity. A third alternative, doubtless less palatable to Windschuttle but no less plausible, is that postmodernism suits the emotional needs and *Weltanschauungen* of today's students, so they seek out those disciplines most thoroughly informed by it. If this were true, historians fretting over emptying lecture halls ought to embrace postmodernism rather than turning their backs on it.

Despite these uncertainties, one thing seems clear: very few historians in America and Europe have been willing to accept those implications of postmodernism that seem most noxious to Windschuttle. They have lived through the fragmentation of the historical field and the time of troubles for master narratives; but they seem for the most part impervious to the doubts about the reality of the past and the ability of historians to come as close as possible to making an exact verbal representation of it. The book which instigated all the discussion about the literariness of historical writing, Hayden White's *Metahistory*, has been all but ignored by the great majority of historians, and this probably is even more true of the great icons of French postmodernism, Lacan and Derrida.[11] Only Foucault has found some few American historians as disciples.[12] Almost all European and American historians who have taken the linguistic turn, as Nancy Partner has wittily observed, have taken it as through a revolving door, and emerged more or less where they entered.

A sample of the fifteen historians who have contributed to this volume—I count myself and Iggers—is very feeble from a statistical point of view, but a survey of these authors may nevertheless present a suggestive index of the degree to which postmodernism has influenced or infected historical thought. I see evidence of such an influence only in the article by Hill (significantly, the youngest contributor). He several times uses the word "imaginary" as a noun, and he cites Derrida's notion of a *supplément*. This certainly shows familiarity with two of the favorite terms of postmodernist thinkers, but I wonder what work these terms actually do in the development of his argument. "Imaginary" as a noun seems to derive from the psychoanalytic theories of Jacques Lacan, which—even by the standards of obscurity regularly achieved by postmodernist writers—are particularly impenetrable. I certainly don't understand why the "global find and replace" option could not have usefully exercised to substitute "ideology" for "imaginary." This would put us in the same conceptual world in which Hill's generally Marxist approach seems congenial. If the intended point is that the "market imaginary of history" is largely or entirely unconscious, the same point can be conveyed by at least one version of Marx's use of "ideology."[13] As for Hill's borrowing Derrida's term *supplément*, more elucidation of what that term does for Derrida would be welcome. Hill seems to acknowledge that his statement "the space of the colony is a 'supplement' to that of the nation, serving to account for an excess that cannot be contained within historical interiority" is not exactly perspicuous, since he introduces his next sentence with "To be clear . . ." and goes on to clarify.

Our fifteen-person sample would have more credibility if it could be expanded to include any women, more people with recent graduate-school experience, and perhaps especially more historians outside Europe and America. Although Lal criticized the Subaltern School as theoretically still subaltern to European theorists (including some postmodernists), Dirlik's paper raises the intriguing possibility that this may not be true of Chinese historians. Their path to postmodernism, if indeed there are Chinese post-modernist historians at all, has been quite different from any found in the West. Although Dirlik also attributes it to political developments, these have been two decades later than Western ones, and not crystallized by any especially eventful year (not 1989, as one might have expected).

There are obvious dangers in trying to understand Chinese historical thought through Western categories, of which "postmodernism" is one. I am sure I would not escape these dangers, even if Dirlik has. Nevertheless, I shall take the license given to a commentator (in this instance somewhat like that accorded to the court fool) to observe that it may be that Westerners have already paid, in Veblen's phrase, "the penalty of taking the lead." Dirlik gives us examples that show that Chinese historians are just as susceptible to some of the sillier excesses of postmodernism as their Western counterparts (which Windschuttle is right to scourge). On the other hand, it would seem that postmodernism in China may profit from what can be learned from it, and can at least achieve the useful task of breaking up the ossified framework of a mechanistic Marxism. It may release creative energies which up to now have been dormant or repressed. We Western historians have no reason to congratulate ourselves that *we*, at least, have no stale and constricting paradigms in need of a comparable wrecking ball. If there is to be global free trade in ideas—the most benign face of a global economy—the intellectual adventures of our Chinese colleagues will deserve our careful attention. As Marx said to his German readers about his accounts of English factories, "De te fabula narratur"—their story is also about you.

References

1. *Poetics*, ch. 6. See the articles "Peripeteia" and "Turning Point" in J. A. Cuddon, *The Penguin Dictionary of Literary Terms and Literary Theory*, 3rd ed. (New York, 1992).

2. The magisterial article by Arnaldo Momigliano, "Time in Ancient Historiography," *History and Theory* 5, *Beiheft* 6 (1966): 1–23, should have quashed this dichotomy, but apparently has not done so.

3. *On the City of God against the Pagans*, Book 4.

4. In this chapter I do use "history" only in that sense; I either use the plural for written histories or refer to them as examples of historiography.

5. A more appropriate word than "demonstrate" might have been "assert," as this issue is much contested, along with other "Africanist" claims about the alleged "theft" of African ideas by the Greeks.

6. On France see the magisterial study by Eugen Weber, *Peasants into Frenchmen: The Modernization of Rural France, 1870–1914* (Stanford, 1976).

7. Hayden White is sometimes said to believe that there is no difference, or no significant difference, between history and novels. It is hard to see how a careful reader of White's work could attribute such views to him, since he has always acknowledged that real events differ from invented ones (see, for example, *Metahistory* [Baltimore, 1973], 6, fn. 5 or "The Fictions of Factual Representation," in *Tropics of Discourse* [Baltimore, 1978], 151). If, as he has written, "history is as much invented as found," it is obviously as much found as invented. Others might want to suggest a different distribution between the found and the invented, but to argue that nothing is found would be as difficult as to argue that nothing is invented. As for the influence of Barthes and Derrida, see Keith Jenkins, "A Postmodern Reply to Perez Zagorin," *History and Theory* 39 (May 2000): 181–200 and the rejoinder by Zagorin, *ibid.*, 201–9.

8. This is the theme of the collection of essays published as *History and . . .*, ed. Ralph Cohen and Michael S. Roth (Charlottesville, 1995). See especially the contribution by Carl Schorske, pp. 382–95.

9. Despite the efforts of Louis Mink to show that for Collingwood historical decisions need not be understood as entirely divorced from the passions of the agent; see "Collingwood's Dialectic of History," *History and Theory* 7 (1968): 3–37.

10. See their statements in the January 2000 issue of *Perspectives*.

11. See my "The Reception of Hayden White," *History and Theory* 37 (1998): 143–61.

12. However Allen Megill describes in "The Reception of Foucault by Historians," *Journal of the History of Ideas* 48 (1987): 117–41, something of the same indifference to his work that I have discovered about the response to White's.

13. On this see Martin Seliger, *The Marxist Conception of Ideology* (Cambridge, England, 1977).

Contributors

Ernst Breisach is Distinguished Professor emeritus at Western Michigan University and an expert on the history of Western historical writing. His many publications include *Caterina Sforza; A Renaissance Virago* (1967); *Renaissance Europe, 1300–1517* (1973); *Historiography: Ancient, Medieval, and Modern* (1983, 1995); and *American Progressive History* (1993). He is currently working on a research project that deals with the postmodern challenge to historiography.

Arif Dirlik is Knight Professor of History and Anthropology at the University of Oregon. His latest publications include *Postmodernity's Histories* (2000) and the following edited volumes, *History after the Three Worlds* (with Vinay Bahl and Peter Gran, 2000), *China and Postmodernism* (with Zhang Xudong, 2000), and *Places and Politics in the Age of Global Capital* (with Roxann Prazniak, 2000).

Benjamin Elman was, at the time that he contributed to this volume, a Visiting Mellon Professor of Traditional Chinese History and Civilization in the School of Historical Studies, Institute for Advanced Study, Princeton. He is now Professor of East Asian Studies and History at Princeton University. His publications include: *A Cultural History of Civil Service Examinations in Late Imperial China* (2000); *Classicism, Politics, and Kinship* (1990); and *From Philosophy to Philology* (1984, 1990).

Toyin Falola is the Frances Higginbothom Nalle Professor in History at the University of Texas at Austin. He is the author of numerous articles and books, and editor of journals and monograph series. A teacher at numerous institutions in various countries since the 1970s, he is the recipient of the 2000 Jean Holloway Award for Teaching Excellence at the University of Texas at Austin.

Eckhardt Fuchs is an Assistant Professor of Education at the University of Mannheim, and is interested in historiographical studies from a transcultural perspective. He held fellowships at the Historical Commission Berlin, the John Kennedy Institute of the Free University of Berlin, and the German Historical Institute in Washington D.C. His publications include *Henry Thomas Buckle: Geschichtsschreibung und Positivismus in England and Deutschland* (1994) and *J'accuse! Zur Affäre Dreyfus in Frankreich* (co-authored with Guenther Fuchs, 1994).

François Hartog is Directeur d'Études at l'École des Hautes Études en Sciences Sociales; his research interest covers both ancient and modern historiography. His most important publications are *Le XIXe siècle et l'histoire: Le cas Fustel de Coulanges* (1988), *Le miroir d'Hérodote: Essai sur la représentation de l'autre* (1991), and *Mémoire d'Ulysse: Récits sur la frontière en Grèce ancienne* (1996).

Christopher L. Hill is Assistant Professor of Japanese Literature in the Department of East Asian Languages and Literatures at Yale University. His research compares cultural formations of modernity in East Asia, North America, and Europe. He has received fellowships from the Mellon Foundation, the U.S. Department of Education, the Japan Foundation, and the Reischauer Institute at Harvard University. His publications include: "Mori Ōgai's Resentful Narrator: Trauma and the National Subject in 'The Dancing Girl'," *Positions: East Asia Cultures Critique* 10:2 (Fall 2002). He is currently preparing a manuscript on the writing of national history in Japan, France, and the United States.

Chun-chieh Huang is Professor of History, National Taiwan University and Research Fellow, Academia Sinica, specializing in Chinese intellectual history, especially Chinese Confucianism, and the study of postwar Taiwan. He has written widely on both subjects in Chinese, English, and Japanese. His publications include *Norms and States in China* (1993) and *Time and Space in Chinese Culture* (1995), which he co-edited with Erik Zürcher; *Cultural Change in Postwar Taiwan* (1992; co-edited with Stevan Harrell); and *Imperial Rulership and Cultural Change in Traditional China* (1994, co-edited with Frederick Brandauer).

R. Stephen Humphreys holds the King Abdul Aziz Al Saud Chair of Islamic Studies at the University of California, Santa Barbara. He has written on several aspects of Islamic and Middle Eastern history: politics and society in medieval Syria and Egypt, contemporary ideologies in the Middle East, and early Arabic historiography. He has been a visiting member of the Institute for Advanced Study, as well as a recipient of several research awards from NEH, SSRC, and ACLS. His books include *From Saladin to the Mongols: The Ayyubids of Damascus* (1977); *Islamic History: A Framework for Inquiry* (1991); and *Between Memory and Desire: The Middle East in a Troubled Age* (1999).

Georg G. Iggers is Distinguished Professor emeritus of European Intellectual History at the University at Buffalo (SUNY) and an internationally recognized authority on historiography. He served as president of the International Commission for the Theory and History of Historiography (1995–2000). A member of the editorial board of *History and Theory* and *Geschichte und Gesellschaft*, he is also the co-editor of *Storia della Storiografia*. His many publications include *The German Conception of History* (1968, 1983); *New Directions in European Historiography* (1975, 1984); and *Historiography in the Twentieth Century* (1997).

Vinay Lal teaches history at UCLA. He has written widely on Indian history, historiography, the cultural politics of sexuality, Indian public culture, the Indian diaspora, and the politics of knowledge systems. He has recently edited *Dissenting Knowledges, Open Futures: The Strange Selves and Multiple Destinations of Ashis Nandy* (Delhi: Oxford University Press, 2000). His *No More Requiems: Politics, Plurality, and Hope in the New Millennium* will appear from Pluto Press in 2001.

Thomas H. C. Lee is Professor of History at City College of New York of the City University of New York. Professor Lee is a specialist in Chinese cultural history, education, and historiography. In the past few years, he has initiated and led an international project, "Chinese and Comparative Historiography," and is the co-chair of the "Chinese Historiography Study Group" at the Association for Asian Studies. Among his many publications are *Government Education and the Examinations in Sung China* (1985) and *Education in Traditional China: A History* (2000).

Richard T. Vann is Professor of History and Letters emeritus at Wesleyan University. He is senior editor of *History and Theory* and president of the International Commission for the History and Theory of Historiography (2000–2005). Besides books on British social and religious history, he is the author of a number of articles on historical writing and theory of history, and he co-edited, most recently, *History and Theory: Contemporary Readings* (1998).

Q. Edward Wang is Professor and Chairperson of the History Department at Rowan University. He is interested in the studies of Chinese intellectual history and historiography, especially from a comparative, global perspective. He has published articles in the *Journal of World History*, *Journal of Contemporary China*, *Storia della Storiografia*, and the following books: *Inventing China through History: The May Fourth Approach to Historiography* (2001); *Postmodernism and Historiography: A Chinese-Western Comparison* (co-authored with Ku Wei-ying in Chinese, 2000) and *Ideas of History in the West* (1998, in Chinese).

Keith Windschuttle is an Australian who has been a lecturer in history, sociology, and social policy at the University of New South Wales, the New South Wales Institute of Technology, and the University of Wollongong. He has published widely in Australian and international academic journals. His most recent book is *The Killing of History: How Literary Critics and Social Theorists Are Murdering Our Past* (expanded edition, Encounter Books, San Francisco, June 2000).

Glossary

An Lu-shan 安祿山
Bunmeiron no gairyaku 文明論之概略
bunmei kaika\shi 文明開化\史
cha-chi ts'e-tzu 箚記冊子
Chang Ch'ao-jui 張朝瑞
Chang Hsüeh-ch'eng 章學誠
Chang Huai 張懷
Chang Feng-pao 張鳳抱
Chang Liang 張良
Chang Tai-yen 章太炎
Chang Wen-chien 張文建
Chao I 趙翼
Chao Ming-ch'eng 趙明誠
Cheng Ch'iao 鄭樵
Chen Chien 陳建
cheng 證
Cheng Ho 鄭和
Cheng Hsüan 鄭玄
Cheng-i t'hung-pao 政藝通報
cheng-shih 正史
Cheng Shih-chü 鄭師渠
cheng-t'ung 正統
Chen Hsien-chang 陳獻章
Chen I-hsiung 陳一熊
Chen Shou 陳壽
Chen Shun-yü 陳舜俞
Chen Tsu-wu 陳祖武
Chen Tzu-lung 陳子龍
Chen Yin-ko 陳寅恪
Che-tung 浙東
chi 記
chia-fa 家法
Chia-li 家禮

Chia Yi	賈 誼	
Chiang Fan	江 藩	
Chiao Ke	膠 鬲	
ch'i-chü-chu	起 居 注	
chi-chuan	紀 傳	
Ch'ien Mu	錢 穆	
Ch'ien Ta-hsin	錢 大 昕	
chih	質	
chih-chih ko-wu	致 知 格 物	
Chih-lin	志 林	
chih-shih pen-mo	紀 事 本 末	
Chi-ku lu	稽 古 錄	
ch'in	琴\秦	
Chin Chü-ching	金 居 敬	
ching-hsüeh-chia	經 學 家	
ching-i chih-chung	精 一 執 中 案	
Ch'ing-ju hsüeh-an	清 儒 學 案	
ching-yen	經 筵	
Chin Lü-hsiang	金 履 祥	
chin-shih	進 士	
Ch'in-shih-huang	秦 始 皇	
Chin-shih lu	金 石 錄	
Ch'iu-ku lu	求 古 錄	
ch'iung-ching	窮 經	
chiu-shih-chia	舊 史 家	
Chou	周	
Chou En-lai	周 恩 來	
Chou K'ai-ch'i	周 開 麒	
Chou-li	周 禮	
Chou Tun-i	周 敦 頤	
ch'üan	權	
Chuang Ts'un-yü	莊 存 與	
ch'uan-hsin yao-tien	傳 心 要 典	
ch'üan-heng	權 衡	
Ch'uan-hsi lu	傳 習 錄	
ch'üan-t'i	全 體	
Ch'üan Tsu-wang	全 祖 望	
Chu Hsi	朱 熹	
Chu I-tsun	朱 彝 尊	

chü-jen	舉人
Ch'un-ch'iu ta-shih piao	春秋大事表
chung	忠
chung-hsing	中星
chün-hsüeh	君學
Chu-tz'u	楚辭
chu-tzu\pai-chia	諸子\百家
Chu-tzu Yü-lei	朱子語類
Ch'ü Yuan	屈原
Chu Yun	朱筠
Erh-shih-erh-shih cha-chi	二十二史箚記
fan-li	凡例
Fan Tzu-yu	范祖禹
Fu hsi	伏羲
Fukuzawa Yukichi	福澤諭吉
Fu Yüeh	傅說
Han	漢
Hang Shih-chün	杭世駿
Han-shu	漢書
Hou Han-shu	後漢書
Hsia	夏
hsiao-chang	消長
hsiao-hsüeh	小學
hsiao-shuo	小說
hsin-fa	心法
Hsing Ping	邢昺
hsin-hsüeh	心學
Hsin li-shih hsiao-shuo	新歷史小說
Hsin-shih-hsüeh	新史學
hsin-shu	心術
Hsin-yü	新語
hsu	序
Hsü Chih-heng	許志衡
hsüeh-an	學案
Hsu Ho-ch'ing	徐河清
Hsun-tzu	荀子
Hsu P'eng-shou	許彭壽
Hsu Shih-ch'ang	徐世昌
Huang	皇

kôtsu	交	通
Kuan Chung	管	仲
Ku Chieh-kang	顧	頡 剛
Kui Hsiao	隗	嚻
Kung An-kuo	孔	安 國
Kung Hsüeh\chen-lun	孔	學 \真 論
Kung Hui	龔	輝
k'ung-t'an	空	談
Kung-yang	公	羊
Kung Ying-ta	孔	穎 達
Kuo-ch'ao Han-hsüeh shih-ch'eng chi	國	朝 漢 學 師 承 記
Kuo-ch'ao Sung-hsüeh yuan-yuan chi	國	朝 宋 學 淵 源 記
kuo-hsüeh\yuan-lun	國	學 \原 論
kuo-hsüeh fu-hsing\lun	國	學 復 興 \論
kuo-shih\ta-kang	國	史 \大 綱
Kuo-ts'ui hsüeh-pao	國	粹 學 報
Kuo-ts'ui hsüeh-t'ang	國	粹 學 堂
kuo-yun	國	運
Ku-pen da-hsüeh	古	本 大 學
Ku-shih-pien	古	史 辯
Ku Tung-kao	顧	棟 高
Ku Yen-wu	顧	炎 武
lei-shu	類	書
li	理	
Liang Ch'i-ch'ao	梁	啓 超
Liang-Han chin-shih chi	兩	漢 金 石 記
Li Ch'ing-chao	李	清 照
Li Kuo-chün	李	國 鈞
Lin Chao-tang	林	召 棠
Lin-ching	麟	經
Lin Tse-hsü	林	則 徐
li-shih-chia	歷	史 家
li-shih chih-hsüeh	歷	史 之 學
Li-shih yen-chiu	歷	史 研 究
Li T'ao	李	燾
Liu Chin	劉	瑾
Liu Chih-chi	劉	知 幾

pien-nien	編	年 記
pi-chi	筆	記
Pi Yuan	畢	沅
Po-li Hsi	百	里 奚
Po Yi	伯	夷
san	散	
San-kuo-chih	三	國 誌
san-tai	三	代
sc	瑟	
Shang	商	
Shang-shu ku-wen shu-cheng	尚	書 古 文 疏 證
sheng-ching	聖	經
Shen Nung	神	農
sheng-yun	聲	韻
Shiga Shigetaka	志	賀 重 昂
Shigeno Yasutsugu	重	野 安 繹
shih	史	
shih[a]	勢	
shih[b]	失	
Shih-chi	史	記
Shih Chieh	石	介
shih-chieh ko-ming	史	界 革 命
shih-hsüeh	實	學 \史 學
Shih-hsüeh wang nali tsou	史	學 往 那 裡 走
Shih-kuan	史	館
shih-kung	事	功
Shih-lu	實	錄
shih-p'ing	史	評
Shih-pu tsung-hsu	史	部 總 敘
Shih-san ching chu-shu	十	三 經 注 疏
Shih-t'ung	史	通
shih-wu ts'e	時	務 策
Shimada Kenji	島	田 虔 次
shu	書	
Shu Ch'i	叔	齊
Shui-hu	水	滸
Shun	舜	
shûron	衆	論

Ssu-ma Ch'ien	司 馬 遷
Ssu-ma Kuang	司 馬 光
Ssu-pu	四 部
Su Ch'e	蘇 轍
Su Ch'in	蘇 秦
Su Hsün	蘇 洵
sui-pi	隨 筆
Sun Fu	孫 甫
Sung	宋
Sung Ch'i	宋 祁
Sung Lien	宋 濂
Sung-yuan hsüeh-an	宋 元 學 案
Sun Hsing-yen	孫 星 衍
Sun Shu-ao	孫 叔 敖
Su Po-heng	蘇 伯 衡
Su Shih	蘇 軾
su-wang	素 王
Ta-ch'üan	大 全
Tai Chen	戴 震
T'ai-p'ing huan-yü chi	太 平 寰 宇 記
T'ai-p'ing kuang-chi	太 平 廣 記
Taguchi Ukichi	田 口 卯 吉
T'ang	唐
T'ang-chien	唐 鑒
tao	道
tao-hsin	道 心
Tao-hsüeh	道 學
T'ao Fu-lü	陶 福 履
tao-t'ung	道 統
Ta-sung hsuan-ho i-shih	大 宋 宣 和 遺 事
ta-t'i	大 體
Teng Shih	鄧 實
t'i	體
Ti	帝
Tien-an-men	天 安 門
t'ien-hsia\chih kung	天 下 \ 之 公
t'ien-li chih tzu-jan	天 理 之 自 然
T'ien Pei-hu	田 北 瑚
Ts'ao Chao	曹 昭

Ts'e-fu yuan-kuei	冊	府	元 龜
Tseng Kung	曾	鞏	
Tso Ch'iu-ming	左	丘	明
Tso chuan	左	傳	
tsûkô	通	交	
Tu Mu	杜	牧	
T'ung-chien Kang-mu	通	鑒	綱 目
T'ung-chien t'i-yao	通	鑒	提 要
T'ung-chih	通	志	
Tung Chung-shu	董	仲	舒
T'ung-meng-hui	同	盟	會
T'ung-shih	通	史	
T'ung-shu	通	書	
T'ung-tien	通	典	
Tu Wei-yun	杜	維	運
Tu Yu	杜	佑	
Tu Yü	杜	預	
Tzu-chih t'ung-chien	資	治	通 鑒
Wang An-shih	王	安	石
Wang Ch'ang	王	昶	
Wang Chien-wen	王	健	文
Wang Ch'in-jo	王	欽	若
Wang Chung	汪	中	
Wang Mang	王	莽	
Wang Ming-sheng	王	鳴	盛
wang-pai chih-pien	王	霸	之 辨
Wang Shih-chen	王	世	貞
Wang Tso	王	佐	
Wang Yang-ming	王	陽	明
Wang Yin-chih	王	引	之 同
Wan Ssu-t'ung	萬	斯	同
Wei Yuan	魏	源	
wen	文		
Weng Fang-kang	翁	方	綱
Wen-shih t'ung-i	文	史	通 義
wu-hsing	五	行	
Wu Po-tsung	吳	伯	宗
Wu Sheng-ch'in	吳	省	欽
Yang Wan-li	楊	萬	里

Yao	堯
Yao Chi-heng	姚 際 恒
yen-chiu	研 究
Yen Hui	顏 回
Yen Jo-chü	閻 若 璩
Yü	禹
Yuan	元
yuan-liu	源 流
Yuan Shu	袁 樞
Yueh	越
Yüeh Shih	樂 史
Yueh-tung chin-shih lueh	粵 東 金 石 略
yung	用
yung-jen	用 人
Yü Ying-shih	余 英 時

Index

A

Abbasid Revolution, 8-9, 93ff
Achebe, Chinua, 216
Adams, Henry, 153
Adams, Herbert Baxter, 153
Adeleye, R. A., 227, 229
Aderibigbe, A. B., 225
Afigbo, Adiele, 225, 227, 229
African historiography.
     See historiography
Africanus, Sextus Julius, 50
Agbebi, Mojola, 212
Ajayi, J. F. A., 221, 227, 229-230
Akintoye, S. A., 227
Alagoa, E. J., 227
Althusser, Louis, 294
American Historical Association, 152,
     273, 277, 337
American Historical Review, 239, 277
American historiography.
     See historiography
Amin, Samir, 170
Amin, Shahid, 256-259, 261, 265-266
anachronism, 8, 60, 62, 64-65, 78, 91
Anderson, Benedict, 192
Anene, J. C., 221, 225, 227
Ankersmit, Frank, 274-275, 298, 302,
     316
anticolonialism, 215, 231. *See also*
     colonialism
antiracism, 215. *See also* racism
Appleby, Joyce, 274
Arendt Hannah, 23-25, 329
Aristotle, 24, 327-328
Armstrong, John, 192
Asiwaju, A., 227
Atanda, J. A., 227
Attoh-Ahuma, 212-213
Auerbach, Eric, 26,
Ayandele, E. A., 227-228, 230
Azad, Maulana, 257
Azikiwe, Nnamdi, 216

B

Baladhuri, Ahmad Ibn Yahyá, 93
Barraclough, Geoffrey, 1-2,
Barthes, Roland, 254, 275, 280, 301, 333,
     335
Beasant, Annie, 248
Becker, Carl, 2,
Beckett, Samuel, 251
Beesly, Edward Spencer, 152
Bengal Renaissance, 244
Berkhofer, Robert, 274-277, 281
Bernal, Martin, 201
Bertens, Hans, 289-291
Bhabha, Homi, 202, 302
Bhandarkar, R. G., 244
Bhattacharya, Neeladhri, 255
Bhattacharya, Sabyasachi, 255
Biobaku, Saburi O., 221, 223-224
Blyden, Edward Wilmot, 213-215, 217,
     219
Bol, Peter, 63,
Bradbury, R. E., 221, 223
Baudrillard, Jean, 275
Breisach, Ernst, 7-8, 328-329, 334
Brew, James, 213
Brumfit, J. B., 68,
Buckle, Henry Thomas, 150-152, 154-155,
     167
Buddhism, 7-8, 113, 121, 129, 188
Bulletin of Concerned Asian Scholars, 309
bunmeishi (history of civilizations), 11,
     167-168, 170, 173, 328
Burke, Peter, 3-4, 147
Bury, J. B., 300

C

Cambridge School, 12, 245-246, 248-249,
     251
Carr, E. H., 278
Carr, Henry, 214

Rosenstone, Robert, 316
Roy, Rammohan, 244
Rudolph, R. C., 128
Rüsen, Jörn, 3-4,
Ryder, Allan, 221, 223

S

St. Augustine, 7, 52-55, 329
Said, Edward, 240
Sarbah, Mensa, 213
Sarkar, Jadunath, 244
Sarkar, Sumit, 242, 254, 265
Sarkar, Tanika, 241
Schama, Simon, 280, 284
Scheid, John, 22,
scientific history, 5, 10, 13, 148-157
Scientific Revolution, 1
Seal, Anil, 246-248, 251
secularism, 245, 262
secularization, 47, 70-71
Seignobos, Charles, 153
semiotics, 278
Sen, Asok, 244
Senghor, Léopold, 214-217
Sen, Keshub, 244
Sharma, R. C., 244
Sharma, R. S., 245
Shiga, Shigetaka, 186-188
Shigeno, Yasutsugu, 134
Shih, Chieh, 62
Siddiqui, Majid, 255
Simiand, François, 153
Simmel, Georg, 156
Sinocentrism, 201
Smith, Abdulahi. See H. F. C. Smith
Smith, Adam, 166, 168, 176-177
Smith, Anthony, 192
Smith, Elizabeth, 278
Smith, H. F. C. (Abdulahi Smith), 221,
    224-225, 228
Smith, Robert, 227
Sobchak, Vivian, 296
social history, 203, 307
Somekawa, Ellen, 278

Southgate, Beverley, 274
source criticism, 5, 13, 149, 153
Spence, Jonathan, 309
Spencer, Herbert, 152-154, 167
Spivak, Gayatri Chakravorty, 240-241,
    279
Ssu-ma Ch'ien, 9, 34, 36-41, 66, 70,
    109, 111-112, 114-120, 189,
    198-200, 203
Ssu-ma Kuang, 8, 62, 68, 70, 73, 75-77,
    102, 109-111, 114, 116, 118-
    120, 198
Sterelny, Kim, 281
Stokes, Eric, 247
Stone, Lawrence, 275
structuralism, 12, 278, 334
Subaltern School, 12-13, 239ff, 333, 337
subjectivity, 300
Su, Ch'e, 63
Su, Ch'in, 70
Su, Hsün, 63-64, 74
Sun Fu, 62, 72
Sung, Ch'eng-chu, 125
Sung, Ch'i, 67-68, 73
Sung Learning, 121, 124-125
Sun, Hsing-yen, 107, 121, 126, 130,
    132, 134
Sun, Yat-sen, 188, 192
Su, Shih, 71

T

al-Tabari, Abu Ja^cfar, 90, 93
Taguchi, Ukichi, 167
Tamuno, T. N., 224, 227
Tagore, Saumyendranath, 244
Tai, Chen, 131, 134
Tao, 6, 8, 32-33, 39-42, 66
Tao-hsüeh (Learning of the Way), 101,
    107, 112, 114, 117-120, 124-
    126
Taoism, 32, 110-111, 121, 129, 195
tao-t'ung, 133
teleology, 336
Teng, Shih, 188-196, 199,

X

Y

Printed in the United States
200815BV00008B/16-21/A